RETURN TO BABYLON

RETURN
TO BABYLON

TRAVELERS, ARCHAEOLOGISTS, AND
MONUMENTS IN MESOPOTAMIA

REVISED EDITION

BRIAN M. FAGAN

UNIVERSITY PRESS OF COLORADO

© 2007 by the University Press of Colorado

Published by the University Press of Colorado
5589 Arapahoe Avenue, Suite 206C
Boulder, Colorado 80303

Previously published by Little, Brown & Company, Boston

All rights reserved
Printed in the United States of America

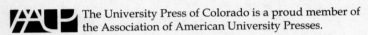 The University Press of Colorado is a proud member of
the Association of American University Presses.

The University Press of Colorado is a cooperative publishing enterprise supported,
in part, by Adams State College, Colorado State University, Fort Lewis College,
Mesa State College, Metropolitan State College of Denver, University of Colorado,
University of Northern Colorado, and Western State College of Colorado.

ISBN: 978-0-7394-8447-0

Design by Daniel Pratt

Printed in the U.S.A.

To Paul
with gratitude for friendship
and much research

When I approached the earth, there was a high flood,
When I approached its green meadows,
The heaps and mounds were pi[led] up at my word.
—PRONOUNCEMENT OF THE GOD ENKI,
FROM THE SUMERIAN POEM "ENKI AND THE WORLD
ORDER," TRANSLATED BY SAMUEL KRAMER

CONTENTS

III. PALACES OF KINGS

IV. TABLETS AND TELLS

V. SCIENCE AND NATIONALISM

PREFACE

Return to Babylon FIRST APPEARED IN 1979 AS A SEQUEL TO A HISTORY OF EARLY Egyptology, *The Rape of the Nile*. The original edition has long vanished into the near-oblivion of dusty library bookshelves, but recent archaeological catastrophes in Iraq have kindled renewed interest in the long history of Mesopotamian archaeology. The quarter century since the first edition appeared has seen a number of important historical studies of early archaeology in Mesopotamia, notably biographies of the cuneiform maestro Henry Creswicke Rawlinson and compelling pioneer Gertrude Bell and a perceptive synthesis of the beginnings of Assyriology. Unfortunately, but for obvious reasons, field research in the land between the rivers has slowed dramatically in recent years, with the notable exception of the discovery of spectacular royal burials in the Assyrian palaces at Nimrud in northern Iraq.

The task of revision was a demanding pleasure that involved extensive rewriting and minor expansion of the original work. Like its predecessor, the revised edition follows a narrative format, which works well. I was pleased to find that my original story was, on the whole, reasonably accurate, although, obviously, modifications were necessary because of new archival research. As a result, I decided to maintain the original structure, keeping the nineteenth-century archaeologists like Paul Botta and Austen Henry Layard as centerpieces of the story. The major changes are in the last two chapters, which cover developments through the twentieth century, the closing one describing the catastrophic events following the two Gulf Wars. As before, I have made no attempt to be comprehensive, focusing on the high points and the major developments rather than describing every important archaeological discovery. I should stress that this is a narrative of discovery, not of intellectual trends, which are of less interest to general audiences. I have added comprehensive notes to this edition, which provide a guide for further reading for each chapter, as well as references and occasional details on people and sites to provide richer detail to the narrative.

Return to Babylon comprises three parts. Part I, "Lost Kingdoms and Biblical Lands," begins with the first accounts of the desolate ruins of Nineveh and Babylon, which seem to confirm Biblical prophecies. I describe the first travelers to visit Mesopotamia and the hazards they encountered during the journey. The few examples of the mysterious cuneiform script to reach Europe puzzled epigraphers and scholars alike. The land between the rivers was still difficult to access when the Danish traveler Carsten Niebuhr recorded the cuneiform inscriptions at Persepolis in Iran in 1764. His pioneering research laid the foundations for the later decipherment of the wedge-like script.

Part II, "Consuls and Cuneiform," begins with the arrival of a young Englishman, Claudius James Rich, as British Resident in Baghdad in 1808. He was only twenty-one years old when he was appointed. A brilliant linguistic and astute observer, Rich visited both Nineveh and Babylon and produced the first definitive accounts of both ancient cities. Unfortunately, he died of cholera in his thirties, but we have accounts of him from other early travelers like James Silk Buckingham and the artist Sir Robert Ker Porter. In Rich's time, Mesopotamia was still far off the beaten track but a strategic place for an overland route for India. The little-known Euphrates Expedition of 1836 sailed downstream to the Persian Gulf in two steamships, one of which was wrecked, opening up the rivers to more foreign contact. Part II ends with the intricate story of the decipherment of cuneiform by a trio of talented scholars, among them the Irish country priest Edward Hincks and Henry Creswicke Rawlinson, Indian Army officer turned diplomat and epigrapher.

Part III, "Palaces of Kings," tells the story of the dramatic excavations into Assyrian cities during the 1840s that began with Paul Botta's diggings at Nineveh, then Khorsabad, which he originally had thought was the Biblical city of Nineveh, and continued with Englishman Austen Henry Layard's campaigns at Nimrud and later Nineveh. These were mere treasure hunts, where the excavators tunneled along the walls of palace rooms looking for bas-reliefs and spectacular finds. It was almost by accident that Layard found King Ashurbanipal's royal library at Nineveh, the discovery that was to throw dramatic light on Assyrian and earlier Mesopotamian history. Botta and Layard were appalling excavators by today's standards, but they placed the Assyrians firmly on the stage of world history.

Part IV, "Tablets and Tells," describes later excavations, fully as crude as those of Botta and Layard, especially in the hands of the controversial Hormuzd Rassam and the French diplomat Victor Place. Their hasty investigations in the north and in the far more complex city mounds of the south led to a scramble for clay tablets that pitted dealers against archaeologists. But the years after 1870 saw a gradual improvement in excavation methods, the discovery of Sumerian civilization in the south by the French diplomat Ernest de Sarzec, and the magnificent German excavations at Assur and Babylon, where Walter Andrae and Robert Koldewey developed effective methods of excavating unfired mud-brick structures. As Koldewey labored at Babylon, Englishman Leonard Woolley excavated Carchemish, a Hittite city on the Euphrates in a dig that epitomizes archaeological practice a century ago.

Finally, Part V, "Science and Nationalism," describes the emergence of Iraq as a sovereign nation and the growing crosscurrents of nationalism that affected the conduct of archaeology in Mesopotamia. Gertrude Bell set up the first antiquities legislation and founded the Iraq Museum in 1923. Meanwhile, Leonard Woolley excavated Ur in one of the great excavations of all time. Increasingly strict laws deterred foreign expeditions from working in the country during the late 1930s. Archaeological survey assumed much greater importance after World War II as multidisciplinary research teams moved into the field, working on such topics as the origins of agriculture. At the same time, the Iraqis assumed increasing responsibility for their own archaeology and conservation activity. All these promising trends ground to a halt with the two Gulf Wars, when uncontrolled site looting followed and professional and amateur robbers ransacked the Iraq Museum. This catastrophe has changed the landscape of Iraqi archaeology forever. The future looks uncertain in this era of rising antiquities prices, insatiable demand from collectors, and poor security in-country. It is hard to be optimistic about Mesopotamian archaeology when the priceless records of its past are disappearing. But one can only hope for a renewal of conservation and research in the near future.

This adventure story is replete with interesting characters, at present with a tragic ending but surely with hope for the future. The stage is set. Let the play begin!

ACKNOWLEDGMENTS

PAUL FRIEDMAN GAVE ME SUPPORT AND WILLING ASSISTANCE WITH THE FIRST edition. Richard McDonough of Little, Brown and Company and my then-agent Henriette Neatrour provided sage advice throughout the project. The late Professor Seton Lloyd gave me valuable insights into Mesopotamian archaeology from the 1930s onward, while David and Joan Oates kindly criticized a draft of Chapter 21. The assistance of the libraries of the University of California at Berkeley, Los Angeles, and Santa Barbara is gratefully acknowledged. The staffs of the Royal Geographical Society and the Society of Antiquaries of London were most helpful. I am also grateful for facilities given to me at the British Museum and Library, at the Public Record Office, and in the Santa Barbara Public Library.

This revised edition owes its gestation to Karl Yambert, then of Westview Press, who interested Darrin Pratt of the University Press of Colorado in the book when he was unable to pursue it further. I'm deeply grateful to Darrin for his enthusiastic encouragement throughout the revision.

Steve Brown drew the maps with his customary skill and assisted with the illustration program. I'm grateful to the various copyright holders who gave permission for the use of images under their control. Credits are given with each picture. Every effort has been made to locate the copyright holders, but anyone with concerns should address them to the author.

AUTHOR'S NOTE

F<small>OR THE PURPOSES OF THIS BOOK, THE TERMS</small> *Iraq* <small>AND</small> *Mesopotamia* <small>HAVE BEEN</small> used interchangeably except in specific and self-evident contexts where a more precise meaning is intended. On occasion, I use such old-fashioned terms as *Babylonia* but always in a historical context. Arab names are spelled in their modern mode and I have used the *Times Atlas of the World* (1977) as a basic yardstick for geographical place-names. Archaeological sites are spelled according to the most common and widely adopted usage in the academic literature; for instance, *Assur* instead of *Asshur*, which is used in many atlases.

Following archaeological convention, all measurements are given in metric except where original quotes are involved. A.D./B.C. is used for dates, as this style is in common use. All radiocarbon dates have been calibrated against tree-ring chronologies.

As is obvious, yet invariably someone gets needlessly upset, quotations from original sources use terms and words in common use at the time, such as *Oriental* and *Orientalist.* I have repeated them here in such specific contexts.

CHRONOLOGY:
10,000 B.C. TO A.D. 1515

	Mesopotamia	Developments Elsewhere
Early Settlement		
By 10,000 B.C.	Early farming in the Zagros foothills	
By 9000 B.C.	Early farmers in northern Mesopotamia	
By 8000 B.C.	First settlement of Jericho	Agriculture in Egypt?
5800 B.C.	Hassuna	
5500 B.C.	Choga Mami and Samarra	
5300 B.C.	First settlement of the Mesopotamian delta and beginning of 'Ubaid period; emergence of Eridu as a city	Pre-Dynastic farmers in the Nile valley
3600 B.C.	Uruk period of Mesopotamian history begins (named after the city of that name)	
3100 B.C.	Jemdet Nasr period begins; writing appears	
By 3000 B.C.	Development of the Sumerian civilization in southern Mesopotamia	Unification of Egypt and the emergence of ancient Egyptian civilization

continued on next page

	Mesopotamia	Developments Elsewhere
Sumerians and Akkadians		
2500–2000 B.C.	Royal cemetery at Ur. Beginnings of Sumerian city-states, among them Kish, Lagash, and Umma. Beginnings of systematic historical records, mainly known from Lagash	Egyptian Old Kingdom Pyramid building
2380 B.C.	Lugalzaggesi of Umma overthrows Lagash and sets up a Sumerian empire, describing himself as "king of Erech" and ruler of territory that extended from the "Lower Sea along the Tigris and Euphrates rivers to the Upper Sea"	
2370 B.C.	Sargon I of Akkad (the Great) over-throws Lugalzaggesi, founds the Akkadian Dynasty, and forms a vast empire that rules not only Sumer but also extends far into Asia and to the Mediterranean	Emergence of Harappan civilization in the Indus Valley
ca. 2200 B.C.	Overthrow of the Akkadians by mountain peoples and the renewed prosperity of Lagash under Gudea and other Sumerian governors	
2140–1945 B.C.	The Third Dynasty of Ur. Surviving ziggurat at the site is built	Egyptian Middle Kingdom
1750 B.C.	Final decline of the Sumerians as the Babylonians assume power in Mesopotamia	
Babylonians and Assyrians		
1790 B.C.	Hammurabi of Babylon establishes rule over the Sumerian domains and a wide area of the Near East	Minoan civilization in Crete. Egyptian New Kingdom
1307–1275 B.C.	Adad-Nariri assumes the leadership of the emerging Assyrian empire based at Assur	Hittite civilization. Mycenaean civiliza-tion in Greece
1115–1077 B.C.	Tiglath-Pileser I	
883–859 B.C.	Ashurnasirpal II (Assyrian capital at Nimrud)	
858–824 B.C.	Shalmaneser III (Nimrud)	Phoenician merchants
744–727 B.C.	Tiglath-Pileser III (Nimrud)	in the Mediterranean
721–705 B.C.	Sargon II (Khorsabad)	

continued on next page

	Mesopotamia	*Developments Elsewhere*
Babylonians and Assyrians (cont'd)		
704–681 B.C.	Sennacherib (Nineveh)	
680–669 B.C.	Esarhaddon (Nimrud)	
668–627 B.C.	Ashurbanipal (Nineveh)	Etruscan civilization
612 B.C.	Collapse of the Assyrian empire in Italy after the sack of Nineveh by the Scythians, Medes, and Babylonians	Darius at Behistun
Babylon and Later Events		
604–562 B.C.	Nebuchadnezzar's empire based at Babylon; he builds the major public buildings of the city	
538 B.C.	Cyrus of Persia overthrows Babylon and establishes Persian supremacy in Mesopotamia	Classical Greece
323 B.C.	Alexander the Great conquers the Persian empire and Babylon	
322–280 B.C.	Seleucus rules Mesopotamia	Rome controls Italy
250 B.C.	Parthian period begins	
A.D. 226	Sassanian kings control Mesopotamia	Roman empire
A.D. 571	Birth of Mohammed and the emergence of Islam	
ca. A.D. 750–1230	Baghdad at the height of its prosperity under the caliphs	The Crusades
A.D. 1515	Mesopotamia becomes al-'Iraq, a province of the Ottoman empire	

Note: Some Assyrian rulers' names are omitted. Dates, especially those earlier than 2000 B.C., are highly provisional.

RETURN TO BABYLON

PART ONE

LOST KINGDOMS AND BIBLICAL LANDS

The Assyrian came down like a wolf on the fold,
And his cohorts were gleaming in purple and gold;
And the sheen of their spears was like stars on the sea,
When the blue wave rolls nightly on deep Galilee.
—GEORGE NOEL GORDON, LORD BYRON,
THE DESTRUCTION OF SENNACHERIB

A LEGACY OF CIVILIZATIONS

And the beginning of his kingdom was Babel and Erech, and Akkad, and Calneh, in the land of Shinar.

Out of that land he went forth to Assyria, and built Nineveh and the city Rehoboth, and Calah,

and Resen between Nineveh and Calah; the same is a great city.

—GENESIS 2:10–12

"DESOLATION MEETS DESOLATION: A FEELING OF AWE SUCCEEDS TO WONDER; FOR there is nothing to relieve the mind, to lead to hope, or to tell of what has gone by," wrote the English archaeologist Austen Henry Layard of Mesopotamia in 1853.[1] The primordial lands of the Biblical Garden of Eden, of Old Testament cities like Babylon, Erech, Nineveh, and Ur, were no more than dusty, forgotten mounds of debris and mud brick. A year later, another English archaeologist, William Kennett Loftus, similarly described the landscape near Erech in southern Mesopotamia: "There is no life for miles around. No river glides in grandeur at the base of its mounds, no green date groves flourish near its ruins. . . . A blade of grass, or an insect, finds no existence there. The

3

shriveled lichen alone, clinging to the weathered surface of the broken brick, seems to glory in its dominion over these barren walls."[2] The desolation of Mesopotamia struck every nineteenth-century European traveler. The fertile and prosperous lands of the Old Testament had become little more than a harsh wilderness inhabited by nomadic tribes.

To devout nineteenth-century Westerners who believed implicitly in the historical truth of the Scriptures—as most of them did—the blasted landscape of Mesopotamia was dramatic confirmation of the dire predictions of the Old Testament prophets. "He will stretch out his hand against the north and destroy Assyria, and will make Nineveh a desolation and dry waste like a wilderness," thundered the prophet Zephaniah.[3] Armed with prophecies like this one, the early travelers and antiquarians wandered over the mounds of the long-abandoned Biblical city of Nineveh in pardonable confusion. What had become of the glorious cities of the Scriptures? Could any sense be made of the chaotic jumble that lay before them? Fortunately for science, Mesopotamia held a strange fascination for many of these visitors. Gradually they replaced the mystery of centuries with a glorious palimpsest of civilizations and cities, of great kings and laboring serfs, of remarkable religious, literary, and artistic achievements.

This book is a story of high adventure and laborious excavation, of brilliant intellectual insights and patient investigation, of high-minded scholarship and blatant chicanery. It is also the story of the Mesopotamians themselves, for centuries exploited and ruled by Macedonians and Persians, Arabs, Turks, and British. The early archaeologists had to pursue their work in the midst of constant political change, of emerging Iraqi nationalism and eventual political independence. Today, Mesopotamian archaeology, threatened by insurgency and uncontrolled looting, is the province of specialists and scholars: experts in cuneiform writing, esoteric art styles, mound excavation, and temple architecture. Their conclusions are more cautious than those of their adventurous predecessors, who lacked both professional training and academic rigor. The Iraqis themselves now run their own antiquities authority and museum, albeit under very difficult circumstances. Under normal circumstances, foreign archaeologists are closely supervised and can no longer help themselves to priceless antiquities with impunity. Today, however, no one is out in the field and the museum is in chaos after a tragic incident of uncontrolled looting and thievery. The great cities of ancient Mesopotamia are alive with

clandestine looters searching for cuneiform tablets and other archaeological treasures. No one knows what the future of archaeology will be
in the cradle of civilization.

The heroic days of Mesopotamian archaeology are gone forever,
but their passing, however nostalgically regarded, did benefit serious scholarship. The pioneers often did irrevocable damage with their
picks and huge gangs of workers, but even so, their achievements
were staggering: the recovery of the long-lost Assyrian, Babylonian,
and Sumerian civilizations, which had been crumbling to dust, and
the discovery of new art traditions that rivaled those of Egypt, Greece,
and Rome. The early archaeologists wrote of Biblical legends come
true, of clay tablets, conquering kings, and great lion hunts. They
showed that the Biblical flood had a basis in Babylonian and Sumerian
literature thousands of years older than the Scriptures. They provided the Victorians with startling vignettes of ancient human societies.
The discovery of the Sumerians and the Assyrians ranks among the
greatest archaeological achievements of the nineteenth and twentieth
centuries.

Iraq is a land of dramatic environmental contrasts with a harsh climate of striking extremes. Mesopotamia—I deliberately use the word
loosely to encompass all of the modern nation of Iraq—is nourished
by the middle and lower reaches of the Euphrates and Tigris rivers, which rise in Turkey and flow into the Persian Gulf. Like Egypt,
Mesopotamia comprises two broad provinces divided by an imaginary line that marks the greatest northern extent of the Persian Gulf
during the warmest millennia of the Ice Age. Originally, the two rivers
had separate estuaries, which can still be discerned near the modern
cities of Samarra and Hit. The south is a low-lying delta formed by
thousands of years of silt deposition by the Euphrates and Tigris. A
crescent of mountain ranges defines the boundaries of the north with
its higher rainfall and better grazing grounds.

At the end of the Ice Age some 15,000 years ago, global sea levels
were as much as ninety meters below modern levels. The Persian Gulf
was a rugged gorge carved out by the then-turbulent waters of the
two rivers. As global warming accelerated, sea levels rose and the gulf

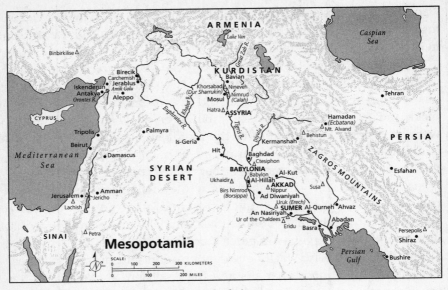

Map of Mesopotamia showing the principal sites.

filled, reducing the gradient of the Euphrates and Tigris. The northern coastline encroached rapidly into what is now southern Iraq, ponding the now-sluggish rivers and causing the spring floods to flow over what became a flat and marshy floodplain. This swampy terrain was probably the homeland of hunters and gatherers, who thrived in the lush marshland with its many species of fish, game, and plant foods. Unfortunately, their sites are buried under many meters of deep river alluvium, which has accumulated year after year.

The environmental stage for our story is set both in the rolling terrain of the north and the featureless, dusty plains of the south. Each offered different challenges to its ancient inhabitants, but they shared one reality—unpredictable rainfall and river floods. Irrigation and water conservation were the keys to survival throughout the land between the rivers with its climate of dramatic, and often violent, extremes.

Mesopotamia had always been off the beaten track for European travelers, and after 1515 was an impoverished and decaying province of the Ottoman empire, ruled by the sultan of Turkey. As for the provincial capital, Baghdad, such was its legendary reputation that European visitors expected to enter a magnificent city of romantic splendor and fabulous wealth. They were invariably disappointed. Baghdad had become a shadow of its former self.

The beginnings of Baghdad were modest. It had been little more than a village until A.D. 762, when the second Abbasid caliph al-Mansur chose it as his new capital. The site was an excellent defensive location and had convenient access to the Tigris, allowing ships to sail downstream to India and even as far as China. In four short years al-Mansur transformed Baghdad into a circular city with double brick walls and four gates from which major highways led to the outposts of the Abbasid empire. The caliph's palace and the Great Mosque stood at the center of the circle. Baghdad was soon known throughout the Mediterranean world and beyond, even as far away as Scandinavia. The Abbasid caliphs made their capital into a great commercial city and a center of sophisticated learning at a time when few European kings could even write their own names. For five centuries, Baghdad enjoyed staggering wealth. When Caliph al-Muqtadir received the ambassadors of Emperor Constantine VII from Constantinople in 917, 100 lions and 16,000 cavalrymen marched in the ceremonial parade. The wealth, exotic tastes, and luxury of the Abbasid court caused such wonder in their own time that they passed into history as an Arabian Nights fantasy preserved by generations of Arab and Western writers. But, in an inevitable reality of history, the Abbasid dynasty lost its vitality. Mongols sacked the city in 1258. One hundred thousand people are said to have perished in the massacre; priceless historical relics and libraries were burned or plundered. Babylon entered a long period of decline. Romantically inclined visitors of the eighteenth and nineteenth centuries were disappointed to find only crumbling palaces and breached walls. Nineteenth-century Baghdad, like the rest of Mesopotamia, lived on its former glories.

The story of Mesopotamian archaeology begins not with casual travelers but with European consuls who served their countries faithfully in remote outposts at Baghdad and Mosul. Today the British embassy in

Baghdad prizes the portraits of its early incumbents. Few diplomatic posts have been blessed with such talented and dedicated occupants. The calm and authoritative Claudius James Rich, who arrived to take up his post in 1808 at the age of twenty-one, gazes down at us. A brilliant linguist and an accomplished Asian scholar, Rich made the first dispassionate surveys of Nineveh and Babylon. He took Mesopotamian archaeology from the realm of travelers' tales into that of scientific fact. He also combined his antiquarian studies with skillful diplomacy. The cuneiform-inscribed bricks he collected at Babylon and Nineveh were among the first Assyrian finds to reach European soil.

Rich's successor, Colonel James Taylor, survived a plague that killed more than two thirds of Baghdad's 150,000 residents in 1831. He was such an eminent Arabist that local scholars were said to consult him on the nuances of manuscript transcription. Taylor was the first European to examine dusty Sumerian mounds, all that remained of the world's first cities in the desolate wastes of the delta country in southern Mesopotamia, but could make nothing of them. He introduced his successor, the Indian Army cavalry officer Henry Creswicke Rawlinson, to the complexities of cuneiform script.

Rawlinson's portrait conveys an air of forthright authority, an impression of a formidable personality. British prestige was never higher than in Rawlinson's day. Even his dogs were said to be greeted with deference in the bazaars. He turned the British residency into a veritable menagerie of leopards, lions, and dozens of smaller animals. Yet this superb diplomat found time to copy and decipher the virtually inaccessible cuneiform inscriptions of Persian king Darius at Behistun near Kermanshah in what is now Iran, which were to serve as the Rosetta Stone of Mesopotamian archaeology. A tradition of diplomacy combined with scholarship survived at the residency into the twentieth century.

Baghdad was a prized post for the type of Englishman who relished Muslim cities and comparative solitude. The British diplomats were normally obliged to stay close to their offices in Baghdad. Although they cheered on the pioneer excavators, they did little digging themselves. But the French government, mindful of the spectacular achievements of Napoleon's scientists in Egypt between 1798 and 1804, encouraged its consular officials to excavate.[4] Paul Émile Botta, a quiet, introspective man, arrived in Mosul, upstream of Baghdad, in 1840, his assignment to find and excavate ancient Nineveh. After an abortive dig into the mounds of Kuyunjik across the Tigris from Mosul, Botta was lucky enough to discover the palace of the Assyrian king Sargon II at Khorsabad, twenty-two kilometers north. The French were so impressed with his finds that they supported a year of excavation with public funds. A later consul, Victor Place, would continue the digs at Khorsabad until most of Sargon's palace was uncovered.

The spell of Mesopotamia fell heavily on one of the most remarkable Englishmen of the nineteenth century, Austen Henry Layard, who came to the Tigris by accident in 1840 while riding from Europe to India. He fell in love with the desert, returned later to excavate the mounds of Nimrud and Nineveh, and wrote two best-selling books on his excavations. A tempestuous, enthusiastic visionary, he was befriended by Rawlinson, lionized by the public, and gave up archaeology at the age of thirty-six to become a politician, then a diplomat. His descriptions of ancient Mesopotamia fired the imaginations of thousands of readers. "The great tide of civilization has long since ebbed," he wrote. "We wanderers were seeking what they had left, as children gather up the colored shells on the deserted sands."[5]

The magnificent Assyrian bas-reliefs in the halls of the British Museum and the Louvre still electrify the visitor today, as they did for the first time more than a century and a half ago. But the surge of public interest caused by the early Assyrian excavations was nothing compared to the sensation in 1872 when a young epigrapher, George Smith, found the greater part of what appeared to be the story of the Biblical flood on some clay tablets from Nineveh in the British Museum. His subsequent discovery of the clay fragments bearing the missing lines of the tale after only a few days of excavation is one of the great coincidences of archaeology. Today it's difficult for us to understand the impact of this extraordinary revelation on a devout public nurtured on the firm conviction that the Old Testament represented recorded history.

The picture gallery of Mesopotamian archaeologists includes many heroes and villains. There are excavators like Hormuzd Rassam, who dug ancient city mounds on a large scale in a frenzied search for tablets and antiquities. He was alternately praised as a great digger and condemned as a robber. There are museum officials like Wallis Budge, who resorted to downright trickery to save cuneiform tablets from looters for the British Museum. Sober and experienced late nineteenth- and twentieth-century German scholars like Robert Koldewey and Walter

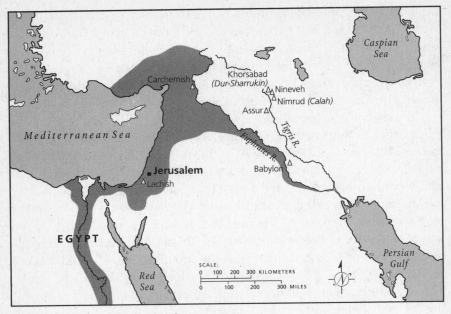

The Assyrian Empire at its height.

Andrae spent season after season reconstructing Babylon and the Assyrian capital, Assur, from seemingly indecipherable mud-brick rubble. The heroic gallery of Mesopotamian archaeology closes with English archaeologist Leonard Woolley, excavator and raconteur extraordinaire, who dug at Biblical Ur in the 1920s and made discoveries that rivaled the spectacular treasures of Tutankhamun's tomb, unearthed by Howard Carter and the Earl of Carbarvon in Egypt's Valley of the Kings in 1922. Woolley was a larger-than-life character, a brilliant improviser and gifted popular writer, who was never at a loss however dire the situation. Like all the early archaeologists, he was a prodigious worker.

The story of Mesopotamian archaeology is rich in lesser figures, too. Sir Robert Ker Porter was an aristocratic romantic whose fine paintings of Mesopotamia influenced the courts of Europe; William Kennett Loftus (quoted previously) dug unsuccessfully in southern Mesopotamia and never quite found the Sumerians; and Gertrude Bell's idealism and political acumen created the Iraq Museum in the early 1920s. Most of the major and minor characters in our story were remarkable people deeply in love with desert life. They had a gift for languages and for getting on with the local people, who helped them on their way or dug in their trenches. It was this ability to thrive in an alien environment that was the key to their ultimate success. In their times a foreigner's word was law. Decisive behavior and a revolver could win the day. If our heroes seem larger than life, it is hardly surprising. They needed extraordinary personal qualities to achieve what they did. Certainly, we shall never see their like again. Today's cautious, highly specialized academic world has moved on from their ambitious enterprises, practicing fine-grained archaeological research unimaginable in Bell and Woolley's day.

The heroic age of Mesopotamian archaeological discovery left a spectacular legacy of early civilization that extends back over 6,000 years. The early excavations revealed startlingly lurid vignettes of early Mesopotamia that flash on the screen of history with dramatic brilliance—kings besieging cities, armies marching on campaign, slaves and prisoners working on great temple pyramids, monarchs hunting lions. The images were arrogant and grandiloquent, larger-than-life, a stereotype of archaeology at its most dramatic and spectacular. Today, the flamboyance of unearthing entire civilizations and Biblical kings has given way to the measured, highly specialized world of multidisciplinary science. Today, we know that Mesopotamian cities appeared well before 5,100 years ago, that some of the roots of civilization between the great rivers extend back perhaps as far as 8,000 to 10,000 years. We look back not just at Assyrian kings strutting in their palaces, ill-defined Sumerian cities, Nebuchadnezzar's Ishtar Gate at Babylon but also at a rich, intricate tapestry of fiercely competing cities and states, quarreling constantly over land and water rights, over territorial boundaries and perceived insults.

The ancient Mesopotamian world was a cosmos of climatic extremes, of violent, authoritarian deities that humans struggled to appease. Thanks to deciphered cuneiform tablets, we can enjoy the titanic struggles commemorated in the *Epic of Gilgamesh,* a classic of ancient Mesopotamian literature; study ancient law cases; learn of the struggles of unwilling students; and consult an ancient farmer's almanac.[6] Instead of chasing elusive Biblical analogies or probing the lives of rulers, a century of research since Leonard Woolley's Ur excavations has drawn aside a curtain into a vibrant world of strong personalities and jostling people crowded into densely populated cities with small houses and narrow streets. A frenzied search for the historical truth of the Scriptures, for spectacular art and clay tablets by the basketful, has given way to a far more personal view of the ancient Mesopotamians. We've learned they were people like ourselves — loving, hating, negotiating with one another, going to war, suffering from hunger, acquiring wealth, and descending into poverty.

Underlying all these discoveries remains one intriguing possibility — that Mesopotamia was the primordial land of Genesis, of the Garden of Eden. "And as men migrated in the east, they found a plain in the land of Shinar and settled there. And they said to one another, 'Come, let us make bricks, and burn them thoroughly.' And they had bricks for stone, and bitumen for mortar. Then they said, 'Come, let us build ourselves a city, and a tower with its top in the heavens, and let us make a name for ourselves, lest we be scattered abroad upon the face of the whole earth."[7] The eleventh chapter of Genesis recounts the legend of the founding of early civilization and of the mythical Tower of Babel. In the course of his search for the earliest Mesopotamians, Leonard Woolley unearthed humble villages of reed-and-mud huts that clustered by the Tigris and Euphrates 5,000 years before Christ.

Fifteen hundred years later, the Sumerian towns of Eridu and Uruk (the Biblical Erech) in the southern delta were already revered ancient settlements. The walls of Uruk were almost ten kilometers around and enclosed an area of nine square kilometers. A high temple dominated the city, gleaming white in the brilliant sunshine. Uruk's architects designed elaborate mosaics of glazed clay cones to adorn hectares of imposing ceremonial buildings in the center of the city. Traders from all over Mesopotamia, from the Zagros Mountains far to the north and from across the Syrian desert, congregated in the city's markets, one of the founding centers of Sumerian civilization.

The kaleidoscope of villages and rapidly growing cities gives way to a picture of the world's first urban civilization, resurrected from years of excavation in desolate mounds, at Telloh, Nippur, Uruk, and elsewhere. The Sumerians were a remarkable people by any standards, brilliant technological innovators who developed the wheel, the sailboat, and cuneiform writing with which to record their religious beliefs and myriad commercial transactions. Their tablets reveal them to be a contentious and pragmatic people who prized wealth, power, and personal freedom. Sumerian literature abounds with apt proverbs and practical advice. "The traveler from distant places is a liar," reads one example. "Keep a sharp eye on your work," admonishes a farmer's almanac.[8] The Sumerians developed philosophical tenets and religious beliefs that were to survive throughout the long history of Mesopotamian civilization. They defined the fundamental relationships of Mesopotamian life in clear terms—those between humanity and its environment, and between humanity and the gods. The elements themselves were the ultimate enemies: from the vast heavens the sun shone pitilessly all summer and violent rains poured in winter, causing floods, suffering, and loss of crops and homesteads. Sumerian civilization lasted, we know, for 1,000 years, until about 2330 B.C., but its teachings lasted far longer and have influenced Judaism, Christianity, and Islam.

Perhaps our most vivid archaeological scenes come from the Botta and Layard excavations at Khorsabad, Nimrud, and Nineveh, digs that unearthed meter after meter of the palace bas-reliefs that were subsequently shipped to London and Paris. We can admire strutting hirsute kings, conquering armies, platoons of deities, and laboring prisoners. Line after line of cuneiform praises the king in extravagant terms. King Sennacherib boasts: "The people of Chaldea, the Aramaeans, the Manneans, [the people of] Que and Hilakku, who had not submitted to my yoke, I removed them hither, and made them carry the basket and mold bricks." He called his royal residence "the Palace without a Rival." This enormous structure contained over seventy halls, chambers, and passages, almost all with finely sculptured reliefs that depicted Sennacherib's military campaigns and hundreds of unfortunate prisoners.[9]

The Assyrian kings appear to us as militant and bombastic imperialists who thought nothing of deporting entire cities or torturing prisoners of war. They created the most efficient army the world had ever seen, a fighting machine that relied heavily on horse-drawn chariots. Neighboring states lived in constant dread of Ashurbanipal, Shalmaneser III, Sargon II, and Tiglath-Pileser III, monarchs who could unleash horrifying vengeance on the slightest provocation. Truly, in the words of Lord Byron, "[t]he Assyrian came down like the wolf on the fold."[10]

One of Austen Henry Layard's greatest discoveries tempers our bloodthirsty impressions of Assyrian life: the library of the last talented

Assyrian monarch, Ashurbanipal. The king was a successful conqueror but also an erudite scholar. Layard stumbled on Ashurbanipal's library and archives, a magnificent collection of cuneiform tablets, in a palace room at Nineveh. Generations of cuneiform experts labored on their decipherment to gain vivid insights into Mesopotamian literature and religion, law, and commercial life. We owe to Ashurbanipal the preservation of two literary masterpieces of ancient Mesopotamia — the *Epic of Gilgamesh* and the *Epic of the Creation*. One can imagine the "Great King, King of the World," listening with delight to stanzas that had been first committed to tablet at least 2,000 years before. The king boasted of his literary achievements, of his abilities at reading ancient scripts from Sumer and Akkad.[11] We can only be grateful for his devotion to learning.

Whatever their scholarly predilections, the Assyrian monarchs lived grandiloquently. When King Ashurnasirpal II celebrated the completion of his huge new palace at Nimrud, he threw a ten-day banquet to which all of the more than 17,000 inhabitants of the city were invited, as well as 52,000 other people from all over his empire. The guests consumed 14,000 sheep, 10,000 skins of wine, and enormous quantities of nuts and dates. Everyone, we are told, went on their way satisfied.

Our final scene comes from the meticulous German excavations of King Nebuchadnezzar's Babylon. Nebuchadnezzar was determined to make his capital the greatest city in the world. His architects and builders labored for years to lay out a vast royal precinct and a long processional way decorated with long lines of glazed-brick bulls and dragons. The Greek chronicler Herodotus tells how it was possible to drive a four-horse chariot along the double defense walls. And Nebuchadnezzar's Hanging Gardens rose tier upon tier to the roof of his palace. The luxuriant displays of flowers and vines that draped the towering walls of his residence were one of the Seven Wonders of the World. Many details of this astounding city come to us from lengthy and highly complex excavations of dry brick heaps.

Nebuchadnezzar's dazzling capital, however, was doomed almost before it was completed. In 530 B.C., a short time after Nebuchadnezzar's death, Cyrus of Persia captured Babylon and laid it waste. The city survived only as a minor provincial capital. The brightly colored palaces and temples soon crumbled to shapeless heaps of rubble as the ancient city slowly vanished into oblivion. Mesopotamia passed under the domination of successive foreign leaders, whose hold on the country was not to loosen until the twentieth century. But the people and landscape remained unchanged, a kaleidoscope of desert nomads and settled farmers, of harsh, hot summers and biting winter cold, of placid rivers and violent storms. In the nineteenth century it was hard to believe that this desolate and neglected land had once witnessed the world's first urban civilizations. To devout Victorians, it seemed that Divine Vengeance had descended on the Garden of Eden. They remembered the dire words of the prophet Nahum: "God is jealous and the Lord revengeth. . . . He rebuketh the sea, and maketh it dry, and drieth up all the rivers. . . . The earth is burned at his presence, yes, the world and all that dwell therein."[12] In Mesopotamia, the Old Testament had come true.

EARLY TRAVELERS

What vows, what rites, what prayers preferr'd,
What songs has the strange image heard?
In what blind vigil stood interr'd
For ages till an English word
Broke silence first at Nineveh?
—DANTE GABRIEL ROSSETTI

THE UBIQUITOUS GREEK TRAVELER HERODOTUS WAS ONE OF THE FIRST WRIT-ers to describe the land between the rivers for outsiders, a place, he said, of "many important cities." Sketchy at best, his description of Mesopotamia, written in 460 B.C., was a secondhand compilation of information based on the campaigns of King Cyrus of Persia and on local folklore. Only Babylon received his sustained attention. The city lay in a broad plain, was heavily fortified, and extended for 1,200 stades (21.8 kilometers) in each direction. The Euphrates divided the city through the middle and the walled city was "packed with three-storeyed and four-storeyed houses and criss-crossed by straight streets, some running right through the city and others at right angles to them going down to the river."[1] Babylon was a city of richly endowed temples, including a bronze-gated sanctuary to the god Bel.

A half century later, in 401–400 B.C., the Greek general Xenophon led 10,000 mercenaries deep into Assyria and Babylonia and back. His army camped near the Tigris in "a large undefended fortification near a city called Mespila," almost certainly Mosul.[2] The fortification was Nineveh, deserted 200 years after it fell to an army of Medes and Babylonians. Xenophon commented on the polished stone foundations topped by a brick wall 30 meters high. But Nineveh was already a desolate ruin, as were other Assyrian cities.

According to the prophet Jonah, even God considered Nineveh a large city, with "wherein there are more than sixscore thousand persons . . . and also much cattle."[3] Nineveh's residents·had plundered Judah and Israel, so its destruction was a matter of rejoicing in the Scriptures. Naturally, early Christian travelers assumed that the Lord had struck down Assyria. It was to be centuries before more accurate accounts of the land between the rivers were available to Western scholars, except to the few expert linguists who had a command of Arabic and a knowledge of Islamic literature. And those who studied Islam were cautious about broadcasting their knowledge. Heresy was a serious crime in medieval Europe.

Between the mid-eighth and early thirteenth centuries, the Arabic-speaking peoples possessed the most cultured civilization in the world. Baghdad and its favored province, al-'Iraq, lay at the hub of Islam. Its scholars engaged in all manner of scientific inquiry: from astronomy and alchemy to mathematics and geography. Generations of illustrious Arab geographers traveled through the province and described its roads and towns. They collected legends and factual information and admired ancient Persian palaces. Their place-name catalogues and essays on manners and customs were so thorough that modern scholars have been able to use them to identify archaeological sites and long-abandoned Abbasid towns. The geographer Muqaddasi, who wrote about A.D. 985, compiled such eloquent summaries of each province of Islam that they have been described as some of the best-written pages to be found in medieval Arab literature. To Islamic wise men, geography was more than a science, it was an art.

The ancient Biblical cities also came under careful Islamic scrutiny. Each learned visitor recorded local tales and walked over the ruins of Nineveh and Babylon. The traveler al-Masudi included Nineveh in his travelogue *Meadows of Gold,* written between 947 and 957.[4] Four hundred years later the Berber geographer ibn-Batuta, whose world-wide travels rivaled those of his contemporary, the Venetian Marco Polo, wrote the definitive Arab account of Nineveh. He admired the imposing buildings of Mosul and its "very fine" bazaar with iron gates surrounded by shops. He added: "In its vicinity is a large village, near which is a ruined site said to be the site of the city known as Nineveh, the city of Yunus (upon whom be peace). The remains of the encircling walls are still visible, and the positions of the gates that were in it are clearly seen."[5] Ibn-Batuta admired the Mosque of Jonah; he described the Christian convent that had preceded it and also the place where Jonah was said to have prayed and performed his devotions. A small village lay on the summit of the Nebi Yunus mound. Its buildings proved to be a major obstacle for early archaeologists wanting to delve into the ancient levels underneath the modern houses.

Despite the work of ibn-Batuta, Masudi, and other Arab scholars, the first European visitors to Mesopotamia had no Islamic scholarship to guide them. Ibn-Batuta and Masudi were not translated into English or French until the eighteenth and nineteenth centuries. Although many medieval pilgrims and crusaders visited the Holy Land and often set-tled there more or less permanently, few of them dared venture east-ward across the lawless Syrian desert to the Euphrates. No one knew much about al-'Iraq except for tales of fabulous and exotic Baghdad and of the horrible fate that could await unprepared foreigners. They had but the Old Testament and Herodotus to guide them. It was be-lieved that near the Euphrates might be found the ruins of the Tower of Babel, tangible proof of the terrifying fury of Divine Vengeance.

We are fortunate that some of the few Europeans to visit al-'Iraq were intelligent and observant men accustomed to recording their travels. The Jewish rabbi Benjamin of Tudela set off from Saragossa, Spain, on a long, circuitous journey through the Near East in about 1160. It was a time of great prosperity for Islam, the period of Saladin and the later crusades. Benjamin made his leisurely way through the south of France, visited Rome and southern Italy, then Corfu, Greece, and Constantinople. From there, he passed some time in the

Greek islands, visited Rhodes and Cyprus, and reached Damascus via the Christian-controlled cities of southern Turkey and the Holy Land. Everywhere Benjamin went he stayed with local Jewish leaders with whom he enjoyed the common bonds of language, religion, and culture. His writings record their names and details of their trading activities. No one knows why he embarked on his extraordinary journey. Perhaps he was looking for an asylum for Jews who were being persecuted in Spain, Germany, and elsewhere. But whatever his motives, Rabbi Benjamin traveled thousands of kilometers on a trip that took him into al-'Iraq when it was prospering under the Abbasid caliphs.

From Damascus, Benjamin went north to Aleppo, then east to the Euphrates and the upper reaches of the Tigris at Mosul. The journey from Aleppo across the Syrian Desert involved joining a camel caravan, which followed a well-trodden route to the Euphrates and beyond. Even a large party did not necessarily guarantee immunity from desert brigands. Each night the caravan turned itself into a virtual fortress. Foreigners took their lives in their hands and were harassed, robbed, and sometimes killed. Most strangers wore local costume both as protection against heat and dust and also as a disguise.

Benjamin found 7,000 Jews living in the "very large and ancient city" of Mosul, which he recorded as being "connected with Nineveh by means of a bridge. Nineveh is in ruins, but amid the ruins there are villages and hamlets. The extent of the city may be determined by the walls, which extend forty parasangs."[6] Rabbi Benjamin, very much a man of the contemporary world, was more interested in Baghdad and the great palace of the caliph than in Nineveh. He admired the palace's extensive park with its fruit-bearing trees and animals. There, "whenever the caliph desires to indulge in recreation and to rejoice and feast, his servants catch all manner of birds, game, and fish." Benjamin marveled at the opulence of the palace, and at "great buildings of marble and columns of silver and gold, and carvings on rare stones . . . fixed in the walls." He also described the caliph's hospitals for the sick and mentally ill—some of them people driven insane by extreme summer heat. As for the caliph himself, Benjamin had only praise: "The caliph is a righteous man, and all his actions are for good." At Ramadan the caliph emerged from his palace and rode in state to the Mosque of Mansur, where he mounted a "wooden pulpit" and expounded the law of the land.[7] Pilgrims came from far and wide to visit the palace and kiss his sleeve, a scarf of black velvet from the hangings of the mosque in Mecca. The large Jewish community of Baghdad lived under his benevolent protection. The twenty-eight synagogues housed famous scholars who were in close touch with Muslim intellectuals.

From Baghdad, Benjamin traveled south for a day to the "ruins of Babylon which is the Babel of old. The ruins of the palace of Nebuchadnezzar are still to be seen there, but people are afraid to enter them on account of the serpents and scorpions." From Babylon, he journeyed to Al Hillah and visited the Jewish community, 10,000 strong. "Thence it is four miles to the Tower of Babel," he wrote. He gazed up at the enormous mass of Birs Nimrod and was duly impressed. "The length of its foundation is about two miles, the breadth of the tower is about forty cubits, and the length thereof two hundred cubits. At every ten cubits' distance there are slopes which go round the tower by which one can ascend to the top." Benjamin scrambled to the summit and admired the thirty-kilometer view. "There fell fire from heaven into the midst of the tower which split it to its very depth," he remembered. The words of the Scriptures seemed to come alive as Benjamin gazed on this extraordinary manifestation of Divine Power.[8]

Rabbi Benjamin wrote an account of his travels in Hebrew, which was then translated into Latin. Long after his death, *The Itinerary of Benjamin of Tudela* was printed in Constantinople in 1543. The book was largely ignored until 1840, when it was translated into English and subjected to scholarly commentary. By that time, other Christian travelers had already published accounts of Nineveh and Babylon.

The educated European of the fifteenth century was largely dependent not on Tudela's book but on *The Voyages and Travels of Sir John Mandeville, Knight.* Purportedly an accurate guidebook for pilgrims to the Holy Land, this entertaining volume titillated and entertained the prospective traveler with a wealth of detail about Mandeville's journey to the East in 1322 culled from classical sources, fables, folklore, and highly unreliable crusaders' and travelers' tales. The book opens with a chapter titled "To teche you the weye out of England to Constantynople." It described the "grete tour of Babel . . . of which the walles were lxiii furlonges of heighte."[9] Nevertheless, *The Voyage*

Birs Nimrod as sketched by the Euphrates Expedition. From Chesney's Narrative of the Euphrates Expedition *(1868).*

was soon accepted as gospel truth, the work of an inveterate traveler of vast experience. Alas, Sir John Mandeville may never have existed, and the author, perhaps Frenchman Jean d'Outremeuse, may never have set foot in Mesopotamia.

Whatever the author's motives, the reader was at least assured of a compilation of available information that the author had culled from many unidentified sources. It was in this spirit that d'Outremeuse (or whomever) sat at home and wrote of ancient Babylon in the "grete Desotes of Arabye." It had been, he said, "fulle long sithe that any Man durst [go] neyhe to the Tour; for it is alle deserte and fulle of Dragonns and grete serpentes, and fulle of dyverse venymouse Bestes." The walls of Babylon, twenty-five "myles" in circumference, contained not only the Tower of Babel but many "Mansions and many grete duellynge places." The "Ryvere of Euphrate" ran through the city, set in a "fair Contree and a Playn."[10] (Actually, King Cyrus of Persia had diverted the river and destroyed Babylon in 530 B.C.)

From the twelfth through the fifteenth centuries a few other visitors followed in Benjamin of Tudela's footsteps. Pethahiah of Ratisbon covered the same ground in the twelfth century and visited the same Jewish communities. A few other clerics—men like Vincenzo Mario di Santa Caterina di Siena, the procurator-general of the Carmelite Order, and Emmanuel de St. Albert, a Dominican—journeyed to the distant land between the rivers to visit Christian minorities. Their reports add little to our knowledge of al-'Iraq. A Bavarian traveler, Johann Schiltberger, journeyed widely in the East between 1396 and 1427 while a slave in the service of various Muslim leaders. "I have also been in the kingdom of Babilonien," he boasted. Then follows the familiar litany of a great city surrounded by long walls, of the Euphrates flowing through the ruins. "The Tower of Babilonien" lay fifty-four stades away, protected by "dragons and serpents, and other hurtful reptiles." His account, dictated upon his return to Bavaria in 1427, reads suspiciously like Mandeville's. No one knows if he really visited the ruins.[11]

By Schiltberger's time Baghdad's fortunes had declined. The Abbasid dynasty had lost its grip on its vast empire after the tenth century as the internal structure of its society decayed. Floods and plagues further weakened Abbasid political and economic power. In 1258, Mongol armies descended on al-'Iraq, sacked Baghdad, and slaughtered the caliph. The Abbasid capital now became a provincial capital of the Mongol kingdom of Persia. The Mongols, in turn, were replaced by the Ottoman Turks, one of many Turkish tribes displaced from the steppes by the Mongol invasions of the thirteenth century. In 1453, the Turks captured Constantinople, which became the center of their enormous empire.

The Ottoman sultan Selim I, known as "the Conqueror," expanded his realms into Persia and Armenia and added Mesopotamia to the empire in 1515. Baghdad, although still the capital of the province of al-'Iraq, became a frontier town against the hostile Persians. The zenith of Ottoman power was in 1566, when the Turks controlled not only the Near East but part of the Balkans, Greece, and much of North Africa. Thereafter the empire embarked on a long period of decline fostered by both internal weaknesses and external political forces. The Ottoman sultans ruled their domains from Constantinople, where they lived in splendor. Each sultan appointed a grand vizier, who ran the day-to-day affairs of state and headed the imperial bureaucracy, known as Bab al-Aali (the "Sublime Porte"). The provincial governors, one of whom was based in Baghdad and another in Mosul, enjoyed some autonomy, but personal initiative was discouraged. A combination of unduly centralized bureaucracy, harsh taxation, and endemic corruption led to gradual impoverishment throughout the empire.

As Americans have discovered in recent years, al-'Iraq's remoteness and fierce climate made communication difficult for a faraway governing power. Its people were sharply divided into several Islamic sects, all of them different from the one the Turks subscribed to. Baghdad never regained its former status and decayed quietly, becoming an obscure backwater suffering under harsh and despotic governance. Except for a half century of Persian rule, from 1580 to 1638, Baghdad was to stagnate in an atmosphere of weak government and in constant fear of desert Arab raids until the late nineteenth century. From 1704 to 1831 Mameluk governors ruled Baghdad with virtual autonomy.[12]

The Ottoman sultans were careful in their dealings with Western nations; thus, trading connections evolved gradually. The French and Venetians were first in the field, trading for silks, "muskadels and Turkie carpets." But Europeans were wary of the Turks and their alleged atrocities and held back from greater involvement in the Ottoman trade until the late sixteenth century. In 1581 the sultan granted the English "Turkey merchants" a seven-year monopoly, which resulted in the formation of the Levant Company. For four centuries the company prospered by trading English wool and cotton goods for spices, silk, dyes, and other Eastern luxuries. The company's coffee imports were behind the coffee-shop boom in London in the seventeenth century. The Levant merchants opened factories in Aleppo and Smyrna (Izmir) through which they channeled much of their trade with remoter areas. Aleppo was an important caravan terminus that enabled English merchants to trade in Persian markets and with Mesopotamia.

The more enterprising traders spent a great deal of time investigating new markets and looking for overland trade routes that would link the Mediterranean with Persia, the Persian Gulf, and India. We know little of these tentative explorations or of the occasional scientists who donned local dress and accompanied caravans into remote Iraq. The German botanist Leonard Rauwolff traveled to the Tigris and Euphrates in 1574. He was amazed at the ruins of Babylon, the "ancient and delicate antiquities that still are standing about in great desolation." Rauwolff described brick arches and fortifications and the Tower of Babel, "which the children of Noah began to build up to heaven." So many vermin infested the tower that one could not approach closer than a kilometer except in winter. Rauwolff went to Nineveh, too, and walked over the Nebi Yunus mound. "It was entirely honeycombed, being inhabited by poor people, whom I often saw crawling out and in large numbers like ants in their heap," he wrote.[13] Like most visitors, he was satisfied that the extensive mounds and ruins near Mosul were the site of Biblical Nineveh.

English merchants were especially interested in the caravan routes to Mesopotamia, for they had begun what became a centuries-long quest, a search for a safe, prosperous overland trading route to India. The Elizabethan chronicler Richard Hakluyt published the report of London merchant John Eldred, who traveled in 1583 "to Trypolis in Syria by sea and from there by land and river to Babylon and Balsara."[14] Eldred left London on a ship called *Tiger* in the company of John Newbery, Ralph Fitch, "and six or seven other honest merchants." They arrived at Tripoli on May 1, 1583, and reached Aleppo three weeks later. Newbery had passed this way two years before and was able to make the necessary contacts to get them on a desert caravan. Dressed in Arab costume, the merchants left Aleppo on May 31 and reached the Euphrates in three days. They then hired flat-bottomed boats and floated downstream in very hot weather, trading with the desert people, "of whom we bought milke, butter, eggs, and lambs, and gave them in barter . . . glasses, combes, corall, amber, to hang about their armes and necks." Their vessels were *kelleks*, wooden rafts supported by inflated goatskins, strengthened with wooden cross-pieces, and fastened together with strong reeds. The boatmen reinflat-ed the goatskins every day and continuously soaked them to prevent accidental bursting caused by the searing heat. Two large oars of split cane served to steer the raft. The passengers perched themselves on the bales of merchandise. Wealthier people bought a wooden bedstead and covered it with a felt awning. The bed stood in the middle of the *kellek* and served as a couch by day and a bed at night. *Kelleks* were a perfect river craft for the Tigris and Euphrates, little changed from an-cient times. The Assyrians depicted *kelleks* on their palace walls nearly 3,000 years ago. Eldred remarked that the people were "very thievish," a complaint echoed by many later travelers.

Once opposite "New Babylon," actually Baghdad, the merchants tried to hire camels, but the weather was too hot and the camels' own-ers did not want to risk their animals' lives. The Englishmen were forced to make do with 100 asses to carry their merchandise on a haz-ardous nighttime journey across the desert. It was during this journey that Eldred stumbled on ancient Babylon, "many olde ruins whereof are easily to be seene by day-light." Eldred made the journey between Aleppo and the Tigris three times, so he had ample opportunity to look at the site. "Here also are yet standing the ruines of the olde tower of Babel, which being upon a plaine ground seemeth a farre off very great," he wrote. The tower was "above a quarter of a mile in compasse, and almost as high as the stone worke of Paul's steeple in London." He commented on the courses of sun-dried brick and layers of matting in the ruins. Baghdad, he observed, "joineth on to aforesayed small des-ert where the olde city was."

John Eldred was above all a merchant. He expressed no surprise at finding the Tower of Babel in the desert and was far more interest-ed in the modern city of Baghdad, "a very great thorowfare from the East Indies to Aleppo." He bought food from "rafts borne upon goat skins blowen up full of wind in maner of bladders" that came from "Mosul[,] which was called Ninivie in olde time," upstream. Eldred's journey ended in Basra and he returned to England. His companions went on to India, where the suspicious Portuguese imprisoned them.

Eldred, Newbery, and Fitch had accomplished their mission: they had explored an established caravan route that Europeans could utilize. It was relatively well-known to foreigners by 1600. The Sherley brothers followed Eldred and visited Mosul and Baghdad in 1598. Sir Anthony Sherley was among many who compared ancient Nineveh to modern Mosul, to the latter's disadvantage. Mosul, he reported, was "a small thing, rather to be a witness of the other's mightiness and God's judgment, than of any fashion of magnificence in itselfe."[15]

John Eldred went on to become one of the founders of the East India Company in 1600, an organization formed to develop new overseas markets for English cloth, which could be exported instead of valuable bullion. The company prospered, so much so that it came to depend with increasing frequency on the overland route from Basra to Baghdad and Aleppo. The company agent in Basra used Arab and Turkish caravans to send travelers and merchandise across the desert in about thirty-eight days. Basra became so important that the sultan recognized a British consul there in 1767. Most people avoided Baghdad, which was politically volatile and liable to frequent plague epidemics.

The merchants brought back travelers' tales of the exotic East that no doubt gained much in the telling. These superficial explorers were castigated for returning with ridiculous stories of other places that defied logic. Were, for example, the Turks as barbarous as everyone made out? Perhaps they were ruled by "another kinde of civilitie." Guides to the "most uncouth countries of the world" now replaced the fables and fantasies of Sir John Mandeville. Their authors compiled them from actual travelers' tales in volumes such as *Purchas his Pilgrimes*, published in 1625.[16] As travel off the beaten track became more commonplace, intellectuals and public figures of the day tried to satisfy their curiosity about Turks, Arabs, and Islam by sponsoring scholarship on these subjects. No less a personage than Archbishop William Laud established a professorship of Arabic at Oxford University in the seventeenth century. Richard Pococke was the first holder of the chair. He traveled widely in the Near East, studied the Egyptian pyramids, and collected Islamic manuscripts. Thomas Roe, the British ambassador in Constantinople from 1621 to 1628, employed agents throughout the Levant to collect on his behalf. Many of the manuscripts described

Arab proverbs, fables, and fairy tales. The *Arabian Nights* was translated into French in 1712. Within a century, such tales were firmly entrenched in European fiction. Pococke, Roe, and their contemporaries were the first scholars to recognize that the civilizations of western Asia had played a leading role in the early development of European civilization.[17]

In 1626, an Italian traveler, Pietro della Valle, returned home from the East with a remarkable collection of curiosities. Valle was born to a noble family in Rome in 1586. He received a good education and spent some time in military service and on an expedition to North Africa. In June 1614 he set off on a long pilgrimage and journey in eastern Mediterranean lands, a trip undertaken, we are told, after a "disappointment" in love. He sailed to Constantinople, then to the Holy Land and Egypt, where he visited Mount Sinai. From Sinai, he journeyed to the Holy Land, Damascus, and Aleppo. His wanderings then took him across the desert to Babylon. He was one of the first European travelers to visit the ancient city.[18]

Valle wandered over the desolate ruins many times. He found it difficult to describe them, for the mass of crumbling bricks and mounds was highly confusing. It was hard for him to believe that a mighty city had ever existed in this dry and flat country. By far the most conspicuous ruin was a huge mass of decaying brickwork in the form of a tower, about 0.8 kilometers in circumference. The four sides of the tower faced the cardinal directions. Finding no signs of stairs or doors, he thought the building was the tomb of the legendary King Belus. It was, he reported, about the size of some of the great palaces of Naples. Mystified by the unfamiliar architecture, Valle walked over piles of baked and unbaked brick, some with reeds and bitumen still adhering to them. Absently, he picked up some strangely inscribed bricks for his collection of curiosities.

Romance found Valle in Mesopotamia. His researches at Babylon were interrupted by frequent visits to Baghdad, where he had fallen in love with a Christian lady named Maani. It took months for him to persuade her family to let him marry her. But in 1616 he succeeded, and the couple left to travel through northern Mesopotamia, where

Pietro della Valle, from the frontispiece of his Travels *(1665).*

Valle copied some cuneiform script from Nineveh bricks. Eventually, he and his wife traveled through Persia as far as the Caspian Sea, where they took part in Persian skirmishes against the Turks. Maani was fearless, apparently oblivious to the dangers of gunfire and hand-to-hand fighting. They saw Shiraz and Persepolis, where Valle copied more cuneiform inscriptions. Maani died of fever in 1621. Her grief-stricken husband had her corpse embalmed and carried it with him to India and Goa. It was not until March 28, 1626, that Valle returned to Rome, where he finally buried his wife.

Valle spent the rest of his life writing of his travels, siring fourteen children by his second wife, and receiving the many visitors who came to see his collections of antiquities and curiosities from the distant East. The Valle collections were justly famous for their two Egyptian mummies, which now reside in the Dresden Museum. But the artifacts that raised the greatest interest were square bricks inscribed with an unknown script. Most of these specimens came from Persepolis. Valle failed to decipher the wedge-shaped characters. He did observe, however, that the thicker ends of the horizontal characters were always on the left and argued that the writing was set down from left to right. Some of the scholars who flocked to Valle's house were familiar with Egyptian hieroglyphs. Already baffled by the complexities of ancient Egyptian, the experts shook their heads in puzzlement. Cuneiform was quite unlike any known script, even Chinese. By April 1652, when Valle died in Rome, no one had been able to decipher even a syllable of cuneiform. But he had left a priceless legacy for his successors, the first specimens of ancient Mesopotamian script to reach Europe. He also bequeathed a long narrative of his travels and some pleasing oratorios.

Valle's cuneiform bricks caused such interest that later travelers began to copy inscriptions and collect additional specimens. But their efforts at copying were fragmentary at best, one of the most widely circulated being a mere two lines of cuneiform copied by an East India Company agent named Flower, who visited Persepolis. Flower's work appeared in the *Philosophical Transactions* of the Royal Society of London in 1693. The sporadic explorations and inquiries of the 500 years since Benjamin of Tudela made his circuitous journey had done nothing but compound the profound mystery that surrounded the ancient cities of Mesopotamia.

CARSTEN NIEBUHR AT PERSEPOLIS

> Here, Nineveh, of length within her wall
> Several days' journey, built by Ninus old . . .
> There Babylon, the wonder of all tongues,
> As ancient, but rebuilt by him who twice
> Judah and all thy father David's house
> Led captive, and Jerusalem laid waste,
> Till Cyrus set them free; Persepolis,
> His city, there thou seest, and Bactra there;
> Ecbatana her structure vast there shews.
>
> —JOHN MILTON, *PARADISE REGAINED*

So far, the European visitors to distant Mesopotamia had gone there for commercial or spiritual reasons without official sponsorship. But the eighteenth century saw a new phenomenon, that of the government expedition. The Renaissance had motivated many governments to support knowledge, learning, and the arts. Some European monarchs sought lasting fame by sponsoring the arts and sciences. When King Frederick V of Denmark decided in 1760 that he would emulate his royal neighbors and embark on a bold cultural program, he thought in terms of botanical gardens and natural history museums. He also decided to send an expedition to Arabia. The idea for the journey had come from the German theologian and Asian scholar Johann

33

Michaelis of the University of Göttingen.[1] Michaelis was unusual for his time in that he refused to believe that the Scriptures were strict historical truth to be taken as *the* account of early history. He thought of them as historical texts to be examined critically. What better way to critically study them than to send an expedition to Arabia? The scientists could study geography, collect plants and animals, and gain insights into Old Testament society by studying the contemporary Arabs. Frederick V seized on the idea with alacrity. The expedition was out of the ordinary, politically important, and potentially a good investment. Contemporary scholarship was passionately interested in science, the Scriptures, foreign countries, and, increasingly, southwestern Asia. The king provided funds for a five-man expedition charged "to make new discoveries and observations for the benefit of scholarship," as well as to collect "valuable oriental manuscripts."[2] Among the five scientists chosen for the expedition was a young man named Carsten Niebuhr.

Niebuhr was born in Friesland on March 17, 1733. His father was a poverty-stricken farmer, who only reluctantly agreed to Carsten's attending school. By the time the boy was sixteen his parents were dead and he was working as a farmhand on a neighbor's farm. Four years later, however, he used a small legacy from his father to obtain training as a surveyor. He attended school in Hamburg and was admitted to the University of Göttingen in 1757, where he studied mathematics under well-known academic Abraham Gottheif Kästner. Kästner soon recognized Niebuhr's intelligence and obtained a scholarship for him to study astronomy. The young man realized he had found his calling and studied with great enthusiasm.

When the Danish government cast around for a fifth member for the Arabia expedition, Kästner recommended his young protégé. Niebuhr spent the next two years learning history, geographical surveying, and astronomy. He learned how to repair his instruments in the field and attempted to learn Arabic, a project he soon gave up in disgust. In October 1760 he found himself in Copenhagen, having been appointed engineer-lieutenant of the expedition.

Niebuhr's colleagues were a varied group: the Swedish scientist Peter Forsskål, a botanist and a theologian with forthright and controversial views; Friedrich Christian von Haven, a Danish philologist; Georg Wilhelm Baurenfeind, an artist; and Christian Karl Kramer, appointed as expedition doctor. It was a tragic combination of personalities. The five explorers did not get along well together. At one point one member of the team tried to poison the others. Invariably the quiet and self-effacing Niebuhr tried to remain aloof from the personal intrigues of his colleagues.

The expedition was to go to Constantinople and Cairo, then through the Sinai and into the Arabian interior. The return journey was to be through Basra, Aleppo, and Smyrna. All the members of the party were to learn Arabic and keep diaries, which they were to send home as frequently as possible. They were to purchase manuscripts, especially those in exotic scripts. Manuscripts that Haven was unable to decipher were to be copied with special care. The scientists were urged to behave circumspectly toward Muslims and to respect local moral values.

The five men left Copenhagen in January 1761. After a stormy voyage and several brushes with British warships, the expedition reached Malta, then sailed on to Constantinople. There, Niebuhr recuperated from a bad dose of fever and the scientists donned Turkish dress. A Turkish vessel carrying a cargo of slave girls carried the party to Alexandria. Forsskål and Niebuhr found themselves occupying a cabin immediately below the women. "Eventually," wrote Niebuhr, "the girls took to tapping on the window as a sign to us that they were now alone; and in this way we both had great fun during the trip."[3]

At Alexandria the slave girls vanished silently and the explorers had their first taste of the Arab world when they saw some Bedouin robbers beaten to death in the street. After taking a boat upstream to Cairo the scientists threw themselves into an orgy of botanizing and mapping. They spent almost a year in Egypt awaiting official dispatches from Copenhagen. Niebuhr compiled a detailed map of Cairo, studied irrigation methods, and measured the height of the Great Pyramid of Giza more than a century before Egyptologist Flinders Petrie completed the first comprehensive survey of the area. He quietly copied hieroglyphs while his colleagues quarreled among themselves about the leadership of the expedition. There was time for Niebuhr, Forsskål, and Baurenfeind to visit "a rather distinguished" Cairene, who allowed them to view and draw the anatomy of a circumcised peasant girl.

In August 1762, dispatches with instructions from Copenhagen finally arrived. After a final party complete with dancing girls, the scientists joined a large, 400-camel caravan crossing the Sinai and reached Suez in thirty-two hours. They rode in its middle section, where the chances of survival in the event of an attack were best. From Suez the travelers sailed down the Red Sea to Jiddah and Loheia. For almost a year they vanished into the deserts of Yemen. Finally, three members of the party reached an English ship at Mocha in August 1763. They reported that Haven and Forsskål had perished from malaria. Six months later, only Niebuhr was still alive and was being cared for by an English doctor in Bombay. But his efforts had yielded the first definitive map of Yemen and a wealth of information about a hitherto-unknown wilderness.

The original plan had called for the expedition to return overland to Copenhagen via Mesopotamia. Niebuhr spent the next fifteen months in India, where he learned English, packed up the surviving expedition notes for dispatch to Denmark, and studied Hindu customs. On December 8, 1764, he boarded a British warship for the Persian Gulf. The ship stopped in Muscat and Bushire. Niebuhr drew a fine map of the gulf, described the island of Bahrain, and bemoaned the unpredictable weather. At Bushire, he disembarked and joined a mule caravan for Shiraz. The trip took eighteen days of arduous travel through the mountains. Rain fell nearly every day and the travelers slept in the open. Fortunately, Niebuhr received hospitality from the only English merchant in Shiraz, who smoothed his way with the governor. This official assured Niebuhr that anyone annoying him would be beheaded immediately. A week later he left on the two-day trip to Persepolis, traveling on a mule and accompanied by a Muslim servant and a guide.

Persepolis had received only occasional European visitors in previous centuries. None of them were as well prepared as Niebuhr, who first saw the valley of ruins at sunset when the columns were bathed in a rosy glow. Enchanted, he wandered among the columns until darkness fell, whereupon he left to find lodgings in the nearby village of Merdast. Every morning he rode out by donkey to the site. He surveyed the ground plan of the palace, studied the architecture, and copied cuneiform inscriptions. Forty-three pages of notes and descriptions and thirty-nine pages of plans, drawings, and copies resulted from his labors. Niebuhr worked absolutely alone, apparently in complete harmony with the local people.

Carsten Neibuhr in local dress.

Niebuhr had arrived at one of the architectural masterpieces of the ancient world. Persepolis lies on a large, bare plain, the Marv Dasht Basin, surrounded by mauve cliffs with sharp contours. It was here, between 518 and 516 B.C., that King Darius decided to build a ceremonial and spiritual center for his empire, as Susa, the administrative capital, was 500 kilometers to the north. It was named Parsa, later known to the Greeks as Persepolis (the Iranian name is Takht-e-Jamshid). In an inscription, the king proclaimed that the god "Ahuramazda was of such a mind, together with all the other gods, that this fortress [should] be built. And I built it secure and beautiful and adequate."[4] Over the next century, later rulers such as Xerxes I (ca. 470 B.C.) and Artaxerxes (ca. 450 B.C.) embellished the city with enthusiasm. The Persepolis we know today is mainly the work of Xerxes. Persepolis continued to flourish under the later Achaemenian kings until it was burnt and destroyed by Alexander the Great in 330 B.C.

The Apadana, the structure used by Darius, Xerxes, and later kings for lavish ceremonies, lies atop an artificial terrace 300 meters long and 10 to 20 meters high. Thirteen of its seventy-two columns still stand on the platform. Two monumental stairways on the north and east sides give access to the summit. Beautiful reliefs showing scenes from the New Year's festival adorn them. They depict processions of twenty-three subject nations of the Achaemenid empire, also court notables, Medes, and Persians, followed by guards with their horses and royal chariots. The delegates in their native costumes bear gifts of gold and silver vessels, weapons, fabrics, jewelry, and exotic animals. Stylized trees separate the different groups in a vast and grandiose display of imperial power. The stairways converge at the top at an entrance gate guarded by bulls and leading to the Throne Hall near the Apadana. Here the king received representatives of subject nations. Scenes of the monarch in combat with monsters represent royal power. Two huge stone bulls guard the north portico. In these building and other structures at Persepolis, the Achaemenid architects evolved a distinctive monumental style that used relief sculpture as an adjunct to monumental construction. Although there are marked similarities to Egyptian, Greek, and Assyrian architecture, the Persian architects used more closely fluted and slender columns than those of Greek temples. The bases are high and often bell-shaped, whereas the capitals are formed from the foreparts of two bulls set back to back. Persepolis is also a royal necropolis. Darius and his successors carved their monumental tombs into the cliff at Naqsh-i-Rustam, 4.8 kilometers northwest of Persepolis.

Totally captivated by this extraordinary place, Niebuhr spent three weeks copying inscriptions. He managed to puzzle out forty-two cuneiform, wedge-shaped symbols in the inscriptions. In the process, he identified three separate alphabets, now known to be Babylonian, Elamite, and Old Persian, but did not succeed in deciphering the script. He also realized that the letters spelled out words. Everyone who subsequently worked on cuneiform developed a healthy respect for Niebuhr's careful work.

Even in the cool hours of the day, the task of copying was demanding. Many of the inscriptions lay high on smooth marble walls, brightly lit with harsh sunlight. Without sunglasses, he suffered from constant attacks of blindness from the white glare. By March 1765 he was near the end of his tether. His Muslim servant became delirious with fever and died in a few days. Niebuhr himself was so debilitated by the exertion and repeated attacks of shivering that he decided to retreat to Shiraz and the blistering heat of Bushire, where he rested for three months. He never returned to his copying work at Persepolis.

Niebuhr now traveled up the Persian Gulf and overland from Basra to Aleppo. It took him months to reach the humid filth of Basra, where he waited in vain for four months for a desert caravan. He traveled as an Arab and assumed the name "Abdullah." His disguise gave him not only security but a pleasing anonymity, something the modest Niebuhr always craved. Because so many robbers were preying on the desert caravans, he decided to travel up the Tigris by boat as far as Baghdad. He shared a cabin with a sick Turk and scared off would-be robbers with a rifle. After a month he tired of river travel and mounted a donkey to visit Al Hillah. He also paused briefly at Babylon and Birs Nimrod. By now most surface traces of the former ancient city had been quarried away by brick diggers, who were still active among the ruins. Like Rabbi Benjamin, Niebuhr was afraid to wander over the site because of the numerous snakes in the long grass. So he contented himself with imagining the city in its days of Biblical glory. He thought that the palace and the Hanging Gardens lay on the east bank of the river. On January 6, 1766, Niebuhr rode into Baghdad, where he stayed for two months, sufficient time to record the names and dates of the last forty-eight pashas. Neither Babylon nor Baghdad made a lasting impression on Carsten Niebuhr.

Desert travel was still out of the question, so Niebuhr joined a Jewish caravan on its way up the Tigris to Mosul. The journey took three arduous weeks at the height of the rainy season. Niebuhr was rarely dry, but he still found time to use his precious astrolabe and sketch some villages. One of them lay opposite Mosul among the ancient ruins of

Nineveh. But the weary traveler added nothing to the outside world's knowledge of the site. On June 6, 1766, he rode into Aleppo and was feted by the European community. From there he journeyed to Cyprus, Jerusalem, and Constantinople. On November 20, 1767, he rode into Copenhagen, where he was greeted with complete indifference.

Times had changed. Frederick V had died while Niebuhr was in Baghdad. Scientific research bored his successor. Niebuhr found himself politely ignored, the sole survivor of a long-forgotten government venture. So he retired to his study on a small official stipend and started to write about his travels and his colleagues' work. A Copenhagen publisher released his books, which were largely ignored by his contemporaries and dismissed as "uninteresting."[5] After ten years of writing, Niebuhr turned down an offer to head a prestigious survey of Norway and became clerk to the council in Meldorf, a small village in western Denmark. He lived happily there in total obscurity with his wife and two children until his death in 1815. By that time leading geographers throughout Europe were using the contributions of this now blind, eighty-two-year-old traveler as a basis for new maps of southwestern Asia. Thus, with his detailed accounts of his journeys and his careful study of cuneiform, humble Carsten Niebuhr had laid the foundations for a new generation of travelers and archaeologists. Tragically, only a few people had the vision to recognize his genius. Among them was General Napoleon Bonaparte, who carried Niebuhr's *Travels in Arabia* with him to Egypt in 1798.

Although Niebuhr added nothing to contemporary information about Babylon, a later French traveler spent considerable time delving into the desolate landscape that Niebuhr had shunned. Abbé Jean de Beauchamp was the Pope's vicar-general of Babylon.[6] Between 1781 and 1785, he traveled extensively in Mesopotamia, visiting Christian residents and exploring the countryside. In 1784 he descended the Euphrates to Al Hillah and Basra, pausing for a leisured inspection of Babylon. He described the mounds there and spent many hours talking to the brick diggers. They showed him clay idols, statues, and inscribed glazed bricks that they had found. One digger led Beauchamp deep into his trenches to look at thick walls and a subterranean canal made of sandstone blocks. Beauchamp was so excited that he hired two men to clear the debris from a "stone idol." It turned out to be a huge basalt lion that was to be re-excavated again and again by later visitors to Babylon. Beauchamp made copious notes and collected a number of inscribed bricks. He also described slabs of solid clay covered with very small writing resembling the inscriptions at Persepolis. But he failed to buy any of the cylinder seals because the brick diggers never bothered to collect them.

Carsten Niebuhr's Persepolis copies slowly disseminated through scholarly circles, providing a new impetus for the study of cuneiform. At the same time, a small trickle of Mesopotamian antiquities began to reach Europe. André Michaux, a French botanist, sent a cylinder seal from Babylon to Paris in 1782.[7] By this time the East India Company had ordered their resident in Basra to obtain some Babylonian inscribed bricks like those reported by Abbé Beauchamp. A small case of Mesopotamian antiquities soon arrived in London, the forerunner of thousands of tons of statuary and other specimens that were to make their way to Europe during the nineteenth century. This sudden interest in Mesopotamia was not entirely academic. The European powers had realized the potential strategic importance of the Tigris and Euphrates. The East India Company tried to foster trading opportunities and better communications in the land between the rivers. In 1783 the company appointed a permanent British agent in Baghdad. Fifteen years later, Napoleon's activities in Egypt caused the company to upgrade the Baghdad agent to British resident and in 1802 the resident received consular powers. Fortunately for science, one of the first holders of this residency was to contribute a great deal to the scholarly knowledge of Mesopotamia.

PART TWO

CONSULS AND CUNEIFORM

Lose no opportunity of making yourself useful, whatever may be the affair which may happen to present the chance. Grasp at everything, and never yield an inch. Above all, never stand on trifles. Be careful of outward appearances. Maintain a good establishment; keep good horses and showy ones; dress well; have good and handsome arms; in your conversation and intercourse with the natives, be sure to observe the customary etiquette.

—HENRY CRESWICKE RAWLINSON

CLAUDIUS JAMES RICH

One of these, a piece of a slab of alabaster with cuneiform writing on it, was located in the kitchen of a miserable house, and it seemed to be part of the wall in a small passage which is said to continue far into the mound.

—CLAUDIUS JAMES RICH

THE BRITISH RESIDENCY IN BAGHDAD ATTRACTED A VERITABLE DYNASTY OF DISTIN-guished Asian scholars, despite being an unpopular posting. The climate was debilitating, the politics volatile, and contact with the outside world sporadic. While officials in their comfortable London and Paris offices worried about the potential strategic importance of the once-glittering city, the solitary resident had plenty of time to sit in his study and pore over ancient manuscripts and cuneiform inscriptions. In May 1808, a young Claudius James Rich, one of the most remarkable of these diplomats, arrived with his wife Mary, a new bride of eighteen, to take up his post.

Claudius James Rich was born in Dijon, France, on March 28, 1787, the illegitimate son of a Colonel James Cockburn. Rich spent much of his childhood in Bristol. When a relation started to teach him the rudiments of the classics, Rich displayed a precocious ability for languages. He learned several modern languages without formal instruction. At the age of eight or nine he was taken to see the fine Oriental library of Charles Fox, a well-known Quaker. Rich was captivated by the exotic scripts, which were quite unlike anything he had seen before. Fox encouraged him to learn Arabic and lent him grammars and dictionaries. Soon Rich had made impressive progress in Hebrew, Syrian, Persian, Turkish, and Arabic under the tutelage of Fox and a schoolteacher who also taught him mathematics. Rich can be compared to Sir Richard Burton, the African explorer of Victorian times, who mastered forty languages, and to another nineteenth-century polyglot, the German archaeologist Heinrich Schliemann, who excavated ancient Troy. One summer's evening Rich met a Turkish gentleman on the hills behind Bristol. The visitor was electrified to be greeted in his native tongue. One can imagine Rich's excitement at being able to use a language he studied from books for so long.

At the age of seventeen, Rich applied for a military cadetship in the East India Company with powerful support from influential friends in Bristol. When he went to India House in London to fill out the necessary appointment forms, he found himself a minor celebrity because of his linguistic skills. The military people introduced him to Charles Wilkins, the company librarian and an expert linguist high in the councils of the company. Wilkins was deeply impressed by Rich's abilities, so much so that he recommended that Rich be given a civil post where his talents could be used to maximum advantage. Rich was appointed a "writer on the Bombay establishment." His fame even reached the august columns of the *Times*, which in reporting his appointment called him a "literary wonder."

Since there was temporarily no vacancy at Bombay, Rich was to serve as secretary to Charles Lock, the newly appointed consul general of Egypt. The appointment would give Rich the opportunity to polish his Arabic and Turkish. In early 1804 he embarked on the store-ship *Hindustan* for Malta, where he was to join Lock. But the *Hindustan* caught fire off Barcelona and was beached. Rich walked ashore with nothing but the clothes on his back. A British merchant befriended him and helped him reach Naples. There Rich lived for three months, waiting for Lock to return to Malta from a trip to Turkey. The three months passed quickly as Rich became fluent in Italian and acquired a passion for music and Italian opera. He arrived in Malta just in time to reach Lock's deathbed. The consul had contracted fever while traveling near Troy along the Dardenelles.

The company allowed Rich to travel to Constantinople to improve his languages. He spent several weeks on a leisurely voyage through the Greek islands, which in those days were infested with pirates. One day a suspicious vessel hove in sight. The captain prepared for a desperate defense, but the ship turned out to be a Turkish merchantman. When Rich and some of the other passengers visited the vessel, Rich was accosted by a richly dressed Turk, who greeted him warmly. Rich was delighted to recognize his old acquaintance of the Bristol hills!

Rich donned Turkish dress and wandered through Asia Minor for fifteen months, mostly on his own. He visited Constantinople and Smyrna, where he enrolled in a school for young Muslim gentlemen. His journeys took him into Syria as far as Aleppo and Antakya, perhaps on confidential official business. In May 1806, he reached Alexandria, where he found a congenial companion in Colonel James Missett, the consul general there. In Egypt, Rich spent his time perfecting his Arabic and learning to ride horses. A Mameluk taught him the management of the scimitar and the lance.

This pleasant interlude did not last long. Rich was ordered to take up his appointment in Bombay late in 1806. Although he had a choice of several routes, he chose the least direct, going overland through Syria and Mesopotamia to the Persian Gulf. Dressed as a Mameluk, he visited Damascus in the company of thousands of devout pilgrims on their way to Mecca. His Turkish host was so taken with him that he offered Rich his daughter's hand in marriage. But Rich declined and pressed on to Aleppo and across the Euphrates through the Turkish foothills to the Tigris. He probably entered Mesopotamia on a *kellek* that carried him downstream to Baghdad and Basra. He sailed for Bombay on the next ship.

While on his travels, Rich had corresponded with Sir James Mackintosh, at that time the recorder of Bombay. This important official took an instant liking to him—they shared an interest in philosophy, languages, and Asian studies. Soon Rich was part of the family, teaching Mackintosh's daughters drawing and painting. James Mackintosh went off on a cruise with his wife, only to return and find that Rich wanted to marry his eldest daughter, Mary. "He has no fortune, nor had he then even an appointment," wrote Mackintosh, "but you will not doubt that I willingly consented to his marriage."[1]

⌒⌒⌒

Rich must have made quite an impression on the authorities in Bombay as well as on his future father-in-law. Four months after his arrival, the company began to look for a suitable man to send as British resident to Baghdad, a man who had experience with the Ottoman Turks and Mesopotamia and a command of the requisite languages. Rich, despite his youth, was the only logical choice. He was appointed resident two months before his twenty-second birthday and married Mary Mackintosh six days later. The young couple arrived in Baghdad at the head of a mounted Indian sepoy guard in May 1808.

Baghdad was so isolated that British and French policy makers of the time knew very little about the city. The sultan of Turkey was afraid of Napoleon and well aware that the province of al-'Iraq lay on any overland route he would take on his way to British India. The decaying city of Baghdad, at the junction of caravan routes and major river highways, occupied the most strategic position in the province. Its bazaars swarmed with spies and secret agents surreptitiously gathering information about the region. The pasha of Baghdad paid only nominal allegiance to Constantinople, for he was a member of the Georgian Mameluk slave dynasties who ruled the affairs of much of the outlying areas of the Ottoman empire at the time. The countryside groaned under his heavy rule. Lawlessness was endemic, the traveler harassed by every village sheikh. Al-'Iraq suffered in silence, its people suspicious of foreigners and alien visitors. British prestige was at a low point.

The day after Rich arrived to take up his post, he called on the pasha and was received politely. Privately, he was unimpressed by the ruler and in public he faced up to him boldly. Rich had a great advantage over other foreigners, for besides his knowledge of Arabic and Turkish he had considerable experience with local psychology. He also possessed monumental patience. Within a few months he had become the most influential foreigner in al-'Iraq. His extreme youth made his dealings with the pasha a constant tightrope. In 1809, matters came to a head when the pasha challenged Rich's diplomatic creden-

4.1 *Claudius James Rich. Copyright the Trustees of the British Museum.*

tials. He was refused entry into the city after a country excursion. With sheer patience and force of personality, Rich quietly turned the tables on the pasha. He refused to leave. Eventually, the pasha's own bodyguard escorted him into the city. The pasha never challenged his authority again.

Life in the residency centered around a large and handsome house "perfectly in the Turkish style." The heat, unmitigated by air conditioning, fans, or refrigerators, was a constant hardship. The Riches left the house only between five and seven in the morning. "The weather is now so warm, we dine on the terrace," wrote Mary Rich. "In less than a month the heat will become so intolerable that we shall be obliged to sleep in the open air."[2] They lived in public during the hot weather. The roof of the residency was divided into open-air compartments that looked down on the city roofs below. The traveler James Buckingham, who stayed with the Riches at the residency, described how at dawn he could look down on "all the families of Baghdad, with their sleeping apartments unroofed, and those near our own abode often in sufficiently interesting situations."[3]

Rich insisted that the British resident live in considerable style and that his wife dress formally for dinner, even when they were on their own. The family letters to Bombay were filled with requests for more and more clothes, for gloves and "trowsers," for books, "a chess board and men, and also a new flute for Claudius."[4] Thirty Indian sepoys under a subadar (officer of the guard) protected the residency. Rich himself raised a small troop of sixteen European hussars. The residency teemed with servants; there was even a Slavic butler. The household lived and occasionally entertained in style. "If I did not come down as well dressed as I should be in Bombay at a party of fifteen or twenty persons, Mr. Rich would be extremely angry," wrote Mary Rich to one of her sisters.[5] Although the East India Company was unsympathetic toward Rich's insistence on a stylish establishment and paid him inadequate living allowances all the time he lived in Baghdad, he was determined to maintain a conspicuous presence. Anything else, he argued rightly, would lower Britain in Turkish eyes. He always called on the pasha in full-dress uniform, accompanied by his guard, drums, and fifes.

Baghdad was no paradise for the Riches, even though they entertained a stream of visitors, both distinguished and not so distinguished. Mary Rich looked out over the dingy landscape with resigned dislike. "The view I have of the renowned city is not the most beautiful," she wrote. "The streets are extremely narrow and the whole town is built of sun-baked bricks which give it a very dirty appearance. There is nothing at all splendid about Baghdad."[6]

The first three years of Rich's term of office were difficult politically. He found himself involved in disputes between company officials; he had to intercede with the sultan on the pasha's behalf—he even offered the pasha's ministers sanctuary when Constantinople arranged for the pasha to be deposed and beheaded. Rich had a reputation for fair dealing and incorruptibility, which enabled him to act boldly. On one occasion some notorious brigands robbed a residency official of his money on the road to Baghdad. Rich calmly invited some visiting British officers to join him and galloped six kilometers after the robbers with his mounted guard. The money was recovered forthwith.

∞∞

Despite the pressures of diplomacy, Rich devoted considerable time to collecting coins and manuscripts as well as other antiquities. During his thirteen years in Baghdad he accumulated a vast collection. His linguistic abilities ensured that he acquired only the best manuscripts, mainly in Chaldee, Armenian, and Syrian. He planned to write a history of western Asia based on materials from his collections, a project he never completed.

In December 1811, he managed to visit Babylon. Diplomatic protocol demanded that he travel in some state, accompanied "by my own troops of Hussars, with a galloper gun, a *havildar* [a sergeant] and twelve Sepoys; [and] about seventy baggage mules." Rich believed that local customs should be respected and attributed his diplomatic success to his sensitivity to the Turks' liking for "state and show." He wrote: "Above all, they have a horror of women being seen or heard. I am inclined to believe that a Turk who overcomes his dislike to this has lost some of his best feelings."[7] Poor Mary Rich! She was obliged to behave like a piece of the resident's baggage, her litter swung between two shafts transported by mules. Mary's maids fared even worse. They traveled in *mojaffas*, cagelike seats that were slung in pairs across a mule's back. The two cages were supposed to balance one another. But one of the attendants was slender, the other very stout. So the lighter woman had to sit on a pile of stones to equalize the weight.

The eighty-kilometer journey took two days and they traveled across numerous dried-up canals and abandoned mounds. The governor of Al Hillah greeted the Riches effusively with his official band, which helped clear away the crowds. Al Hillah lay three kilometers from Babylon's dusty mounds. Rich found it almost impossible to get a general impression of the site so he set his hussars to work as surveyors. Rich rode the length and breadth of the ruins, a somewhat hazardous undertaking as the mounds were composed of loose earth and were full of large holes made by brick diggers.[8]

Most of the Riches' ten-day stay was devoted to exploring the huge mounds of brick and earth that lay on the left bank of the Euphrates. Rich noted the northern mound, which he called Babil. A mile to the south lay another mound he labeled El Qasr. A third he named Omran ibn Ali. He paced out measurements, sketched the mounds, and tried to survey the architectural features of what we now know to be the inner city. He explored the larger ruins and compiled a survey plan that was the first systematic map of Babylon. The brick diggers of Al Hillah were hard at work extracting fired bricks from the ruins, many of which bore inscriptions. Some well-placed gratuities ensured him a steady supply of these inscribed bricks for his collection. When he came across some gaping holes in the ruins, he employed some workmen on his own to dig deeper. To his delight, they disinterred a skeleton in a coffin, which was removed piece by piece in a thoroughly nonarchaeological fashion.

On December 19, 1811, the party rode out ten kilometers from their camp southwest of Babylon to the vast mass of Birs Nimrod. "The morning was at first stormy," wrote Rich, "but as we approached the

4.2 *View of Babylon. From Chesney's* Narrative *(1868).*

object of our journey, the heavy clouds separating, [we] discovered the
Birs frowning over the plain, and presenting the appearance of a circular hill, crowned by a tower, with a high ridge extending along the foot
of it." He felt somewhat disappointed, for the clouds prevented him

from "acquiring the gradual idea," as he approached from afar, as he had done with the pyramids. But there were consolations, as Rich tells us at his romantic best: "Just as we were within the proper distance, it burst at once about our sight, in the midst of rolling masses of black clouds partially obscured by that kind of haze whose indistinctness is one great cause of sublimity, while a few strong catches of stormy light, thrown upon the desert in the background, served to give some idea of the immense and dreary solitude of the wastes in which this venerable ruin stands."[9] Hastily he measured and sketched the Birs, which he estimated to be seventy-two meters high, an enormous, oblong mound of decaying and vitrified brickwork.

Rich returned from Babylon with sufficient sketches and notes to write a "Memoir on the Ruins of Babylon," which appeared in the Viennese journal *Fundgraben des Orients* in 1813.[10] The article contained his plan of the ancient city and a description of its major features. Rich kept his Biblical speculations to a minimum and concentrated on straightforward exposition. The article was soon reprinted in England, where it caused great interest on account of Babylon's Old Testament associations. The reviewers praised Rich's "classical and oriental learning" and his "natural fruits of knowledge." He found himself an authority on ancient Mesopotamia, so much so that when a Major Rennell published a critique of the memoir in 1816, Rich felt obliged to return to the site to double-check his original work. His *Second Memoir on Babylon* appeared in 1818 and was to remain the definitive survey of the site until the 1890s.[11] Rich did little to untangle the confusion of ruins at Babylon — the task was beyond the archaeological methods of his day — but he provided generations of travelers with a map that gave at least some reliable information on the legendary city. He had no time for a truly comprehensive survey, nor did he do any excavation except for cleaning off Abbé Jean Beauchamp's celebrated lion. Yet, the few finds he did bring back formed the nucleus of the Mesopotamian collections in the British Museum and his memoirs captured the public's attention.

So great was the stir caused by Rich's two memoirs that Lord Byron immortalized them in his poem *Don Juan*, a tribute paid to few academic authors:

> . . . Claudius Rich, Esquire, some bricks has got
> And written lately two memoirs upon't.[12]

DIPLOMACY AND ARCHAEOLOGY IN BAGHDAD

These ruins consist of mounds of earth, formed by the decomposition of buildings, channeled and furrowed by the weather, and the surfaces of them are strewed with pieces of brick, bitumen, and pottery.

—CLAUDIUS JAMES RICH

AFTER FOUR YEARS IN BAGHDAD, THE TORRID SUMMERS AND THE CONSTANT STRAIN of political intrigue had undermined Claudius James Rich's health. His temper was not improved by constant bickering with his superiors in Bombay, who considered him a young upstart. So, at Mary's urgent pleading, he applied for, and was granted, a three-month overseas leave.

In October 1813, they set off for Europe, riding with official Ottoman *tatars* (couriers) to Constantinople. He found Vienna, Paris, and London so stimulating that he dreaded the prospect of returning to his post. Through the influence of his father-in-law, he managed to prolong his leave for months. He dined with the Duke of Wellington and was astonished by the violinist Nicolò Paganini's virtuosity in Milan. He talked archaeology with scholars both in England and on the Continent, men he had corresponded with for years, and found that they considered him an important scholar. As he relaxed and enjoyed himself, Rich gradually recovered his health. Such was his influence that an attempt by company officials in India to dismiss him from Baghdad was overruled imperiously from London. A week after Napoleon's defeat at Waterloo, the Riches began the long overland journey to Baghdad. The trip was a slow one, for Rich deliberately tarried two months in Constantinople and a month in Mosul, awaiting definitive information from London on his status with the company. Finally, in March 1816, the Riches resumed their sojourn in Baghdad.

Rich had managed to visit a number of scholarly colleagues in Europe, among them Joseph von Hammer-Purgstall, who was associated with the Academy of Oriental Languages in Vienna.[1] Hammer had taken a close interest in Carl Bellino, a promising student at the academy, and recommended him to Rich as a potential private secretary. Rich took to the young man immediately and he accompanied the family in early May 1816 with the title of official interpreter. He was given a horse, which he hated, and the run of Rich's library. The new private secretary was an immediate success. Mary remarked on his loyalty, industrious character, and passion for Oriental languages. Claudius found him a kindred spirit with a priceless asset—he had an uncanny knack for accurately copying cuneiform inscriptions. Rich had found that his European colleagues were more interested in accurate copies of cuneiform characters than anything else. Bellino could take much of this burdensome task off his hands.

It was just as well that Rich had additional help, for Baghdad was in turmoil. The effendi Daud, the pasha's brother-in-law, succeeded in deposing and executing the pasha and took over the pashalik. The Turks and Persians were at loggerheads and Arab insurrection was in the wind. Baghdad was full of executions, treachery, and warring factions. The resident remained pointedly neutral. Even during these troubled weeks, Rich's morning office hours were a formal audience attended by senior government ministers every day. "Everything was conducted with great decorum," wrote an early guest of the Riches. "Nothing could be more evident than the high degree of respect with which these interviews inspired the visitors."[2] No important official decisions were made without Rich's approval and imprimatur.

∽∽∽

Any traveler en route to the Persian Gulf made a beeline for the hospitable residency. A steady stream of visitors provided the Riches with welcome social diversion. Fortunately, most of their guests were literate and articulate people who were not only entertained but entertaining. One such visitor arrived at the residency gates in rags in July 1816. The ragged figure turned out to be James Silk Buckingham, a well-known traveler who enjoyed wandering through the East.[3] Buckingham was a charming and widely read man. He spent months in Baghdad and later published his impressions of the city and life at the residency.

Buckingham had traveled overland from Aleppo to Mosul and Baghdad with a small caravan under the patronage of a wealthy Mosul merchant, who insisted he dress like an Arab to the skin, with turban, tarboosh, and red silk sash.[4] He wore a "damascus sabre," a Turkish musket, small carbine, and pistols. Buckingham traveled light for safety, with a pipe and tobacco bag, a metal drinking cup, a pocket compass, memorandum books, and an ink stand. These items filled one saddlebag, the other held the chain fastening for his horse. A "small Turkey carpet" served as bed, table, and prayer mat, and a woolen cloak sufficed for bedding. He tucked his money in a cummerbund around his waist, but these precautions did not prevent him from being stripped of many of his possessions. He hated caravan travel. The camels ambled along at 2.5 miles per hour, and every nomad band extorted a harsh tax from travelers. At Mosul, he attached himself to two *tatars*, government couriers who were carrying official dispatches to Claudius Rich. The tatars traveled at full speed. On one occasion, Buckingham found himself riding eighty kilometers in six hours at full gallop. This lightning progress ended when the couriers ran out of horses. So Buckingham joined a Baghdad mule caravan. He found himself riding an overladen animal in appalling heat, not an enchanting experience. It was so hot that he jumped in a river fully clothed, then mounted his slow-moving animal without drying off. The intense heat blistered his face and lips; dust inflamed everyone's eyes. The rich carried parasols, while the poor—like Buckingham—had to be content with the scanty protection of their cloaks.

On July 16, 1816, the gates of Baghdad appeared eight kilometers ahead. The city guards stopped Buckingham from entering so they could inspect his load. He sat cross-legged in the dust by the gate and tried to smoke his pipe. A Turkish guard promptly snatched it from his mouth, asking him how he dared smoke when the pasha was about to pass on the way back from his morning ride. Soon the pasha and his troop of gaily dressed Mameluk guards swept past, accompanied by an ill-disciplined troop of foot soldiers dressed in cast-off military coats and muskets purchased from the British residency. He was impressed by the awe with which the onlookers greeted the pasha: everyone rose and made some gesture of respect. The pasha returned the salutations with great dignity. Two Englishmen—John Hine, the residency doctor, and Bellino—rode at the back of the procession. Buckingham heard their conversation and was smothered in the dust from their horses' hooves. But he forbore to identify himself in this public place.

Once the pasha was inside Baghdad, Buckingham boldly produced his revolver and pushed his mule past the gate. The onlookers cheered at the embarrassment of the Turkish guards. Buckingham made his way to the tatars' headquarters, identified himself as an Englishman, and was escorted to the British residency. There, as the guest of a large and luxurious establishment, he relaxed for the first time in months, reveling in baths, good food, a comfortable bed, and the welcome company of Claudius and Mary Rich.

The residency was formed from several houses converted into a single large dwelling with two courtyards. One of them served as a riding ground, surrounded with numerous rooms and galleries. Vaulted subterranean chambers, called serdabs, served as a daily refuge from the intense summer heat. The Rich establishment rose at dawn, bathed, and went riding until eight o'clock, when everyone met for breakfast. Rich then received official visitors in audience, after which everyone returned to the serdabs until sunset. Dinner was served on one of the terraces, the household gathering in formal evening dress for a leisured meal that lasted until ten o'clock. Beyond Hine and Bellino, the residency housed numerous dragomen, janissaries, grooms, and servants, as well as a company of Indian sepoys who acted as bodyguards to the resident. Their drums and horn calls regulated the life of the household. A large yacht lay in constant readiness; fine horses were instantly available for guests. Everything, wrote Buckingham, was calculated to impress the local people with the prestige of the resident and his country. He found a small but entertaining European community in Baghdad, of which Rich was the undisputed leader. The only other diplomat was the new French consul, a Monsieur Vigoroux, whose establishment consisted of a single dragoman, a few servants, and a tumbledown abode. The few Christians worshipped at the convent, presided over by a Carmelite monk called Padre Vincenzo.

Buckingham rested and amused himself by recording the temperatures during a typical calm summer's day when the brazen sun shone unmercifully from a dusty sky. His thermometer stood at 44°C at dawn, 49°C at noon, 50°C at 2:00 P.M., and 45°C at midnight. Many people died from the heat. Buckingham, however, managed to wander through the narrow streets with local guides a few times. After dark he visited bazaars and coffeehouses thronging with people clothed in colorful apparel. He would sit for hours in the middle of the famous Bridge of Boats, contemplating the brilliant stars in the heavens reflected in the placid water of the Tigris as it rippled past the boats. Buckingham was always interested in women and discovered that the pasha maintained a harem of Georgian girls. "It is permitted only to the Faithful, however, to possess white slaves . . . so that the Georgians and Circassians fall exclusively to the enjoyment of the orthodox," observed Buckingham. "Sceptics and heretics must content themselves with the sable beauties of Nigritia, Soudan, and Madagascar."[5] History does not relate whether Buckingham diverted himself in this way.

Except for excursions to Babylon and Ctesiphon, Buckingham spent much of his time laid low with fever and closeted in the residency.[6] He consoled himself with Rich's library and the fine collection of "cylinders, amulets, idols, and intaglios of the most curious kind" in Rich's study. Buckingham admired the clay seals with "inscriptions in the arrow-headed character, such as has been found at the ruins of Persepolis, Babylon, and Nineveh." Unfortunately, Buckingham was obliged to limit his occupations to "such light reading as would beguile the time; for the powers of the mind were so unhinged by the influence of the climate, as to be incapable of close application to any subject requiring much thought."[7]

Buckingham's greatest pleasure seems to have been spending time with the Riches themselves. Nearly ten years later he published his book on Mesopotamia, in which he praised Claudius Rich's "boundless generosity" and "unremitting zeal for the interests of science and general knowledge."[8]

Two years later, in October 1818, the Riches entertained another well-known visitor, the noted traveler and artist Sir Robert Ker Porter.[9] Ker Porter's introduction to Rich's prestige was dramatic. One hundred and thirty seven kilometers from Baghdad he stopped to rest at a village inn and sent a messenger on ahead to inform Rich that he would arrive soon and that his travel funds were running low. Rich's kavass (dragoman) soon arrived with a purse of several thousand piasters, which he presented to the landlord. When the landlord of the inn found out that his guest was short of money, he came in with a large bag of piasters, merely requesting that the money be repaid to a friend of his in Baghdad. Ker Porter was astounded at this unheard-of gesture of trust. "Simple," replied the landlord, as he explained that the British resident had such a good reputation and such power that he knew his money was absolutely safe.

Armed with these unexpected funds, Ker Porter pressed on to Baghdad. His companions were so sick that they rode in basketlike carriers flung on either side of a mule's back. A day later they were met by an imposing Turk guarded by two well-mounted Arab horsemen armed to the teeth. Thinking that he was in the presence of a high government official, Ker Porter prepared to pay his respects. To his astonishment, the Turk salaamed and brought him greetings from the British resident, a letter, and a purse of 1,000 piasters. Two days later, Ker Porter was escorted into an airy room overlooking the Tigris and greeted warmly by Claudius and Mary Rich.

In Ker Porter, Rich found a kindred soul. He examined his visitor's sketches, notably those of Persepolis and the undeciphered inscriptions on the Great Rock at Behistun in Persia, which later was to provide so many clues to the decipherment of cuneiform. The two men and Bellino discussed the problems of copying and translating the mysterious script. Rich had been in poor health for a while. Ker Porter's welcome conversation sent him back to his manuscripts and inscriptions with renewed vigor. The academic debates at the residency did not prevent Ker Porter from enjoying the hospitality of Baghdad's wealthier inhabitants. He attended dinners and entertainments and saw male dancers dressed in linen and coins perform violent dances "by twisting the body into all kinds of odious postures, accompanied by a machine-like dodder of the head, which is duly answered by a wriggle from the back, or hips."[10]

Ker Porter had come to Baghdad with the intention of visiting Babylon. The countryside, however, was so unsettled that Rich sent not only Bellino but also an armed escort with him. Ker Porter was in a state of eager anticipation, his mind full of the city walls nearly 100 kilometers in circumference, the brass gates, the Hanging Gardens described by Herodotus, and the ultimate destruction that had beset the "daughter of the Chaldeans." What he found was a solemn sight, the "majestic stream of the Euphrates wandering in solitude, like a pilgrim monarch through the devastated ruins of his kingdom." He deplored how the scene had changed: "These broken hills were palaces; those long undulating mounds, streets; this vast solitude, filled with the busy subjects of the proud daughter of the East. Now, *wasted with solitude,* her habitations are not to be found."[11]

More than any traveler, Ker Porter was impressed by the desolation of Babylon, the utter destruction extolled by the Scriptures. Here, indeed, was powerful demonstration of the Lord's handiwork. He paused at Birs Nimrod to admire that "stupendous work arrested before completion." That this mound was the Biblical Tower of Babel seemed beyond doubt. "It does not seem improbable," he wrote in wonder, "that the fire-blasted summit of the pile, its rent wall and scattered fragments, with their partially vitrified masses, may be a part of that very stage of the primeval tower which felt the effects of the divine vengeance."[12]

As he and his party approached the silent mass of brickwork on a second visit, they saw several dark figures moving along the summit of the ruin. Their immediate thought was of robbers. But Ker Porter was amazed to see "two or three majestic lions, taking their air upon the heights of the pyramid." He was deeply moved, remembering the utter destruction of Babylon foretold by the prophet Isaiah: "But wild beasts will lie down there, and its houses will be full of howling creatures."[13]

Meanwhile, Carl Bellino had been hard at work copying the cuneiform inscriptions in the residency library, including those on "a small earthen vase covered with cuneiform" from Nebi Yunus at Nineveh (the vase is now known as the Bellino cylinder). He had been corresponding with European experts, to whom he sent copies of his work. Rich arranged for him to be elected to the Bombay Literary Society, an honor that delighted Bellino. His "Account of the Progress Made in Deciphering Cuneiform Inscriptions," which had been published in the society's journal in 1818, was widely read and praised.[14] The hard-working and obscure young man was making a major contribution to the decipherment of cuneiform.

∽∽

In spring 1820, Rich planned an official journey to the higher elevations of Kurdistan, where he could escape the summer heat. He organized the trip with care, for Kurdistan was a remote and little-visited territory for foreigners in the 1820s. He felt he should travel in official splendor, accompanied by most of his household and a guard of twenty-five sepoys. As usual, Mary Rich had to bounce along in her mule-borne litter until the caravan reached remote country where she could mount a horse.

The Kurdistan trip took the Riches into the Zagros Mountains and Kurdish provinces of Persia, where they held court for tribal rulers and studied local customs. Rich even slipped away in disguise to witness the dancing in a local Arab wedding. The British cavalcade arrived back on the plains at Mosul in October so that Rich could examine Nineveh across the Tigris from the town. Difficulties with Pasha Daud in Baghdad caused the Riches to spend five months in Mosul. Their stay was saddened by Bellino's death from fever, a heartfelt loss to both Claudius and Mary.

Rich spent many days examining Nineveh. "The area of Nineveh, on a rough guess, is about one and a half to two miles, broad, and four miles long," he wrote. "The Mount of Kuyunjik is, except at its west and part of its eastern face, of rather an irregular form. Its sides are very steep, its top nearly flat; its angles are not marked by any lantern or turret." Rich's party measured the height of the mound — 13 meters. It was 210 meters in circumference. "It evidently has had building on it, at least round its edges," reported Rich. "Stones and bricks are dug or ploughed up everywhere. There were also other buildings further in the mount, and at a place where they had been digging into it, we saw the same coarse grey stone, shaped like the capital of a column such as at this day surrounds the wooden pillars or posts of Turkish or rather Persian verandahs."[15]

As the party wandered over the surface of Nineveh they came across the stone and earth floors of long-abandoned houses and thousands of potsherds and brick fragments. The finds included "a piece of fine brick or pottery covered with exceedingly small and beautiful cuneiform writing." Rich visited the small village of Nebi Yunus, which flourished on the summit of one of Nineveh's tells.[16] He delved in kitchens and living rooms in search of inscriptions and artifacts. He found that the inhabitants regularly dug up cuneiform inscriptions. But they were terrified of undermining their dwellings. Rich crouched over cuneiform-covered bricks, now part of kitchen walls, and persuaded one woman to allow him to record an inscription set into the modern plaster wall of her small room. Rich was tantalized by these inscriptions, but the labyrinth of houses in the village prevented him from digging into the mound below. So the Riches contented themselves with visiting the imposing Mosque of Jonah on the north end of the mound. The entire population of the village assembled to gaze at the strange sight of some Europeans admiring the view from the terrace of the mosque, but no one objected to their presence. The spectators were heard to mutter that Rich was working out whether the mosque was a suitable gun emplacement to bring a cannonade to bear on Mosul.

The local people kept on reporting almost-forgotten discoveries of fine statues in the mounds. Much of Mosul was built of stone and mud brick quarried from them. In one place Rich was shown a quarry where "some years ago, an immense bas-relief, representing men and animals, covering a grey stone of the height of two men was dug up from a spot a little above the surface of the ground." Apparently everyone in Mosul trekked out to see it. Then the quarrymen broke it up for building stone. The only way to recover valuable specimens was to buy them from the walls of local houses. One beautifully inscribed slab was literally talked out of the houseowner's wall in Nebi Yunus. "It is now safely lodged among my other curiosities," wrote Rich happily.[17]

Rich embarked on an ambitious project to map the entire complex of mounds. He was fortunate in having the services of his military escort, whom he dispatched in all directions to measure mounds and fortifications. Sometimes the sepoys could survey a site without anyone taking notice, whereas Rich would have been followed by dozens of curious spectators. In the meantime, "Delli Samaan, my curiosity-hunter," was dispatched to hunt out antiquities from the local bazaars and villages. Rich ranged widely over the countryside in every

Mosul and Nineveh, with the mound of Nebi Yunus in the foreground. From Chesney's Survey (1850).

direction, trying to establish the boundaries of the ancient city. Time and time again he came across erosion gullies or stream banks where floodwaters had cut through ancient midden deposits to expose mud-

brick courses or stone walls that lay intact below the surface. Claudius and Mary amused themselves by carving their names into a stone wall by a well. "Some traveler in after times, when our remembrance has long been swept away by the torrent of time . . . may wonder, on reading the name of Mary Rich, who the adventurous female was who had visited the ruins of Nineveh," he wrote. "He will not be aware that, had her name been inscribed at every spot she had visited in the course of her weary pilgrimage, it would be found in places compared with which Mosul is the centre of civilization."[18]

Rich continued to explore the countryside whenever the weather allowed. But heavy rains often confined him to the town, where he watched the locals open Mosul's Bridge of Boats to let the Tigris flood unimpeded. He also puzzled over his plans of Nineveh, certain that all the mounds he had measured were of the same age. An earlier visit many years before had convinced him that the major buildings were confined to the mounds of Nebi Yunus and Kuyunjik. These mounds were the "citadel or royal precincts, or perhaps both, as the practice of fortifying the residence of the sovereign is of very ancient origin."[19] Later excavations were to prove him right.

Between his archaeological expeditions, Rich searched for ancient manuscripts preserved in local monasteries and convents. He was horrified to learn that the monks of one monastery had destroyed a library of 500 manuscripts some years before as they had no use for them. "Manuscripts are fast perishing in the East," he wrote, "and it is almost the duty of a traveler to rescue as many as he can from destruction." Rich spared neither time nor money in acquiring as much as he could, wherever he traveled. He found that the manuscripts held little value for their owners until the time came to haggle over price. Then, "with that avidity for money which is so undisguised in the East, they express unwillingness to part with them, in order, too generally, to secure a large sum being offered for them."[20] Fortunately for science, the manuscripts collected by Claudius Rich ended up in the British Museum, purchased for the then-enormous sum of 7,000 pounds. A letter from the museum written in 1836 reveals that they possessed 800 volumes of Rich's manuscripts, a definitive collection of Syriac and Arabic documents.

On March 3, 1821, the Riches started for Baghdad on a *kellek*. They floated downstream through intensely cultivated country. After forty-eight kilometers, they came to the ancient mounds of Nimrud, where Claudius, Mary, and a working party disembarked for a difficult walk to the conspicuous mounds.[21] The ruined ziggurat at the northwest corner of the site could be seen from far away, but Rich found it difficult to trace the edges of the city among the plowed fields. The visitors wandered over the mounds, saw traces of buildings like those at Nineveh, and collected burned bricks inscribed with cuneiform. Rich was elated to find one brick bearing "writing larger than that at Babylon." The rafts were waiting, so Rich had only enough time to make some simple measurements and to observe that "these ruins singularly illustrate those of Nineveh." They floated downstream for the next ten days, enjoying the countryside and admiring the skill of the boatmen in navigating through intricate passages, sandbanks, and low islands.

Dispatches awaited Rich at Baghdad, one of which was an offer of a senior job in Bombay. He accepted this new position, but the volatile Pasha Daud rescinded British trading rights in the pashalik and refused to allow the resident to depart. Rich learned that the pasha planned to take him prisoner, so he fortified the residency and had his sepoys man the barricades. The pasha's infantry started a surprise advance on the residency but backed off when they saw Rich's preparations. In any case, their commander and most of the townspeople were firm friends of the Riches. When the pasha's ministers came to negotiate, Rich demanded the removal of the besieging troops. The ministers refused, whereupon he grabbed a stick and angrily drove the ministers from the residency gates. The pasha had no option but to allow Rich to depart. The Riches left on the residency yacht to the accompaniment of a tumultuous send-off from their friends. They sailed to Basra and then on to Bushire, on the Persian Gulf, where Claudius paused to await instructions.[22] He sent Mary on to Bombay in a passing ship. They never saw each other again.

Bored in the sweltering heat of Bushire, Rich thought of Ker Porter's dazzling stories of Persepolis and decided to travel to the ruined city before continuing to India. He timed his visit to coincide with a full moon. Both Niebuhr and Porter had recorded the inscriptions, so Rich, free of tiresome diplomatic protocol and the need to sketch, could indulge his imagination. The ancient city did not disappoint him. As he approached the ruins the moon rose behind the backdrop of mountains. "Ages seemed at once to present themselves to my fancy," he wrote.[23]

After this unashamed archaeological indulgence, Rich traveled on to Shiraz. A few days after his arrival, cholera descended on the city. Over 6,000 people died in a few days. The wealthier inhabitants fled the town, but Rich insisted on staying behind to quell the panic and aid the sick. On October 14, 1821, he developed symptoms of cholera after a warm bath and died within twenty-four hours. He was only thirty-four years old.

THE EUPHRATES EXPEDITION

The ascent of the Euphrates will be easy compared to what has just been overcome, and which has demonstrated that both rivers are navigable at all times with ease.

—FRANCIS CHESNEY

THE CLOSING YEARS OF CLAUDIUS RICH'S RESIDENCY IN BAGHDAD HAD SEEN HIM increasingly preoccupied with what was to become the dominant issue of Eastern politics for decades—"the Eastern Question." Napoleon's abortive campaign in Egypt in 1798 had raised the specter of an enemy power blocking British access to India by an overland route. By the end of the Napoleonic Wars, Russia was beginning to examine her eastern frontiers and the Dardanelles with interest. Her more aggressive foreign policies raised another persistent worry, that of a Russian invasion of India with the compliance of Afghanistan and Persia. The French wanted to control the Syrian coast, and the Germans were eyeing the Persian Gulf. Everyone expected the Ottoman empire, with its shrinking economy and cumbersome bureaucracy, to crumble and evaporate, leaving behind a political and economic vacuum. As successive sultans tried to reform their government, almost invariably without success, a complicated checkerboard of patronage, political and economic manipulation, and espionage ebbed and flowed over the region. In the long run, the greatest impact of the Eastern Question was the exposure of even the remote provinces of the Ottoman empire to new and alien European ideas. The slow changes that resulted from these ideas led in part to a rising tide of Arab nationalism that culminated about the time of the First World War.

Baghdad lay at the center of the Eastern Question. The city's strategic position in Mesopotamia made it an obvious military and administrative center for a potential invader. About 100,000 people lived there in Rich's time. He and his successors never forgot the strategic importance of Baghdad, even if the city itself was decaying into ruins and had become a shadow of its former glory. "It bears a name, and a certain respectability in the East," reported Sir Robert Ker Porter in 1818, "solely from the circumstance of its situation being a central depot . . . from its lying on the main road of traffic between so many distant counties, to receive, and protect, and set forward on their business, all the merchants and merchandise which pass to and fro from Baghdad."[1] As Constantinople took more and more authority into its own hands, Baghdad and its pashalik sank into greater poverty. Constant grain shortages caused the pasha to force thousands of poorer people from the city. The expelled poor starved in the desert, wandered in the harsh foothills, or, more often than not, joined robber bands and supported themselves by pillage and murder. Even large caravans were in constant danger of attack, for the pasha's authority was confined to Baghdad. The government taxed peasants so heavily on their crops that they grew as little corn as possible. When revenues fell, the tax collectors resorted to extortion and beatings. So the farmers fled their land and joined the swelling city population. Most serious of all, the government neglected to maintain the irrigation works and embankments that checked the floodwaters of the Tigris. Baghdad was a vulnerable city, and its rulers were living on borrowed time.

∞∞

The crisis came in March 1831, while Rich's enemy, Pasha Daud, was still in power. That spring a few cases of plague appeared in the bazaars, isolated occurrences that mushroomed into an epidemic in a few short weeks. Rich's successor, Colonel James Taylor, closed the British residency at once to keep the plague outside the buildings. All supplies for the household were delivered through apertures in the wall and passed through water before being touched. Letters and papers were fumigated before opening. While the Europeans went into quarantine, the locals fled to the countryside. But the plague still spread. By April 10, 7,000 people had died in the eastern parts of the city. Then a sepoy in the residency contracted the disease. Taylor immediately packed up his effects and fled to Basra. Fortunately, the residency boats were moored beneath the walls of the house and everyone could get away without contact with the townspeople. The only British resident not to leave was a Christian Brethren missionary, the Reverend A. N. Groves, who insisted on staying behind to minister to Christians who had taken shelter in his house.

Between April 16 and 21, about 2,000 people a day were dying. So virulent was the disease that people scarcely dared bury their dead relatives. Many families bought up stocks of winding sheets before the supply ran out. One of Groves's servants told him she saw fifty bodies being carried off for burial within 200 meters. To cap this misery, the Tigris rose in flood and inundated much of western Baghdad. Part of the British residency collapsed into the river. Bands of desert Arabs roamed the outskirts of the city and robbed those who fled. Food supplies were depleted, cemeteries were overflowing, corpses were buried in the streets. Many people were completely demoralized and stayed at home waiting for death. Families left infants in the streets to die, and the dead lay stacked on mules to be carried away for burial. Dogs mangled and devoured freshly buried corpses.

By April 26, over 4,000 people a day were succumbing to the plague. More than a third of the city's population had left; many more had perished. On April 27, Groves recorded that the Tigris had undermined a long length of the ancient city walls, which had collapsed. The floodwaters rushed into the Jewish quarter. Within hours, over 7,000 mudbrick houses melted in the flood water, killing at least 1,500 people. The survivors camped on higher ground, hastily throwing the dead into the Tigris. The survivors crowded into smaller and smaller spaces, so the disease struck even harder. The floodwaters also trapped many refugees, who drowned or lost their possessions to robbers. It was not until the beginning of May that the floods receded and the plague abated. The death rate fell gradually; the epidemic ended on about May 26.[2]

By the time the floodwaters retreated, thousands of Baghdad's population had perished. Only a small cluster of buildings on higher ground and a few mosques with strong foundations still stood. The city walls encompassed a barren wilderness of ruined foundations and stagnant pools. It was months before life returned to a semblance of normalcy. The government's already weak administrative grip on Baghdad and the countryside weakened even more. Several pashas murdered their predecessors. Arab sheikhs living within and near Baghdad did what they pleased. Matters improved after 1831, when Mameluk power in Baghdad finally evaporated and the sultan was able to appoint his own pashas. Yet, Mesopotamia's troubles were not over as minor plague epidemics returned in two successive years, killing another 5,000 to 7,000 people each time.

Traveling to Mesopotamia during such troubled times took considerable courage and ingenuity. A few explorers like Richard Mignan and James Baillie-Fraser ventured onto the desolate plains between the rivers in Babylonia, accompanied by only a small party of armed Arabs. Baillie-Fraser was probably the first European to visit Tell Muqayyar, the site of the Biblical Ur of the Chaldees.[3]

In 1834 Baillie-Fraser found Baghdad a gutted town. The city walls, with their courses of well-worn brick and fortified towers, still looked imposing. He enjoyed the narrow roads and brick houses whose projecting windows overhung the streets. The sitting rooms of houses across the street from each other were sometimes joined. Occasionally, Baillie-Fraser found himself "illuminated by a beam from some bright pair of eyes shining through the half-closed lattice." The river frontage boasted "a long range of imposing, if not absolutely handsome" buildings shaded with palm trees. A constant bustle of boats and rafts carrying horses, camels, and people passed to and fro. The bazaars were dilapidated and in ruins, many of the shops neglected and unoccupied. The largest bazaar was near the Mosul Gate, a busy place where the headless trunks of executed criminals were exhibited to the public. Above all, Baghdad was noisy, filled with every imaginable din. As Baillie-Fraser sat on his balcony over the street, he was beset by cocks crowing in a nearby yard, the sepoy's reveille call at the British residency, dogs barking, donkeys braying, and herds of sheep and cattle passing through the streets early in the morning. The Arabs, he complained, "rush along in droves . . . hallooing to each other and to all they pass, often maintaining a conversation at the top of their tremendous voices, with some equally clear-piped brother, at a quarter of a mile's distance."[4]

The East India Company and the British government were concerned not only about Russia but also about finding fast and reliable land and sea routes to India. They sought to address these concerns through diplomacy in Constantinople and exploration of new routes to India that would maximize the benefit of steamship travel up the Red Sea and in the Mediterranean. The diplomatic effort was in the hands of the British ambassador in Constantinople, the formidable and powerful Sir Stratford Canning, known to Englishmen and Turks alike as the Great Elchi (*elchi* is "envoy" in Turkish).[5] Canning believed that the Ottoman empire "was rotten at the heart" and spent many years trying to institute reform. He fostered a policy that bolstered the Ottoman sultans to protect British trade and communications. His main worry was Russia. Al-'Iraq was of lesser importance except as a possible highway route between Europe and India. Canning's influence with the sultan was enormous. He presided over a glittering embassy with almost military precision. An autocrat and a firm believer in the doctrine of the divine rights of ambassadors, he was to play a leading part in organizing early excavations in Iraq.

With Canning's diplomatic backing, British officers and embassy officials quietly explored many of the sultan's domains. The search for an overland route to India, however, was pursued on a larger scale. In the late 1820s, the East India Company drew up a staff document that asked a number of specific questions about possible overland routes to India via Syria and Mesopotamia.[6] In particular, the document stressed the importance of discovering whether the Euphrates was navigable and for what distance and, above all, whether it could be traversed by steamship. In 1830, Captain Francis Chesney of the Royal Artillery, who was a rocket expert and a surveyor based in Constantinople, was sent on a trip through Syria, Egypt, Iraq, and Turkey to areas where the provincial governors' loyalty to the sultan was in doubt. He started off by visiting Egypt in 1829, where he studied the idea of an isthmus canal and showed that such a waterway was technically feasible as far as sea levels were concerned. "The practical question," he wrote, "appeared to be one of expenditure."[7]

In late 1830, Chesney traveled across the Holy Land and Syria to the Euphrates, floated downstream on a *kellek,* and visited Baghdad and Basra. He returned to London in 1832 to find that his preliminary surveys had caused quite a stir. Two years later, he was summoned to an audience with King William IV, appointed leader of the Euphrates Expedition, promoted to colonel, and given 20,000 pounds to spend on the enterprise.

The Euphrates Expedition of 1836 is an obscure chapter in the annals of exploration. Chesney was to transport two prefabricated iron steamers from the Syrian coast to the banks of the Euphrates 225 kilometers away, assemble them, and determine whether both that river and the Tigris were navigable. The official charge was to survey the northern part of Syria, explore the basins of the Euphrates and Tigris rivers, test the navigability of the former, and report on potential markets for British and Indian goods.[8] Although a major objective was to open a regular steamer route to India, the organizers were also interested in opening Mesopotamia to external trade on a scale unknown since the days of the caliphs.

Chesney threw himself into this enormous task with his characteristic energy. He recruited officers from the navy, the army, and the East India Company and arranged for skilled artisans, marines, and seamen to be posted to the expedition. His equipment included not only the two prefabricated paddle steamers *Tigris* and *Euphrates* but a diving bell, tools for mining coal, Congreve rockets, and numerous guns and ammunition.[9] Two years' provisions had to be carried overland as well, including dried meat and wine.

The expedition reached the mouth of the Orontes River on the Syrian coast in April 1835. The cumbersome steamer components, especially the keels and boilers, were floated as far up the Orontes as possible, then transferred to stout carriages. Heavy carts carried the boilers and hull sections. Some carts were even rigged with square sails, but these sails did little to help them over the muddy plains. Chesney's officers hired pack animals and dozens of laborers, three times more, he reported, than would have been necessary in Britain to do the job. While most of the officers and men were busy moving the disassembled steamers inland, a small group of surveyors began the laborious task of running levels from the coast to the Euphrates to establish the feasibility of a canal from the Mediterranean to the river.

The transportation of the steamers to the Euphrates occupied more than nine months of backbreaking work. Many officers and men were felled by fever or alternately baked by the sun and drenched by record rains and floods. The worst part of the journey was a steep hill near Lake Amik Gölü. A zigzag track had to be built up the slope. Forty pairs of oxen and a hundred men eased the boilers up the hill. Once over the summit, the heavy loads were floated across the lake and dragged 190 kilometers to a newly constructed stockade at Birecik on the Euphrates, christened Port William after the expedition's royal patron.

Three months later, on March 16, 1836, the *Euphrates* set off on her first trial trip. A few days later, both steamers sailed in convoy downstream, preceded by a small advance party who sounded the river. The local people were astonished at Chesney's "supernatural" genius in moving vessels without sails or oars. He cashed in on his supposed magic by employing hundreds of laborers to haul the steamers off uncharted shallows. When some desert Arabs stole a corporal's brass buttons, a small party of officers and men rode out to remonstrate with the marauders. They nearly fell into a trap and would have been cut off had it not been for a "rapid demonstration in light infantry order," which enabled the party to return to the shelter of the steamers' rockets and guns. Later, Chesney invited the sheikhs to dinner, which was preceded by a timely demonstration of rocket firepower that had them hastily proclaiming their peaceful intentions.

Hampered only by coal shortages, the survey went smoothly until May 21. Then tragedy struck. The two steamers were proceeding quietly downstream at midday when dark and ominous clouds blew up from the southwest. The steamers were about to enter the rock passage of Is-Geria. Since there was no room to turn around, the steamers pressed on, intending to secure alongside the bank as soon as possible. Just as they were making for the bank, the storm struck with winds of hurricane force. To avoid a collision with the *Tigris,* the *Euphrates* had to back-paddle. The crew secured her to the bank with great difficulty, combating steep waves more than a meter high. By keeping her engines full ahead, she managed to stay in one place. But the *Tigris* touched the bank, bounced off, and drifted helplessly in midstream. The wind heeled the steamer on her beam-ends. Water broke through

The Tigris *and* Euphrates *sailing in company downstream, on the Euphrates. From* Chesney's Narrative *(1868).*

the skylights, open windows, and paddle boxes, extinguishing the boilers. *Tigris* foundered and capsized only eighteen meters from shore in pitch-darkness and flying dust. The thirty-four crew mem-

bers had clustered at the stern. They jumped for their lives. Chesney found himself swimming in a cornfield accompanied by his sodden Bible. The storm ended as quickly as it had begun. When the survivors assembled at the *Euphrates,* they found fifteen of their party, as well as four Arabs, missing.[10]

Everyone agreed that the survey should continue, so Chesney sailed south to Basra, where the *Euphrates* arrived in June, burning empty casks to fuel the last sixty-nine kilometers. He then sailed her over the open sea to Bushire, carried out essential repairs, and ascended the Tigris to Baghdad. The river was so shallow that the Arab pilots had to swim and wade ahead of the steamer in places to spot the channel. On August 30, 1836, the *Euphrates* steamed triumphantly through the Bridge of Boats at Baghdad to be greeted by the British resident and the entire population of the city. An attempt to ascend the Euphrates ended in failure when the engines suffered a serious breakdown. By this time the funds of the expedition were too low to permit another attempt.

The Euphrates Expedition showed that a regular steamer service upstream was impracticable on account of the many shallows and rapids. Nor was the technology of steam power advanced enough to stem the rapid current of the Euphrates narrows. There was no advantage to a steamer service anyhow, when letters could reach Baghdad from Damascus by camel in eight or nine days. Chesney's reports noted that the Euphrates flowed through desert country inhabited by nomads. He complained that there was nobody to civilize or convert. So the East India Company quietly shelved the overland route through Mesopotamia. But the expedition generated some lasting benefits. The Lynch brothers, one of whom served on the *Euphrates,* decided to take advantage of the river surveys, which had been mapped by Chesney on a scale of two miles to the inch. They had three river steamers shipped out from England via the Cape of Good Hope and put them into service on the Tigris between Basra and Baghdad. For years, the Euphrates Steam Navigation Company carried mail, horses, merchandise, and people up and down the river. The steamships provided a vital link with the outside world that made Baghdad less dependent on the whims of desert sheikhs.

Thanks to the Euphrates Expedition, Mesopotamia became much more familiar to the Western world. Every traveler to Baghdad carried Chesney's river maps with him. The archaeologists and adventurers who came after him were traveling in territory that was no longer a remote outpost of the eastern world. The pace of scientific research increased accordingly.

CUNEIFORM DECIPHERED

I aspire to do for the cuneiform alphabet what Champollion has done for the hieroglyphics.

—HENRY RAWLINSON

WHEN SIR ROBERT KER PORTER ARRIVED IN BAGHDAD IN OCTOBER 1818, HE carried many pages of copies of the cuneiform inscriptions left by the Persian kings at Mount Alvand near Hamadan (the ancient Ecbatana) and on the Great Rock at Behistun, thirty-two kilometers east of Kermanshah. Carl Bellino and Claudius Rich had urged him to publish his copies from Behistun, where the perpendicular rock faces were carved with inscriptions in three languages. "What a treasure of information doubtless was there to the happy man who could decipher [the scripts]," he wrote in his *Travels*, published in 1821. "It was tantalizing to a painful degree, to look at such a sealed book, in the very spot of mystery, where, probably, its contents would explain all."[1]

The Great Rock demonstrates vividly the megalomania of the Persian kings. One hundred and eleven square meters of rock face were carefully smoothed and the weak portions consolidated with a mixture of rock and lead. Dozens of artisans burnished the surface to a high polish. Then artists carved a huge bas-relief surrounded on three sides by inscriptions in Old Persian (414 lines), Elamite (263 lines), and Babylonian (112 lines). The relief is 5.4 meters wide and more than 90 meters above the ground. It depicts King Darius standing in triumph over Gaumata, a rival for the throne. Two officers attend the monarch, while the god Ahuramazda hovers overhead. Darius's foot rests on his rival's stomach as he pronounces sentence on nine other rebel leaders. "Eight of my family have been kings," boasts Darius in the inscriptions, which recount how Ahuramazda helped the king put down Gaumata's rebellion in 522 B.C.

Ker Porter's drawings of Behistun and its inscriptions excited widespread interest in Europe. He had spent many weeks copying the trilingual Persepolis inscriptions, too. His pictures of flying bulls and columns of cuneiform were compared favorably with those made by Carsten Niebuhr many years before. Although it would be a quarter of a century before Behistun was copied accurately and deciphered, by the time Ker Porter's *Travels* appeared a small international community of scholars had begun to argue and correspond about cuneiform. Each new inscription was passed from hand to hand, for accurate copies were in chronically short supply. The experts had developed a healthy respect for Niebuhr's careful work and his identification of forty-two different letters in an alphabetic method of writing, in which letters spelled out words.

In 1798, Bishop Friedrich Münter of Copenhagen, a well-known historian, published two papers on Persepolis in which he argued that Niebuhr's Class I script was alphabetic and that his Classes II and III were syllabic and ideographic, respectively.[2] Furthermore, each class was not only a different language but a different type of writing as well. He also proved that the Persepolis inscriptions were the work of the Persian Achaemenid dynasty and speculated that the Class I script was Old Persian, an Indo-European language. Although

French artist Eugène Flandin's sketch of the Great Rock of Behistun, which gives an excellent impression of the inaccessibility of the inscription. From E. Flandin and P. Coste, Voyage en Perse *(Paris: Imprimerie impériale, 1851).*

Münter never worked on cuneiform again, he had provided some of the vital groundwork for its decipherment. So did the French scholar Abraham Hyacinthe Anquetil-Duperron, who learned how to read and interpret Old Persian by comparing it with Indian manuscripts he had collected. His works, published in 1768 and 1771, gave the decipherers the necessary linguistic insights to tackle Niebuhr's Class I script. Another French scholar, Antoine Isaac Silvestre de Sacy, translated later Persian inscriptions and revealed the stereotyped titles of Persian kings.[3] Each monarch was addressed as "____, great king, king of kings, king of ____, son of ____, great king, king of kings." This information was of incalculable value to the new generation of decipherers, among them Oluf Gerhard Tychsen of Rostock, Germany. In 1798, Tychsen correctly identified four characters and the critical symbol that separated individual words from one another. His work was of great benefit to the man who finally was successful: Georg Friedrich Grotefend.

Grotefend was born at Münden in Germany and studied philology at University of Göttingen. In 1797, he embarked on a long, uneventful career as a schoolteacher and eventually became director of the Hanover Lyceum. But this quiet man was a philological genius. He first became involved with cuneiform at the age of twenty-seven, when a friend asked him if it would ever be possible to decipher the script. So Grotefend acquired some copies of the Persepolis inscriptions and sat down to attempt what many people thought was impossible. In 1802, he presented some preliminary conclusions to the Göttingen Academy of Sciences. His contribution, "Commentary on the Persepolitan Cuneiform Writing," took over where Münter and Tychsen had left off.[4]

Grotefend began by confirming Pietro della Valle's conclusion that the cuneiform script was actually a form of writing, written in a horizontal direction and read from left to right. When he began to look closely at the inscriptions, Grotefend found an astonishing diversity of cuneiform types. From his detailed knowledge of the history of Persepolis, he knew that the Persian king Cyrus had conquered the Babylonians around 538 B.C. This information, he believed, suggested that at least one of the three Persepolis scripts was Old Persian. The columns of cuneiform danced in front of Grotefend's eyes as he patiently compared the lines of characters. The middle column was alphabetical, he felt, and written in Old Persian. And a group of signs and another single sign reappeared time and time again. Grotefend hypothesized that this group stood for "king" and that the isolated character represented a divider between words.

So far so good. Selecting the Old Persian inscriptions for further study, Grotefend recalled Sacy's description of more recent royal inscriptions that gave the Persian king the title "great king, king of kings." Had this formula been used in earlier times with earlier inscriptions? He selected two short inscriptions that Niebuhr had copied from above the heads of royal figures. When he compared these cuneiform groups with each other, he found that the beginnings and ends of the inscriptions were different, but in between the texts were basically similar, the minor differences being those, perhaps, of genitive significance. Each final group of characters ended with genitive signs. Perhaps, he thought, they represented the same formula as that described by Sacy: "____, great king, king of kings, king of ____, son of ____, great king, king of kings."

After much close reasoning, Grotefend was able to identify not only a group of characters that meant "king" but signs that were the names of rulers, which were repeated again and again. Who were these kings? Grotefend checked through the Persian king lists to see whose names coincided most closely with the Persepolis characters. He eliminated Cyrus, Cambyses, and Artaxerxes and found himself left with Darius and Xerxes. Their names fitted perfectly. When Grotefend came to convert the Greek names of the Persian monarchs into Persian form, he found he could add other letters to those he had already deciphered. He ended up with the names of two kings: "Darius, son of Hystaspes," and "Xerxes, son of Darius."

Grotefend eventually succeeded in identifying ten signs and three proper names by using Anquetil-Duperron's Old Persian studies. Although his translations of Persepolitan inscriptions turned out to be full of errors, they gave the essence of the meaning. In 1805 he published a fuller account, which spurred great interest. The discussions generated by his work began a long tradition of close collaboration among experts in several European countries. Unfortunately, Grotefend started to overstate his achievements and claimed more for his translations than was justified. He eventually ceased to play a leading part in the translation of cuneiform and died in comfortable obscurity in 1853.

Grotefend's successors corroborated many of his results and kept chipping away at the philological problem. By its very nature, the study of cuneiform tended to attract quiet, scholarly men rather than flamboyant adventurers. These often introspective scholars wrote to one another constantly, reporting each minor advance or new inscription. They worked in cluttered studies, often holding down jobs as teachers or ministers at the same time. Cuneiform studies knew no national boundaries, for Danes, Englishmen, Frenchmen, and Germans shared their results freely. Among them were the French philologist Eugène Burnouf and the Norwegian scholar Christian Lassen. In 1836 each published a treatise on the Old Persian of the Persepolis inscriptions, drawing wide attention.

By then, it was obvious that the end of the road had been reached with the Persepolis inscriptions. They were too short and of too limited a vocabulary for verification of decipherment. What was needed was an accurate copy of the lengthier Behistun inscriptions. But how to get it? Ker Porter, and others who had made the attempt, had tried using a telescope to defeat distance and lack of visibility, but the results had proved unsatisfactory. Then an unlikely person, a cavalry officer named Henry Creswicke Rawlinson, produced accurate copies by climbing up to the virtually inaccessible cuneiform.

Soldier, political officer, and philologist of genius, Rawlinson comes across a little larger than life.[5] He was born into a wealthy English county family on April 11, 1810. Henry displayed a remarkable flair for horsemanship at an early age and became a superb shot as a teenager. Although an average student, he showed a natural aptitude for languages. With these talents, he was a logical candidate for the Indian Army. He sailed for India at seventeen. The voyage lasted four months, a fortunate circumstance, for it brought Rawlinson into close association with Sir John Malcolm, the governor of Bombay and a scholar in his own right. Malcolm spent many hours with Rawlinson talking about manuscripts and Oriental languages. He gave the young officer a lifelong interest in Persian dialects and ancient languages.

Once in India, Rawlinson spent five years enjoying the fast-moving sporting and social life of his regiment—dinner parties, theatricals, horse racing, and hunting. The officers of the Bombay Grenadiers were a dashing lot, but none could touch Henry Rawlinson. When he took on all comers for a wager of 100 rupees at any sport, he found no takers. On one memorable occasion, he accepted a bet that he could ride from Poona to Panwell, a distance of 116 kilometers, in four hours. Rawlinson arrived in Panwell in three hours and seven minutes, leaving a trail of exhausted horses behind him. Despite all the entertainment, Rawlinson spent many hours studying Hindi, Marathi, and other languages, including Persian. He acquired a reputation not only as a dashing young officer but as a linguist as well.

In 1833, Rawlinson was appointed staff officer of a military mission to Persia. The mission was to train the Persian army to defend against a possible Russian invasion, a limited response to official concern about Russian designs on Persia. The first two years of the mission were rather humdrum. Rawlinson was saddled with routine drills and political duties, but since he also served as interpreter and middleman between the shah and the British, he had ample opportunity to improve his Persian. He particularly enjoyed Shah Mohammed Mirza's chaotic coronation, enlivened by the sight of the newly crowned but obese king waddling to the throne and then perching the diamond-studded crown on his head with a fat hand. Rawlinson endeared himself to the shah by reciting Persian poems, something no British officer had done in Tehran before. In 1835, the shah sent Rawlinson to act as adviser to his brother, the governor of Kurdistan.

In the intervals of raising and training Kurdish regiments, Rawlinson pondered over the ancient inscriptions of the Persian kings and examined several rock-cut texts during his travels. After a month at his Kermanshah base, he found time to ride out to the Great Rock of Behistun, only thirty-two kilometers away. He stared at the trilingual inscriptions and the huge figures over ninety meters above him. Behistun, he realized, held the key to cuneiform. With single-minded intensity, he spent his free time for the next two years copying the more accessible parts of the inscriptions. He had no scientific literature or philological experience to guide him, just a tough and well-disciplined mind. Unbeknownst to him, Burnouf and Lassen were about to publish their partially deciphered versions of these inscriptions.

The task would have daunted even an expert mountaineer with sophisticated equipment, and Rawlinson had no ropes or ladders. The rock was bare, often precipitous, and always slippery. Luckily, he was in excellent physical shape. Using makeshift scaffolding and risking his life every time he perched on one of the narrow, rocky ledges, Rawlinson managed to copy half the Old Persian inscriptions in two years of regular visits. His work at Behistun had to be squeezed in be-

Henry Creswicke Rawlinson in middle age.

tween other duties, for the governor kept Rawlinson busy. He was called to quell mutinies of Kurdish soldiers and rode enormous distances in the mountains. This hectic life took its toll. He contracted a severe fever that could only be cured by sick leave. He decided to spend a month in Baghdad under the care of the British residency doctor. While there, he became friends with then-resident, the scholarly Colonel James Taylor, and sat down to master Arabic in the congenial atmosphere of the residency. Taylor was deeply interested in cuneiform and gave his guest every chance to examine the clay tablets in his collection.

During the winter of 1836–1837, Rawlinson was posted back to Tehran, where he devoted himself seriously to the decipherment of the Behistun inscriptions. By this time he had succeeded in copying almost the entire first column of the Old Persian script and parts of the remaining columns. He concentrated on the royal titles "Darius the king, son of Hystaspes" and "Xerxes the king, son of Darius." Once the royal titles were identified, Rawlinson proceeded to decipher other proper names. He compiled an alphabet by comparing phonetic values and names with possible Greek equivalents, obtained from classical sources and medieval geographers. By late 1837, he had succeeded in deciphering the first two paragraphs of Old Persian.

In 1840, the French artist Eugène Napoléon Flandin, on a mission with architect Pascal Coste to copy all the ancient monuments and inscriptions in Persia, arrived on his own at Behistun. He found the ascent to the inscriptions a daunting prospect, even with the two ladders he had brought from Kermanshah. He managed to reach the ledge below the inscriptions by climbing up with bare feet, but he was unable to copy them, as his perch was too narrow. He later said, "[I] climbed the mountain for nothing, and the reward for my troubles was that I could only state simply that the inscriptions are all cuneiform, engraved in seven columns, each containing 99 lines, and that above the figures, there are several more little groups of similar characters."[6] He climbed down with great difficulty, his fingers and toes bloodied by the sharp rock. At the time, Flandin had no idea that Rawlinson had already copied much of the inscription.

Rawlinson's Persian mission ended in 1839, so he returned to political service in India and served with distinction in the Afghan War. In 1843, he was at a loose end, but a fortunate meeting with the governor general of India, Lord Ellenborough, secured for him the vacant residency in Baghdad, an appointment that would involve light political duties and abundant opportunities to work on deciphering cuneiform. To this outdoorsman, the arduous discipline of hours of scholarship was tiresome, especially in the intense heat, so Rawlinson built a cool summerhouse on the banks of the Tigris. An ingeniously contrived waterwheel turned by the river kept the temperature of his study to a mere 32°C. He amused himself by taming wild animals, including a young lion and a leopard named Fahed. Fahed stayed with Rawlinson for many years, eventually finding a permanent home in England in the Bristol Zoo. Rawlinson used to visit Fahed frequently, stepping up to the bars of the cage and calling his friend. Fahed would approach, lie on his back, and let Rawlinson tickle his head and ear. One day a keeper rushed in. "Sir, sir," he cried, "what are you doing? The animal's very savage and will bite you." Rawlinson merely smiled calmly. "No, I don't think he'll bite me. Will you, Fahed?"[7] Fahed answered with a loud purr and would not let him stop his caresses.

For all his preoccupation with cuneiform and his pets, Rawlinson was a highly successful and respected diplomat. Like his predecessors, he was a political force for the Turks to reckon with. British prestige never stood so high in Baghdad as in his day. Years later, Wallis Budge of the British Museum met an aged retainer from the residency who confirmed widely circulated rumors that Rawlinson had once knocked two recalcitrant Baghdad ministers' heads together. The servant remarked that had Rawlinson taken his dog, put his English hat on its head, and sent the dog to the Serai, all the people in the bazaar would have made way and bowed to him.

Six months after his arrival in Baghdad, Rawlinson was able to take a long trip to Persia and to the Great Rock. He planned to copy the Old Persian inscription in its entirety, leaving the Elamite and Babylonian texts for later. He managed to copy both the Persian and Elamite inscriptions in a relatively short time, using makeshift scaffolding and scrambling all over the rock face in the hot sun. He then decided to come back another time, with more elaborate equipment, to copy the more inaccessible Babylonian sections. Characteristically, he insisted on returning to Baghdad through the Zagros Mountains, country rarely visited by Europeans.

Rawlinson's new Behistun copies gave him access to far more accurate cuneiform material than he had been able to draw on previously. In 1847 he dispatched a memoir titled "The Persian Cuneiform Inscriptions at Behistun" to the *Journal of the Royal Asiatic Society*.[8] His paper was an absolutely trustworthy decipherment of Persian cuneiform that was soon accepted by other cuneiform scholars. This academic contribution gave Rawlinson an international reputation and access to the linguistic work of many colleagues throughout Europe, among them Edward Hincks and Jules Oppert. He found that he had, quite independently, progressed as far as they had.

∾∾

The son of a distinguished Protestant minister, Edward Hincks was born in 1792 and developed an interest in Eastern manuscripts while at Trinity College in Dublin. He entered the priesthood and accepted the living of Killyleagh, forty-eight kilometers south of Belfast, in 1825 and held this post for forty-one years. Hincks devoted his abundant spare time to ancient languages. He published a Hebrew grammar in 1832 and an article on hieroglyphs in 1846. In 1846 he also read a paper containing some observations about cuneiform that led this humble, absentminded man to devote most of his life to its decipherment, more because of an interest in Biblical chronology than in the script itself. Despite his contributions, he remained an obscure character, embittered perhaps by his lack of recognition in scholarly circles. In 1853, the British Museum gave him a two-month appointment to work on the Nineveh inscriptions, but, except for that appointment, the Church never gave him time off to pursue his lifelong interest. Hincks, however, conducted an enormous correspondence with fellow experts and followed the early excavations at Nineveh and Nimrud with great interest (see Chapters 9 and 10). He also worked closely with Layard on the inscribed bas-reliefs from the Assyrian royal palaces. His cuneiform studies ran closely parallel to those of Henry Rawlinson, with whom he had an ambiguous love-hate relationship for years. Hincks, who died in 1866, deserves more credit for his work on decipherment than he has often received.

Jules Oppert was born in Germany in 1825 and went to France to teach German in 1848. A short, pugnacious man with deep-set, bright eyes, he became closely involved with the decipherment of the Khorsabad inscriptions found by Paul Émile Botta in his excavations described in Chapter 8. Oppert was one of Lassen's students and did most of his important work after cuneiform had been at least provisionally deciphered. He was a brilliant linguist, at home in at least six modern languages and several ancient Semitic dialects. He was a member of Arabist Fulgence Fresnel's archaeological expedition to Mesopotamia in 1851–1855 (see Chapter 12) and then devoted the rest of his life to Assyrian cuneiform and Sanskrit, becoming a professor of Assyrian philology and archaeology at the College de France in 1869.

Oppert worked sporadically with Hincks and Rawlinson. Together they put the decipherment of Old Persian on a firm footing and became known as the Holy Triad of cuneiform studies. In later years Oppert was hampered by failing eyesight, so he devoted much time to encouraging young students, whom he then, half jokingly, accused of stealing his ideas. At conferences he would keep up a running commentary on his colleagues' papers in an undertone. At one memorable meeting, a German colleague chose to attack Oppert in French, which he assumed was Oppert's mother tongue. Oppert tried repeatedly to jump to his feet and interrupt but his neighbors held him down by his coattails. Finally, with a sudden jerk, he literally tore himself free and rushed to the platform in the ragged remains of his coat. Shaking his long white hair, he denounced the speaker in vigorous and much-applauded German. Although autocratic and overbearing at times, Oppert was a brilliant raconteur who could recite Persian, Arabic, and Turkish poetry for hours at a time.

Like his contemporaries, Rawlinson attacked the problem of decipherment at the point of least resistance, by using the royal titles and their Greek equivalents to reconstruct the alphabet. Then, using recent grammatical studies on Old Persian, he compared cuneiform words with those in known languages of approximately the same date. Such decipherment was relatively simple, for the Persian script was alphabetical with only thirty-two characters, not forty-two as Niebuhr had originally thought.

To decipher the Elamite columns of inscription was straightforward, but the Babylonian script was another matter. Even a superficial examination of the available Babylonian inscriptions from Mesopotamia confirmed that the script had hundreds of characters. Some signs seemed to represent several different symbols, even words. Alternatively, several characters could be used for the same word. Even worse, none of the experts trying to make sense of the inscriptions seemed to agree with each other.

In 1847, Edward Hincks achieved a minor breakthrough when he managed to decipher a number of vowels, syllables, and ideograms. Three years later, he used Paul Botta's minute studies of cuneiform letters and words from the excavations at Khorsabad (Chapter 8) to prove that the Babylonian script was not alphabetical but syllabic and ideographic. In other words, the signs represented syllables, which were combined in different ways to make words. Alternatively, each sign might represent a whole word.

While Hincks was working on vowels and syllables, Rawlinson made his third trip to Behistun in September 1847. This time he brought ladders, ropes, pegs, nails, and an entourage of expert climbers to the rock face. Some of them were small wiry boys who were more agile than mountain goats. The ladders enabled Rawlinson to reach the narrow ledge below the lines he had copied previously. He verified his copies but still could not reach the other parts because of the overhangs. The local cragsmen told him it was impossible. Eventually a "wild Kurdish boy," who came from a distant village, offered to have a go. He climbed up a narrow cleft to the left of the inscription and drove in a peg. Hanging ropes from the peg, he tried to swing over to another crevice, but the rock projected too far. So, carrying a rope with him, the boy clawed his way across the precipice, literally hanging in midair. Eventually he rigged up a cradle between pegs in the two clefts. Again hanging in midair, the boy made paper impressions of the inaccessible inscriptions under Rawlinson's anxious supervision.

Rawlinson now could work with the entire 112 lines of Babylonian text, lines that could be deciphered with the aid of the Persian translation. He soon added another element to Hincks's discoveries, the proof that the same sign could stand for more than one sound or meaning. Once he understood this polyphonic feature of Babylonian cuneiform, Rawlinson progressed rapidly. Soon he could read about 150 characters and understood the meaning of some 200 words of what turned out to be a Semitic language (now known as Akkadian). In 1850 and 1851, he published his copies and provisional decipherment of much of the inscription. Hincks used Rawlinson's work to add even more values to the cuneiform, ending up with about 350 readings.[9]

Henry Rawlinson's Behistun study evoked great public enthusiasm. His copies were hailed as the Rosetta Stone of cuneiform and displayed at the Royal Asiatic Society's rooms and in the British Museum. The impressions were exhibited on and off for half a century but were eventually partially eaten by the mice that infested the museum. By that time, however, they were of little more than historical interest.

Many of Rawlinson's colleagues, although admitting his remarkable mountaineering exploits, challenged the idea that the Babylonian script was polyphonic. How could such a confusing script be used as a writing system if it meant different things to different people, they wondered? The controversies raged until 1855, when Jules Oppert, the third member of the "triad," published a review of the decipherment problem in which he endorsed the Hincks-Rawlinson readings and added some new signs that had more than one value. He also had the advantage of a flood of new material from the first excavations in Mesopotamia, including actual syllabaries prepared by ancient scribes for their own use.

Much of Oppert's new material had come to him from Rawlinson's good offices. Because of Rawlinson's strategic position in Baghdad, he could examine the latest clay tablet finds as they passed through Baghdad on their way to London or Paris. His office acted as an informal clearinghouse for new discoveries at the time Austen Henry Layard began his spectacular digs at Nineveh and Nimrud in the late 1840s (see Chapters 9 and 10). Layard's second excavations at Kuyunjik in 1850–1851 came just as Rawlinson had finished with Behistun. The dig turned up part of King Ashurbanipal's royal library, a veritable treasure-house of cuneiform tablets that threatened to overwhelm the decipherers with new data. The library contained syllabaries, lists of different cuneiform symbols, and a mass of grammatical information. The same excavations even yielded a list of religious and legal terms in both Sumerian and Semitic. Rawlinson was the first to examine a great mass of tablets from Kuyunjik with a knowledgeable eye. He wrote in high excitement that "the collection gives us a most curious insight into the state of Assyrian science while Greece was still sunk in barbarism. . . . Altogether, I am delighted at the splendid field now opening out. The labour of carrying through a complete analysis will be immense; but the results will be brilliant."[10]

By 1849, Rawlinson had served for over twenty-two years overseas without a single home leave. Exhausted, he returned to England to find himself a celebrity. The queen entertained him at dinner and he lectured to many learned societies and enthusiastic popular audiences as well. Four years later he finally resigned from Baghdad and the company service. He received a knighthood and became a director of the East India Company, devoting the remainder of his career to diplomacy, politics, and Indian affairs. He, however, never lost interest in cuneiform and spent years working with Jules Oppert and others on the Nineveh tablets in the British Museum.

The supreme test of the triad came in 1857, when W. H. Fox Talbot, a mathematician and astronomer who was also a pioneer photographer, attempted to translate some Assyrian texts. He took an unpublished 810-line inscription of King Tiglath-Pileser I (1115–1077 B.C.) from Assur, translated it, and sent his version to the Royal Asiatic Society in a sealed envelope. Then he suggested that they ask Hincks and Rawlinson to independently do the same. The three sealed translations could then be compared. The society formed a five-man learned committee to supervise the test and invited not only Hincks and Rawlinson but Oppert to take part as well. Two months later the seals on the four envelopes were broken. The committee found that each man had made the same general sense of the inscription and that many paragraphs agreed so closely that no one could doubt that Babylonian cuneiform had been deciphered.

Oppert had annotated his translations with comparisons from six Semitic dialects, part of an ongoing study that led to his most important work, *Déchiffrement des inscriptions cunéiformes*, a lucid and comprehensive survey of cuneiform writing insofar as it was known to that date. From that moment, serious criticism of decipherment ceased.[11]

The decipherment of cuneiform ranks as one of the more remarkable scientific achievements of the nineteenth century. In 1800, not one word of the script could be deciphered. By 1860, several hundred inscriptions had been at least partially translated. Rawlinson was to be seen around the Department of Oriental Antiquities at the British Museum for the next twenty years as he patiently worked on the multivolume compilation *Cuneiform Inscriptions of Western Asia*, a compendium of accurate copies of cuneiform tablets. Generations of students were to benefit from his encyclopedic knowledge of Assyria and from Oppert's polemical encouragement. In the decades that followed the Royal Asiatic Society's test, dozens of scholars from all over Europe collaborated to read thousands upon thousands of Assyrian, Babylonian, and, later, Sumerian texts. The credit for this academic triumph belongs to a handful of scholars and part-time enthusiasts who not only pursued cuneiform with an almost single-minded intensity in the study and in the broiling Mesopotamian sun but trained a new generation of Assyriologists to refine their work. Without their efforts, the great pioneer excavations in Mesopotamia would have been little more than glorified treasure hunts.

PALACES OF KINGS

Sennacherib, . . . wise stag, prudent ruler, shepherd of mankind, leader of widespread peoples, am I. . . . Assur, father of the gods, made all of mankind bow down at my feet; he elevated me to be shepherd over the land and people.

—INSCRIPTION FROM THE
ASSYRIAN KING SENNACHERIB AT NINEVEH

EXCAVATIONS AT KHORSABAD

I have only been M. Mohl's tool. . . . I therefore owe all my discoveries to others, for I have in reality worked on the basis of ideas which were not my own, using resources which were not mine either. The true honour for the discoveries therefore falls to those who delivered these ideas and these resources, and the only praise to which I can aspire is that I have had the luck to be able to make use hereof.

—PAUL ÉMILE BOTTA

GENERAL NAPOLEON BONAPARTE PLANNED HIS CAMPAIGN IN EGYPT AS FAR more than a military venture. He arrived with a corps of civilian experts in quest of knowledge—information on antiquities, agriculture, demography, folklore, and many other subjects. The campaign ended in failure, but the investigations of Napoleon's scientists had as lasting an impact on Europe as the Eastern Question had. Napoleon's small army of scholars was intoxicated with ancient Egypt and published their findings in an exquisite multivolume work, the twenty-volume *Description de l'Egypt,* published from 1809 to 1828. The *Description*'s magnificent folios caused a sensation throughout Europe, for they revealed the glories of ancient Egypt in all their fascinating detail to people who were only dimly aware of that early civilization.

Correspondingly, the 1820s and 1830s witnessed a surge of interest in Egyptian antiquities. Diplomats and travelers descended on the Nile and removed mummies and other artifacts by the thousands. The British and French consuls combined their sporadic diplomatic activities with collecting. These part-time acquisitors sold their collections to the highest bidder, often the British Museum, the Louvre, or another public institution.[1] Inevitably the currents of nationalism flowed strongly, as the major museums competed for prize specimens and collections. It was only a matter of time before governments sponsored excavations in the eastern Mediterranean with the objective of adding treasures to national collections.

The French Asiatic Society had several members who were deeply involved in cuneiform studies. Julius von Mohl, a much respected Asian scholar, and other prominent members examined inscribed bricks and read Claudius Rich's *Memoirs* on Nineveh and Babylon with great interest.[2] A lack of inscriptions hindered the members' research, so they urged the government to appoint a suitably qualified consul to represent them in Mosul, one who might dig, in the traditions of the *Description,* in the mounds of ancient Nineveh. Such excavations, they argued persuasively, would not only provide more inscriptions and artifacts for the Louvre but also enhance France's reputation as a leader in the fine arts. The government responded by appointing Paul Émile Botta as consul in Mosul. Officially, he was to look after French political interests there. Unofficially, he was to carry out excavations at Nineveh. In making this point, perhaps his superiors remembered the words of the Egyptian traveler and diplomat E. de Verninac Saint-Maur: "Antiquity is a garden which belongs by natural right to those who cultivate and harvest it."[3]

Paul Émile Botta was the son of a well-known Italian doctor and historian, who became a French citizen. Botta was born in 1802, studied medicine, and then joined an expedition around the world from 1826 to 1829. During this long scientific excursion, he learned to smoke opium while in China and opium smoking formed the sub-

Paul Émile Botta by E. Champmartin, 1840. Courtesy of Musées Nationaux, Paris.

ject of his medical dissertation. Botta was a gaunt, serious-minded young man who craved adventure. He entered the service of Pasha Mohammed Ali of Egypt as a military physician. His duties gave him a chance to learn several Asian languages, study natural history, and travel deep into what is now the Sudan, where he collected 12,000 insects. He acquitted himself so well that he was appointed French consul in Alexandria in 1833. For the next seven years Botta became familiar with the monuments of ancient Egypt, although there is no evidence that he excavated any sites. He also found time for a lengthy journey into desolate Yemen, an experience he recorded in a widely read book.[4] Perhaps it was on the strength of this experience that the French government appointed Botta their consul in Mosul in 1840.

Mosul was a remote consular assignment, even then a town rarely visited by Europeans. Few foreigners had much polite to say about it. Wrote Charles Edward Mitford, who visited the town in the 1840s when traveling with Austen Henry Layard: "Mosul is an ill-constructed mud-built town, rising above the banks of the Tigris, and backed by low hills; in the center is a tall brown ugly minaret very much out of the perpendicular. . . . [T]he ground between the walls and the town is occupied by stagnant pools, ruins and the dead bodies of camels and cattle, which is enough to breed a pestilence; the bazaars are mean and dirty."[5]

Botta soon settled in. His fluency in Arabic, gained by years of residence in Egypt and Yemen, rapidly made him well-known to the inhabitants. He spent his ample spare time wandering through the ruins of Nineveh and haunting the bazaars in search of antiquities. He bought everything ancient he could lay his hands on—including inscribed bricks, pots, and clay tablets. Every time he bought a piece, he tried to track down its place of origin. But the sellers were vague and they were puzzled by his questions, for they pointed out that such finds could be made everywhere. In December 1842, Botta decided to look for himself by digging into the large mounds across the river— those purported to be ancient Nineveh.

Botta's first target was the conspicuous mound of Nebi Yunus, where the villagers who lived near the Muslim shrine of Jonah were constantly finding inscribed bricks and other artifacts. A storm of protest descended around his ears from the guardians of the shrine, who accused him of desecrating a holy place. Botta was forced to move his excavations to the nearby mound of Kuyunjik. There he dug for several months, finding many alabaster fragments and some inscribed bricks. The excavations, however, were largely fruitless because he was digging in the near-sterile upper levels of the huge city mound and, unlike his successors, did not dig deep into the mound. Botta had never excavated an archaeological site before and he did not have any experience digging into city mounds.

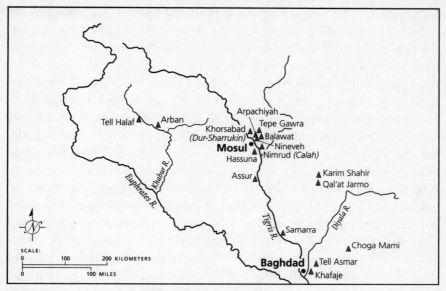

Archaeological sites in northern Mesopotamia.

In March 1843, Botta's luck changed. A villager from Khorsabad, twenty-two kilometers north of Kuyunjik, called on him with some inscribed bricks for sale. He told the consul that there were large numbers of inscribed bricks and other finds of the sort he was looking for in the mound under the village of Khorsabad. His own stove was built out of ancient bricks. Botta did not believe these exaggerated tales, the like of which he had heard many times before. To get rid of the man, he sent a couple of workers home with him to dig for awhile in the reported mound. A week later, one of the men returned in great excitement. Their first few spadefuls of earth had uncovered richly carved walls adorned with strange animals.

Paul Botta rode to Khorsabad posthaste. He was astounded by the exotic bas-reliefs exposed in the walls of the small pit: bearded men in long gowns, winged animals, and other wild beasts. The figures were quite unlike anything he had seen in Egypt and were totally unfamiliar to European eyes. After copying the finds, the consul moved all his diggers to Khorsabad. Within a few days the workers had exposed a whole frieze of sculptured limestone slabs from the palace of an ancient king.

Botta pondered his new finds for a time and then wrote a dispatch to Julius von Mohl in faraway Paris. He boldly claimed, "I believe I am the first to discover sculptures which may be assumed to belong to the time when Nineveh was still flourishing."[6]

The discoveries at Khorsabad made banner headlines in Paris and fired French clerics and intellectuals with excitement. Consul Botta had discovered a wholly "new" ancient civilization, one at least as old as that of the Egyptians and perhaps even older. Furthermore, unlike ancient Egypt, this civilization had emerged from an utterly desolate landscape. No traces of its temples and palaces survived aboveground. It had vanished completely from the face of the earth as Biblical prophets had said it would. The prospect of proving the historical events in the Old Testament captured the Europeans' imaginations. The French government responded to the Khorsabad discoveries magnificently. In the tradition of research that had brought the Napoleonic savants to the Nile, the authorities provided Botta with 3,000 francs to continue his work on an enlarged scale. The consul pressed on with his digging, but conditions grew increasingly difficult as neither the officials in Constantinople nor in Mosul understood what he was doing. They were convinced he was treasure hunting.

Even among the notoriously corrupt Ottoman empire officials, the pasha of Mosul was known for his excessive corruption. Mohammed Keritli Oglu was a short, fat man with only one ear and a single eye, who had suffered from smallpox in his youth. His gestures were uncouth and his voice harsh. Austen Henry Layard, who had many dealings with this gentleman, remarked that his character put hypocrisy beyond his reach (see Chapter 9). One of the pasha's favorite tricks was to pretend he was dead. Those of his subjects who rejoiced lost all their property. And woe betide those who entertained the pasha. They would often find themselves burdened with a tax to compensate for the wear and tear on his teeth. The pashalik of Mosul groaned under his harsh burden of the pasha's excessive taxation as villagers unable to pay their taxes fled to the countryside and lived by robbing travelers.

Sensing a golden opportunity to make money, the pasha harried Botta at every turn. Convinced that the consul was digging for gold and buried treasure, he sent minor officials to watch over the excavations. They checked every small patch of dirt for gold and were under strict orders to bring all metal objects back to Mosul. When Botta's workers were threatened with torture if they did not deliver treasure to the pasha, they threatened to quit.

Next the pasha gave the consul permission to build a house on the mound at Khorsabad. When it was finished, he promptly informed the authorities in Constantinople that Botta had built a fortress from which to dominate the countryside. This "fortress" was so flimsy that early rains washed part of it away. Finally, in October 1843, the pasha forbade any further excavations on the orders, he said, of the Constantinople government. Botta protested at once to the French ambassador to the Porte and attempted to save the recently unearthed precious sculptures from damage by shoring them up with timber. But the villagers stole the wood at night. Botta became more and more frustrated. Antiquities were turning up everywhere and he was constrained from dealing properly with them. The workers digging around the foundations of his house unearthed a large bull's head. The house had to be modified so that the bull could be excavated at leisure. Fortunately, the house's flimsiness meant that it was easily modified.

We have every reason to condemn the pasha's behavior, and there is no question that he was both difficult and unpleasant. But one should remember that Botta had absolutely no official documents allowing him to dig or remove antiquities from the city until 1844. The pasha, as the man in the middle with demeaning and capricious superiors, was in a difficult position. If he allowed the excavations to proceed, orders might arrive stopping them and he would be in an untenable situation. Add xenophobia and religious intolerance, especially on the part of Europeans (Botta and Layard were notable exceptions), and one can understand that day-to-day life was volatile for all concerned.

Meanwhile, things were moving in Paris. The Académie des Inscriptions et Belles-Lettres, which had already obtained the first government grant for the excavations, now prevailed upon the ministers of the interior and education to complete the excavations in a manner worthy of the French Government. The ministers were persuaded to provide not only an increased subvention but the services of a young draftsman named Eugène Napoléon Flandin, who had previously made an unsuccessful attempt to record the inscriptions at Behistun, to draw and record the precious alabaster sculptures before they fell apart in the hot sun. Flandin was an experienced archaeological artist who had been on an expedition to Persia and had published several books on ancient monuments.[7] He was instructed to go out to Mosul via Constantinople, where the French ambassador would hand him a special firman (permit) for the excavations, which would overrule the pasha of Mosul. Finally the ministers ordered Botta to send all the sculptures that were in fit condition to Paris. They also authorized a special publication that would inform the world of the Khorsabad discoveries.

The French ambassador worked long and hard on Botta's behalf, navigating among the intricacies of Turkish and Islamic law. Eventually the sultan issued a firman that authorized both excavation and the purchase of houses in the village on the mound, which Botta had to demolish to get at the buried palace underneath. The consul was also allowed to occupy his famous base house until the end of the dig. The ambassador took so long acquiring the firman that Flandin did not reach Mosul until May 4, 1844, a full year after Botta's first Khorsabad finds.

The consul could now proceed without interference. He began by purchasing the land under the village and the place where the inhabitants were resettled, a process that provoked excessive demands from dozens of villagers and, of course, the pasha. Then he recruited a labor force. The locals were unwilling to work, for their lives depended on agriculture and they could not leave their fields. Many of them were superstitious about working on the mound, too. But Botta was in luck. For some months the Mosul area had been flooded with Christian refugees who had fled to the plains in the face of Kurdish raids. Many of them had settled near Khorsabad and were only too glad to work for modest sums. They were, said Botta, "very robust and docile" and good workers. He and Flandin deployed more than 300 of them across the ancient palace. They dug more or less continuously until October 1844.

Flandin found the work of copying arduous and slow-moving. It took him weeks to record the finds Botta had already made. When that task was complete, he made a plan of the elaborate palace emerging from the soil while Botta copied all the inscriptions. The work was very difficult for both men. The consul had to commute from Mosul, for diplomatic business required his regular attention. Flandin was less accustomed to the heat and dirt and the frustrations of daily life in a distant, exotic land. But the fascination of the new art styles kept both men going, even in July 1844, when the populace of Mosul demolished and looted a new Dominican convent in the town and assassinated one of the missionaries. For some hours, Flandin's life seemed to be in danger at Khorsabad, but Botta managed to get reinforcements to him in time.

By October the two men had excavated the outline of a huge, elaborate building. The word *excavate* is used loosely, for they had no idea of controlled, scientific archaeological work. Their workmen merely followed the decorated alabaster walls of the palace wherever they led. Digging became harder when they ran out of decorated walls and had to follow inconspicuous mud-brick features. Their techniques of excavation were simply too rudimentary for delicate tasks like tracing mud walls. All Botta really wanted to find were stone palaces and fine sculpture. After a while he and Flandin gave up, for trial trenches on other parts of the mound yielded no traces of stone palace walls. Perhaps, thought Botta, the stones had been removed for other purposes after the great palace was abandoned. In fact, what he had found was the palace of the Assyrian king Sargon II (721–705 B.C.). It was some time before Botta learned the name of the monarch whose palace he had excavated. No one could yet read cuneiform.

Today, we know that in the late eighth century B.C., Sargon II had ordered the construction of a new capital, known as Dur-Sharruken. Sargon himself chose the site. He personally supervised the laying out of the fortified, four-sided compound of the city with its seven gates. His new palace rose at the northeast side of the quadrangle, on a vast artificial mound. A ziggurat and lesser temples formed part of his splendid residence, which contained dozens of chambers, storerooms, and passages. When the king died on one of his military campaigns, his successor, Sennacherib, moved downstream to Nineveh and abandoned Dur-Sharruken. Khorsabad contained but a single palace with no overlying occupation, which is why Botta was successful here and not at Nineveh.

During the memorable summer of 1844, Botta and Flandin had cleared room after room, corridor after corridor, all lined with sculptured bas-reliefs of gods, humans, and animals.[8] In the bas-reliefs, the Assyrian king was depicted at war, besieging cities, hunting game, and engaging in elaborate religious ceremonies. Cuneiform inscriptions covered the walls between the bas-reliefs. Imposing human-headed and winged lions and bulls guarded the palace gates. Never before had six months' excavation yielded such incredible treasures.

On November 9, 1844, Flandin left Mosul for Paris, carrying a huge portfolio of Khorsabad drawings with him. He promptly exhibited them to the Académie des Inscriptions and the public. It is difficult for us to imagine the extraordinary sensation they caused. We are familiar with the Assyrians as Biblical figures and as a historical fact. But, to the European of the mid-nineteenth century, the Assyrians were a shadowy people, fierce conquerors who had conquered and deported the Israelites. Many scholars seriously doubted whether they existed. Botta proved them wrong. He had brought the Old Testament to life, found a whole new civilization, and unearthed a palace with bas-reliefs showing Assyrian monarchs engaged in warfare and conquest.

The Académie des Inscriptions set up a scholarly commission to review the drawings and the excavations. Its members warmly praised the work of Botta and Flandin and recommended immediate publication of the material for the benefit of artists and scholars. Their recommendation came only six months after Flandin's arrival in Paris. The sumptuous *Monument de Ninive,* which included four volumes of drawings and one of text, appeared between 1846 and 1850 and became an immediate classic admired by layman and scholar alike.[9]

While Flandin was being lionized in Paris, Botta stayed in Mosul to complete the copies of the inscriptions and to execute the last part of the French government's instructions, the removal of the best bas-reliefs for exhibition in Paris. Although the sultan of Turkey had given reluctant permission for the finds to be exported, Botta was faced with a formidable task. No one in Mosul, or elsewhere in Mesopotamia for that matter, had ever moved delicate antiquities a meter, let alone twenty-two kilometers over rough country from Khorsabad to the banks of the Tigris. Some of the stone blocks weighed two or three tonnes. Botta almost despaired at times during the frustrating months of packing. He was obliged to saw up the larger pieces. Wood was in short supply, so he could not make packing cases. He protected the delicate bas-reliefs with strong beams that formed a framework round the stone, a crude protection that fortunately proved effective.

These packing problems were nothing compared to the challenge of actually moving the sculptures. Botta decided to build a huge cart. He had to set up a special forge to make the axles, which took six weeks to construct. His original plan had been to have water buffalo or oxen tow the cart, but not enough animals were available. So 200 men strained and heaved at ropes attached to the cart. The huge wheels constantly bogged down in the soft, rain-soaked plain. In places the road had to be covered with boulders or planks. It took Botta eight months of exhausting labor to move the sculptures from Khorsabad to Mosul. One bronze-headed lion had to be abandoned when the cart collapsed. It was burned for gypsum by the locals. Fortunately the Tigris was still high enough for the precious blocks to be loaded on *kelleks* for the long journey to Basra. Despite every precaution during loading, one worker died when he was crushed between a sliding block and the sculptures already on board. The *kelleks* had to be strengthened with outsized timbers and extra inflated goatskins. The journey downstream was a nightmare, for the heavily laden rafts were uncontrollable in rough water. One load of sculpture and bas-reliefs of Assyrian kings went to the bottom. Undeterred, Botta dispatched another consignment that reached Basra safely. In March 1846, the French vessel *Cormorant* loaded the precious antiquities. The consul, now recalled to France, personally supervised the unloading at Le Havre on the English Channel in December. The following May the first Assyrian room opened in the Louvre to great popular acclaim.

After returning to Paris, Botta spent his time working on *Monument de Ninive* and lecturing on his finds. By all accounts he was a pleasant and easygoing man except when under opium's seductive influence, which caused him to rage about the perfidy of the English. Austen Henry Layard remarked that one could not blame him for his opium addiction after the frustrations of Khorsabad.

Botta never returned to Mosul. On the establishment of the Second Republic in 1847, the Mosul consulate was abruptly discontinued. He was assigned to a minor post in Lebanon, never returned to archaeology, and died in 1870. By that time, the Assyrian civilization had become one of the best known ancient civilizations.

LAYARD OF NINEVEH

Your cases arrived all right and we have been regaling our antiquarian
appetites on the contents ever since. . . .

I look upon them as of more value than Pompeii or Herculaneum,
and view every new inscription as equal to gaining one of the lost
decades of Livy.

—HENRY RAWLINSON

CONSULAR OFFICIALS LIKE PAUL BOTTA WERE ACCUSTOMED TO ENTERTAIN-
ing the occasional travelers who passed through their remote outposts. European visitors were an event in Mosul, a chance for news
of the outside world. Botta was therefore delighted when a young
Englishman named Austen Henry Layard called on him in 1842 while
traveling from Baghdad to Constantinople. The two men had much
in common—an interest in diplomatic gossip and local politics and
a passion for archaeology. Botta was just starting to dig at Kuyunjik.
Layard was a young adventurer, without a job or any archaeological
experience, but talking to a fellow archaeology enthusiast reinforced
Layard's determination to dig in Mesopotamia. When he eventually

did so, Layard expanded Botta's work on a huge scale. He became one of the heroic archaeologists of the nineteenth century, an era of dramatic excavations and legendary discoveries.

∞∞

Austen Henry Layard was a remarkable man by any standards. During his long life he was in rapid succession a law student, a traveler and explorer, an archaeologist, a writer, a diplomat, a politician, and an art critic. He perhaps is best described as energetic and enthusiastic. Merely reading Layard's journals, correspondence, and public writings is exhausting because his boundless energy and enthusiasm for solitary travel and the beauty of remote places leap off the pages.

Layard was born in Paris on March 5, 1817, to an English family who preferred to live abroad. Most of his childhood was spent in Italy. His education was sporadic, much of it acquired by voracious reading. His parents encouraged him to think independently, indulge his curiosity, and cultivate his powers of observation. Layard's formal education ended in 1834, when he left school in England and became a clerk in a wealthy uncle's law firm in London. He hated his new life. Money was short, his lodgings small and cramped, the work repetitive and dull. The wintry streets of London were a far cry from the open spaces of Italy. Ambitious young Layard felt caged in and stultified at the prospect of a steady legal career. He spent summer vacations traveling as far afield as Finland, Russia, and Italy. Serious tensions developed in the family over his future.

In 1834, Henry's uncle Charles, a prosperous merchant in Ceylon, suggested he set up a legal practice there. He introduced Layard to Charles Edward Mitford, a thirty-two-year-old businessman who had decided to start a coffee plantation in Ceylon. Mitford, who suffered from chronic seasickness, planned to make as much of the trip as possible on horseback through the Ottoman empire to Baghdad, and on to Kandahar and India. At first he was hesitant about shouldering the responsibility for a twenty-two-year-old who was a bad horseman and had never been beyond Europe. Layard, however, soon won him over with his enthusiasm and careful preparations that included lessons in trigonometry and surveying.

Austen Henry Layard in Albanian dress, painted by Henry Phillips. From the frontis-piece from Layard's Autobiography *(London: John Murray, 1903).*

Layard and Mitford traveled across Europe in July 1839. In the Balkans, Layard bought his first saddle. "The first day we rode sixteen hours, the second fourteen, and the third twenty-six without stopping," he wrote home.[1] He must have had a seat made of steel. A few weeks later, the travelers called on a Montenegrin prince who accommodated them in a room that looked out on forty-two gory Turkish heads impaled on posts, relics of a skirmish the week before. Layard carefully recounted all the details to his nervous family in London.

After two and a half months on the road, Layard and Mitford passed through Constantinople. In January 1840 they arrived in Jerusalem after a rough journey across Syria and Turkey, where they had slept in their cloaks under the stars. Layard was intoxicated with his new life and made notes on every ruin they passed — Roman, Greek, or older. Four shillings a day fed Mitford, Layard, a Greek servant, and their horses. From Jerusalem, Layard insisted on making a solo journey south to the ruined city of Petra, which lay in a remote defile occupied by hostile Bedouin tribesmen.[2] Accompanied by only a young boy and everyone's dire predictions, he set off through the desert to Amman, the ancient Rabbath-beni-Ammon of Biblical times. The Bedouins at Petra demanded money and nearly killed him when he refused to pay. Another group of Arabs robbed him of all his possessions and held him hostage. For days Layard wandered with the nomads while they argued over his fate. He enjoyed this experience, for he saw many archaeological sites and gained an understanding of the Arab character, which served him in good stead later on. The Arabs had dual characters. The same man would be grasping, deceitful, treacherous, and cruel on one occasion, and on another generous, faithful, trustworthy, and humane. By the time he rejoined Mitford in Aleppo unharmed, Layard was an experienced desert traveler.

Laden with only seven kilograms of baggage each, the two travelers arrived in Mosul in early April 1840. Layard insisted they stay two weeks so he could examine the mounds of Nineveh thoroughly. The desolate earthworks made a profound and lasting impression on him. In the countries he had recently visited, Greek and Roman temples and theaters rose out of the natural landscape with dramatic effect, so that even the casual visitor could not help but mentally reconstruct ancient buildings and cities from the surviving ruins that lay before him. But at Nineveh, Layard wrote, "he is at a loss to give any form to the rude heaps upon which he is gazing. Those of whose works he is contemplating, unlike the Roman or the Greek, have left no visible traces of their civilization or of their arts; their influence has long since passed away. . . . The more he conjectures the more vague the results appear."[3] He vowed to return and dig into the silent heaps of bricks and occupation debris.

On April 29, Layard and Mitford set off for Baghdad on a *kellek* that would float them the 482 kilometers downstream. Guided by a single boatman who never seemed to sleep, the two men passed Nimrud, watched birds, and looked for more ancient mounds. The world of the *Arabian Nights* surrounded them on every side — the fragrant oases, the creaking waterwheels, the cry of the muezzin calling the faithful to prayer. Even more impressive was their reception at the British residency, where Colonel James Taylor, a slight and wizened man in late middle age, greeted them hospitably. Layard and Mitford spent two months at the residency, enjoying the company of the small European community. They tried to learn Persian as preparation for the next stage of their journey. Layard spent many hours examining Taylor's magnificent library of Arabic and Persian manuscripts and heard about Henry Creswicke Rawlinson's work at Behistun. Taylor enjoyed teaching his young visitor, who absorbed knowledge about Mesopotamia like a sponge. At the time, some young naval officers were using Captain Francis Chesney's *Euphrates* steamer to survey the waters near Baghdad. Layard explored the delta in their company and visited the major archaeological sites, including Ctesiphon and Babylon. The sighting of the latter moved Layard to ecstasies of delight over its desolation and deserted mounds.

All too soon it was time to travel to Persia. After seeing Behistun, Layard realized he wanted to spend much more time in Mesopotamia rather than settling down in Ceylon. Mitford was all for pressing on, so the two companions parted company. Alone, Layard traveled to Esfahan in Persia, where he obtained permission to visit the Bakhtiari nomads who lived in the remote and unsettled mountain country of the region.

Layard's ultimate objective was to reach the site of Susa, the Biblical Shushan.[4] The nomads lived in the midst of fertile, highland plains that could be reached only by steep mountain tracks over high passes. He could trace the line of route by the blood from the horses' hooves. The local chiefs lived in fortified castles or temporary encampments near the river valleys that crisscrossed the plains. Swampy rice fields alternated with rocky hillocks and fertile grasslands where the

Bakhtiari grazed their herds. The local people greeted Layard with great suspicion, convinced that he was an English officer sent to spy out the land for a possible expeditionary force against them. When he tried to travel alone across the plains, the tribesmen robbed him of his compass and watch. They were so hostile and made his life so uncomfortable that he was convinced they might try to kill him. Just when he was about to leave in despair, he managed to cure a chieftain's son of fever with quinine and Dr. Dover's Powder.[5] He was promptly adopted as a member of the chief's family and became such a trusted adviser to the rebellious tribe that the Persian government tried to arrest him. Layard escaped and fled to Baghdad, only to be robbed of all his possessions a few kilometers from the city. Meanwhile, his family was very anxious to learn of his whereabouts and asked the British Foreign Office to make inquiries in Persia. When the British ambassador asked the vizier about him, that eminent personage snorted with exasperation. "That man!" he cried. "Why, if I could catch him, I'd hang him. He has been joining some rebel tribes and helping them."[6] None of this information reassured the Layard family.

Austen Henry Layard was now an expert on Persian and Mesopotamian affairs, so much so that Colonel Taylor sent him to brief the British ambassador in Constantinople and deliver dispatches. Layard rode upstream to Mosul in fifty hours through the great heat of May 1842. There he was able to spend three days with Paul Botta. They took a great liking to one another, inspected Nineveh and Khorsabad, and talked of digging together. Layard left Mosul determined to excavate at Nineveh one day.[7] Three years were to pass before he achieved his ambition. In Constantinople the ambassador, Sir Stratford Canning, liked Layard so much that he retained him as part of his staff. Layard worked for the British embassy as an unofficial attaché engaged in sensitive intelligence work. He enjoyed his confidential role immensely but occasionally hankered for more freedom, especially when his family started complaining about his prolonged absence from England. "How I long for a black tent, a horse, a flock of sheep, and a wife in the solitary mountains," he wrote.[8]

Unfortunately, the ambassador would not allow Layard to leave. But even Canning became interested when Flandin laid out his drawings at the British embassy. Henry Rawlinson, among others, had written from Baghdad, urging that Layard be sent to dig at Nimrud, where heavy rains had exposed stonework and cuneiform-inscribed bricks. Rawlinson had started corresponding with Layard about archaeology earlier in the year. "I should be exceedingly glad indeed if the Ambassador and through him the Government could be induced to take an interest in the antiquities of this country. It pains me grievously to see the French monopoly," he wrote.[9] His letters and Layard's pleadings finally persuaded Canning to agree to a two-month survey at Nimrud with Layard acting as his personal agent.

Layard was overjoyed. He arrived in Mosul in October 1845, announcing that he had come to hunt boar along the Tigris. By this time, Botta had left and his successor, M. Rouet, was eager to maintain French supremacy in archaeology. Fortunately, Christian Rassam, the British vice-consul, was a building contractor, so the excavating tools could be made secretly in his workshop. On November 8, a *kellek* bore Layard and his small party downstream to a tiny village called Naifa, near ancient Nimrud. Layard spent a restless night in the village. His mind would not relax. Palaces and sculptures danced through his brain; he imagined himself in the streets of an ancient city.

The next day he paced over the mounds while his six newly recruited local workers brought him bricks and a fragment of bas-relief. He set the laborers to dig at likely spots. Almost immediately they uncovered a large chamber lined with cuneiform-inscribed slabs in the northwest corner of the mound. The same day, Layard moved some men to the south side, where they found more stone-walled chambers. On the very first day of excavation, Layard had found not one Assyrian palace but two. His first trenches had unearthed the North West Palace, built by Ashurnasirpal II (883–859 B.C.). This imposing structure covered 2.75 hectares, although Layard did not excavate all of the chambers. His southerly trenches had revealed the so-called South West Palace, built by a later monarch, Esarhaddon (680–669 B.C.). Layard was thrilled when the earth inside the first chamber yielded some magnificent ivory figures, including a crouched sphinx and a king.

Even greater excitement lay in store. By November 28 the workers digging at the site of the South West Palace had tunneled their way 4.5 meters into the mound when they uncovered a mass of sculpted tablets. These tablets, which are now known to date from the reign of Tiglath-Pileser III (744–727 B.C.), had originally adorned his magnificent palace, of which no trace now remains. Some sixty years later, King Esarhaddon, in a fit of unaccustomed economy on the part of Assyrian monarchs, dismantled his predecessor's residence and planned to re-use his sculptures. But Esarhaddon's residence was never finished. Many of the sculptures were abandoned in the unfinished structure after his death in 669 B.C. They depicted, Layard wrote, "a combat with warriors in chariots, a second the siege of the city, both designed and executed with considerable spirit." He reported to Canning that "the sculptures could be removed with little care and are well worth sending to England."[10]

At this critical moment a messenger arrived from the pasha of Mosul, the infamous Mohammed Keritli Oglu, forbidding all further excavation. Layard promptly saw red, jumped on his horse, and rode furiously into Mosul. On the way he puzzled over the sudden order. As far as he knew, the pasha had no grounds for complaint. No official objections had been raised in the first few weeks of digging. In Mosul, Layard found the pasha all smiles. The pasha assured Layard that he could continue digging at Nimrud. Mystified, Layard rode downstream and resumed the excavations. He had hardly begun when he was summoned to Mosul again. This time the pasha told him he was stopping the excavations for Layard's own protection. His life would be in danger if he continued to disturb the Muslim burials on the mound. In vain Layard protested that he had never seen a burial marker on the mounds. After two fruitless days of argument he rode back to Nimrud, only to find the site littered with gravestones that had sprung up overnight. Eventually Captain Daud of the pasha's staff sheepishly confessed that he had been ordered to move gravestones from nearby cemeteries onto the site and had done so for the past two nights. "We have destroyed more real tombs of the true Believers in making sham ones than you could have defiled," he complained to Layard. "We have killed our horses and ourselves in carrying these accursed stones!"[11] So Layard quietly bribed the friendly captain to keep some small-scale excavations going.

The French consul was the cause of Layard's difficulties. Upon hearing news of the British excavations, he had sent men all over the countryside to open mounds and claim sites. Layard was forced to do likewise, at the same time urging Canning to give him more money so that he could transport some of his finds to England before Botta's sculptures, delayed in Basra, could reach Paris. He also begged for an official firman from the sultan that would overrule the mischievous pasha. But Canning, worried about the mounting expenses, did nothing and just waited to see what future months would bring.

In the heat and dust of November 1854, Layard now started to speculate about the identity of the buried city he was uncovering. Henry Rawlinson wrote from Baghdad, congratulating him on the finds and arguing that Nimrud was the original Nineveh. When the two men met in Baghdad at Christmas, they took a liking to each other and debated for hours about cuneiform, archaeology, geography, and languages. The trouble was that no one could yet read Babylonian cuneiform, so the identity of Nimrud was still a tantalizing mystery.

Layard's stay in Baghdad was not all archaeology and cuneiform. "At Baghdad, there are remarkably pretty women," he remarked. "Provided your dwelling is convenient, the ladies make no difficulty in walking in, not only when you want them, but uninvited." He horrified his mother by writing that he had so many "wives" he would be glad to be rid of them.[12]

Events in Mosul were now turning in his favor. The pasha had been replaced by a new official, who encouraged the continuance of the excavations. Layard could now return to Nimrud, accompanied by Hormuzd Rassam, the seventeen-year-old brother of the British vice-consul, who was to act as his assistant. They set up their camp on the mound itself, so Layard had a panoramic view of the green floodplain dotted with black tents and huge flocks. He took care to call on the local sheikhs with gifts, thereby averting a raid on his camp. On returning from such a visit on February 20, 1846, Layard sighted two Arab horsemen riding furiously toward him. They reined their horses up on their haunches and urged Layard to follow. "Hasten, O Bey," they cried, "for they have found Nimrod himself!"[13] Layard found an excited group of workmen clustered around a heap of baskets and cloaks. Dramatically, they withdrew the coverings. An enormous alabaster head with an imposing beard and a fine headdress rose out of the ground. Layard realized at once that they had uncovered the upper part of a winged bull, like those found by Botta at Khorsabad. The face bore a calm and majestic expression. The Arabs had been terrified when they first came across the figure. One man dropped his basket and was said to have never stopped running until he reached Mosul.

That evening the joyful Layard and his workers celebrated with several slaughtered sheep, music, and dancing. The excavations were mobbed by sightseers the next day, some from as far away as Mosul. The frightened workman who had fled from the site had announced in the bazaar that Nimrod had appeared. The town was in an uproar. The pasha asked Layard to hold off further work until the furor died down. So, while two or three men dug around the walls of the newly uncovered palace and duly discovered a second pair of winged lions, Layard spent hours contemplating the enigmatic figures and their meaning.

As the weeks passed and more and more palace sculpture came to light, Layard became concerned about his position. He was excavating without a firman, which meant that he could export nothing. The only chance of government support was a dazzling appeal to the public. So far he had spent only eighty pounds as opposed to Botta's large sums. He become ever more frustrated as the weeks passed. Again, he urged Canning to take action but without success. The ambassador was wait-ing for the right moment to approach the government. Layard recom-mended publicity with a capital P. "Botta owes his success with the French Government in a great measure to the notice taken by the pub-lic of his discoveries," he wrote to Canning.[14] In the meantime, Layard decided to honor the laws of hospitality and throw a party for the local tribes. He roasted fourteen sheep for his visitors, who danced all night and celebrated for three days. It was no coincidence that Layard's ex-cavations were largely trouble-free.

In mid-May 1846, three months after the discovery of the great bulls, Layard received the long-awaited firman granting him permis-sion to dig and export antiquities to England. He read this momentous document by "the light of a small camel-dung fire, the document which secured to the British nation the records of Nineveh, and a collection of the earliest monuments of Assyrian art."[15] Unfortunately, however, he was so short of money that the excavations had to remain on a small scale for the time being. Even so, his men had now tunneled deep into the mound. A steep flight of crude steps led into the depths of the North West Palace. The deeper the tunnels penetrated, the more beau-

One of Layard's tunnels at Kuyunjik, sketched by F. C. Cooper. Copyright the Trustees of the British Museum.

tiful the sculptures. Visiting tribespeople would crowd close and gasp in amazement at the figures of kings and soldiers, servants and wild beasts. The workers were now as interested in the dig as Layard was. They cursed and spat at the bearded male figures, declaring they were idols, whereas they patted and kissed the cheeks of eunuchs, declaring they were beautiful women. When new sculptures were emerging from the ground, they would work like madmen, uttering savage war cries and letting their matted hair fly in the wind.

Layard's mode of operation, although unconscionable by today's standards, was direct enough. He simply tunneled into the huge mounds and went on digging until he hit a fine sculpture or a stone-walled palace room. His deep tunnels led along the walls of the rooms and ignored or destroyed the contents of the chambers. Although Layard was more conscientious than most of his contemporaries, he never forgot that the continuation of the excavations depended on a steady flow of fine sculptures for export. Everything was subordinated to this objective. Nimrud soon looked like a cratered battlefield.

He now had found so many sculptures that he had to start crating them before the locals destroyed them. So he drew on family funds. He struggled along in summer temperatures of 47°C or more, packing ten crates of sculptures wrapped in felt and matting, some of them nearly three meters square and a third of a meter thick. It was a miracle that no slabs were broken as they were laboriously loaded on a *kellek* for the journey downstream to Baghdad.

After a summer in the Kurdish highlands, Layard returned to Mosul in October. He found letters from Sir Stratford Canning announcing that the British Museum had taken over financial responsibility for the excavations with a grant of 2,000 pounds to cover all expenses incurred so far and for future work until June 1847. Layard was furious at the stingy financial provisions. Evidently the museum had no idea of conditions in Mesopotamia, nor had they allowed for Layard's remarkable abilities. The pompous instructions from the museum trustees advised Layard to be extremely careful not to injure any sculptures and to avoid incidents with the locals. Layard complained to his uncle that he was being treated like a master-bricklayer. The trustees did not realize how lucky they were to have Layard. Where a lesser man might have returned home, he set aside his pride and tried to do as much as he could with this limited budget. The truth was that he was enjoying life in Mesopotamia. He had built himself a substantial mud-brick house with a thatched roof. Unfortunately, the rains had come before the walls were covered so Layard had living grass for wallpaper the entire winter. The Christian workers lived in a house on top of the mound near the winged lions, where Layard also built a storage hut for small finds. The Arabs pitched their tents in three different areas according to their tribal affiliations. Forty tents stood near the entrances to the trenches, another forty around Layard's dwelling, and the balance by the Tigris at the spot where the sculptures were loaded onto the *kelleks*. These encampments provided Layard with an effective defense against possible raiders. Everyone was armed to the teeth, ready to fight at a moment's notice.

The dig had acquired a considerable staff. Hormuzd Rassam paid the workers and did the accounts. He got on well with the locals and "soon obtained an extraordinary influence, among the Arabs, and his fame spread through the desert."[16] Beyond grooms and servants, Layard employed two carpenters and a stonemason from Mosul. The workers were divided into digging parties of eight or ten Arab basket-carriers, who carried away the loose earth, and two to four pickmen, who loosened the soil. Layard himself cleared the soil away from bas-reliefs or delicate small objects, as he could not trust his diggers not to damage them. The digging teams were carefully composed of Arabs from different tribes so that he would get wind of any plotting or learn if his people were appropriating antiquities for sale. He worked hard to create goodwill and to keep his teams interested in their work.

Layard had great power in the eyes of his employees, but his workers were sometimes hard to control. On one memorable occasion, a visiting tribesman murdered the mother of a young girl he wanted to marry. Layard delivered the murderer to the authorities in Mosul but found no one at Nimrud willing to marry the girl. "I married her, therefore, to an inhabitant of Mosul," he wrote calmly. In appreciating Layard's extraordinary archaeological achievements, one must also recognize his remarkable sensitivity and skill in managing the human side of his excavations. By his generous hospitality and firmness, he achieved miracles where his successors with better facilities were far less successful. He worked hard, rising at daybreak, spending all day supervising the digging and packing, and then copying inscriptions and bas-reliefs until midnight. Yet, it was his willingness to manage his workers that made the biggest difference. The desert Arabs found life rather dull sometimes and would make mischief as a result. One evening Layard was riding home to his house when he saw his workmen driving a huge herd of sheep before them with brandished swords and loud war cries. The sheep belonged to the villagers of Nimrud. Layard asked the yelling Arabs for an explanation. "Oh, Bey," they cried, "it is not for a man to carry about dirt in baskets, and to use a spade all his life; he should be with his sword and his mare in the desert. . . . Let us then believe that these are sheep we have taken from the enemy, and that we are driving them to our tents!"[17] And with that, they scattered the bleating sheep in all directions. The local shepherds were not amused. Layard was shrewd enough to roll with the punches. He also understood that decisive behavior was essential.

The Nimrud excavations kept on producing extraordinary results. Layard finally realized that he had uncovered two phases of occupation. The North West Palace was contemporary with Botta's palace at Khorsabad, but the South West Palace was somewhat later since it had been built using some of the sculptured slabs from the earlier structure. The dig had yielded thirteen pairs of winged lions and more magnificent bas-reliefs of a ruler on military campaign conquering a foreign nation. Layard was especially interested in some scenes that showed men crossing a river on rafts made with inflated skins, just as they still did in his own time. Although many small objects were destroyed in the tunneling, the dig revealed pieces of armor, ornaments, helmets, fine alabaster vases, and many other artifacts depicted in the bas-reliefs. One of his most remarkable finds came from the center of the mound, where the workers had been set to work trenching behind the first winged bulls found at the site. Layard was about to abandon the fifteen-meter-long trench when the diggers came across a magnificent black obelisk lying on its back. The obelisk was carved on four sides with twenty small bas-reliefs. Above, below, and between them were 210 lines of cuneiform inscription, looking as fresh as the day they were carved. The bas-reliefs depicted the king and his attendants receiving tribute. Henry Rawlinson was delighted with what he called "the most notable trophy in the world." He roughly translated the inscription just before the publication of *Nineveh and Its Remains* in 1849: "The tribute of Jehu, son of Omri: I received from him silver, gold . . ."[18] The rest of the text listed Jehu's gifts. Excited Biblical historians recalled how Jehu had become king of Israel after killing Joram and destroying the ruling house of Ahab, who had been killed at the battle of Ramoth-gilead in 850 B.C. (described in I Kings 22). He had broken alliances with Judah and the Phoenicians and had paid tribute to the Assyrians. Today the black obelisk of King Shalmaneser III is one of the British Museum's most prized possessions.

The excavations at Nimrud continued until mid-May 1847. One load of sculptures and artifacts had already gone down the river by *kellek* the previous December. So Layard began to move one of the great bulls to the Tigris in preparation for a second load. He was determined to take at least one of these mythical beasts to London where, he knew, it would be a spectacular exhibit. His troubles began when robbers stole a load of felt, mats, and raft materials only a few kilometers upstream of Nimrud. Layard realized that his camp could be in danger if he let matters slide. So he boldly rode out to the robber sheikh's tents and demanded his possessions back. The sheikh received him courteously and denied all knowledge of the theft. Layard made a sign to his dragoman, who handcuffed him before the bystanders could move, and then he jumped on his horse and dragged the chief out of the camp.

The tribesmen were taken completely by surprise. Although well armed, they made no effort at resistance. Layard regaled the sheikh with horror stories of the pasha's jail and the tortures that awaited him. By the time they reached Nimrud, the sheikh was so terrified that he confessed. Tales of Layard's ruthless methods soon circulated, as he knew they would. The packing materials were returned the next day.

While the packing continued, Layard combed Mosul for timber to build a large wagon on which the larger sculptures could be moved. He bought Botta's iron axles from the French consulate and assembled a massive wagon of wood beams braced with iron hoops. Strong loops were fixed to both ends of the cart so that both workers and buffalo could haul the heavy loads. Meanwhile, the laborers dug a huge trench sixty meters long and about seven meters deep from the excavated figures at Nimrud to the plain below. Layard then removed the earth and the mud-brick walls behind the first bull that he had found so that it could be lowered onto its back. Next, he had the figure wrapped in felt and mats to prevent chafing and tied with ropes so that it could be lowered to the rollers behind it. This step was the trickiest part of the operation, for the ropes at Layard's disposal were too small and it was feared they might give way.

Lowering the great bull at Nimrud. Layard (atop the cutting) and Hormuzd Rassam (center foreground) supervise the task. From Layard's Nineveh and Its Remains *(1849).*

On March 18, 1847, the great day came. Greased rollers lay behind the bull, which was supported by wooden braces. A team of workers manned the lowering tackles, while some strong individuals stood

by the braces, with instructions to ease them slowly as the bull was lowered to the ground. Layard stood on the mound above the bull and ordered the wedges supporting the figure removed. The bull still stood upright, so six or seven men tilted it until the lowering ropes took the weight. The heavy figure slowly descended as the lower workers propped it with the beams and the ropes strained against the load. The shrill of Kurdish pipes increased as the men yelled their war cries. The women spectators screamed and gesticulated. So loud was the din that Layard was unable to make himself heard in the confusion. In desperation, he threw clods of earth at the noisiest workmen to get their attention, but his actions were in vain. All was well until the men below were forced to remove their beams as the bull neared the ground. The dry ropes creaked, strained, and then parted with a twang. The bull crashed onto the rollers in a cloud of choking dust. The workers collapsed in confused heaps on the ground. A sudden silence fell. Layard jumped into the trench expecting a shattered figure. To his delight, the bull was intact and positioned in the correct place on the rollers. The workers went wild with joy, seized the women's hands, and started dancing.

The bull and, shortly afterward, the winged lion were dragged to the banks of the Tigris with superhuman effort as they bogged down in the sand and nearly capsized in potholes. A band of marauders tried to steal the felt packings one night, but Layard's guards beat off the attack with their rifles. As a result, the bull's flank bears the mark of a rifle ball.

Layard had decided to float the two figures all the way to Basra by *kellek*. None of the Mosul boatmen would venture beyond Baghdad, so Layard hired a Baghdad skipper for the long journey. The raft contractor turned up with a single assistant and two donkeys laden with deflated skins. Layard argued ferociously with the villainous-looking skipper and eventually prevailed on him to build a higher-than-usual wooden framework so the crew could squeeze under the sculptures at Baghdad and reinflate the skins without unloading them. After a strike for higher wages that Layard easily frustrated, the figures slid down a ramp onto the *kelleks'* greased frameworks. About thirty cases of small objects and many bas-reliefs were loaded on the same rafts. As he watched the laden rafts disappear downstream, Layard mused on the strange destiny of their burdens. Once the adornment of royal palaces, they had been neglected for centuries. Now they were to cross the Mediterranean and be displayed in the British Museum.

For some time Layard had been planning a dig at Kuyunjik, which lay across the Tigris from Mosul and was the site where Botta had dug unsuccessfully in 1842. Although Botta had claimed that Khorsabad was ancient Nineveh whereas Rawlinson had thought Nimrud was the place, Layard was convinced that Kuyunjik was the great city. By now he was sufficiently knowledgeable about Assyrian palaces to realize that Botta had not dug deep enough into the tell. The Assyrians had built their palaces on huge brick platforms. Thus, when the palace walls collapsed, the platforms were covered by deep sterile deposits, which had to be removed to expose the original structure. Once the surface of the platform was located, all one had to do was to trench along its surface to find the palace walls.

Layard planned to dig at the southwest corner of Kuyunjik. When the French consul heard of this plan, he promptly claimed the site as French property in an effort to thwart British excavation. Fortunately, the pasha imperiously overruled him and Layard began digging. In a few days his workers located some badly burned alabaster bas-reliefs. After a month's hectic work, Layard had uncovered nine chambers of a palace similar in design to those of Nimrud and Khorsabad and containing bas-reliefs of the king at war, besieging a city, and returning from battle in triumph. Time was so short that he was only able to make some hasty drawings and to send to England one fragment of sculpture—a fisherman with a wicker basket on his back.

For some time, details of Layard's discoveries had reached England through his letters to his family and from newspaper articles contributed by occasional visitors to Nimrud. The journalist J. A. Longworth had fascinated the readers of the *Morning Post* on March 3, 1847, with an account of his descent into the tunnels of the North West Palace. "The portly forms of kings and viziers were so lifelike, and carved in such true relief, that they might almost be imagined to be stepping from the walls to question the rash intruder on their privacy. . . . All these figures, the idols of a religion long since dead and buried like themselves, seemed actually in the twilight to be raising their desecrated heads from the sleep of centuries; certainly the feeling of awe which they inspired me with must have been something akin to that experienced by their heathen votaries of old."[19]

The first load of sculptures from the excavations went on display in the British Museum on June 25, 1847, the day before Layard left Mosul, and caused great excitement. Unfortunately, Layard at the time was ill with fever and exhausted by the heat and long, lonely hours of copying inscriptions. He left Mosul accompanied by a large armed

The Nimrud bull on its way to the Tigris. The great mounds of the ancient city are in the background. From Layard's Nineveh and Its Remains *(1849).*

party that included Hormuzd Rassam, who was going to Oxford. In Paris, Layard found himself the celebrity of the hour. Paul Botta and other fellow scholars admired his sketches of Kuyunjik. When he arrived home, he found that London was agog for details of the excava-

tions. He dined in great houses, lectured to learned audiences, and
called on the trustees of the British Museum, who had good reason
to be delighted with their agent's work. They immediately applied to
the government for a large grant to cover the publication costs for the

Nimrud excavations, but the grant was just as promptly turned down on grounds of economy.

Undeterred by this rejection, Layard wrote to the trustees in January 1848, urging a major archaeological expedition to Mesopotamia. He recommended a large-scale excavation, one financed to the tune of 4,000 or 5,000 pounds for just the first year. He pointed out that the French and Prussian governments had gained great prestige by their munificent support of archaeological expeditions to Egypt.[20] He now urged the British to take the lead in Mesopotamia, where even casual excavations had yielded spectacular palaces and magnificent sculpture. Besides, Layard cautioned, the Porte had recently decided to start an imperial museum in Constantinople and had issued orders for excavations to be carried out on likely mounds. Thus, future foreign expeditions might be discouraged as a result. The proposal fell on deaf ears, but Layard was given permission to write a book about Nineveh on his own initiative. He grabbed the chance with alacrity, planning "a slight sketch" of the ancient city. He added: "I think the book will be attractive, particularly in America where there are so many Scripture readers."[21] Unfortunately, Layard was in very poor health. Writing was an effort and reading even more so. He spent most of 1848 staying with friends while he compiled his "slight sketch" and corresponded with Rawlinson about cuneiform.

In October 1848 fifty cases of Nimrud antiquities arrived after a long and circuitous journey from Basra to London via Bombay. The precious cargo had been transferred to another vessel in India and had sat on the quays of Bombay harbor for some time. When Layard supervised the unpacking at the British Museum, he was distressed to find that the cases had been rifled. It transpired that British residents in Bombay had opened the precious cases out of curiosity. Some pieces had even been stolen, but the British Museum did not care. They were delighted to be in the possession of so large and fine a collection. The trustees wrote to the foreign secretary, acknowledging the debt they owed Canning and Layard: "The entire collection will undoubtedly be regarded as one of the most important contributions to the materials of archaeological science which has been made in recent times."[22] But the government offered no money for further excavations. Layard's own future remained far from secure. In December 1848 he returned to Constantinople, where the Foreign Office had given him an unpaid position as an attaché at the embassy. It appeared that his archaeological career was over. He left the completed manuscript of his early excavations in the hands of John Murray, the London publisher who had handled the works of Lord Byron and many celebrated travelers.

Early in 1849, *Nineveh and Its Remains* appeared in the bookstores and became an immediate best seller. The reviewers waxed lyrical. On February 9, 1849, the *Times* described the book as "the most extraordinary work of the present age." Layard, said the reviewer, was one of the "most enterprising travelers" to be found "in the annals of our modern history."[23] *Nineveh and Its Remains* is remarkable for its enthusiasm, liveliness, and vivid descriptions of the Nimrud finds. Some people were surprised at the depth of Layard's knowledge, but they had never realized how many long hours he had spent in Taylor's and Rawlinson's libraries in Baghdad or how well he spoke the local languages. Now Layard was accepted as a respected scholar as well as a competent archaeologist. Other scholars were impressed by his command of the diverse literature on the Assyrians, and the general public was intrigued by the incredible adventures he had undergone in Mesopotamia and by the relevance of his discoveries to the Old Testament. *Nineveh and Its Remains* highlighted a deep mystery that, wrote Layard, "hangs over Assyria, Babylonia, and Chaldea. With these names are linked great nations and great cities dimly shadowed forth in history." The new excavations had yielded bas-reliefs of the Assyrian kings and their subjects, of wars and conquests. Once Babylonian cuneiform was fully deciphered, people would be able to read the inscriptions on the walls of the newly discovered palaces. In the meantime, most readers were content with Layard's claim that he had revealed the "most convincing and lasting evidence of that magnificence, and power, which made Nineveh the wonder of the ancient world, and her fall the theme of the prophets, as the most signal instance of divine vengeance."[24]

NIMRUD AND KHORSABAD

A few hours more and they were to stand no longer where they had stood unscathed amidst the wreck of man and his works for ages. It seemed almost sacrilege to tear them from their old haunts to make them a mere wonder-stock to the busy crowd of a new world. They were better suited to the desolation around them; for they had guarded the palace in its glory, and it was for them to watch over it in its ruin.

—AUSTEN HENRY LAYARD

ALTHOUGH *Nineveh and Its Remains* WAS THE SENSATION OF LONDON, ITS AU-thor languished in his unpaid post at Constantinople, certain that he would never excavate in Mesopotamia again. But he had underesti-mated the power of public opinion. The trustees of the British Museum became uncomfortably aware that they had acquired a magnificent collection of about 40,000 pounds' worth of antiquities at practically no cost. When Albert, prince consort, and government ministers visit-ed the Assyrian exhibit and learned that the new treasures had cost the country almost nothing, the pressure on the museum grew. Ministers and influential scholars urged the museum to fund excavations for Austen Henry Layard to find more sculptures.

The government finally acted. The prime minister arranged for a ship to be sent to Basra to pick up the bull and lion from Nimrud that were still awaiting transport to England. In belated recognition of his services, the Foreign Office appointed Layard attaché in Constantinople at a salary of 250 pounds a year. Meanwhile, the museum trustees granted him a further 3,000 pounds for renewed excavation. Layard was instructed to concentrate on Nineveh, collect more sculptures, and record as much of the art and inscriptions as possible.

Layard was horrified at the small size of the grant. His party was to include a young and talented artist, F. C. Cooper, and Humphry Sandwith, an English physician. Hormuzd Rassam left the comforts of Oxford to join the expedition. He did so somewhat reluctantly, for he was enjoying university life. All three men were to be paid from the subvention, but after the salaries were subtracted, there was little money left for the excavation and transport of finds. Once again, Layard had no option but to make the most of a bad situation.

On August 28, 1849, the expedition left Constantinople for Mosul, traveling across eastern Armenia and Kurdistan through the mountains near the upper reaches of the Tigris. As they descended onto the Mesopotamian plains, the heat became oppressive. Raiding parties were everywhere. When a large party of horsemen neared, Layard sounded the alarm. The two parties approached each other warily. There was a shout of joy as the strange horsemen turned out to be a group of headmen from Mosul who had ridden sixty kilometers to greet Layard. The journey became a triumphal progress. Layard stopped to visit friends. His workmen and their families lined the route and kissed his knees. As Mosul and the brooding mounds of Nineveh rose from the plain, Layard's groom arrived with his horse readied for him to ride. The travelers drew up at Layard's home as if he had never left. His old servants were already at work, the household running on oiled wheels. Layard felt as if he had been on a summer's ride.

During his absence, the British vice-consul had kept a few men at work on Kuyunjik to ward off the French. For a while, Layard's friend Henry Ross, a local English businessman, had watched the diggers, but he had recently left.[1] Layard found little had changed. He walked through the deep, elaborate tunnels dug by Ross's workers. Wooden beams or earthen pillars supported the roof. Sculptures and broken clay vessels projected from the dimly lit walls. Layard gazed at the bas-reliefs along the southern wall of a great hall. Although much damaged by fire, they clearly described a military campaign, from the royal advance into battle to the triumphal return of the king. The Assyrian armies engaged the enemy in close combat among hills and by streams. Mounted archers and spearmen pursued their foe and trampled them underfoot as they begged for mercy. The returning troops threw the severed heads of the vanquished in heaps before their officers. Row after row of prisoners and great loads of booty paraded past the king. Two gigantic, human-headed bulls guarded the wide doorway at the side of this hall.

As he examined Ross's finds, Layard's mind was busy with preparations for digging. He recruited his old workers, who arrived from far and wide, and set small parties of men to work clearing further chambers in the palace. By October 12, when the work began in earnest, over 100 laborers and their families were camped at Kuyunjik. Hormuzd Rassam supervised and paid the work force and relieved Layard of the day-to-day burdens of administering the excavation, thereby enabling him to travel to neighboring sites and work at his beloved Nimrud. There, Layard decided to investigate the great conical mound in the northwest corner of the site that served as a landmark for kilometers around. During the previous excavations, Layard had sunk a twelve-meter shaft into solid mud brick from the summit. He now started to dig sideward into the base in the hope of better results.

He spent several days at Nimrud supervising the new excavations and renewing his contacts with the local sheikhs. One morning he rode up to the mound to find a group of strange horses picketed on the stubble. He was greeted by a dragoman who silently pointed to Henry Rawlinson wrapped in his cloak and sleeping soundly in an excavated chamber. Rawlinson was on his way to London for his first home leave in twenty-two years. He had come down with fever on the way from Baghdad and was exhausted, having ridden to the site in the hope that the exercise would cure him. For a few hours, he inspected the excavations, examining exposed inscriptions on the walls. "Much interesting talk on Assyrian matters," wrote Layard about his visit, but Rawlinson worsened the next night and rode with difficulty into Mosul. He managed but a short visit to Kuyunjik, upset by continued malaise and the death of one of the British consul's servants from a horse kick. Rawlinson's sojourn in the area was surprisingly brief, but he was sick and his primary interest was inscriptions, not excavations and ruins.

During his all-too-brief tour, Rawlinson surprised Layard by telling him that he had changed his mind about Nimrud. Originally he had thought that Nimrud was ancient Nineveh and dated to about 2500 B.C. Now, he felt that much of Assyrian history was pure myth and that Nimrud was not Nineveh but the site of Biblical Calah, dating from 1300 to 1200 B.C. Since the earlier dating had appeared in *Nineveh and Its Remains,* Layard was somewhat perturbed by the new chronology. Yet, he could hardly blame Rawlinson, for no one had fully deciphered the royal inscriptions; thus, sudden telescoping of chronologies was to be expected. "I know not how to console you for the loss of those fifteen centuries of which Major Rawlinson is determined to curtail you," wrote Sir Stratford Canning from Constantinople, where Rawlinson had stopped briefly. He urged him to find "an antidiluvial dynasty . . . under the old mound."[2] We know today that Rawlinson was closer to the mark.[3]

The excavations continued throughout the fall and winter of 1849–1850. Layard commuted between Kuyunjik and Nimrud while Cooper, the artist, lived in Mosul and rode out to Kuyunjik every day. By the end of November several new chambers had been cleared, including most of a huge hall thirty-eight meters long and twenty-seven meters wide, the walls of which were covered with elaborate sculptures. Two enormous human-headed bulls guarded the entrance. The hall's west wall told the story of the conquest of a hill-country people.

Some unique bas-reliefs adorned the north wall, showing how the Assyrian kings transported their huge, human-headed bulls from quarry to palace. On one, a huge block of stone lies on a round-bottomed boat on the Tigris. Wooden wedges and beams hold the precious cargo in position. Nearly 300 laborers drag the boat with huge cables, while an overseer sitting astride the stone supervises the work gang.

Another relief shows the finished sculpture on the banks of the river. Only minor details remain to be completed. The sculpture rests on a huge sledge, carefully supported by wooden beams mounted on rollers. Four large cables, with smaller ropes fastened to them, are attached to the corners of the sledge. Gangs of laborers, each with one of the smaller ropes over his shoulder, drag the sledge along. As it moves forward, men insert levers behind it to give momentum. Kneeling workers add wedges under the levers while others sit on them to provide additional weight. The superintending officers stand or kneel on the bull. One is beating time, another blowing a trumpet. Slaves draw carts full of spare beams and wedges behind the sledge; still others carry ropes and saws. The king in his ceremonial chariot, shaded by a parasol and attended by eunuchs, supervises this operation and the next one, a scene where his people build artificial platforms for a palace and for moving a bull into place. The huge figure is being dragged and levered up the artificial mound. Hundreds of captives, many of them wearing fetters, are hard at work under the king's watchful eye. A last scene shows the bull, now held in a vertical position on the sledge, being moved to its final resting place. Beams, crossbars, and wedges keep the precious load upright. "In moving the winged bulls and lions now in the British Museum from the ruins to the banks of the Tigris, I used almost the same means," wrote Layard.[4] It must have been an extraordinary experience to gaze at scenes depicting the construction of the very palace he was excavating. According to the reliefs and inscriptions, the monarch appears to have taken a personal interest in every detail of the construction, down to the use of exotic stone: "At the command of the god white limestone for the construction of my palace was discovered in the district of Balatai," Sennacherib boasted.[5]

For some time Layard had been corresponding with the Reverend Edward Hincks in Ireland about the cuneiform inscriptions from his excavations. With the help of Hincks and Rawlinson, it was now possible to identify some of the kings on the bas-reliefs. Hincks eventually provided a provisional decipherment of the inscription accompanying the winged bull scene: "Sennacherib, king of Assyria, the great figures of bulls, which, in the land of Belad, were made for his royal palace at Nineveh, he transported [thither]."[6] It was now certain that Layard had been digging Sennacherib's "Palace Without a Rival," built in about 700 B.C. at Nineveh.

While working on Sennacherib's palace, Layard started another set of tunnels in a high mound in the northwest portion of the earthworks surrounding Kuyunjik. By the end of November the workmen had uncovered a huge gateway facing open country and guarded by two fire-damaged and unfinished human-headed bulls. They were 4.5 meters long, bore feathered wings, and had hairy bodies. The gateway itself was almost five meters wide and paved with huge limestone slabs that Layard used to trace the passageway. A mass of charcoal and burned brick covered the stone sentinels, for the gateway had been destroyed before completion. Layard remembered the prophet Nahum: "The gates of your land are wide open to your foes; fire has devoured your bars."[7] Visitors to the excavations came upon the bulls after progressing through dim tunnels lit by small air shafts. They were invariably impressed. "Between them Sennacherib and his hosts had gone forth in all their might and glory to the conquest of distant lands, and had returned rich with spoil and captives, amongst whom may have been the handmaidens and wealth of Israel," Layard wrote. "Through them, too, the Assyrian monarch had entered his capital in shame, after his last and fatal defeat."[8] The large limestone slabs still bore the ruts of Assyrian chariot wheels.

Layard now set laborers to dig on the east side of Sennacherib's palace near a human-headed bull found in 1848. Soon he found the entire southeast facade of the palace, over fifty-five meters long. Ten huge bulls and six gigantic human figures surrounded the entrance. Bas-reliefs showing the king's conquests occupied much of the facade. One hundred and fifty-two lines of inscriptions on the great bulls described Sennacherib's early reign and many details about the Assyrian religion and the construction of the palace.

Even more sensational discoveries came from a large chamber full of bas-reliefs that depicted the siege and capture of a large and heavily fortified city. A huge Assyrian army camps before its walls. Battering rams and earthworks are in place. While the defenders put up a desperate resistance, part of the city has already fallen. Sennacherib sits in judgment over the captives. An inscription above the king's head reads: "Sennacherib, the mighty king, king of Assyria, sat on the throne while the booty from Lachish passed before him."[9]

Layard was thrilled. He had found an original depiction of the capture of a city mentioned in the Bible, seized by the Assyrians in 700 B.C. Sennacherib's army besieged Lachish when the Assyrians demanded tribute of the rebel king Hezekiah. In the Old Testament we read: "In the fourteenth year of King Hezekiah[,] Sennacherib king of Assyria came up against all the fortified cities of Judah and took them.

"Sennacherib, king of the universe, king of Assyria, sat upon a throne while the booty of Lachish passed before him." Part of the Lachish frieze that commemorates the king's capture of the city in 701 B.C. From the Palace of Sennacherib at Nineveh. Copyright the Trustees of the British Museum.

And Hezekiah, king of Judah, sent to the king of Assyria at Lachish, saying, 'I have done wrong; withdraw from me; whatever you impose on me I will bear.'"[10] He was told to pay 300 talents of silver and 30 of gold, so outrageous a tribute that Hezekiah had to strip gold and silver from the temple of the Lord. But Sennacherib was not satisfied. His armies camped in front of Jerusalem and threatened to take it. But the Assyrian host was decimated by a sudden plague and Sennacherib never achieved his objective. He was murdered in the temple at Nineveh by his sons. Now Layard had found not only his palace but the actual record of his Judean campaign. When Rawlinson deciphered Sennacherib's inscriptions, he found reference to Hezekiah, the capture of forty-six cities, and a tribute of 800 talents of silver and 30 of gold, a remarkable correspondence to the Biblical account. Sennacherib boasted extravagantly that he had carried off 200,150 people, old and young, male and female, into captivity. With such vivid confirmation of Old Testament events emerging from ancient Nineveh, it was hardly surprising that Layard became a popular hero.

Meanwhile, the excavations under the conical mound at Nimrud were making progress. The laborers tunneled into the base at bedrock for twenty-five meters before coming to a solid masonry wall six meters high. They then tunneled along the stone wall until they emerged at the end. A huge mass of collapsed brick and mud covered this foundation, which Layard said were the remains of a square tower, not a pyramid. The structure had been cased in baked mud brick, the cone formed of sun-dried blocks. Convinced that a royal grave lay under the structure, he tunneled with difficulty through the stone base. No tomb came to light, so he tunneled at right angles to the center of the stone structure, then about two meters into bedrock, without result. A long galley did lie, however, on top of the stone foundation, vaulted with sun-dried bricks and blocked at both ends. Layard conjectured that this was the long-ago desecrated burial chamber of the king who had built the tower. Deeply disappointed, he was forced to content himself with estimating the height of the structure at about sixty meters.

As these tunneling operations were in progress, another gang of workers prepared to move the two huge human-headed lions found in 1846. Early one morning Layard was startled by gunfire and women's screams. He dashed from his house to see a group of spear-toting horsemen driving away the locals' cattle and sheep while the bereaved owners fired at the raiders. The women, armed with pitchforks and tent poles, were trying to rescue their animals. Layard grabbed a horse and boldly rode up to the leader of the raiding party. He demanded the cattle and sheep back, promised redress for an earlier theft of camels, which turned out to be the cause of the raid. The leader reluctantly agreed, but Layard had considerable difficulty in stopping the hostilities. His own laborers advanced on the raiders, brandishing swords and spears. Others gathered up bricks from the excavations and were ready to pelt the strangers with antiquities. At this moment, Layard's greyhounds spotted a wild hare and took off in headlong pursuit. Everyone's "love of the chase overcame even their propensity for appropriating other peoples' property."[11] The marauders took off in wild pursuit, dropping their booty behind them.

Despite this noisy interruption, the lions reached the Tigris safely. Every available worker pulled or levered the carts as dozens of horsemen wheeled around the cavalcade, shouting war cries. "The procession closely resembled that which in days of yore transported the same great figures," wrote Layard. "As they had been brought, so were they taken away."[12] It was months before the lions reached Basra. The flooding Tigris covered them with silt as they lay on the bank. Once under way, one of the lion-carrying *kelleks* went out of control and washed over a flooded embankment downstream of Baghdad. Fortunately, Captain Felix Jones, then skipper of the *Euphrates*, boldly took the steamer into shallow water alongside the stranded raft and rescued its historic treasures.

The Nimrud excavations continued to yield remarkable discoveries, particularly those of the chambers near the floor, which were in an excellent state of preservation. Layard supervised the removal of the earth fill from a chamber in the North West Palace that had once overlooked the Tigris. The fill contained a series of copper vessels and jars, many of which fell to pieces as they were uncovered, an all-too-familiar litany of nineteenth-century excavators. Bronze bells with iron tongues, cups and dishes, studs and bottoms of ivory and mother-of-pearl, and many fragments of horse and chariot trappings lay inside these receptacles. Cauldrons sat on bronze tripods with feet in the shape of bulls' hooves or lions' paws. Circular flat vessels and fragments of a throne came to light. A whole array of decorated bronze dishes, plates, bowls, and cups came from a single floor-level chamber. Layard lifted as many as possible in groups and sent them to the British Museum in that state, so they could be cleaned up at leisure. The same chamber yielded weapons, fragments of military armor, glass bowls, shields and spears, and also iron saws and picks. He removed some delicate ivory ornaments with great difficulty, for the fragments tended to crumble to dust when exposed to the air. Layard spent days removing the fill of this rich chamber and regretted he had no time to remove the contents of other rooms, because he was too busy tunneling round the walls in search of bas-reliefs.[13]

Despite his spectacular finds at Nimrud and Nineveh, Layard was at his best when on the move. He preferred finding new sites and visiting local sheikhs to the monotony of excavation. He sometimes found the tensions of excavation unbearable. The expedition's physician, Humphry Sandwith, was totally uninterested in archaeology and preferred to idle away his time hunting or riding. Cooper, the artist, was so ill with fever that he could hardly draw. Layard had to check the details of his work every day. Cooper was homesick for his wife, too, and made for a very poor companion. Visitors could be even more of a trial. Percy Badger, an ardent missionary and the brother-in-law of Christian Rassam, turned up in Mosul. He was busy writing a book on the local Christians and spent much time at Nineveh examining the excavations. Layard took a violent dislike to Badger, partly because he had a deep distrust of intolerant and quarrelsome missionaries. Consequently, the atmosphere in camp became rather strained.

Two other English visitors introduced tensions of a different kind. Captain Stewart Rolland and Charlotte Rolland were a young couple traveling to visit friends in the east. Stewart found the country very attractive because he could keep fine horses by the Tigris for almost nothing. Charlotte became entranced with archaeology when she witnessed the discovery of the rutted gateway road at Kuyunjik. Both of them liked Layard immensely. While Stewart helped supervise the workers, Charlotte worked on clearing and packing the finds. Soon the Rollands had moved into Layard's house at Nimrud. Even in these intimate surroundings, they all remained fast friends. Inevitably, tensions arose after a few months, perhaps because Layard may have been attracted to Charlotte Rolland. She accompanied him on many of his Bedouin visits, sitting behind him on a fast-riding camel. His letters hint at an attraction between them, for he refers to her "good nature" and kindness to the local people. His diary refers circumspectly to painful scenes and violent quarrels when Stewart Rowland started to beat his wife. Layard suggests in other letters that the captain had gone slightly mad and had to be restrained. Eventually, he was obliged to tell them to go back to England as soon as possible.

∞⌒∞

By March 1850 the Nimrud and Nineveh excavations were well advanced. Layard had managed to stretch the British Museum's 3,000-pound subvention to cover much more excavation than he had originally anticipated. Although the wage overhead for the Europeans was relatively high, the local labor costs were much lower, so Layard could manipulate his budget. He paid his workers about four pence a day, the foremen a little more. Cooper, the artist, received 200 pounds a year and 30 for an outfit, whereas Layard was granted 200 pounds for his own equipment. He deployed his digging teams where finds were most plentiful, occasionally throwing a feast or buying an ox for his laborers. There is no doubt that the museum got a spectacular bargain for its modest grant.

Most of the British Museum subvention had been expended by March, so Layard decided to take off on a long-planned trip to the Khabur Valley west of Mosul. He traveled in some style, taking along a huge hospitality tent that could entertain 200 guests. The Khabur River flowed placidly through fields of bright spring wild flowers, a paradise after the muddy plains near Mosul. Layard visited the mound of Arban, where floodwaters had exposed two much-damaged winged bulls of a simpler style than those at Kuyunjik.[14]

A month's digging into the tumulus revealed a fine lion and another pair of bulls opposite the first two. But the diggings were somewhat of a sideline. Layard spent most of his time visiting the local tribes. He was later to write a long account of the Khabur peoples, remarkable for its vivid descriptions of Arab hospitality, blood feuds, and women who wore necklaces of "coins, coarse amber, carnelian beads and cylinders, mostly Assyrian relics picked up amongst ruins after ruins."[15] Deserted, grass-covered village mounds could be seen on all sides.

On his return, Layard was delighted to find a new series of bas-reliefs emerging at Kuyunjik depicting nearly thirty meters of a procession of servants bearing "fruit, flowers, game, and supplies for a banquet, preceded by mace-bearers."[16] There were attendants carrying dates and baskets of pomegranates, apples, and bunches of grapes. Some men bore partridges, hares, and even strings of locusts, a highly prized Assyrian delicacy. Huge bas-reliefs of the fish-god Dagon guarded small rooms that contained thousands of clay tablets and cylinders. The archives filled each room to a depth of more than a third of a meter, many of them in fragments from the collapse of the roof. The tablets and cylinders were covered with minute cuneiform signs, characters so small they could only be read with a magnifying glass. "The documents appear to be of various kinds," wrote Layard. "Many are historical records of wars, and distant expeditions undertaken by the Assyrians; some seem to be royal decrees, and are stamped with the name of a king, the son of Esarhaddon."[17] There were lists of gods and registers of temple offerings, even lists of sacred days and tables of values of cuneiform letters.

Within a few weeks, Layard had filled six crates with clay tablets, with many more to come. He had uncovered the royal library of Ashurbanipal, a find that was to place the scientific understanding of the Assyrians on an entirely new footing. "They furnish us with materials for the complete decipherment of the cuneiform character," he wrote later, "for restoring the language and history of Assyria, and for inquiring into the customs, sciences, and we may even add, literature of the people." Then he stated prophetically: "But years must elapse before the innumerable fragments can be put together, and the inscriptions transcribed."[18] The task took generations.

The Nimrud excavations were yielding important finds as well, especially from a buried temple near the ziggurat. This temple yielded a sculpture of an "early Nimrud king" in an arched recess and sculpted in very high relief. The great entrances to this temple lay to the east. Two human-headed lions nearly 5 meters high and 4.5 meters long formed the main door. A second temple lay thirty meters east of the first, its entrance also flanked by two lions with bristling manes. Hincks and Rawlinson deciphered the temple inscriptions, which commemorated the king's military campaigns and many conquests. The detailed chronicles of royal deeds surprised Layard and the cuneiform scholars, for they were more complete than those of the ancient Egyptians. Three hundred and twenty-five lines of inscription on a huge monolith in the second temple recorded the building and rebuilding of the North West Palace, as well as military expeditions conducted with savage cruelty. Prisoners were burned alive, impaled on stakes, or otherwise tortured. Soldiers slaughtered women and children indiscriminately.

By early summer 1850, Layard and his companions were exhausted by the increasing heat, the constant strain of dealing with their volatile work force, and the primitive working conditions. In later years Layard was to remember his stay among the nomads and workmen at Nimrud with nostalgia, but in reality camp life was very uncomfortable indeed. Everyone lived in primitive mud-brick huts that teemed with lice and fleas. Bitterly cold north winds whistled over the city in winter. At times pools of water on the mound froze over. The camp could become a muddy quagmire after a few hours of rain. The first few weeks of spring were pleasant, but then the sun would bake the plains dry and sear the camp in debilitating, shimmering heat. Strong winds brought sandstorms and almost unbearable discomfort.

Layard's large hut actually boasted glass windowpanes. He had a dilapidated couch but little other furniture. The remaining members of the party fared worse and often ate their meals seated on the ground. Everyone lived on much the same food as the local people — a diet of rice and vegetables with occasional feasts of sheep or goat meat. They were able to supplement the local foods with a few expensive European luxuries, like jam and tea. Although Dr. Sandwith had a small chest of medicines, there was little he could do to treat the recurring dysentery and fever that laid them all low. The only treatment for more serious ailments was to retreat to the cooler air of the Kurdish highlands. Fortunately, most members of the party were living an active, healthy life out-of-doors in all weather. Thus, serious illnesses were the exception rather than the rule despite poor sanitation.

No nineteenth-century excavator could afford to ignore his local neighbors. The local laws of hospitality dictated that Layard entertain anyone who visited his camp. Thus, the constant stream of visitors pausing at Nimrud to look over the excavations took a great deal of Layard's time. He found himself entertaining sheikhs and Turkish officials, shepherds and former workmen, and along with the occasional European. He was well aware that hospitality was a sacred duty in a land where there were no lodging houses and the traveler had the harsh realities of the desert to contend with. A guest could never be turned away or harmed, not even one's deadliest enemy. Shrewdly, Layard used his obligations as a host to further his archaeological objectives. By flattering his guests and giving generous hospitality he managed to forestall any plans for an armed raid on the camp. He also made sure that all Europeans carried arms and did not stray far from camp alone, and he maintained a twenty-four-hour guard at the excavations.

When it was clear that everyone was feeling the strain of the difficult work, Layard shut down the Nimrud excavations and once more
set off, this time for the Kurdish highlands. He again left a gang of
workmen tunneling into Sennacherib's palace at Kuyunjik, where
they soon found bas-reliefs of campaigns in the lower Mesopotamian
marshes, military victories, prisoners of war, and day-to-day life in the
king's domains. In the fall, Layard returned to pack nearly 100 crates
of bas-reliefs and other finds, which he floated safely downstream to
Basra. He left Mosul on October 16 for an uneventful ride by *kellek* to
Baghdad. He was lucky. The countryside was in open rebellion against
the Turks and no one was safe. One of his rafts was attacked but the
crew beat off the raiders, killing several of them.

Layard had come to Baghdad with plans to shift his operations to
Babylonia and specifically to dig at Babylon itself. He found Baghdad
an island in a sea of rebellion; its only safe means of contact with the
outside world was the British East India Company's steamer *Euphrates*
still under the command of Felix Jones. When unsettled conditions
delayed him in Baghdad, he sent some of his experienced laborers
from Mosul to work on mounds near the city but with little result.
On December 5, 1850, he set out for Al-Hillah and Babylon, where he
befriended the local pasha. This kindly gentleman presented him with
two lions. The younger one soon died of mange, but the second, a full-
grown specimen, was well known in Al-Hillah. He was a friendly beast
whom everyone liked except the butchers, because the lion would occupy their stalls and not allow them back until he had eaten all their
stock. When not eating meat, the lion would chase fisherfolk from
their wicker boats and eat the succulent catfish they had just landed.
"The pasha," wrote Layard cynically, "rather encouraged [this] mode
of obtaining daily rations, which, although of questionable honesty,
relieved him from butchers' bills."[19] When not hungry, the lion would
lie in the sun and allow little boys to pet him.

The Babylon excavations were a disappointment. The ruins were
very different from the relatively compact tells and earthworks at
Nimrud or Nineveh. Babylon was a veritable sea of mounds, thus very
hard to survey and excavate. It was impossible for Layard, and for

Claudius Rich before him, to correlate the historical descriptions of the great city with the ruins he saw. There were no signs of city walls or the famous palace of Nebuchadnezzar with its Hanging Gardens. Nevertheless, Layard put his diggers to work on the two principal mounds—Mujelibe and the Kasr. The workers tunneled deep into the mounds at different levels but found little more than masses of mud bricks. Layard investigated the underground chambers originally dug into by Rich forty years before. Rich had found modern skeletons in wooden coffins. Layard found more of them. A foul smell permeated his tunnels, a scent of decaying wood and wild animals. He was puzzled by the lack of bas-reliefs. All he found were huge quantities of glazed bricks in brilliant colors. He bought a few cylinders and small gems from the local dealers in Al-Hillah but found almost nothing himself.

The Babylon discoveries fell far short of Layard's expectations. He doubted whether the site would be worth investigating on a large scale. After all, he rationalized, if Alexander the Great had employed 10,000 men to uncover the rubbish from the temple of Belus and had failed to find it, it was likely that his small group of Arab workmen would be unsuccessful. The truth was that his crude excavation methods were not up to the complex task of tracing buildings or individual levels in the mounds. Without the familiar bas-reliefs to go by, he was at a complete loss on how to proceed.

Layard had wanted to dig at Birs Nimrod as well, but the country was too unsettled. A heavily armed escort accompanied him there. The soldiers promptly fell onto a party of Arabs, stripped them of their cows and sheep, and severely wounded their owners, who would have been killed if Layard had not objected. Peace restored, he climbed to the summit of the Birs and gazed over a vast, marshy landscape. The analogies between Birs Nimrod and the collapsed Assyrian temples at Kuyunjik and Nimrud were obvious, he thought. "The ruin is a specimen of the perfection of the Babylonian masonry," he wrote.[20] He refused to speculate as to its association with the Tower of Babel in the Scriptures, preferring to associate it with the ancient city of Borsippa, an interpretation favored by both Rawlinson and modern scholars.

In January 1851, Layard rode further south into Babylonia with the intention of digging into the tells at Nippur and Uruk. The desolate plains of the region were little known to Europeans, although William

Kennett Loftus had carried out some abortive excavations at both sites in 1849. Because political conditions were now exceedingly dangerous, Layard sought the protection of the sheikh of the Marsh Arabs, in whose swampy country of reed-hut villages Nippur lay.[21] He was greeted by the sheikh's sons, who arrived in black boats built of rushes and bitumen that skimmed over the water with remarkable speed. The sheikh's village was all mats and reeds, the houses divided by canals. Layard was forced to live in the mosquito-ridden village, where, at least, he was safe from robbers and wild animals. He rented two large boats to act as commuter ferries for his men. The workers dug into the mounds of Nippur for several weeks and found large numbers of glazed earthenware coffins dating to the Parthian period (250 B.C.–A.D. 226). These coffins contained human remains that almost invariably crumbled to dust as they were uncovered. Deep trenches revealed massive brick foundations and cuneiform-inscribed bricks but none of the spectacular finds associated with Nimrud or Kuyunjik. Again, Layard was discouraged: "I am much inclined to question whether extensive excavations carried on at Nippur would produce any very important or interesting results."[22]

Political conditions were now deteriorating rapidly in the delta, so much so that Layard was unable to reach Uruk. He surely would have been murdered if he had tried. Then he contracted pleurisy and fever from the marshy environment, becoming so weak that he resorted to desperate measures and took a dose of blistering fluid used on sick horses. This drastic remedy gave immediate, if temporary, relief. He rode the whole way to Baghdad, almost collapsing from fever, but he arrived unscathed. His workers were less fortunate. Desert robbers stripped them of all their possessions.

After a few weeks of rest in Baghdad, Layard had recovered sufficiently to return to Mosul. There he found Thomas Septimus Bell, a young artist sent out by the British Museum as a successor to Cooper, who had been invalided home. Bell turned out to be competent and hardworking, although young and inexperienced. Layard set him to work at once copying newly discovered bas-reliefs from Kuyunjik. Sennacherib's palace was still yielding artistic treasures. Four new chambers contained scenes of Assyrian armies returning from successful campaigns with prisoners and loads of booty. Another series depicted royal soldiers fighting marsh peoples in reed boats just like those Layard had recently used at Nippur.

⟨⟩⟨⟩

By April 1851, Layard had had enough. Although the British Museum was pressing him to continue, he was fed up with their inadequate financial support and complained bitterly about the amount of his own money he had been obliged to spend. He was justifiably proud of his accomplishments at Kuyunjik and Nimrud. No less than "seventy-one halls, chambers, and passages" in the palace of Sennacherib had been opened, and their walls were covered with, "by a rough calculation, about 9,880 feet, or nearly two miles, of bas-reliefs, with twenty-seven portals, formed by colossal winged bulls and lion-sphinxes."[23] And only a small proportion of the palace had been fully examined.

But Layard, the perfectionist, was obsessed with his failure to uncover anything of value at Babylon and Nippur and his inability to reach the great mound at Uruk. Above all, he was depressed about the state of the country. Political conditions had deteriorated sharply in recent months and travel was exceedingly dangerous, even for Europeans. He was tired of insolence from townspeople and the complexities of Arab hospitality, even if his memories of desert tents were to remain his most lingering and nostalgic experiences of Mesopotamia. He left Mosul on April 28, 1851, never to return to Nineveh or Nimrud again. The excavations were left in the charge of Christian Rassam and young Bell, who drowned in a swimming accident while sketching reliefs at Bavian soon afterward.[24] They were instructed to maintain a British presence at the site to prevent the French from moving in on the excavated palace. No large-scale operations were contemplated. They were simply to await new instructions from the British Museum.

Layard arrived in London in July 1851 and was swept into a social whirl. He was lionized by the Duke of Wellington, Lord Cowley, and other prominent men. When the crates of bas-reliefs from Kuyunjik and Nimrud arrived at the British Museum, Layard spent long hours supervising the unpacking. At the same time he felt increasingly bitter about the offhand attitude of the museum trustees to his discoveries. Outspoken by nature, he complained loudly about their cluelessness about local conditions and their desire to do everything on the cheap, staffing the expedition not with an artist of Flandin's stature but with a young, inexperienced man who knew nothing of the country or the people. He was well aware of the furious competition for Assyrian antiquities that was about to break out and complained to the secretary

The reception of the Nineveh sculptures at the British Museum. From the Illustrated London News, *February 28, 1852. Courtesy the Illustrated London News Picture Library.*

of the museum that the trustees were allowing the French to overtake them. Relations between the museum and Layard soon became distant at best. Layard retreated into seclusion to write a sequel to *Nineveh and*

Its Remains, which was still selling well, while thousands of Londoners flocked to the British Museum to see his latest discoveries. Eventually the sheer weight of public opinion goaded the trustees into casting

A fanciful reconstruction of Nimrud's palaces along the Tigris by Thomas Mann Baynes, featured in Layard's second series of sketches, published in 1853. HIP/Art Resource, NY.

around for a successor to Layard, who had refused to go out again. It was a year before the museum renewed its work at Nineveh.

In January 1852, Layard's fortunes improved dramatically. A change of foreign secretary brought Lord Granville to the Foreign Office. He promptly appointed Layard his undersecretary. The appointment caused some surprise but was widely acclaimed as a just reward for the discovery of Nineveh. As it turned out, the job lasted only eleven days, for the government resigned in crisis, and Layard with it. He now stood for Parliament and in July was elected Liberal member for the constituency of Aylesbury in Berkshire, west of London. Since a political career was less demanding in those days, Layard was still able to spend much time in society and working on his new book.

A fascinating stay with the Reverend Edward Hincks in his remote country parsonage at Killyleagh gave Layard new insights into the thousands of lines of inscriptions from Kuyunjik and Nimrud. Hincks had the rare combination of talents that make up a successful decipherer—an ingenious mind, great linguistic abilities, and inexhaustible patience. For years, he had pored over the history of the Assyrian kings and had deciphered the names of Sargon, Sennacherib, and Esarhaddon. Now he was working on the main bodies of the inscriptions, the texts that followed the standard formulas of kingly titles. Layard was able to use his preliminary results, and those produced by Hincks's rival Henry Rawlinson, to attempt a general account of the Assyrian kings in his new book. *Discoveries in the Ruins of Nineveh and Babylon with Travels in Armenia, Kurdistan, and the Desert* was published by John Murray in March 1853. The public eagerly devoured its 700 pages.

Layard's second book is more authoritative, the work of a man who knew he had discovered a unique civilization. The decipherment of cuneiform had enabled him to develop a provisional chronology of the Assyrian kings, one that, he readily admitted, would be altered radically when his new clay tablets from Kuyunjik were deciphered.

He attempted a description of the Assyrian state, which he considered a confederation formed from many tributary states. He stressed the independence of each ruler and their perpetual internecine warfare. His book, he claimed, revealed the truth behind the Biblical references to the Assyrians and the Israelites. The nonpayment of tribute led to an Assyrian military expedition, the reduction of a few towns, and the enslavement or resettlement of their populations—interest, as it were, on the unpaid tribute. Throughout *Nineveh and Babylon*, Layard returns again and again to the connections between the Old Testament and his archaeological finds. This association, he knew, was the crux of the profound interest in all things Assyrian on the part of the general public. For all his scholarly pretensions, he was a journalist and popular writer by inclination.

Austen Henry Layard's archaeological achievements are staggering, especially for a man with no formal training. He had no idea how to keep records of finds or different archaeological levels. He simply worked out his own solutions as he went along. Anyone visiting Nineveh, Nimrud, or the British Museum is amazed at the results he obtained with inadequate financial resources, no special equipment, certainly no cameras, and, on his first expedition, no skilled assistance except that of Hormuzd Rassam. The British Museum owns sheet after sheet of drawings of bas-reliefs made by Layard's own hand that are the only record of finds he was unable to ship home. Unfortunately, he could not sketch them all. Hundreds of bas-reliefs and inscriptions were found but never recorded and are now lost. Layard had the great archaeologist's instinct for the vital rather than the trivial and a nose for discovery that led him unerringly to royal palaces and spectacular finds. His prodigious energy made up for many of his scientific shortcomings.[25]

Layard gave up archaeology after the publication of *Nineveh and Babylon*. He was only thirty-six years old. He then embarked on a successful career as a politician and a diplomat, eventually becoming British ambassador in Madrid and, later, Constantinople. No carefully trained archaeology students stepped into his shoes to take over where he left off. His successors were little more than treasure hunters, out to acquire as much loot for the major museums or their private gain as they could. It was almost half a century before the self-taught amateurs and treasure hunters were replaced by systematic, careful, scientifically trained excavators.

TABLETS AND TELLS

Colonel Rawlinson was daily thus employed in a most inclement season: book in hand, sometimes seated in a swamp, sometimes protected
only by an umbrella from the torrents coursing down from above, he
persevered and succeeded in obtaining copies of all the legible tablets
uncovered within the mounds both of Nineveh and Nimrud.

—JAMES FELIX JONES

EXCAVATIONS IN BABYLONIA

The news of this discovery of the cylinders at the Birs seems to have
flown far and wide on the wings of fame, for since my return to
Baghdad I have been besieged by applications to employ "the magic
compass" in extracting treasures that are believed to be buried in the
courtyards or concealed in the walls of the houses; often in the very
"boudoirs" of the ladies.

—HENRY RAWLINSON

AUSTEN HENRY LAYARD WAS EFFECTIVELY IRREPLACEABLE AT NINEVEH AND
Nimrud. Not only had few people ever dug there but hardly anyone in
England had even visited the area. Clearly, any excavation would have
to be under the general supervision of Henry Rawlinson in Baghdad,
even if he had no time to direct it in person. The trustees of the British
Museum asked him to suggest someone. After extensive consultation
and correspondence, Rawlinson recommended one of the few people
with archaeological experience in Mesopotamia, the geologist William
Kennett Loftus. Rawlinson was particularly impressed with Loftus because he was a man of initiative and resource who was not afraid to
work in dangerous territory. Determined and aggressive, Loftus was

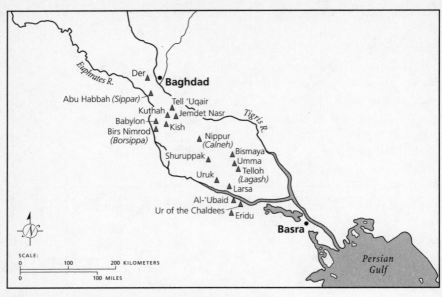

11.1 *Archaeological sites in southern Mesopotamia.*

very much a man of action who was happiest in the field. His excavation experience had been acquired on the desolate mounds of southern Mesopotamia, which Rawlinson believed held the clues to early Mesopotamian civilization. Conceivably, he felt, the British Museum could be persuaded to expand their operations into the south at the close of the Nineveh dig.

Loftus had gained his first archaeological experience while serving as the geologist on a boundary commission charged with mediating a complex frontier dispute between Persia and Turkey. The commission's work brought Loftus to al-'Iraq in 1849, the year Layard's first sculptures from Nimrud went on exhibition in London. In December, the members of the commission were to travel by steamer from Babylon to Ahvaz, in present-day Iran, on their way to the disputed areas. Always eager for adventure and a change of routine, Loftus obtained permission to take an alternative route overland from the Euphrates to the Tigris to examine the geology of the marshes on the way. Accompanied by his friend Harold A. Churchill, Loftus traveled light with a small armed guard. Even so, their lives were in danger, for the tribes of the desert and marshes owed allegiance to no one. As they rode toward the Tigris, Loftus was amazed by the abundant traces of ancient civilization littering the desolate plains — canals, earthworks, and earthen mounds stood as the remains of ancient cities that had once been flourishing settlements. He made a special point of visiting the mounds of Uruk (described in Chapter 1).

As the two men approached Uruk, they saw the mounds of the ancient city towering above the grass-covered plain. Herds of gazelle grazed on the new grass and bounded away to safety when the guards pursued them with loud cries. Loftus noted: "Three massive piles rose prominent before our view. The whole was surrounded by a lofty and strong line of earthen ramparts, concealing . . . all but the principal mounds." Loftus and Churchill spent two hasty days at the site, trying to draw at least a rudimentary plan of the mounds and fortifications. Loftus wrote: "Each step that we took, after crossing the walls, convinced me that [Uruk] was a much more important place than had been hitherto supposed, and that its vast mounds, abounding in objects of the highest interest, deserved a thorough exploration."[1] The two travelers reached the boundary commission's camp full of enthusiasm for the new site. Their sketches and reports, along with their few small finds, so interested the commission leader, Colonel W. A. Williams, that he allowed Loftus to return to Uruk for a few weeks of digging.

Loftus was on the road within a few days, accompanied by four servants, two guides, and fifteen horses and mules. The protection of a local sheikh enabled him to work in relative safety. For three hectic weeks he rose at dawn and labored all day in the fine dust. It was exhausting work made even harder by the extremely cold nights. On his first visit Loftus had noticed dozens of clay coffins outcropping from the Uruk mounds. "Even the tombs of ancient Thebes do not contain such an aggregate amount of mortality," he wrote.[2] The coffins lay in every corner of the site. Loftus tunneled as deep into the artificial platform as he dared — some nine meters — and still came across a solid mass of burials. Urns and large dishes contained skeletons, but most common of all were glazed, slipper-shaped clay coffins. The lids were cemented in place with lime mortar and ornamented with elevated ridges and figures of warriors. The rich, green enamel on the exterior contrasted with the blue on the inside. All these "slipper" burials dated to the Parthian period and were obviously of recent date.[3]

The coffins sometimes contained skeletons that crumbled to dust when exposed to the air. Rings, amulets, bangles, and gold ornaments often accompanied the bodies. Over the years the local Arabs had

The slipper coffin makes its way from Uruk to the Euphrates. From William Kennett Loftus's Travels and Researches *(1857).*

broken open hundreds of coffins in search of gold ornaments. Loftus observed them at work. The grave robber would drive a spear into the soft soil until he struck an obstruction. Then, burrowing like a mole, he would grub and pick his way to his quarry, break open the lid, and root around among the bones with his dagger in search of gold. The

coffin was then broken into pieces to get at others below. Most of the mounds were honeycombed with burrows and broken potsherds that testified to centuries of treasure hunting. On several occasions coffins unearthed during the excavations were rifled while Loftus's back was turned.

Every time he tried to separate a coffin from its tightly packed neighbors, it fell apart. After breaking at least 100, he devised a method using a mixture of paper, flour, water, and gum that enabled him to lift three to send home to the British Museum. Even so, the operation caused Loftus much anxiety, for his exuberant workers had to carry the extracted coffins over fourteen kilometers across rough ground to the Euphrates. The porters almost danced the coffins to the river, their companions feigning mock attacks that caused the laborers to lift their spears in defiance and almost drop their precious burden. When the coffins reached the river, the local villagers staged a mock funeral with wailing and dancing. Loftus could do nothing but watch as his precious finds were tossed to and fro by the crowd.

While Loftus resumed his work with the commission, Rawlinson and others were poring over the tablets and inscriptions from Kuyunjik in the north. The more Rawlinson examined the Layard finds, the more convinced he became that the ancient texts would provide useful pointers for future excavators of the southern Mesopotamian mounds. He theorized that Uruk and Ur had been settled first. The names designated in the ancient texts would identify localities where the descendants of Noah established the first colonies, whose names became famous in later times and were associated with city-states. Rawlinson's hypotheses caused widespread interest. He became eager to start new excavations at Uruk and other tells and was convinced that the mounds would yield finds as spectacular as those from Khorsabad, Nimrud, and Nineveh.

Just as Loftus was about to set out for Kuyunjik to take up his appointment as Layard's successor, the British Museum decided to send him to Susa instead. As it turned out, the Susa excavations were unsuccessful, and Loftus returned home in 1852. At this juncture, the Assyrian Exploration Fund—a private body formed by prominent figures, including Albert, prince consort—appointed him to dig in southern Mesopotamia. Forthwith he made elaborate preparations to return to Uruk. A well-known French artist, William Boutcher, and a friend, Ker Lynch, accompanied him.

In 1852, Uruk presented an even greater scene of desolation than it had in 1849. The river had not flooded in recent years and the resulting drought had driven the local people elsewhere. Loftus had great difficulty recruiting laborers. The logistics were a constant worry. His supplies had to come from a small town many kilometers away. Camels brought water to camp from the river and also to Uruk, which was fourteen kilometers from Loftus's base. Blinding sandstorms developed on all but the calmest days, enveloping the excavations in dense clouds of choking dust. Sometimes the workers got lost on their way back to camp. But the aggressive and determined Loftus persisted.

Uruk is the largest archaeological site in the south, consisting of a series of long mounds that extend over an area nearly ten kilometers in circumference. A canal once flowed through the site. On either side of its now-dry bed lie mounds of occupation debris up to fifteen meters high. The most imposing structures, now crumbled masses of brickwork and rubbish, lay in the southwest portion and include the remains of three ziggurats and a huge Parthian temple. Loftus concentrated his first efforts on the highest mound, a pyramidal heap of sundried brick named Buwariyya ("reed matting") over sixty-one meters square. He tunneled into the mound and found some brick buttresses and also layers of unbaked brick and reed mats. He quarried further in search of inscribed cylinders but found none and assumed they had been destroyed when the structure collapsed.

Loftus's primary objective was to find bas-reliefs and art objects like those from the Assyrian palaces. So he moved his workers over to a "walled quadrangle" 260 meters from Buwariyya. This structure, known as the Waswats in Loftus's time, consisted of a series of courts, gateways, and enclosures that seemed like a possible site for a palace. The structure stood on a huge artificial platform over fifteen meters high and was covered with deep deposits of collapsed brick and occupation debris. The masses of decaying brickwork made the excavations very hazardous, especially since materials for shoring trenches were unobtainable.

Loftus concentrated on finding walls, the insides of which might be adorned with sculptures. He uncovered a long facade, which he estimated to be over fifty-three meters long. The plain wall was adorned with stepped recesses and had once been decorated with terracotta cone bricks. It had evidently been plastered in antiquity. The exterior was relatively easy to excavate, but the interior was a different matter. An entrance lay at the northeast side, leading to a large court flanked by rooms on either side. The walls were so thick that Loftus was convinced for a while that he was digging into a solid structure. Eventually he managed to clear seven chambers, but no sculptures came to light, just plastered walls and the remains of date-wood beams. The only traces of decoration were some fragmentary glazed bricks. "Rubbish . . . completely filled every chamber; so that, having ascertained the non-existence of sculpture in two apartments, I did not deem it advisable to explore further," Loftus commented. The bricks used in the construction of this edifice were all marked with a deeply impressed triangular stamp or with "an oblong die bearing thirteen lines of minute cuneiform characters."[4] The Uruk architecture was quite different from that of the northern palaces. Loftus surmised that the difference was attributable to the lack of suitable stone for sculptures in southern Mesopotamia; thus, it was hardly surprising that the ancients had used the local building materials. He had just uncovered the first Sumerian building known to modern times.

Loftus now sank some trenches into a nearby smaller structure on a level with the desert. He uncovered a nine-meter length of a wall built of terracotta cones each about nine centimeters long. The cones were arranged in semicircles with their rounded bases facing outward. "Some had been dipped in red and black colour," he wrote, "and were arranged in various ornamental patterns." The site was littered with thousands of these cones, which "were undoubtedly much used as an architectural decoration."[5]

The three months that Loftus spent at Uruk did little more than scratch the surface of what was obviously a highly complex and long-occupied settlement. Loftus was somewhat disappointed by the results of his diggings. He blamed his lack of success on the absence of building stone, the inaccessibility of the place, and the huge deposits of Parthian burials that mantled most of the site. His portable finds were especially disappointing: a scatter of inscribed cones and bricks and a few tablets. But he had demonstrated that Uruk was worth future exploration.

Rawlinson followed the progress of Loftus's excavations with great interest. As his long-term office in Baghdad drew to a close in 1853, he managed to free time for some southern excavations on his own. Soon after Loftus's departure for England, Rawlinson dug briefly at Birs Nimrod. By then Rawlinson was wise in the ways of Mesopotamian architects and searched for commemorative cylinders in the corners of the great mass of brickwork, which had long been identified as a ruined ziggurat. He unearthed a series of clay commemorative cylinders recording how "Nebuchadnezzar, king of Babylon," had rebuilt and repaired the "building named the Stages of the Seven Spheres which is the wonder of Borsippa."[6] Rawlinson published the cylinders in the Journal of the Royal Asiatic Society, the first positive identification of Birs Nimrod as an actual Babylonian location rather than the hypothetical Tower of Babel.

Not content with this triumph, Rawlinson now sent J. E. Taylor, the vice-consul at Basra, on exploratory journeys into Babylonia in search of early Biblical cities. Taylor spent some time at a series of low mounds near the town of An Nasiriyah that were 2,700 meters in circumference and associated with a two-storied structure about twenty-one meters high. These ruins, collectively known as Muqayyar ("bitumen" or "cemented with bitumen"), are a high spot on the low-lying plain and are often isolated by the floodwaters of the Euphrates. Pietro della Valle had collected some cylinder seals here in 1625, and James Baillie-Fraser had visited the site in 1835. In the manner of the day, Taylor tunneled into the heart of the two-storied structure, which was one of the best-preserved Babylonian temples because it was free of the debris of later millennia. He soon was convinced that the "whole building was built of sun-dried bricks in the center, with a thick coating of massive, partially burnt bricks of a light red color, with layers of reeds between them."[7] Pausing to admire the buttresses and drainage holes, Taylor now turned his attention to the southwest corner of the temple, where he found a perfectly preserved inscribed cylinder in a niche in the bricks 1.8 meters below the surface. Three other cylinders came from similar niches in the remaining corners, along with another even more important cylinder in the north wall.

Excavations elsewhere at Muqayyar yielded inscribed bricks, dozens of burials, and abundant traces of lengthy urban occupation. The cylinders and bricks found in the temple structure proved to be highly informative, forcing Rawlinson to reevaluate his earlier theories. He now correctly identified Muqayyar as the Biblical Ur of the Chaldees, associated in Genesis with the patriarch Abraham. The temple turned out to be that of the moon god Sin. It had been built by a king named Ur-Gur about 2700 B.C. and restored 2,000 years later by the Babylonian monarch Nabonidus, whose commemorative clay cylinder Taylor recovered. Each of Nabonidus's commemorative inscriptions ended with a prayer for his eldest son, Belsharusur, none other than the Biblical Belshazzar, whose feast was spoiled when the fingers of a man's hand appeared and wrote on the plaster of the wall of the king's palace.[8] Belsharusur served as coregent with his father and was the last Babylonian king. Taylor's excavations at Muqayyar remained the only source of information on Ur until well into the twentieth century.

Taylor also dug into Abu Shahrain, a smaller complex of mounds south of Ur, where he found traces of a large ziggurat and inscribed bricks that later identified the site as the Sumerian city of Eridu.[9] Rawlinson now had solid historical data from cuneiform records to modify the provisional identifications of Biblical cities he had published in 1852. His new identifications of the locations of Ur and Eridu have stood the test of time. Perhaps fortunately for archaeology, the country round Ur and Eridu was so robber-infested that Turkish authorities insisted that anyone visiting Ur sign a letter releasing the Ottoman government from any responsibility for their safety. Because of these dangers, few European travelers visited these two sites until the twentieth century, by which time archaeological methods were vastly improved.

The English were not the only Europeans interested in digging in Babylonia. The news of Loftus's early work at Uruk reached Europe just as the French were considering a new official expedition. No less a personage than the French minister of the interior, Léon Faucher, was in London in the summer of 1851, both to visit the Great Exhibition and to view the Assyrian finds in the British Museum. He examined them meticulously, then sent a request through diplomatic channels for permission to make plaster casts of some of the originals for the Louvre. He returned to Paris convinced that the French government should become involved in Mesopotamian excavations a second time; otherwise, all the prizes would fall into alien hands and French prestige would suffer. Armed with a special report from a commission of the

Académie des Inscriptions, Faucher requested and obtained a grant of 78,000 francs from the Commission of the Budget for the Scientific and Artistic Expedition to Mesopotamia and Persia. The expedition was to be led by Fulgence Fresnel, an experienced Arabist and former consul at Jiddah. Jules Oppert was the linguist and cuneiform expert of the party, and Félix Thomas served as artist and architect. They arrived in Mosul in March 1852.

The expedition set off for Baghdad after three weeks of preparatory work at Khorsabad, Nineveh, and Mosul. Fresnel, Oppert, and Thomas spent over three months in Baghdad, debating what to do next. Rawlinson had strongly advised them to work in Persia rather than Babylonia on account of the disturbed political conditions outside the towns. But in July 1852, a rumor in the bazaars announcing the discovery of a golden statue of Nebuchadnezzar at Babylon spurred Fresnel into action. Accompanied by two regiments of Turkish troops on their way to Al Hillah, the three men began excavations in the Ksar mound at Babylon. The results were discouraging at best. They found the usual inscribed bricks, stamped, so Oppert showed, with nearly forty different signs, and glazed tiles with fragments of mosaics on them. Trenches sunk into other mounds nearby and into the summit and base of the so-called Babil tell were just as disappointing. The French worked in the Babylon area for nearly two years, gathering a scatter of antiquities and inscribed bricks from dozens of mounds and ruined buildings. Fresnel and Oppert, however, were unable to explore the vast site fully and they did not throw any new light on the topography of the ancient city. Perhaps their most significant discovery came from a mound adjoining Birs Nimrod. A small, dated tablet identified the great mass of brickwork as the remains of ancient Borsippa. Unfortunately for Oppert, his translation did not appear until Henry Rawlinson had already identified the site from his own excavations there.

The French expedition ended in February 1854. Oppert returned to France via Mosul, where he spent six weeks with Victor Place, the new French consul, helping him decipher many of the inscriptions from his excavations at Khorsabad. Félix Thomas also went to Mosul and assisted Place in the marathon task of recording the details of Sargon's palace. Fresnel remained in Baghdad and died of fever there the following year. The expedition's finds were tragically lost in the Qurna disaster of May 1855, when Arab raiders overturned the rafts bearing a huge load of Mesopotamian antiquities from both Assyria and the south (see Chapter 12). In spite of these challenges, Oppert willingly shouldered the burden of publishing his colleagues' work. His two-volume monograph appeared in 1859 and was notable for its brilliant analysis of the inscriptions from Khorsabad, Nineveh, and Babylon and for Thomas's fine drawings.[10] Despite Oppert's work, the finds from the southern sites were unspectacular compared with those from Khorsabad. It was a quarter of a century before anyone dug scientifically into the ancient cities of the south.

THE ROYAL LION HUNT

The third scene represents the king with his attendants spearing a lion, which had evidently sprung on the chariot, and foiled in his revenge, viciously grasps in his terrible jaws the chariot wheel.

—HORMUZD RASSAM

WHILE THE FRENCH BUSIED THEMSELVES IN BABYLONIA, HENRY RAWLINSON was still trying to find a permanent successor to Austen Henry Layard in Assyria. With William Kennett Loftus excavating at Susa and then at Uruk, the problem became urgent, for there was a danger that the British government would withdraw its grant of 1,500 pounds for renewed Assyrian excavations. Not only that, but the French had reactivated their consulate at Mosul. In August 1851, Léon Faucher, the Minister of the Interior, had obtained funds not only for the scientific expedition but also for an 8,000-franc renewal of the Khorsabad excavations.[1] The French foreign ministry scrutinized their personnel files for an energetic young diplomat who could direct their new Assyrian excavations before appointing Thomas Victor Place as the new French consul at Mosul.

Victor Place was born in Corbeil on July 18, 1818, the son of a wealthy merchant who lost all his money in speculative investments when his heir was sixteen years old. The young Place had subsequently made his way in the world on his own and became a career diplomat at the age of twenty-one. He was regarded as a bright young man and served as secretary to a special mission to Haiti and as a junior consul in Cadiz, Naples, and the Republic of Santo Domingo. He served as consul in Mosul for three eventful years, from May 19, 1851, to November 20, 1854. Place had no archaeological qualifications whatsoever. "I recognize that one of the principal interests attached to the Mosul Consulate is the discovery of the monument at Nineveh," he wrote. "The administrators of the Museum have encouraged me to concentrate my attention on this."[2] But he had to beg a copy of Botta and Flandin's *Monument de Ninive* from the Louvre. No one seemed interested in training him to excavate. He traveled out to Mosul with Jules Oppert and Félix Thomas, two of the three members of the French scientific expedition that was to operate in the south at the same time as Place dug at Khorsabad. Place arrived in Mosul with a firman from the sultan that authorized him to dig more or less anywhere he wished. The Académie des Inscriptions had told him to occupy as many sites as possible as fast as he could.

Diplomatic secrets seldom lasted long in Mesopotamia. Rawlinson got wind of the Académie's instructions even before Place arrived in Mosul and promptly increased the tempo of excavation at Kuyunjik at his own expense. At the same time he arranged to meet with Place at Samsun on the Black Sea to negotiate a division of sites for excavation. They reached a harmonious agreement whereby Place was given a clear field at Khorsabad, and the British retained Sennacherib's palace at Kuyunjik. Rawlinson raised no objection to Place's working at the northern edge of Nineveh nor was exclusion from Nimrud mentioned. Minor sites were apparently considered fair game for everyone. Rawlinson hastened back to Mosul and directed the Kuyunjik laborers to concentrate on a chamber called the Hall of Bulls, which was yielding large numbers of inscribed tablets. At the same time he importuned the museum for both a director and an artist, preferably individuals of mature years.

The museum ignored Rawlinson's pleas and sent out Charles Hodder, another young and inexperienced artist who knew nothing of the East and even less of archaeology. He reached Mosul on April 10, 1852, where he found an impatient Rawlinson trying to manage the excavations in Sennacherib's palace until his arrival. No major sculptures had been found for months, merely a steady stream of clay tablets, which filled eight large boxes. "The labour of carrying through a complete analysis will be immense; but the results will be brilliant," he observed.[3] Rawlinson was taken aback at Hodder's youth and inexperience but set him to work on the bas-reliefs from the palace. In the meantime, Rawlinson watched the French and again tried to recruit Loftus, whose Susa excavations had proved abortive. Loftus soon left for Uruk, even though political conditions were chronically unsettled.

For some weeks, Rawlinson enjoyed the company of Felix Jones of the Indian Army. Captain Jones was an expert surveyor and former captain of the *Euphrates* but now was in command of the river steamer *Nitoris*. Jones had accompanied Rawlinson to Behistun on the second visit and had rescued Layard's Nimrud lion from the floodwaters of the Tigris two years before. The British Museum had now commissioned him to make a detailed survey of the area between the Tigris and the Great Zab rivers, "yielding," they said, "to a general desire of seeing a complete picture of Assyria in her present desolation." The survey took several months, but Jones was delighted to find that Rich's map of Nineveh was accurate. His own survey, he said, stamped Rich's "narrative with the broad seal of truth." Jones's map was the primary source on Nineveh for nearly a century.[4]

Meanwhile, Victor Place had arrived in Mosul to find that only 8,000 francs of the government subvention could be used for Assyrian excavation. The rest was reserved for the scientific expedition to Babylonia. Under the arrangement sanctioned by Paris, Fulgence Fresnel was in charge of all excavation, including Khorsabad, which put Place in a difficult position. Fresnel was by all accounts a genial and kind man, a cosmopolitan figure with a taste for opium-smoking, but even his tact could not prevent a rift with Place, who insisted on autonomy in the north. Place told his government that they hadn't given him enough money. But, with the aid of Botta's foreman and many of his former workers, Place reopened the Khorsabad excavations. For some weeks his laborers found almost nothing, so he talked of abandoning the site. Rawlinson again offered him the northern part of Kuyunjik, an offer Place declined, for he felt it would be difficult to avoid encroaching on Layard's long-held preserves. Just as Place was about to give up, his workers came across some bricks inscribed with King Sargon II's name. From then on, Place never considered giving up the excavation. For two years Place excavated the remaining chambers of Sargon's palace on the summit of Khorsabad, an area three times larger than that explored by Botta. Like Layard, he dug the site by tunneling around the walls of each room. His objective was to reconstruct the ancient appearance of the palace and find bas-reliefs and inscriptions. He succeeded brilliantly. Fortunately he had the services of the French scientific expedition's artist, Félix Thomas, who returned from Babylonia just in time to work on the intricate details of the sculptures and bas-reliefs before the finds were shipped downstream. Place recovered not only the floor plan of the palace but also four outlying gates flanked by bulls and other fine sculptures. Although his excavations did not yield as many bas-reliefs as Botta's, they produced dozens of small objects in clay, glass, and metal. Even the bakery and Sargon's wine cellar full of painted storage jars came to light.

Place was able to publish a reconstruction of Sargon's palace in his sumptuous monograph *Ninive et l'Assyrie,* which appeared in Paris in 1866 through 1869. Even if his complex tunnels made an accurate survey difficult and if at times he attributed to the Assyrian architects a concern for symmetry that, in fact, they may never have had, Place's excavations showed that Sargon's city had covered at least 300 hectares. His palace stood on a huge brick platform that supported the royal residence, several temples, a ziggurat, and a large open plaza. The northwest wing consisted of large halls decorated with winged bulls and bas-reliefs that glorified Sargon's deeds in peace and war. Each room had walls from about three to five meters thick to provide insulation against the heat of summer and the cold of winter.[5]

Place's excavations were a scientific contribution of lasting value, for his reconstruction was based not just on observations in the field but on deciphered inscriptions as well. His monograph remained the standard source on Khorsabad until 1927, when the site was reopened. Tragically, nearly all his finds perished in the wreck of a raft near Basra in 1855, in the same mishap that wiped out the scientific expedition's work and many British finds (described later in this chapter).

Henry Rawlinson returned to his post in Baghdad soon after Place started work at Khorsabad and was informed that the trustees of the British Museum had decided to appoint Layard's former assistant, Hormuzd Rassam, as director of excavations under Rawlinson's general supervision. Although reluctant to leave the comfort of Oxford, Rassam was gratified to receive such an important appointment, which allowed him two years of excavation in Assyria. He arrived in Mosul in October 1852 and took up residence in the home of his brother Christian Rassam, the British vice-consul. Mosul was full of gossip about the French excavations at Khorsabad. Place had followed his official instructions and put teams of sixteen workers digging into sites all over the countryside in the hope of claiming their contents for France. By all accounts, Place was a quiet, conscientious diplomat of impeccable integrity. His new British rival was a very different type of person, one who at best can be described as ambitious, devious, and ruthless in his methods. Hormuzd Rassam's abrasive personality exacerbated the rivalry that surrounded most of his operations in Mesopotamia.[6]

Hormuzd Rassam had served as Layard's loyal and hardworking assistant, a superb mediator between a respected foreigner and his workers. Now he was to stand on his own feet, a local man fully accepted by the people of Mosul as a long-standing member of their community but employed by a foreign organization. Unquestionably, Rassam had been strongly influenced by Layard and the long periods of time he had spent in England. He espoused English customs and mannerisms but was acutely aware of his "inferior" native status in the eyes of many Englishmen. He desperately wanted to be recognized as a great archaeologist. He assumed that the way to succeed was through spectacular finds and shiploads of antiquities. He assumed, wrongly, that people would not care exactly how he came by them.

Rassam's mettle was tested soon after his arrival. He learned that an inhabitant of Nebi Yunus had unearthed a huge, human-headed bull while digging a cellar for his house. Nebi Yunus was the one Nineveh mound where no one was allowed to dig because of the mosque on its summit. When news of the find reached the vice-consulate, Christian Rassam sent Hodder to draw it. But the young artist returned home empty-handed. Place had already hurried to the scene and had tried unsuccessfully to remove the bull. Convinced that treasure lay under the mound, the pasha of Mosul now intervened. He informed all parties that the Turkish government needed antiquities as much as anyone and sent a large gang of convicts to dig away at the site. He did, however, allow Hormuzd Rassam to copy the inscriptions. The pasha even asked him for some experienced workers to assist his convicts. The excavations lasted for nine months but were hampered by the high prices the landowners asked, even of the pasha, for digging on their property and by the heavy chains the convicts always wore. At the end of the excavation, there was little to show for the work except two human-headed bulls, a bronzed lion, and an inscribed marble tablet, which indicated that Sennacherib had built his stables and military warehouses there.

In intervals between his time spent watching the French, Rassam sent laborers to dig as close to the limits of French territory at Kuyunjik as he dared. He was expecting Place to start work on his Nineveh concession shortly. Meanwhile, he packed up the already-famous bas-reliefs of the siege of Lachish found by Layard (see Chapter 10) and scattered teams of laborers on dozens of obscure mounds around Mosul, most of which yielded absolutely nothing. Since Place's men were operating near Nimrud, Rassam also reopened that site and dug in an area east of the Central Palace. The dig soon revealed shattered fragments of a huge obelisk. It had stood near a great doorway guarded by a stone bull and lion, both bearing inscriptions of Ashurnasirpal II. The North West Palace was still yielding a seemingly inexhaustible supply of bas-reliefs, this time of the king hunting lions. Unfortunately, the sculptures were badly damaged.

Both Place and Rassam had their eyes on the large mounds of ancient Assur, another Assyrian capital on the Tigris, downstream of Mosul on the confluence of the Great Zab River. Assur had been investigated very superficially by Layard some years before. Before Rassam had arrived, Place had worked there, attracted to the locality by its legendary fame as the first city built by the god Assur when he came to the land of the rivers. But the dig had proved unproductive and the French had moved elsewhere. When rumors of Rassam's plans reached the French consulate, Place, according to Rassam, hastened to reestablish his excavations first. One of Rassam's brothers was getting married, so he delayed his departure for the celebrations. The day before the wedding he heard that Place's guides had set out. Immediately, he and Hodder leapt aboard a large *kellek* with their equipment and some workers and floated down to Nimrud. From there Rassam organized a party of ninety men and reached Assur in three days. While he was en route, a galloping messenger from Mosul brought him letters from Place protesting that the French had prior claim. Rassam claimed he could not understand the grounds for Place's complaint. After all, Layard had found as much as anyone had there. So he ignored the complaints and pressed on, spurred by reports that the French were also on their way. Delayed by a storm, Rassam arrived later than he planned, but he immediately sent a small gang of laborers with Hodder across the Tigris to claim possession of the choice spots. There were loud cheers when a Union Jack rose on the summit of the highest mound. But, as Rassam himself approached, he heard sounds of conflict and war cries. He arrived in time to prevent bloodshed between his men and the French, who had just arrived. The unfortunate French overseer was being kept at bay, the rival Arab guide was stretched out full-length on the ground, and the two work gangs were almost at blows. With considerable difficulty, Rassam managed to establish peace. The French, who had come overland with few tools or supplies, were permitted to dig on the eastern side of the mound while Rassam commandeered the best locations. When an indignant Place turned up three days later, he had no option but to agree to an unfavorable — at least to the French — apportionment of the mound between the two nations.

Although the French soon abandoned their trenches in disgust, Rassam persisted for three weeks. The results were disappointing, for the mud-brick buildings on the mound had crumbled. Layard had earlier found an inscribed terracotta cylinder bearing the name of king Tiglath-Pileser I on the site. During later visits, Rassam found two others at the corners of a square masonry platform. Tiglath-Pileser's inscription served as the basis for the Royal Asiatic Society's cuneiform decipherment exercise in 1857 (see Chapter 7).

The intense competition surrounding the Assur excavations became typical when Rassam started operations. Rival gangs of workers chased each other over the countryside. A site was abandoned after superficial examination if it produced nothing. Both parties were looking for palaces, sculptures, gold, and other treasure.

During the summer of 1853, Rassam spent much of his time packing sculpture for shipment overseas to fulfill promises made by Henry Rawlinson. The British Museum received many prize pieces; others went to the Louvre, for Rawlinson had given Place permission to ship duplicates from Nimrud. A fine collection including some magnificent and unique examples of Assyrian artistry went to the Crystal Palace Company, the commercial organization operating the great Exhibition Hall in London. This collection eventually ended up in the Berlin Museum when the company later disposed of its assets. Rawlinson has been criticized for dispersing this material to a commercial company, but in fairness to him it should be said that he was primarily concerned with saving as much sculpture as possible from certain destruction.

Even the Americans started to collect some finds. An American missionary, the Reverend W. F. Williams, applied for permission to ship some duplicates to the Smithsonian Institution in the summer of 1852. With the approval of the American ambassador in London, the trustees of the British Museum, and Henry Rawlinson, a number of Ashurnasirpal's bas-reliefs were exhibited at various cities in the United States.

When cooler weather returned, Rassam again scattered his workers over more than 300 kilometers of the local countryside. He concentrated his main efforts, however, on the northern sector of Kuyunjik, where, he felt, the only chance of spectacular results lay. By this time Rassam seems to have been getting desperate for success. His funds were nearly exhausted and Hodder was sick. He became convinced that the only way to achieve results was by digging forbidden ground ceded to the French by Rawlinson. Rassam rationalized his actions, observing that Place had never tried to dig on his concession in the year or more since he had been ceded it. Furthermore, the landowner had been paid off by the British for years; thus, Rassam assumed he would prefer that the English, rather than the French, excavate there. In his desperation he resolved on a secret dig at night.

On December 20, 1853, Rassam took a small team of trusted laborers to dig by moonlight at three spots in French territory in an area where Layard had sunk some shallow trenches. Rassam ordered his men to dig much deeper, stopping work each day at dawn. The first night yielded accumulations of painted bricks and inscribed marble fragments; the second, a marble wall, which petered out after a few meters. Rassam was deeply disappointed, for, impetuously, he had reported the discovery of a new palace to Rawlinson and the British Museum the day before. So the third night he oversaw the men himself, digging around the short marble wall. The men worked in shifts without respite in a frantic search for the alleged palace. After three hours of work they uncovered a magnificent bas-relief of an Assyrian king standing in his chariot about to set out on a lion hunt. The sculpture formed part of a wall in a long hall into which the men were tunneling blindly. Suddenly the earth fell away from the side of the wall, revealing the king in his chariot. The workmen paused in astonishment. "Images," gasped one of them and everyone pressed forward to wonder at Ashurbanipal in his chariot. The workmen sang and danced for joy. "For a moment I did not know which was the most pleasant feeling that possessed me, the joy of my faithful men or the finding of the new palace," remarked Rassam.[7]

The early part of the night's work had been a nightmare for Rassam. Word of his nocturnal diggings had filtered out in Mosul. He was not afraid of the French but he was worried about the Ottoman authorities, who were, he knew, fascinated with buried treasure. The discovery of the palace relieved his anxiety, for it was an unwritten law that whoever excavated a palace had rights to it. "Thus," wrote Rassam proudly, "in my position as agent of the British Museum, I had secured it for England."[8] He now boldly kept a new shift of workers digging in the daytime. Place was at Khorsabad when news of Rassam's coup arrived. He hastened to Kuyunjik to find his rival and the new discovery surrounded by hundreds of fascinated spectators. He protested the trespass but to no avail. Rassam calmly told him that Rawlinson had had no authority to give away the concession, for the British had indemnified the landowner since Layard's time. After acidly congratulating Rassam on his good fortune, Place left, uttering threats of protests to higher authority.

"In my lordly sport, they let a fierce lion of the plain out of his cage, and on foot I shot him with arrows but did not kill him." Detail from one of Ashurbanipal's lion hunt bas-reliefs at Nineveh (ca. 645 B.C.). Copyright the Trustees of the British Museum.

By the end of that remarkable day, Rassam's team had cleared all the upper part of the hall. A sequence of bas-reliefs, about 1.5 meters high, depicted the story of the entire lion hunt. Ashurbanipal enters his chariot while attendants prepare the horses and hand him weapons. In the first relief that came to light, the king stands in his chariot about to set off. Then, in succession, the king is depicted in vigorous pursuit of a lion, bow drawn. The monarch spears his prey, then engages another lion in combat. Additional reliefs picture him in other heroic postures of the chase. The haunting depiction of a lioness, dying in agony, is part of the sequence. So are scenes of caged beasts waiting to be released for the hunt, as are pictures of all the bustle of a royal hunt and the ceremonies associated with it. Above the reliefs extended courses of crumbled, sun-dried bricks painted with other hunting and war scenes, most of which had perished in the intervening centuries.

When Rassam started to clear the floor of this remarkable chamber, he came across a great concentration of clay tablets thickly strewn about in apparent chaos. One has the impression that Rassam regarded tablets as somewhat of a nuisance in the midst of his palace. He simply instructed his men to gather them up and stack them in packing cases. Had he realized that this cache was to turn out to be one of the most important treasures of information on the Assyrians ever recovered, he might have been more careful. Just over three years before, Layard had recovered a part of Ashurbanipal's library in two small chambers in the South West Palace. Now Rassam, working in the North West Palace, had stumbled across the main body of Ashurbanipal's archives, stored in the great hall of the royal residence, a most unlikely place for a library. Rassam never bothered to record the exact provenience of the priceless archive. He casually wondered whether the tablets had been stored in the hall after the king's death while Kuyunjik was under siege. In retrospect it seems probable that the library was kept on a floor above the great hall and tumbled down when the hall ceiling collapsed. A team of British Museum experts was still unpacking, cataloguing, and deciphering Ashurbanipal's library twenty years later. The king, who had scholarly pretensions, had ordered his scribes to search for and copy all known examples of cuneiform literature. Thus, the library was a priceless repository of literature, historical records, and myths, among them the Babylonian version of the flood story, deciphered twenty years later by George Smith (see Chapter 13).

Every worker at Rassam's disposal labored at the North West Palace in teams of seven, including a digger, a basket filler, and five carriers. Soon, another long chamber appeared southwest of the lion-hunt hall. Its bas-reliefs depicted an orchard with tame lions and dogs exercising among the trees. A nearby room bore scenes of Ashurbanipal's military campaigns in Persia. Two pairs of colossal mythical figures, one with a lion's head and an eagle's talons, guarded the chamber. These hideous personages were the equivalent of the winged bulls and lions found at the entrances to other Assyrian palaces. Much of the palace had been destroyed and later quarried away for building materials. Rassam had no option but to make a superficial examination of his new palace, for the discovery came, as these finds often do, just as he was running out of funds and preparing to return to England. As it was, he postponed his departure for three months to clear the rooms southeast of the lion-hunt hall. By this time he was working alone. Hodder had come down with an intestinal complaint so serious that he had to be sent to Baghdad for medical attention before returning home. Rassam had no one to help him record the elaborate bas-reliefs before their removal. His excavations were hurried and careless. Rawlinson was so preoccupied with official business in Baghdad that he could pay only a flying visit to Mosul to see the finds. He quickly selected the best pieces for shipment and offered the duplicates to the French for the Louvre.

It was six months before Rassam had discovered the North West Palace that a group of influential people in London had formed the privately endowed Assyrian Exploration Fund with the intention of carrying on work in Mesopotamia once official funds ran out. This new digging sponsor came as somewhat of an irritant to Rawlinson, Rassam, and Place, for it introduced another competitive element in an already-crowded field. An annoyed Rawlinson suggested that the fund work in the south. Yet the fund's artist, William Boutcher, proved of value to Rawlinson, who prevailed on Loftus to release the artist to work at Kuyunjik when Loftus's excavations proved unproductive. Boutcher reached the North West Palace in time to receive a briefing from Rassam and to carry on where Hodder had left off. His drawings are the only surviving record of Ashurbanipal's spectacular residence.

In early April 1854, Rassam all but closed down the excavations at Kuyunjik and Nimrud, leaving Boutcher with a single team of excavators. Reaching England after a bitterly cold journey, he discovered that the trustees had obtained another 1,500 pounds from the treasury specifically for the removal of the North West Palace sculptures. They promptly asked him to return to Nineveh, which he agreed to do. On the eve of his departure, however, he was offered an appointment as a political administrator at Aden under the East India Company, a post that offered permanent employment. The trustees allowed him to accept this opportunity and informed Rawlinson that the grant was still available and should be used. This information put Rawlinson in a difficult position. By now he had reluctantly authorized Loftus to dig at Kuyunjik after Rassam's departure but had made it clear that only the museum had a concession to remove sculptures from that site.

Rawlinson may have distrusted Loftus's motives, for he had learned that Loftus's employers had been offered 500 pounds by Kaiser Wilhelm IV of Prussia to assemble some sculptures for his collections. Wilhelm IV had already supported the Lepsius Expedition to Egypt in 1842 to 1845, which had yielded fine scholarly results. Apparently he did not want to miss an opportunity to make a mark in Assyria as well.

Loftus dug for weeks on the west side of the North West Palace without result. He was planning to give up when his workers found a wall of sculptured slabs at a level six meters below Rassam's cuttings. By then, the new trench threatened to undermine the North West Palace and the British Museum's excavations. An agitated Christian Rassam, who was watching over the situation for Rawlinson, put six gangs of workers on the old dig in an attempt to forestall any raiding of palace bas-reliefs. Two British organizations were now in direct competition. Just when the situation was becoming untenable, news arrived that the Assyrian Exploration Fund had decided to merge its efforts with those of the British Museum. To Rawlinson's relief, Loftus and Boutcher promptly became museum employees. They unearthed magnificent garden scenes and more hunting pictures. The rooms in which the new reliefs were found were marked on a master plan compiled by Boutcher, which Rassam published many years later without acknowledging the source.

Boutcher's drawings were widely admired. Those examples that have survived justify this admiration. He was also eager to try photography and ordered an instrument from Paris, but it never reached him. Unlike in Egypt, where photographers like Francis Firth were working as early as 1857, Mesopotamia's ancient mounds did not receive real photographic attention until the 1880s, by which time irreparable damage had been done to the ziggurats and royal palaces.

By the end of 1854 the first excavations in Assyria were drawing to a close. Henry Rawlinson felt that his work was done. He left Loftus to select forty cases of Kuyunjik finds that were to follow eighty cases of Rassam's lion hunt reliefs and tablets to London. The remainder of the Kuyunjik materials were given over to the French or abandoned. Onto heavily loaded *kelleks* Place had packed 235 crates, including material

A kellek carrying a Nimrud bull. Painting probably attributable to F. C. Cooper. Courtesy of the Victoria and Albert Museum, London. The Rodney Searight Collection.

from Kuyunjik and Nineveh for the Louvre and the British Museum, as well as his Khorsabad finds. Kaiser Wilhelm IV had twenty-four cases in the same shipment. The *kelleks* reached Baghdad safely but were delayed there because of a shipping shortage caused by the Crimean War. In spite of warnings from Rawlinson that political conditions were highly unsettled downstream and that the flood embankments could burst suddenly, the convoy left Baghdad on May 13, 1855. Five days later, marauding tribesmen attacked and plundered the *kelleks* near Qurna. The marauding tribesmen tipped the crates into the Tigris and killed several of the crew. When news of the disaster reached Basra, frantic attempts were made to salvage the precious cargo. The salvagers recovered seventy-eight crates of the original shipment, twenty-six of them destined for the Louvre. Kaiser Wilhelm never received his sculptures and only two crates of Place's Khorsabad finds ever reached Paris. The loss to science was incalculable. Fortunately, the fifty crates containing Ashurbanipal's lion hunt were not shipped until the following year and reached England safely.[9]

A few months before the Qurna disaster, the Assyrian Exploration Fund wound up its affairs. All the British Museum's funds were exhausted, so Loftus's Kuyunjik excavations were never published, partly on account of "the present disturbed state of the East."[10] When the fifty crates of his finds arrived in London, the museum had to store them in the basement because there was no space to put their contents on display. The trustees had already decided not to apply for further government support for Mesopotamian excavations. All the palaces of Assyria had apparently been discovered and most of their treasures removed. So much sculpture had been found that there was a positive embarrassment of Assyrian kings in London and Paris. The public had lost interest in the subject as the sensations of the Crimean War crowded the front pages of the newspapers. Only scholars continued their passionate interest in the hundreds of cuneiform tablets shipped home by Layard, Rassam, and Loftus.

Henry Rawlinson left Baghdad for the last time in 1855. His forceful visits to the British Museum ensured that decipherment, classification, and study of the Kuyunjik tablets continued. Loftus died of heatstroke aboard ship on his way home in 1858. Victor Place returned to Paris in 1856 to write his study of Khorsabad. What he felt about the Qurna disaster is not recorded. He never returned to archaeology but continued his diplomatic career in Turkey and New York until his death in 1875. The French were as disinterested in further excavations as their rivals. When Place's successor in Mosul applied for official funds to dig, the minister in Paris turned down his request. The government had spent enough. Nearly twenty years passed before foreign archaeologists dug in Mesopotamia again.

THE DELUGE TABLETS

Whenever I found anything of interest, it was my practice to examine the most likely parts of the collection, and pick up all the fragments that would join, or throw light on the new subject.

—GEORGE SMITH

As the Crimean War ended in 1856, the focus of Assyrian scholarship shifted from the field to the quiet of libraries and museums. A small band of cuneiform scholars sifted through the huge archives of clay tablets from Ashurbanipal's library at Kuyunjik. Since the tablets were the property of the British Museum, the experts tended to congregate in London. Scholars from all over Europe visited the cramped study room of the Department of Oriental Antiquities. The work of translation took years to complete, for many of Ashurbanipal's tablets were in a poor state and had never been sorted, pieced together, or even cleaned properly. There were no textbooks on cuneiform or Assyrian grammar. Everything had to be learned firsthand by copying, translating,

187

and annotating tablets and by relying on the experience of older scholars. Henry Rawlinson and his friend Jules Oppert were instrumental in
training the Assyriologists who were to make even closer correlations
between the Scriptures and ancient Mesopotamia than the pioneers
had succeeded in doing.

In 1862, Rawlinson had published a provisional chronology of
Assyrian history that provided a basis for comparing Assyrian events
with the Old Testament. "The order and duration of at least thirteen
reigns have been ascertained without the possibility of a considerable
amount of error," he wrote.[1] The philologist Edwin Norris, who had
published the authoritative Elamite version of the Behistun inscriptions
in 1855, spent years working on an Assyrian dictionary.[2] Although it
remained unfinished at his death in 1872, the three volumes that were
published were invaluable as a basic source on Assyrian vocabular-
ies and were set alongside a steady stream of grammatical studies from French scholars like Joachim Menant, who worked on King
Hammurabi's Babylonian inscriptions.[3] By 1876, Assyrian was a widely
studied script but still based almost entirely on the Kuyunjik tablets.

The Department of Oriental Antiquities at the British Museum was in
the genial charge of Samuel Birch, one of the most influential Asian
scholars of the late nineteenth century. Birch reported to the secretary of the museum but relied heavily on colleagues like Rawlinson
for advice and overseas contacts. Incredible although it may seem,
Birch never visited Egypt or Mesopotamia. Yet his tiny, cramped office over the museum heating plant was a major center of Egyptology
and Assyriology in Europe for half a century. Birch was a vigorous,
hardworking man of "generous build." He sported a short, white
beard in later life and a mustache trimmed, it was alleged, to make
him look ferocious. Whatever the weather, he wore a black broadcloth
coat and light trousers. His black, chimney-pot silk hat was, his friend
Wallis Budge wrote, "quite the worst in the museum, which is saying
a good deal." One American visitor described him as part jockey and
part bishop.[4]

Birch bore the brunt of the mass of Near Eastern correspondence
that descended on the museum. He advised scholars all over the world

about cuneiform, hieroglyphs, and excavations. Visitors—including serious scholars, dealers, and publishers, but also casual inquirers and the inevitable cranks—arrived in droves, too. Conspicuous were the "experts" on Biblical chronology who were trying to reconcile newly translated tablets from Nineveh with the Scriptures. They invariably would begin by challenging the accuracy of the translation, before producing large charts that purported to give the exact day and month, even the hour, when events in the Bible had occurred. Birch always remembered the gentleman who, when asked when Adam and Eve were expelled from the Garden of Eden, consulted his chart and replied, "They were turned out at sunset on Friday the twentieth day of the month Tebheth, four thousand, seven hundred and thirteen years before Christ."[5] It transpired that they had lived in the garden for eighty-nine days, seven and a half hours. Argument with such visitors was useless, so Birch used to sit back and let them run on until they ran out of patience, breath, and ideas.

Birch was also busily engaged in acquiring Egyptian and Mesopotamian antiquities from dealers in the Near East and all over Europe. Although official excavations had ceased after Rassam's expedition in 1855, unofficial diggings, especially near Baghdad, supplied a steady stream of cylinders, tablets, and other antiquities for museums and collectors on both sides of the Atlantic. A flourishing illegal trade started in Baghdad and ended in dealers' stores near the British Museum and the Louvre. Nearly all these finds had no known provenience. Forgeries were commonplace.

Birch had another invaluable quality. He encouraged enthusiastic young scholars to become involved in the work of his department. He allowed them free access to his records and the departmental collections on condition that they work seriously at translation or tablet preparation. As a result, his hospitable office and study room became a mecca for gifted students, among them a reclusive clay tablet sorter, George Smith.

Smith was the classic ivory-tower scholar, a quiet and shy man with a nervous manner whose only interest in life appeared to be Assyrian texts. He was an engraver's apprentice by trade but became interested in cuneiform while very young, having read Rawlinson's work and corresponded with him. "He had a broad, high forehead, and keen eyes set rather close together," wrote Wallis Budge, who commented on his "curiously pointed fingertips."[6]

Smith succeeded in deciphering a new account of Shalmaneser's war against Jehu, the king of Judah, which caused considerable interest when it was published in 1866. Soon he was hired by the British Museum to assist Rawlinson in the preparation of additional volumes in his series, *Cuneiform Inscriptions of Western Asia*, which had first appeared in 1861.[7] From 1867 to 1871, Smith closeted himself in a small room in the museum and produced a series of important translations of Assyrian and Babylonian history. The staff of the department saw little of him because he kept to himself. He was absorbed in translation and neglected cataloguing for the more exciting and arduous work of interpretation. His main preoccupation was Ashurbanipal's library. He divided hundreds of tiny fragments into seven broad categories of subject matter, one of which was mythology.

In 1872, Smith began sorting through the mythology tablets. Suddenly, he came across "half of a curious tablet which had evidently contained originally six columns." He scanned the columns and noticed in the third one a reference to a ship resting on the "mountains of Nizir, followed by the account of the sending forth of the dove, and its finding no resting place and returning." Smith immediately knew what he had found: "I saw at once that I had here discovered a portion at least of the Chaldean account of the Deluge."[8] The earnest students in the study room were electrified when Smith laid down the tablet on the table, jumped up, and rushed around the room in a great state of excitement. When he calmed down, Smith reexamined the first fragment and found it covered about half the story. A more thorough search of the pile revealed eleven other fragments of the same epic. Oppert and Rawlinson had found traces of this legend before, but it was not until Smith pieced it together that its true significance was appreciated.

It was a thoroughly dignified and formally dressed George Smith who lectured to an overflow audience of the Biblical Archaeological Society on December 3, 1872. Rawlinson presided over the meeting, which was attended by Prime Minister William Gladstone and a distinguished gathering of archaeologists, philologists, and theologians. Smith's lecture was a tour de force of modesty that generated pro-

13.1 One of the fragments of the eleventh tablet of the Epic of Gilgamesh, *which gave George Smith a version of the Babylonian story of the flood. The tablet came from Ashurbanipal's library at Nineveh. Copyright the Trustees of the British Museum.*

longed discussion afterward. "The meeting," said the *Times* in a glowing review next day, "concluded at a late hour."[9]

Smith revealed a version of a deluge myth that showed marked resemblances to the story of the flood in Genesis. He translated for his lecture audience the eleventh tablet, the one that dealt with the "Chaldean Deluge." The hero Izdubar learns from a seer named Hasisadra how he survived a great flood sent by the gods to punish humankind. The tablet told how Hasisadra made a large ship, which was planked and caulked with bitumen. Into it he loaded all his family and, he added, "the beast of the field, the animal of the field, the sons of the people, all of them, I caused to go up." Then the flood came and "destroyed all life from the face of the earth." It rained for six days and nights but cleared on the seventh. The ship went aground on the "mountain of Nizir." Hasisadra "sent forth a dove and it left. The dove went and turned, and a resting place it did not find, and it returned." Eventually a raven was dispatched and did not come back. So Hasisadra released the animals, became a god, and lived happily ever after.[10]

George Smith was well aware that the texts he had discovered were by no means the only account of the Babylonian flood. He suspected, rightly, that they could be traced to even earlier myths. We know now that that they were part of a masterpiece of Sumerian and Akkadian literature—the *Epic of Gilgamesh*. The flood story comes from the eleventh tablet of the epic. Gilgamesh hears the tale of the flood from the mouth of its hero, Atramhasis ("exceedingly wise"). The original Babylonian flood legend came from another poem, the *Epic of Atramhasis*, which was a history of humankind. A large part of this epic is lost, but enough is known about its content for scholars to reconstruct the original story of the flood in reasonable detail. The Sumerian prototype of the Babylonian *Epic of Atramhasis* was found in the archives at Nippur years later, 100 lines of the original 300-line epic.

All versions of the flood story are a highly dramatic narrative of gods and people. The *Epic of Atramhasis* tells how the world was created and how the gods felt that someone should be in charge of it. The mother goddess Mami created the first man, made of the flesh and blood of a minor god mixed with clay. Humankind is born, the first cities built, and kingship established. But the world's population becomes so numerous and troublesome that the chief god, Enlil, decides to destroy humanity with a great flood. The devout king of Suruppak, Atramhasis, is warned of the impending flood by the god Enki. He builds a large boat, taking aboard his family, some craftsmen, and the "beasts of the field." Gilgamesh then hears the sequel, which is lost in the original *Epic of Atramhasis*. The deluge destroys everyone else, but Atramhasis's ship floats on the waters and grounds on Mount Nisir (Pir Omar Gudoun) east of the Tigris. He sends out first a dove, then a swallow, to reconnoiter the earth. When they return, he dispatches a raven, who never comes back. Atramhasis and his crew then recolonize the world. As a reward for his faith, Atramhasis and his wife are granted immortality by Enlil. Gilgamesh fails in his quest for the same eternal life, for death is the lot of mortals.

Smith's revelations caused an ecclesiastical and scientific sensation. Public interest in Mesopotamian archaeology enjoyed a dramatic revival after twenty years of indifference. The museum displayed the so-called Deluge Tablets, which drew large crowds. But the account was incomplete. In his lecture Smith had told how he had managed to piece together most of the epic from duplicate tablets. But there remained tantalizing gaps, especially one of seventeen lines from the first column of the first tablet. The *Daily Telegraph* newspaper saw a unique opportunity for a dramatic story and promptly offered the British Museum 1,000 guineas for a new excavation at Nineveh to find the missing lines, provided that Smith led the expedition and sent regular accounts to the paper.[11] The trustees accepted the offer. Smith took a six-month leave of absence and left for Mosul on January 20, 1873.

The shy and retiring Smith was hardly an ideal choice as director of a major excavation. He had never traveled outside Europe and he had no experience with handling Arab workers, let alone conducting an excavation. In those days lack of excavation experience was no disqualification, for no one had thought deeply about archaeological technique. One must admire Smith's single-minded courage and devotion to his beloved tablets, for his health was far from robust. He first traveled to Paris to visit the Louvre, where he inspected the Khorsabad finds. Then he continued his trek, traveling through Marseilles, Palermo, and Antioch in Syria. After only a day in Antioch, he was on the road for Mosul. The journey took a month, Smith's first taste of Eastern travel's vagaries and flea-infested lodging houses.

The pasha of Mosul received Smith courteously enough but declared that instructions from Baghdad prohibited foreigners from inspecting or excavating any archaeological sites in his district. When the pasha forbade Smith even to look at the sites, Smith called on the French consul for help, because there was no British representative in Mosul at the time. When that plea failed, he decided to float down to Baghdad while awaiting the firman from Constantinople that the British Museum had applied for months before. He stopped briefly at Nimrud and Assur and spent a valuable month at the British residency while he visited Babylon, Birs Nimrod, and other sites. Like so many travelers, Smith lamented the lack of excavation at Babylon and longed for a chance to dig in the mounds there. He realized they were a potential gold mine of information and would no doubt confirm the records on already-deciphered tablets in London.

The firman came through in April 1873. Back in Mosul, Smith found Layard's old foreman, Toma Shishman, who was now very fat and short-winded. He claimed to know everything about the Nineveh mounds and asserted that his services were indispensable. Smith was not impressed and in any case planned a small-scale excavation at Nimrud first. He hoped to find additional inscriptions that would throw light on the reign of the relatively unknown monarch Tiglath-Pileser II (967–935 B.C.), as well as to verify information from previous-ly excavated and deciphered tablets. Smith had a powerful intellectual weapon. He was fluent in cuneiform, which enabled him to identify buildings and sculptures and decipher inscriptions on the spot. At Nimrud, which had fallen on bad times since Layard — and his excava-tion funds — had departed, Smith focused his attention on the Temple of Nebo, where he duly found a tablet describing Tiglath-Pileser II's reign. The excavations continued for a month, during which time he checked inscriptions unearthed by Layard in the South West Palace, attempted to find foundation cylinders in the huge ziggurat tunneled into twenty years before, and uncovered new chambers in the South East Palace. The finds, by Layard's standards, were far from spectacu-lar, but Smith obtained some valuable inscriptions.

On May 7, 1873, Smith turned his attention to Kuyunjik, starting ex-cavations at three locations in the library areas of Sennacherib's South West Palace and at the southeast corner of Ashurbanipal's residence. Unlike his predecessors, Smith had no interest in bas-reliefs, just in terracotta cylinders and clay tablets. Any form of excavation was dif-ficult, for the palace sites were honeycombed with abandoned tunnels and deep trenches. Some inscriptions came to light in Sennacherib's precincts, but the North Palace of Ashurbanipal was a mess. The lo-cal people had turned the stone slabs exposed by Rassam into build-ing materials. Smith had to shift heavy boulders with crowbars to get at the archaeological deposits. The work proceeded slowly until the evening of May 14, when Smith sat down to examine the cuneiform tablets found during the day's work. To his amazement, one of them "contained the greater portion of the seventeen lines of inscription belonging to the first column of the Chaldean account of the Deluge, and fitting into the only place where there was a serious blank in the story."[12] As soon as the tablet was copied, Smith telegraphed the *Daily Telegraph*, which published the sensational discovery on May 21, 1873. The missing fragment had come to light only a week after the Kuyunjik digging began.

To Smith's astonishment, the *Daily Telegraph* instructed him to close down the excavations. They had achieved their editorial objective and were no longer interested. Smith had enough time to sift through the debris of previous excavations and find some more interesting cylinders and tablets, including some dealing with creation legends, but he dutifully left Mosul on June 8 after only a month of digging. Some months passed before the finds reached London, because the Turkish authorities at the port of Izkenderun seized them as illegal exports. Only the direct intervention of the British ambassador in Constantinople secured their release. The tablets now reside in the British Museum, labeled "DT," for *Daily Telegraph*.

The complete Deluge Tablets continued to cause a sensation in London, so the British Museum decided to send Smith out on a second trip to Nineveh in order to benefit from the rest of the sultan's firman. Thus, only four months after returning home, Smith was on his way to Mosul again. He found the Turkish authorities far from welcoming. The sultan had decreed that half of all the finds must go to the Imperial Ottoman Museum in Constantinople. When Smith pointed out that his objective was to find fragments of inscriptions, the authorities laughed in disbelief. From this point on he excavated in an atmosphere of distrust, forbidden to work anywhere other than at Kuyunjik.

For years, Smith had been convinced that Layard's library chamber in Sennacherib's palace contained but a portion of the royal archives. Layard had just shoveled an irregular mass of tablets into baskets and shipped them in crates to England in bulk. Smith believed that the tablets found by his predecessor had fallen into the chamber from second-story rooms when the palace was destroyed. To test this hypothesis, he excavated an oval area about 213 meters in circumference, ordering his workers not to tunnel into the mounds and to begin by removing the huge piles of excavated soil from the surface of the deposits. He recovered many tablet fragments from these heaps in the process, then he dug through the hard-packed upper levels of the mound. At first only modern objects came to light. Cuneiform tablets became plentiful as the trenches penetrated to greater depths. Smith was clearing the fill from halls and chambers that Layard had tunneled through by following the walls. Numerous tablets containing invaluable bilingual lists, historical and mythological data, and histories of Sargon II, Ashurbanipal, and other monarchs came from the floors. Eventually over 3,000 tablets came from three months of excavation. Smith's hunch had proved correct.

At the beginning, Smith had employed only forty men, but the pressure of time imposed by the firman, which would expire in March 1874, was such that he engaged more and more diggers until an army of nearly 600 men labored away. "When they were at work, the mound presented an interesting appearance of bustle and activity," remarked Smith in one of the classic understatements of archaeology.[13] It was a miracle that he found anything at all in the chaos. To add to his anxieties, the Turkish authorities were a nuisance, constantly interfering with the dig. They charged him with desecrating Muslim graves and accused him of not paying adequate rent for the land. At times the weather was so cold that pools of water on the mound were frozen all day. Then the Tigris overflowed and the vast labor force had to be ferried across the river from Mosul by boat.

On March 21, 1874, Smith closed down the dig and prepared to leave for England. But the pasha of Mosul claimed half his finds and only let him depart when the sultan of Turkey gave orders that he be allowed to leave provided he left half his duplicates behind. Although the bookish Smith lacked the authority and experience that Botta and Layard had enjoyed in their dealings with the authorities, the scale of his operations show that he was no weakling and was determined to achieve his declared objectives. In the 1870s, it was far harder to work in Mesopotamia than in Layard's day, for the Turkish government was now well aware of the significance and value of Assyrian antiquities. Fortunately for science, the objectives of the British Museum's operations had shifted from sculpture to small objects, especially to clay tablets, so Smith was able to take most of his finds with him.

The furor over the Assyrian tablets continued unabated upon Smith's return to London. He succeeded in matching many of the tablets from his new excavations with those from his earlier diggings and Layard's collections. In 1875, the museum sent him out for a third dig, but this time he went to Constantinople first, so he could help the British ambassador obtain a new firman. He waited there for five months, eventually arriving at Mosul in March 1876, too near summer to start work. He decided to return to London at once and, against everyone's advice, insisted on crossing the desert to the Mediterranean in the heat. Already weary from months of negotiation and arduous travel, Smith contracted dysentery about four days' ride from Aleppo and died on August 19, 1876. Right up to his final days, he worked on his cuneiform tablets, including a remarkable specimen that gave an account of the construction of the temple of Belus at Babylon. The ziggurat had been built with seven great steps, then capped with a temple that was visible from a great distance.

The British consul in Aleppo shipped Smith's possessions and his precious tablets to London. His travel notes showed that he had worried about the safety of his finds to the end. As he lay dying, he scribbled in his small notebook that the thirty-five tablets "are in my long boots . . . in my trunk." His last entry was true, if pathetic: "[M]y work has been entirely for the science."[14]

Smith's unexpected death created a vacuum at the British Museum. The tremendous surge in public interest over the Deluge Tablets had not passed by the dealers in Baghdad, who promptly sent large new shipments of cylinders and tablets to London, Berlin, and Paris. Birch and Rawlinson were worried by the increased illegal traffic. Clearly the new tablets came from unexcavated sites in the south, tells like Nippur and Telloh. A group of influential scholars urged the museum trustees to apply for a firman to dig not only in Assyria but in Babylonia as well. They pointed out that the epic poems from the Kuyunjik libraries made repeated reference to Uruk, Eridu, and other much earlier cities in the south, which promised rich rewards for those patient enough to excavate them over a long period of time.

The trustees agreed that further excavation was desirable, but the problem was finding a suitable archaeologist to direct the work, someone familiar with tell excavation and local conditions. It so happened that Hormuzd Rassam had just resigned his political appointment in Aden after a fascinating and checkered term of office that took him as far afield as Zanzibar and Abyssinia.[15] He had been asked to work with George Smith and had refused, but now he accepted the unsalaried post as director of excavations. His appointment heralded the beginning of a new scramble for Mesopotamian antiquities, one that focused not on sculptures but on archives, cuneiform tablets, and cylinders.

Rassam's appointment was one that the trustees would regret more than once.

GATES AND PALACES

The people of Balawat declared . . . that rather than disappoint me, they would turn up the bones of their forebears themselves, happen what may.

—HORMUZD RASSAM

THE OCCASIONAL SOCIAL REFORMS OF NINETEENTH-CENTURY TURKISH SULTANS placed considerable emphasis on public education and included the founding of the Imperial Ottoman Museum of Antiquities. The beginnings of the museum go back to the mid-nineteenth century, but at that time the collections consisted of little more than some scattered archaeological finds dumped in an ancient church courtyard. In 1877, the sultan decided to reorganize the museum along the lines of the Bulak Museum in Cairo. His purpose was not only to house some local antiquities in the East but also to stem the rapidly increasing traffic in illegal antiquities that had been centered in Baghdad since the 1850s.

The sultan designated a quaint early Turkish palace, the Tshinili Kiosk, as the museum building. The first Turkish director general of the museum was Osman Hamdi Bey, a quiet yet effective man who had received art training and a legal degree in Paris. After an early career as a government administrator in Baghdad and elsewhere, Hamdi Bey found his niche in his new position. Hampered by inadequate funds and government apathy, he nevertheless succeeded in making the museum a viable repository for antiquities and managed to obtain the funds for a larger permanent building. Hamdi Bey collected antiquities from all over the Ottoman empire and directed excavations in Lebanon and Mesopotamia for the Turkish government. Anyone applying for a firman had to negotiate with him on the details. Hamdi Bey was highly sensitive to the interests of his government. He revised the antiquities laws in 1881, making them even more stringent. The new permits specified precise physical and time limits for the excavations and gave instructions for the finds' disposal. Every excavation was required to pay the wages of a Turkish government commissioner, who joined the dig and supervised the work on Constantinople's behalf. For a quarter of a century the dedicated and hardworking Hamdi Bey — a "slightly built" man with a pair of dark, extraordinary eyes that looked through one and beyond — controlled the destiny of excavations in al-'Iraq.[1]

The Imperial Ottoman Museum had only just been founded when Hormuzd Rassam arrived in Constantinople to negotiate a new firman for Assyrian excavations. Forewarned by George Smith's difficulties in 1876, Rassam was prepared to be patient. After three and a half months, he left empty-handed. Anglo-Turkish relations were at a low ebb; the British ambassador, Sir Henry Elliot, unsympathetic; and the sultan downright hostile. Just as the British Museum was giving up hope, the Foreign Office appointed Austen Henry Layard as the new British ambassador to Constantinople in April 1877. Although Russia and Turkey were at war and the sultan was preoccupied with military affairs, Layard approached him personally. Such was the weight of his authority and prestige that a firman on very generous terms was forthcoming at once.[2]

Hormuzd Rassam, painted in Turkish costume, as a subject of the sultan, by F. C. Cooper, 1851. Copyright the Trustees of the British Museum.

Rassam reached Mosul and Baghdad in December and started work at Kuyunjik on January 7, 1878. He had not been near an archaeological site for almost twenty years. A great deal of archaeology had been carried out in Europe and Egypt since then, and excavation techniques were slowly changing for the better. But Mesopotamian archaeology had remained a backwater, unaffected by the new, more rigorous excavation methods pioneered by German scholars at Samothrace and

Olympia in Greece since 1874.³ Rassam was unaware of these developments. His instructions from the museum trustees were simple and specific: "Find as many fragments as possible from the libraries of Assurbanipal [sic] and the completion of the records which were already amongst the national collection in London."⁴ Rassam, however, had set his sights higher. He remembered the fame and fortune that had come Layard's way a quarter century before. Unwilling to concentrate all his energies on such a tame undertaking as the acquisition of mere clay tablets, he decided to look for new, unexplored sites that would yield spectacular finds like Layard's lions and sculptures. Finds like those magnificent bas-reliefs, he felt, would gratify the British public, "especially those who valued such discoveries either for their Biblical or literary studies."⁵

As soon as Rassam's arrival became known, dozens of Layard's former workers and even their sons and relatives descended on Mosul. He wanted 400 or 500 men, an expense that was bound to strain his limited purse. For some reason the tribesmen liked working for Rassam, probably because he was a respected local man and employment options were limited. So he took advantage of them and paid only about three fourths of the regular laborer's wage for the Mosul area. As a result he was able to engage many more men than otherwise would have been possible. His long experience of labor problems under Layard enabled him to get away with this economy, sweetened as it was with the occasional gift of an ox for a feast. Within a few weeks, the digs at Kuyunjik and Nimrud were in full swing.

Rassam conducted the Kuyunjik and Nimrud excavations at a distance, but he employed Christian overseers who knew something of inscriptions and clay tablets. Instead of following the walls of Ashurbanipal's palace, they continued Smith's work, clearing chambers and breaking down brick walls that were in the way. The overseers found numerous tablets and the most important find, a cylinder with 1,300 lines of cuneiform inscription describing the conquests and empire of Ashurbanipal. Nimrud yielded a temple built by Ashurnasirpal II, located near the North West Palace. Unfortunately, the walls were gone and the beautiful glazed ceiling tiles lay in thousands of fragments.

Rassam was operating with a temporary, telegraphed firman that spelled out no restrictions. When the official one came—which imposed strict conditions, including a provision for sharing finds with the Ottoman government—Rassam kept it to himself. Without Layard in Constantinople and his own friends in Mosul, he would have been in trouble. The sultan had specified that an official Turkish commissioner, on salary from the British Museum, was to be present at all excavations. This clause had been removed from the temporary firman on the insistence of Layard, who also had pulled strings to allow Rassam to export everything. The new breed of firman, which did not make these concessions, was restrictive even for a highly responsible excavator. For a plunderer like Rassam, the new restrictions made it impossible for him to achieve his objectives. Even using all his diplomatic and bargaining skills, he could not secure a firman granting him permission to excavate in the old-style manner that had been commonplace in Layard's day.

Some time before, a villager digging a grave into the Assyrian city mound at Balawat, twenty-four kilometers east of Mosul, had come across a large bronze plate embossed with human figures. He had broken it up and sold it to the French consul and some of Rassam's friends. One of the friends in turn sent some fragments to Rassam, who hastened to investigate. He was relieved to find that the discovery had been made in a part of the mound that was devoid of modern gravestones. The local villagers, however, would be certain to object if he dug there, on the grounds that he might disturb nearby recent burials. So Rassam came to terms with the landowners and started work with his own men, knowing that trouble would come as the first spadeful was turned. He was right. Yelling villagers forced the dig to stop, as Rassam knew they would. After prolonged negotiations, he promised to employ some local people to watch for graves and to stop digging when necessary. To Rassam's relief, his stratagem worked and there were no further problems.

The next day the workers came across huge bronze panels lying at an angle in the ground. The tops lay a meter beneath the surface, the bases four and a half meters below it. The plates had to be removed in large pieces, for they started to crack when exposed to the air. They proved to be the coverings of a huge gate with double doors, originally hung from a wooden frame. Each door had seven two-meter bronze panels set in cedar wood. The bronze hinges had rotated in stone sockets. The plates bore scenes of Shalmaneser III's conquests in southern Mesopotamia. "The plates, which are embossed with a variety of subjects, such as battle scenes, triumphal processions and religious performances, are divided into two panels surrounded by a border of rosettes," wrote Rassam.[6] He had found the bronze gates of Shalmaneser III, now one of the great treasures of the British Museum. Balawat has since been proven to be the site of a temple to Mamu, the god of dreams, and of a palace called Imgur-Enlil, which was entered through the bronze and cedar gates Rassam had found.

The Balawat excavations were a constant source of anxiety for Rassam. The local workers, concerned about grave desecrations, quarreled with his regular crew. Bitterly cold winds blew over the site and nearly froze the night watchmen who guarded the gates. He told his men to recover the bronze work as fast as possible and to tunnel into other parts of the mound. A second pair of bronze gates, these belonging to Ashurnasirpal II, set on brick platforms emerged near the first ones. A temple housing a "marble coffer, containing two beautifully inscribed tablets hewn of the same material," was discovered at the north side of the site.[7] The burned-down temple contained inscriptions and a large quantity of human bones. Although these burials were obviously ancient, the local workers raised such a hullabaloo that the bones had to be reburied. Rassam also found an Assyrian well, which he cleared to the bottom in search of treasure thrown into it in time of danger. He found nothing. So troublesome did the local people become that Rassam decided to remove the bronze gates and shut down the excavations.

Naturally, the trustees were delighted with Shalmaneser's bronze gates. They decided to take advantage of Layard's presence in Constantinople by applying for another firman, this time a permit that would enable Rassam to dig in Assyria, Turkey, and even Babylonia. While awaiting word from Layard, Rassam returned to Mosul in November 1878 to be greeted by a huge crowd of well-wishers. He opened up Kuyunjik again and went looking for new sites to excavate. For two months he visited large numbers of mounds and dug feverishly at Nimrud and again at Assur, with little success. A severe attack of fever so reduced his energy that any work was a supreme effort. He also was frustrated. Everywhere huge sites awaited excavation, many of them, presumably, full of spectacular finds. Yet he found little. His methods were too crude and the days of "digging up" were now numbered. Spectacular finds would only come from carefully planned, systematic excavations conducted under close supervision for months, even years, at a time.

⚬⚬⚬

In January 1879 Rassam, incredibly, found himself in possession of a two-year firman that enabled him to excavate in three different provinces of the Ottoman empire at the same time. Thanks to Layard, Rassam now held the permit of his dreams. He immediately hastened to Baghdad, where the British representative, a Colonel Nixon, agreed to keep an eye on excavations south of the city when Rassam was elsewhere.

Rassam's first target was Babylon, so he took some trusted overseers and set up his headquarters at Al Hillah. His arrival created great concern among the local brick diggers, who had quarried Babylon for generations. Recently, some Baghdad merchants had bribed them to collect cylinder seals and other small antiquities for export to Europe and the United States at 100 times their Babylon price. Their clandestine diggings were easily combined with brick quarrying, so much so that the workers would contract with two or three dealers, then break up cylinder seals and sell parts of the same specimen to different people. Rassam had even bought a Babylonian cylinder that had been sawed in half with such a crude saw that nearly a centimeter of the inscriptions had been destroyed.

Shrewdly, Rassam moved in on Babylon by hiring a brick contractor from Al Hillah to negotiate with the diggers. The contractor agreed to pass on all the inscribed bricks he received, while Rassam made a similar arrangement with the other diggers. In this way he obtained a temporary monopoly on all finds from the site. When a few dealers tried to bribe his men, Rassam quietly turned a blind eye, for his monopoly arrangement worked well. He got most of the antiquities and the diggers received both a wage and also the profits from the plain bricks.

In addition to ensuring a monopoly on casual finds, Rassam started large-scale operations at the site. After a few abortive days on the Kasr, he moved his men to more promising mounds nearby, where he opened huge trenches in search of palaces on the scale of those in Assyria. Although no large stone structures or sculptures were likely to come to light, Rassam felt sure he would recover at least the rooms of a brick-built palace. "By following a certain method," he wrote, "we came upon signs of standing walls, which surprised my diggers not a little."[8] But the major finds were few and far between, although he did unearth some cylinder seals. Just like Loftus before him, Rassam employed excavation methods that were simply too unsophisticated to trace mud-brick structures. Furthermore, Rassam did not have the patience to dig at one site for any length of time. So while he was still working at Babylon, he also began digging at Birs Nimrod, where he found brick diggers feverishly looking for antiquities. He used the same tactics as at Babylon and placed a few work gangs to excavate in four different spots. He found a large but insignificant building erected by Nebuchadnezzar, numerous glazed bricks, and little else.

Leaving his overseers in charge, Rassam took a boat downstream to visit the large mounds of Telloh, which had been identified as the site of the city of Girsu, part of the Sumerian city-state of Lagash. He described the mounds as "very curiously shaped," which suggested to Rassam that they might contain the treasure he sought. Telloh was over a kilometer in circumference and consisted of a series of mounds, including one in which the French vice-consul in Basra, Ernest de Sarzec, had found in 1877 to 1878 a series of diorite statues and many inscriptions on mud bricks (see Chapter 16). Rassam's firman did not extend as far south as Telloh. Nevertheless, he gathered some local people and set to work on Sarzec's site. He dug into the highest mound, recovered a mass of clay cone bricks, two inscribed gate sockets, and a series of red stone maceheads, which, he said, were "a kind of weight." Sarzec had left the largest of his diorite statues in the mound, reburying it for protection. Rassam calmly dug it up "to take a squeeze of the inscription on it for the British Museum" and left it exposed.[9] The local people broke it up after his departure.

After three days, fighting broke out among Rassam's workers at Telloh, so he abandoned the excavations. He was furious when he learned that Sarzec was already negotiating for a permit for Telloh. To head off Rassam, the cunning Frenchman had kept quiet about his application. When Sarzec's Telloh excavation proved a success, Rassam remarked pettishly that he would have found as fine statues as the French if he had been able to dig a few days longer.

Rassam continued his frenetic travels as he made his way upstream, again digging into likely sites. He traveled on horseback, by boat, on foot, and in dust storms, torrid heat, and blinding rain. All manner of travelers hung on his coattails, including Swiss tourists, military missions, and officers' wives, one of whom had to spend the night shivering under a tarpaulin in a rainstorm. "I could not invite her to share my tent, for fear of causing scandal," Rassam pompously remarked.[10] Back in Mosul, he closed down the digs at Assur and Nimrud, where his excavations had been unproductive, and advanced on his ultimate target—the mound of Nebi Yunus at Nineveh, hitherto unexcavated because of the violent objections of the guardians of the mosque on its summit. Rassam was confident he could outwit them even though others before him had failed.

During his months of work at Kuyunjik, Rassam had taken care to employ plenty of Nebi Yunus villagers. He visited their homes and cultivated the acquaintance of the leading inhabitants, as well as the priests. After a while, a number of prominent families suggested that he dig in their backyards. Rassam also went one step further. He quietly purchased two or three tumbledown houses with the consent of the shrine's guardians (who were paid a fee), with the intention of digging under the foundations and then giving the land and the materials necessary to rebuild back to the original owners. Quite naturally, the owners were delighted. The mosque guardians were equally pleased when Rassam not only negotiated with them about off-limits areas around the mosque but agreed to erect some baths within the sacred precincts. Of course, he would be able to keep any antiquities found in the deep foundation trenches he would dig in order to build the charitable baths.

After his carefully negotiated plans were in place, Rassam was eager to start work at once, but the local authorities in Mosul demurred and referred the matter to Constantinople. After prolonged negotiations and inquiry after inquiry, the minister of public instruction flatly refused permission for the Nebi Yunus excavations. Rassam vainly assailed the officials responsible for the decision as being anti-British. Even Layard's influence could no longer help him; Rassam was now persona non grata in Constantinople. Nebi Yunus remains unexcavated to this day. We can be thankful that Rassam's workmen were prevented from ruining a series of Assyrian public buildings that one day may fill in many of the gaps caused by the haphazard excavations of the nineteenth century.

Hormuzd Rassam's archaeological career was now nearing its close. He returned for a last season under the Layard firman in 1880, this time at the beginning of the summer. He crossed to the Euphrates from Aleppo with a mule train to save time, reaching the river at Hit, where he engaged a bitumen boat in which to float down to Babylon. The heat was intense, reaching 41°C even on the river. At Babylon Rassam nearly collapsed from heat prostration. Although he found that his overseers had unearthed plenty of clay tablets, the excavations were unproductive by Rassam's standards. He retired for the summer months to dig near Lake Van in Turkey and returned to Mosul in the fall for a further season in Babylonia. He always believed that there was a chance that the authorities might relent and allow him to dig at Nebi Yunus. During this time his nephew Nimrud was overseeing small-scale excavations at Kuyunjik, looking for clay tablets.

In fall 1880, Rassam came south with the objective of widening his excavations beyond Babylon and Birs Nimrod. This time he had his eye on the ancient Babylonian site of Kuthah, a huge tell over eighty-five meters high that lay twenty-four kilometers northeast of Al Hillah. He also planned to search for the Biblical city of Sepharvaim (the Babylonian Sippar). Kuthah, locally known as Tell Ibrahim, was relatively inaccessible, so Rassam concentrated on Sippar, which he finally located at Abu Habbah, a tell thirty-two kilometers southwest of Baghdad, which Rassam had come upon almost by accident.[11] The ruins of the walled city contained a small ziggurat. Still not sure of the city's identity, Rassam hastened to dig there, camping close to a nearby shrine and supervising the excavation in person. This time success rewarded his efforts. The workmen uncovered a chamber paved with bitumen. Some impulse caused him to break through the floor. To his astonishment, a terracotta box containing a magnificent inscribed marble tablet came to light. The tablet, known as the tablet of Shamash, bore a relief of the sun god seated in a shrine and commemorated the restoration of the god's temple at Sippar by King Nabuapalidinna. An inscription in front of the shrine identified the city and the name of the temple from which it came.

Rassam continued to dig at Abu Habbah at intervals until 1882. He estimated that a complex of buildings consisting of at least 400 rooms surrounded the ziggurat. He excavated about 170 of them, from which he removed large numbers of inscribed cylinders and tablets. The Sippar archives were preserved on unbaked clay. Eventually he recovered between 60,000 and 70,000 tablets, a large number of which fell to pieces before he could have them baked. It took years to decipher the piles of tablets. Most of them were business records concerning sacrifices, the manufacture of jewelry and other objects, and affairs of a complicated bureaucracy of priests, scribes, and temple officers. The tablets also included revenues of the great temple of Shamash for generations, like the accounts of a large commercial concern. One cylinder recorded how Nabonidus, the last king of Babylon, had a passion for antiquarian pursuits. The cylinder described how he decided to check his historical records by digging into the cities of his predecessors. Eighteen cubits below the surface Nabonidus came across a foundation stone that had been laid by Naram-sin, the son of Sargon of Akkad. According to the cylinder, Nabonidus was gratified to uncover an artifact "which for 3,200 years no previous king had seen."[12]

Except for his discovery of the clay tablets, Rassam was disappointed by his Abu Habbah diggings. And the hasty month he spent at Kuthah wasn't any more rewarding. "I had no less than twenty tunnels and trenches opened in it," he wrote. "There were no indications whatever in them to give me any hope of discovering Babylonian remains."[13] He found only some bricks inscribed with Nebuchadnezzar's name and surmised that they had been brought there from elsewhere. His tunnelings missed the Babylonian city of Kuthah completely, because it was buried six meters below the surface.

Rassam kept his overseers scattered all over Mesopotamia perennially searching for a spectacular palace or finds that would enrich the British Museum's galleries in his name. Although the trustees were delighted with the Abu Habbah tablets, Rassam continued to search for buried treasure with methods that horrified the Turkish authorities. When his firman expired in July 1882, he waited in Baghdad in the vain hope that the Porte would renew it. Once it became clear that the sultan had no intention of letting him loose on Mesopotamia again, Rassam went back to London. But he left local workers posted at each of his major sites to protect them against unauthorized excavations. He fully expected to return.

A SCRAMBLE FOR TABLETS

I was then standing near a small pyramid situated at the westerly limit of the mound, which I was told contained a golden model of the ark in which Noah and his family were saved from the Deluge, and that the second father of mankind had it buried there as a memorial of the event.

—HORMUZD RASSAM

THE BRITISH MUSEUM CONTINUED TO PAY HORMUZD RASSAM'S WATCHMEN IN Mesopotamia for four years while the cuneiform experts in London sifted through the Abu Habbah archives. Rassam visited the museum regularly to meet with Samuel Birch, Austen Henry Layard, and Henry Rawlinson, in the hope that he would be employed to dig more sites. In 1886, Birch began to receive disturbing reports from Baghdad about the sanctity of sites under British Museum guard. His correspondents reported that the museum's guards were apparently conniving in illicit excavations at the sites under their charge and indeed were themselves engaged in illegal digging. A German scholar confirmed this information when he wrote that a party of his academic friends had bought a fine collection of antiquities at Nineveh from Rassam's watchmen. Even more distressing, his friends had purchased no less than 300 Babylonian tablets from the guardians at Abu Habbah. The close-knit network of Assyriologists buzzed with rumors when one of Birch's former assistants, William St. Chad Boscawan, reported that the Berlin Museum had recently acquired magnificent collections of Babylonian commercial and legal tablets from a Baghdad dealer.[1] These specimens could only have come from one of Rassam's guarded sites. Since most of the European dealers retained Boscawan as a cuneiform consultant, the museum took his report seriously. Rawlinson was consulted and suggested that the trustees apply for a new firman to dig at Kuyunjik. At the same time, the person appointed to oversee the excavations could try and locate the source of the tablets and other specimens that were reaching Europe illegally. This time the trustees rejected Rassam in favor of Wallis Budge, a young Assyriologist who was to achieve international fame as a collector and a popularizer of Mesopotamian and ancient Egyptian archaeology.[2]

Wallis Budge was a precocious youth whose family had served in the East for generations. His schooling was harsh but proved useful in later life, for his teachers encouraged him to study Hebrew and the historical background of the Scriptures. At an early age he met Charles Seager, a prominent Semitic philologist of the time. Seager introduced Budge to Samuel Birch and to cuneiform at about the time George Smith was working on the Deluge Tablets. When Birch gave Budge the run of his office, Smith told him the only way to learn cuneiform was by "copying a piece of text each day, and, by trying to transliterate the signs in it."[3] The industrious Budge found himself taking informal classes in Egyptian hieroglyphs and cuneiform. There were no textbooks, so everyone copied down the script from the blackboard and handed in his translation at the next session. Budge was soon in close touch with all the early Assyriologists: Rawlinson, Oppert, and even Layard, who urged him to go out and dig rather than study inscriptions. Budge made other influential friends, too, among them Prime Minister William Gladstone, who was one of those who helped him gain admittance to Cambridge University to study Semitic languages in 1878.

By this time Budge was producing a steady stream of translations of Assyrian tablets. During the next five years he added Arabic, Ethiopic, and Talmudic literature to his repertoire. In 1883 Gladstone and others nominated him for an appointment as an assistant in the Department of Oriental Antiquities at the British Museum under Samuel Birch. Budge was to spend his entire productive and controversial career in the service of the museum. He now found himself faced with the prospect of becoming an Egyptologist as well, for the department was so understaffed that all staff members had to acquire competence in a whole range of archaeological and historical fields.

Budge's newly acquired Egyptological skills led to his first collecting expedition to Egypt in 1886 to 1887, a mission that taught him the wily tricks of tomb robbers and antiquities dealers and enabled him to smuggle twenty-four cases of antiquities out of the country under the furious nose of the British consul general, Sir Evelyn Baring. The trustees of the British Museum were delighted. Budge's acquisitions were of fine quality and had been obtained at very moderate cost. A born collector, Budge was a sociable person with a penchant for bargaining and an eye for new acquisitions. He had the gift of ignoring official regulations and getting away with activities that would have landed most men in jail. The British Museum recognized him for what he was—a superb acquisitor.[4]

Just as he was about to leave for Baghdad, Budge received information that a unique collection of clay tablets had been found at Tell el-Amarna in Egypt, tablets that bore, his correspondent said, a remarkable resemblance to cuneiform tablets that had been brought to Cairo from Baghdad some years before. Budge realized that this discovery was potentially of great importance because the tablets might throw light on the relationships between Assyria and Egypt in Old Testament times. So he traveled to Baghdad via Egypt, acquiring the Amarna tablets on the way. They turned out to be a unique archive of diplomatic correspondence of great historical value, which Budge spirited out of Egypt in the face of determined opposition from officials of the Egyptian Museum.[5] Unrepentant, Budge sailed for Basra and then traveled by river steamer to Baghdad, a city that did not impress him.

There was, he complained, "appalling noise and confusion" that he thought "indescribable." Although the residency had rented a house for him, Budge hesitated to live in it because it was far from the river, the main highway for the city. Fortunately, the captain of the *Comet*, an Indian Merchant Service steamer, invited him to stay onboard. The berth gave him far more freedom of action, something Budge needed if he was to be an effective collector. In Baghdad, he found himself pursued by irate customs officials who were convinced he was carrying contraband whiskey. In fact, the box he carried contained the precious Amarna tablets. After much yelling and commotion, the captain of the steamer managed to persuade officialdom that Budge was no drug or alcohol smuggler.

For all his devious ways, Wallis Budge was meticulous in making official contacts. He called on Colonel William Tweedie, the British consul general, who was at the end of a long and distinguished career in government service. Budge recalled being ushered into the presence of a "tall, spare man, of military bearing, and he possessed the calm demeanour and quiet dignity which I have noticed to be characteristic of the official who has had much experience in dealing with orientals of high rank."[6] Tweedie wore "a sort of turban cap" and was wrapped in a cloth cloak to ward off the chill of the winter morning. Budge was mildly disconcerted when his host started talking not about antiquities but about the Arab horse and its pedigree. Then he realized that Tweedie was sizing him up and weighing his letters of introduction from Rawlinson and others.

After some minutes of rambling conversation, Tweedie spoke very frankly. He could do little to help Budge. British prestige in Baghdad was a pale reflection of what it had been in Rawlinson's day and, in any case, the British Museum had no power to appoint guards at Mesopotamian sites. Furthermore, the local people would always steal antiquities and Budge could not stop it. Tweedie pointed out that Rassam was very unpopular with the authorities, for he never finished a dig and hopped from one site to another. Besides, the Turkish inspector of antiquities in Baghdad was well aware of the purpose of Budge's visit and had called on Tweedie to point out that no foreigner was allowed to deal in antiquities. In other words, Budge could visit sites and eat at the residency, but he had better behave himself. "I can promise to give you a new kind of curry every night for a month at a stretch," ended Tweedie, "so good a cook has God given me." And with these words, he gave Budge lunch and a tour of the residency with its fine portrait of Rawlinson and magnificent stained-glass windows.[7]

After this strange interview, Budge spent hours wandering around the bazaars and made a point of visiting as many dealers as possible. He learned that the wealthiest dealers lived in the meanest hovels. As Budge became trusted, he found that the dealers would produce high quality antiquities and exquisite jewelry from secret cubbyholes and cellars. He quietly added choice pieces to his British Museum collection, using techniques that had paid dividends in Egypt: show an appreciation for fine things, pay fair prices, and take time to buy.

Budge also called on the Turkish inspector of antiquities, who complained loudly about Rassam and promptly introduced him to more dealers. For the next few days, he busied himself buying up hundreds of Babylonian tablets from Abu Habbah and other sites already sampled by the British Museum. Many of the dealers were none other than the very guards appointed by Rassam to guard the museum's interests. He was now certain that the London rumors were true. He carefully packed away the tablets in twenty-five wooden boxes and, to avoid customs officials, smuggled his purchases on board the *Comet* at night, loading them on the side that faced away from the customs house. The prices he paid were fully 300 percent lower than those in London, so low in fact that he became suspicious. It turned out that the dealers and the authorities had made a deal, whereby he would be arrested upon departure and the tablets confiscated and then returned to the dealers, for a consideration. But they had met their match in Wallis Budge. He calmly announced that he was off to Al Hillah to buy more tablets. The watchers relaxed their supervision of the steamer after Budge vanished. Meanwhile, the skipper of the *Comet* quietly departed for Basra with a visiting Persian nobleman on a state visit to India aboard. Budge learned a few days later that his precious tablets were safely on their way to England locked in the strong room of a British India mail steamer.

Budge's blatant smuggling was soon common knowledge. He found himself much criticized for actions he considered entirely ethical. After all, he argued, he was only recovering property stolen from British Museum sites. "I felt," he wrote many years later, "that I had done what anyone would have done who had the welfare of Babylonian and Assyrian archaeology and his employers' interests at heart."[8] His only regret was that he had to spend more public money to recover property that had come from excavations financed by the museum in the first place. Budge, however, had no worries. He had powerful backers, among them Henry Rawlinson, who had urged him: "With all your gettings, get tablets."[9]

Budge next traveled to the major sites in Babylonia excavated by Hormuzd Rassam. He found illegal digging in full swing. Babylon's mounds had now been stripped of most of their bricks. The diggers quarried in old excavation trenches, extracting bricks by day and antiquities by night because they feared that Turkish officials would confiscate them. Years of illegal digging had virtually destroyed Abu Habbah. Rassam's former workers smuggled tablets into Baghdad every month. One of the laborers willingly admitted his thefts. After all, he said cheerfully, no one pays my wages. Budge bought over 750 tablets from local dealers and workmen and made contacts for future sales. At the same time, he acquired a knowledge of how the illegal antiquities trade worked, which was right under the often-compliant noses of the Turkish authorities. Being a collector himself, he could sympathize with the tricks played by the workers to smuggle tablets into Baghdad. One man at Abu Habbah would walk into town wearing a long cloak with hidden pockets full of tablets. Others would smuggle their finds in loads of bricks or charcoal. The dealers bought everything that came in and promptly sold their stocks in Berlin, London, or Paris. The demand for tablets was inexhaustible as the major European museums tried to acquire as many as they could. Budge bought all the specimens he could afford. Again he smuggled his finds past the authorities, who then telegraphed the sultan for permission to detain him. Fortunately for Budge, a friendly postal official arranged an accident to the telegraph wires near Baghdad, and Budge got away safely.

Wallis Budge returned to London full of self-righteous indignation about the chicanery of the watchmen and dealers. He urged the British Museum to fire all their retainers in Babylonia. Significantly, no Kuyunjik tablets were coming on the London market, for it seemed that Hormuzd Rassam's nephew Nimrud was watching closely over the excavations. Most of the Babylonian antiquities reaching London came from Abu Habbah. There was nothing anyone in Europe could do to stop the illicit digging there.

The British Museum decided to reopen their excavations at Kuyunjik, specifically to recover as many tablets as they could. The museum had started to compile a catalogue of the Kuyunjik tablets. Obviously it should be as complete as possible. The trustees dispatched Budge to Constantinople to apply for a new firman in person, working both through the British ambassador, Sir William White, and the director of the Imperial Ottoman Museum. He stayed in Constantinople for seven weeks, exercising his considerable charm on Hamdi Bey and the minister of public instruction. Unlike many other scholars who did their best to insult the Turks, Budge had the gift of getting on with them and understood their sensitivities. But only the personal intervention of the British ambassador with the sultan finally produced the firman. The conditions were specific and stringent. The British Museum might retain any clay tablets found, but all other finds were to go to Constantinople. A Turkish commissioner would be present at the excavation at all times, his salary paid by Budge. Since the proposed excavations had a highly specific purpose, Budge agreed to the conditions. Although it was now December, which left little time for winter digging, he set off for Mosul at once, accompanied by the British ambassador's son. They traveled by a steamer full of mutinous Turkish soldiers as far as Antioch, then overland to Mosul via Aleppo and the village of Jerablus on the Euphrates, where Budge examined the ancient mounds of the Hittite and Roman city of Carchemish (see Chapter 18). The journey was arduous and cold. Shummar tribesmen looted their caravan just short of Mosul.

Once safely in Mosul, Budge stayed with Nimrud Rassam, before renting the front part of an old house, where he hoped to get some privacy. It was a vain hope. Neighboring families dumped their garbage in his courtyard; their chickens flew into his stable. All the cats and dogs of Mosul fought at his front door.

The sultan's firman made the preliminary arrangements for the excavations an easy matter, especially since Budge "facilitated" the process with some timely gifts. He walked over Kuyunjik with Nimrud Rassam and decided to start on a modest scale by sifting through the heaps of dirt left by Hormuzd Rassam's excavations of 1852 to 1854. Fifty workers sorted through the contents of the chambers at the southwest corner of the mound, where Rassam had found

Ashurbanipal's library. Eventually 200 men joined the excavations, which lasted until the end of June 1889 and for an additional three weeks in November 1890. Nearly 600 tablets came from old spoil heaps and unexcavated chambers. Budge spent much time soothing the Turkish commissioner, who turned out to be ineffectual and timid, so much so that he spent most of his stay in Mosul. In his spare moments Budge purchased manuscripts from dealers. In February 1889, Budge left the excavations under the supervision of Nimrud Rassam and traveled to Mosul and then Baghdad by raft, glad to escape the sordid little town. "The smells in the town were numerous and powerful at the best of times," he commented, "but with the coming of warm weather, the reek from the tanneries down by the bridge became more penetrating, and when to this the fumes from the hot sulphur springs to the north of the town were added, the result is easier imagined than described."[10]

In Baghdad, Budge received a cool reception from the dealers. They had not forgotten his strategies of a year before. But the official atmosphere in Baghdad was transformed. A new British consul general had been appointed, Colonel Adelbert Cecil Talbot, whose diplomatic skills were more polished than those of the eccentric Colonel Tweedie. Budge received a personal call from the pasha and many formalities were waived. Customs officers hardly inspected his baggage. "It seemed to me that most Turkish rules and regulations were especially made to be broken — on payment by the breaker," remarked Budge cynically.[11] He succeeded in buying all the Abu Habbah tablets he could afford without any difficulty — and with official help.

After an interval in London, Budge made one more visit to Mesopotamia, this time in 1890. He returned to Mosul to collect the Kuyunjik tablets found in his absence, crossing the desert to Mesopotamia overland from Damascus in twenty-three days. Everyone had warned Budge not to use this route, but he refused to listen. He was lucky. His muleteer guides were both honest and clever men, who managed to avoid the Arab raiders that beset the caravan tracks. He spent three weeks in Mosul closing down the Kuyunjik excavations and packing the finds, then waiting for a firman to dig at Der in southern Mesopotamia, a site thirty-two kilometers from Baghdad known to contain numerous tablets.[12] Budge had purchased some finds from there the previous year. As usual, the permit application was delayed interminably. This time the officials' were involved in large-scale chicanery.

As Budge's *kellek* neared Baghdad, he was hailed by a tribesman, who told him that the Baghdad authorities had been digging at Der for months. The actual excavations had been entrusted to local dealers. Budge's informant revealed that the dealers and their overseers had recovered hundreds of cylinder seals, three rooms of clay tablets, and dozens of coins. They had smuggled their finds into Baghdad, where they awaited his pleasure.

Budge was speechless with rage and frustration, but there was nothing he could do. Any excavations would be a mockery, despite their respectable legality. His Arab friend could not understand his anger. "Be not sad of heart," he cried. "We have all the tablets in Baghdad, we are your friends, and we have kept all the tablets for you. You will buy them and they shall get out of the country quickly, and you will be able to live with your English friends in Baghdad and not be obliged to sit in the desert with the jackals and the vultures and burn by day and freeze by night. You will have plenty of rice to eat and clean water to drink, and there are now many oranges in Baghdad."[13] Budge's reply is not recorded.

Meanwhile, the pasha of Baghdad blandly denied all knowledge of any illegal excavations. So Budge turned to the dealers and bought 2,500 tablets in three evenings, all of them from Der and many of unique historical value. He packed these into boxes and sent them to Basra at once before purchasing another 7,000 less important tablets to be sent off later. His only consolation was that the market was depressed and prices were low. Not content with purchase alone, Budge talked discreetly to some of the illegal diggers and established that there were probably some isolated pockets of tablets still awaiting recovery at the site. A week after his arrival in Baghdad, the long-delayed firman finally arrived. In late January 1891, Budge set out for Der. The excavations started in pouring rain, but 200 men were soon swarming over the mounds, opening up the extensive trenches started by the illicit diggers.

As usual, the firman stipulated that a Turkish commissioner be present at all times. An elderly gentleman, immaculate in "bright red wool tarbush, fez, a black frock coat, light trousers, and patent shoes," sat on a sofa outside his special tent. This unassuming, very religious gentleman never visited the excavations but his servant watched everything with a lynx's eye. It was he who told Budge that the workers were selling a lot of his tablets on the side to Baghdad dealers, despite careful security precautions. The inspector advised him to buy the illicit finds back from the dealers. Once the men became aware of his strategy, they brought the tablets directly to Budge in exchange for regular bonus payments. Thus, he paid them to be honest. "Of course," wrote Budge, "this was to compound a felony, but it was the only practical way of obtaining the tablets."[14]

Leaving Nimrud Rassam to supervise the excavations, Budge traveled downstream in search of yet more tablets, purchasing more fine collections from Abu Habbah and other mounds. The weather was so wet that the Der excavations had to be curtailed in late February. By this time Budge was satisfied that he had not missed anything significant and that most of his proposed excavation area had been gutted before his arrival. He dismantled his excavation on February 19, 1891, and rode back to Baghdad. To his frustration, he met a funeral cortege on the narrow path that led to the city. Ten men and four women trudged along with a loaded bier. They chanted and wailed as they monopolized the track. Fuming at the delay, Budge rode up to the Bridge of Boats behind the mournful procession. He was disconcerted to learn that the mourners had told the bridge guards he would pay their toll charges. There was nothing to do but to pay up, for the mourners had even told the guards the deceased was Budge's personal friend! It turned out the funeral was a fake. Budge's dealer friends had used the funeral to smuggle a large consignment of tablets into the city.

Budge had many friends interested in his finds. They gave him much sage advice on how to circumvent rules and regulations, so he was never at a loss for a stratagem or an ingenious solution to an export problem. Wallis Budge believed that all Baghdad officials were bribable (he was probably right) and that the safest place for clay tablets was out of Mesopotamia, where they could be deciphered and studied after cleaning and restoration. This time Budge returned to London not only with 2,500 cuneiform tablets but with over 200 priceless Arabic, Syriac, and other manuscripts exported by the simple expedient of donating a comfortable sum of money to the pasha's favorite Baghdad charity. He also left the city with long-term connections that gave him a regular conduit for purchases of tablets and cylinder seals from local dealers.

The following year, Budge became acting keeper of the now-renamed Department of Egyptian and Assyrian Antiquities in the British Museum, a sign that the trustees approved of his collecting activities. But by no means was everyone fond of Wallis Budge. His smuggling was looked upon with disfavor in some academic circles. The local overseers who had lost their jobs as a result of his investigations were only too eager to bad-mouth him to foreigners in Baghdad. Hormuzd Rassam was particularly unhappy. Sensitive as he was about his reputation as an archaeologist, he considered the dismissals a personal affront. Disturbing rumors about Budge's reports on his activities in Baghdad reached his ears almost weekly. Soon the two men were barely speaking to each other. In the second week of July 1891, Budge was talking to Rassam, Layard, and others in the Assyrian student room at the museum when he suddenly accused Rassam of being a party to the theft of Assyrian antiquities from British Museum sites. He went on to say that the Abu Habbah tablets sold to the department and the Berlin Museum had been exported by overseers who were in fact Rassam's relations. Furthermore, the British Museum's consignments from its own excavations at the site had consisted of "rubbish." The prize tablets, he alleged, had gone elsewhere. Layard, who was already upset with the museum because he felt they had downplayed Rassam in their displays, tried to convince Budge that he was mistaken. Rassam demanded an apology from the principal librarian of the museum, who wrote back that Budge denied he had ever made the alleged statements. When Layard pursued the matter, Budge prevaricated in what Layard called a "mean, shuffling, and untruthful manner." He wrote to a friend: "I may say they [Budge's charges] were pressed upon me."[15]

Budge had sent a report on the Baghdad situation to his supervisors. In his confidential document he made several charges. He alleged not only that the corrupt overseers were Rassam's relatives but that Rassam himself had sold antiquities from official excavations to dealers in Baghdad and London. Rassam, he continued, had never visited his excavations but lived comfortably in Baghdad, smuggling spirits into the city. This confidential report caused the principal librarian to advise Budge to lie low.

While the British Museum attempted to placate Layard, Rassam seethed with anger. Against all advice, he sued Budge for slander and sought 1,000 pounds in punitive damages. The columns of the *Times* and other newspapers hummed with comments as the case awaited trial. Questions about Budge were now asked in the House of Commons. How many missions had Budge undertaken with public funds? How much had he spent and where had the funds come from? The first lord of the treasury replied that a special grant had provided funds and urged members not to ask for more specific details as it would be detrimental to the public interest. The fact was that the nation had acquired remarkable antiquities at a modest cost. Even if questions were being asked by Budge's colleagues, the museum was very happy with his work.

Rassam and Budge came to court for five days in late June 1893. After hearing from plaintiff, defendant, and Layard on Rassam's behalf, the jury decided in Rassam's favor to the tune of 50 pounds. Budge's museum colleagues promptly paid the damages, and the trustees covered his legal fees. Rassam's reputation suffered more than Budge's did, for the papers made it clear they felt the case was a frivolous one. "While we admit the general justice of the verdict," wrote the *Times*, "it is impossible on the whole not to regret that the plaintiff did not take the advice of his friends . . . and refrain from bringing the action."[16] The *Daily News* went even further and described the trial as "a sort of antiquarian festival. These distinguished persons have not been in the intimacy of Assurbanipal [*sic*] for nothing. Their measures of time are not as our measures: otherwise the better part of a week would hardly have been devoted to the settlement of such a case."[17]

Hormuzd Rassam continued to seethe impotently until his death in 1910. He appealed to the Archbishop of Canterbury, a museum trustee, for a renewed investigation of the affair. When that got him nowhere, he withdrew from any involvement in Assyriology and retired to Hove on England's south coast to write a book on his excavations. The completed manuscript, *Asshur and the Land of Nimrod*, was rejected by several London publishing houses before it eventually found a home in the United States, where it appeared in 1897. Rassam's magnum opus is dedicated to his late friend and supporter Austen Henry Layard, who had died three years before. Unfortunately, the book is a disappointment after his mentor's brilliant narratives; at best it is a self-serving document, a defensive and smug account of an archaeological career full of chicanery and intrigue. Rassam's inferiority complex peeps through on many pages, as he tries to defend his methods and ethics. The book did him no good, for archaeological colleagues were now openly attacking his methods, which more closely resembled rape and pillage than scientific excavation.

The tragedy of Hormuzd Rassam was that he and, to a certain extent, Wallis Budge were anachronisms. Just at the moment when Rassam was trying to justify his actions, the first long-term excavations into the very southern mounds he had tried to pillage began. These excavations revealed the hitherto virtually unknown Sumerian civilization and unmasked the palaces and temples of ancient Babylon from their desolate isolation of centuries.

SUMER DISCOVERED

Famine was severe, nothing was produced,
At the small rivers, there was no "washing of the hands,"
  The waters rose not high.
The fields were not watered.
  There was no digging of [irrigation] ditches.
In all the lands there was no vegetation,
  Only weeds grew.

—SUMERIAN EPIC

AS EARLY AS 1872, GEORGE SMITH HAD PREDICTED THAT HIS "CHALDEAN ACCOUNT of the Deluge" was a late version of a folk legend that had been in existence for untold centuries. Once the cuneiform experts in Europe began to decipher the mass of new tablets from Wallis Budge's and Horzmud Rassam's investigations in Babylonia, they realized that Smith had been on the right track. The Assyrians had copied a literary tradition that had come from the Babylonians, who had in turn copied it from yet another people. Had an early urban civilization in southern Mesopotamia served as a prototype for both the Babylonian and Assyrian cultures?

Another French diplomat proved that there had been. In January 1877, Ernest de Sarzec, a consular official with considerable experience in Ethiopia and Egypt, was transferred to Basra as vice-consul. Sarzec was about forty years old and an active, tall man. He had, we are told, "expressive features" and was familiar with desert life. He combined his consular duties with a profound interest in Asian art. At the time, Basra was a torrid outpost of the Ottoman empire. It had a sleepy trade with India and a very small European colony that suffered greatly from fever and lethargy. Sarzec was too active a person for an obscure life of soporific trade and occasional desert hunting excursions. He decided to spend his leisure time exploring the ancient civilizations of Babylonia. While on a visit to Babylon and Birs Nimrod, he got in touch with dealers and illicit diggers. Soon afterward, he strengthened his dealer contacts in Basra through a prominent local Christian and steamship operator, J. Asfar, who dealt with antiquities on the side. Asfar introduced him to local merchants who regularly bought artifacts from tribes upstream. The diggers kept on talking about a site called Telloh, where inscribed bricks, cones, and an inscribed torso of a man had come to light. Asfar urged the new consul to investigate Telloh more closely and perhaps even dig it.[1]

Sarzec made secret preparations for an excavation. Well aware that Hormuzd Rassam was charging around Mesopotamia with bands of laborers, he said nothing publicly and took the risky step of digging without an official firman. This scheme, he felt, was the best way to claim the site, which in any case was under only nominal Turkish jurisdiction. The old adage of possession being nine-tenths of the law seemed to apply. The real political power lay in the hands of the local pasha, Nasir, who had founded the town of Nasiriyah and named it after himself. Sarzec had sedulously cultivated Nasir. As a result he could travel and excavate anywhere he liked in the pasha's domains.

Only two months after arriving in Basra, Sarzec was hard at work at Telloh on the first of a series of brief excavation campaigns.[2] Telloh consisted of 6.5 kilometers of sites extending along the bank of a dried-up canal that formed a branch of the Shatt-el-Hai. Sarzec spent two preliminary seasons in 1877 and 1878 digging massive trial trenches in the principal mounds. The first time he rode over the largest of them, he picked up part of the shoulder of a magnificent diorite statue. He started his excavations on the fifteen-meter mound from which this fragment had eroded. The workers soon unearthed a platform of un-baked bricks upon which a substantial building had once stood. In a recess in the outer northeast wall of the building, Sarzec's laborers recovered the torso of the figure from which the inscribed shoulder had come. Sarzec was unable to remove such a large piece, so he took an impression of the inscriptions on it and buried the statue under soft earth. It was this statue that Rassam subsequently uncovered in his hasty illegal dig of 1879 and that was destroyed by locals after Rassam left it exposed (see Chapter 14).

Once Sarzec had established the general character of the building on the platform, he set his men to work across the entire site in long rows. Telloh had not been reoccupied in later times, so this technique produced a rich haul of tablets, jars, inscriptions, and two large ter-racotta cylinders that commemorated a ruler named Gudea.[3] The ex-cavations also yielded large quantities of cuneiform inscriptions that were the most comprehensive ever found from the earliest periods of Mesopotamian history.

Clearly Telloh was the site of a very early city, one where the tem-ples and other buildings were not mantled in meters of debris from later occupation or in deposits of Parthian slipper coffins. Sarzec sus-pected he had found a complete early settlement of a hitherto-unknown Mesopotamian civilization far earlier than that of Babylon. So con-vinced was he of the importance of his finds that he obtained a leave of absence from his consular duties, sailed to Paris, and tried to es-tablish his work on a more permanent basis. The Ministry of Foreign Affairs referred him to Leon Heuzey, the curator of the Department of Oriental Antiquities at the Louvre.[4] Heuzey at once recognized the sig-nificance of the Telloh finds, which he identified as a magnificent col-lection of early Mesopotamian art and artifacts of a previously largely unknown type, except for a couple of isolated statues acquired for the Louvre some years before. Heuzey at once committed the Louvre to acquire the Telloh material for 130,000 francs. He encouraged Sarzec to return to Basra and carry on the excavations at his own expense until the French ambassador could obtain a firman for Telloh before anyone else got wind of the finds. His application beat Rassam's to the punch and the French secured official permission for a long-term campaign of excavations on the mysterious city.

Sarzec remained on leave in Paris until 1880, when he returned to Telloh accompanied by his new wife. This time the French government subsidized the excavations. He returned to Telloh almost every year until 1900. His first official season (1880–1881) was devoted to a thorough and unhurried examination of the great building he had found during the 1877–1878 season. Sarzec was soon able to announce the finding of nine other large diorite statues, as well as fragmentary bas-reliefs and numerous inscriptions. The workers probed deeply into foundation walls of structures buried below the major ziggurat, recovering pre-Babylonian artifacts and art objects far older than anything dug up before.

Sarzec returned to Paris in triumph in the summer of 1881, bringing a huge collection of Sumerian art with him. These finds caused a considerable stir when exhibited at the Fifth International Congress of Orientalists in Berlin and before the French Academy in Paris. In 1884, Heuzey published the first part of his magnificent *Découvertes en Chaldée par Ernest de Sarzec,* the first compendium of information on the Sumerians. Sarzec had uncovered the world's earliest literate society.

For years Edward Hincks, Henry Rawlinson, and others had suspected that a more primitive script and civilization had preceded the Semitic Babylonian culture. In a January 1869 lecture, Jules Oppert had argued that the early rulers of the south were often called "king of Sumer and Akkad." Thus, he argued, the non-Semitic peoples who had preceded the Semitic Akkadians should be called "Sumerians."

At the time, most cuneiform experts disagreed with Oppert, arguing that there was simply not enough material from the clay tablets in the Kuyunjik archives to document the Sumerians. In any case, the Ashurbanipal archives were assembled at least 1,000 years after the demise of Oppert's new civilization. Only a few inscriptions from delta sites were known, and those were of very limited value.

Sarzec's excavations had changed everything. The inscriptions and tablets documented the history of Lagash, a Sumerian city-state of the third millennium B.C. Lagash had been ruled by a series of powerful governors. Six of Sarzec's diorite statues depicted Gudea, the seventh and most famous of them. The Sumerian statues brought the Assyrian bas-reliefs found by Paul Botta, Austen Henry Layard, and Hormuzd Rassam into a new focus. Fully 1,500 years earlier than the Assyrians, the Sumerians were producing works of art that exhibited

Dolerite statue of Gudea of Lagash, ca. 2120 B.C., now in the Louvre. Scala/Art Resource, NY.

a naturalism and freshness not found in the later bas-reliefs. One of the first examples was a bas-relief called the Stela of Vultures, which dates to about 2400 B.C. and depicts a group of armed men and their leader marching in formation. The Sumerian king Eannatun had erected the stela to mark the boundary between the state of Lagash and its archrival Umma. Their respective rulers quarreled incessantly about irrigation water through the centuries. The stela attracted the attention of best-selling author H. G. Wells, who once described natural man as "a spasmodic and untrustworthy fighter." When he wrote about the Sumerians, he said: "There you see him in a sort of phalanx, advancing with his shield locked with that of the next man and their spears at a level making an invincible line. All down the changing historical record that body of disciplined infantrymen appears and reappears."[5]

Despite his success where others had failed previously, Sarzec's excavations could hardly be described as scientific. His laborers simply followed mud-brick walls and recovered as many small finds as possible. Few plans of the excavations or the structures survive. At least Sarzec had the sense to realize that systematic, long-term excavation would provide much greater dividends than hasty diggings in search of caches of tablets. His efforts at systematic exploration saved much of the site from destruction by tablet hunters.

Unfortunately, dealers still descended on Telloh each time Sarzec wound up his excavations. His security was so lax that the illicit diggers could work openly in the daytime. Many of the tablet hunters were former Rassam laborers who were continuing their lucrative arrangement with Baghdad dealers. They smuggled their tablets into the city hidden in the usual flowing cloaks or in baskets of fruit. For months the tablet dealers had searched feverishly for the royal archives and official tablet repository of Lagash. While Sarzec was away, they eventually found it in a small, compact mound whose small chambers were packed with thousands of baked clay tablets. Just as the archives came to light, Sarzec returned to Basra and heard the rumors of a spectacular illegal discovery. The diggers hastily covered up their find and started work elsewhere on the site until he was again out of the way. They denied all knowledge of the find and managed to prevent Sarzec from digging in the small mound. Some time later the diggers opened up the chambers at leisure and sold 35,000 to 40,000 tablets to the Baghdad dealers. The Lagash archives were exported to museums all over Europe and the United States, to be followed in later years by larger antiquities, including more Gudea statues. Telloh was so large that adequate policing of its precincts was almost impossible. But the plundering of the excavations should in no way detract from Sarzec's remarkable achievement, sandwiched as it was between consular duties in Baghdad and Basra.

Sarzec's finds rekindled interest in the excavation of southern Mesopotamian cities throughout the scholarly world. The Germans began a systematic excavation at Babylon in 1900 after a lengthy series of preliminary investigations. They were preceded by excavations at Nippur, under the sponsorship of the University of Pennsylvania, that began in 1888.

American interest in Mesopotamia stemmed from a profound concern with the historical veracity of the Old Testament. After the publication of Layard's books, no Asian scholar could overlook the connections between the Bible and archaeological sites in Mesopotamia. The result was the formation of the American Oriental Society. "England and France have done a noble work in Assyria and Babylonia. Now is the time for America to do her part. Let us send out an American expedition," cried a speaker at the society's annual meeting in New Haven in 1884, where the finds from Telloh were discussed.[6] The society formed a committee to raise funds and elected a prominent journalist as the chairman. The Archaeological Institute of America was given $5,500 to send out a party of American scholars to spy out the land and look for promising excavation sites. Dr. William Ward led the Wolfe Expedition to Babylonia, which was named after Catherine Lorillard Wolfe of New York, who had given most of the money for the trip. The expedition followed in William Kennett Loftus's footsteps and visited many of the major sites, cameras and surveying instruments in hand.

Ward submitted his report to the institute in June 1885. He recommended large-scale excavations, but his ideas met with little enthusiasm, for popular interest in Mesopotamian archaeology had already faded. Nothing might have happened had it not been for the Reverend John P. Peters, newly appointed professor of Hebrew at the University of Pennsylvania. Peters was an energetic and hard-driving man who began teaching courses on Semitic and archaeological topics at the university in 1886 to titillate the interest of the educated, affluent public. He received strong support from the provost of the university and from Edward White Clark, a prominent local banker who headed a fund-raising drive in the city. From 1888 to 1900, the community raised over $100,000 to support American excavations in Babylonia, especially at the site of Nippur, the Biblical Calneh.[7]

The fund-raising drive and overall direction of the "Babylonian Exploration Fund" were in the hands of a fifteen-person committee. Peters was named director of the first expedition; Hermann Hilprecht, the newly appointed professor of Assyriology at the university, was secretary. Plans for the expedition matured rapidly, with several members, among them Hilprecht, agreeing to serve without salary. The committee rooms at the university buzzed with activity: firman applications were written and plans for the purchase of tablets devised. Unfortunately, no one had a clear idea what conditions would be like in the field.[8]

Peters spent three frustrating months in Constantinople obtaining a firman. He encountered malicious gossip, indifference, and open hostility, much of it caused by his own grandiose demand that he be allowed to dig several sites at once. After a shaky start Osman Hamdi Bey and Peters became good friends, which helped accelerate the permit. Eventually, the six members of the expedition converged on Aleppo and Baghdad in late 1888. Peters met his Turkish commissioner, whom he found to be living at the house of a notorious dealer, a former headman on Hormuzd Rassam's excavations. The dealer was a general merchant who had conducted a considerable business in antiquities since Rassam's departure. The Turkish commissioner had a well-known reputation for taking bribes. The Germans digging at Babylon told Peters to keep the commissioner drunk, well fed, and happy by systematic bribery. Peters also kept him in line by threatening to expose his thefts of tablets to the authorities and, consequently, had little trouble. The commissioner did help the expedition find some experienced diggers at Babylon who were expert at locating tablets and mud-brick structures. Small wonder, for they made their living by illegally digging for antiquities.

The firman allowed the Americans to dig either at Birs Nimrod or Nippur. After a brief visit to the former, everyone agreed they should concentrate on Nippur. Thus, while Peters and the expedition's Turkish commissioner rode to the miserable town of Diwaniyah to pay their respects to the local authorities, the rest of the party, accompanied by twenty-two trained workers from Babylon, their families, and a caravan of animals loaded with equipment, struck out for Nippur. The three-day journey only confirmed the rumors they had heard about tribal blood feuds and highly unstable political conditions. At one point a group of raiding horsemen descended upon the column, which somehow managed to evade them. On the third morning the ziggurat and mounds of Nippur appeared, towering above the plain. Hilprecht's heart sank. Even at a distance he could see that at least fifty years would be needed to dig Nippur adequately: "What would our committee at home have said at the sight of this enormous ruin, resembling more a picturesque mountain range than the last impressive remains of human constructions?"⁹

Nippur lay amidst a wilderness of swamps and dried-up canals. Bands of hostile tribesmen watched from a distance as the Americans approached. "Greeted by the wild dance and rhythmical yells of some fifty 'Afej warriors who had followed our movements from a peak of the weather-torn ruins, we took possession of the inheritance of Bel," recalled Hilprecht. They pitched their tents on the summit of the southwestern portion of the ruins, a windy vantage point that provided an all-round view and, therefore, some warning if a surprise attack was planned. The Arab workmen erected reed and palm-leaf huts in a square around the tents. The huts served as stables, kitchens, storerooms, and workshops and as protection from "sand storms and the thievish inclinations of the children of the desert."¹⁰

While Peters received tribal visitors, Hilprecht and the other Assyriologists combed the surface of the site to choose the places to excavate. Hilprecht was anxious to dig in a large, open area northwest of the conspicuous temple precincts, where he expected to find storerooms and tablets. The impetuous Peters disregarded his expert colleague's advice and set workers to dig a small mound in an area where Parthian slipper coffins had come to light and the early pre-Babylonian levels were far below the surface. Once additional laborers were available, Peters consulted with the expedition architect and dug into the corners of the ziggurat in search of foundation cylinders. The first ten days of digging yielded only a few inscribed bricks and an isolated cuneiform tablet bearing the name of King Sargon I of Akkad. Peters began to get worried. He saw his funds evaporating without tangible results to show for them. At this point, Hilprecht again urged a dig in the northeast section of the ruins and asked for a few workers to dig some trial trenches. After considerable hesitation, the worried Peters agreed and gave him two gangs of laborers for a week to prove or disprove his hunch. Within a few hours, tablets emerged from the trenches. By the end of the first six-week season, Hilprecht had recovered more than 2,000 tablets, most of them dating to around 2000 B.C. The better-preserved specimens, found in a baking kiln, were for the most part records of business transactions; the rest were literary, mathematical, and medical texts. The literary tablets, most of them fragments, made Hilprecht suspect that he was close to the temple library. Peters allowed him five extra gangs of diggers in March, but the excavation ended when time ran out, a few meters from a series of tablet-filled chambers that Hilprecht was not to discover for eleven years.

Peters continued to concentrate on the ziggurat, at one point directing 250 workers as they trenched through rock-hard mud brick and rubble. For nine weeks the Americans dug on uneventfully.

Funds were running out fast when serious trouble erupted between the Hamza and Behahtha tribes of the 'Afej, both of whom claimed the mound and insisted on furnishing laborers for the dig. The workmen would shout war cries and insults at the foreigners and quarreled with the Turkish escort, who took delight in picking fights with them. To add to the strain, no one had any privacy. Tribesmen wandered unmolested through tents and storerooms. The camp could be seen from kilometers away and was under no sheikh's protection. It would only be a matter of time before someone raided it. The Americans were surprisingly naive, for they omitted to build a guesthouse for visitors and to provide hospitality for those who called on them. They were horrified by the local people and their morality. The locals held the Americans in open contempt and threatened again and again to burn down the camp. In April, a bread oven was destroyed and four sheep stolen. Rumors whispered that the Americans' horses would be the next to go. On April 15, the Turkish guards frustrated an attempt to steal the horses and fired on the intruders. Unfortunately, one of the thieves was killed by a rifle bullet through the heart. The next four days were full of anxiety. Compensation was offered and refused and the emissaries beaten. Angry horsemen pressed on the camp. The excavations were closed down and preparations made for immediate departure. On April 18, the tribesmen set fire to the reed huts of the camp before dawn. In minutes the camp was a pile of smoldering ashes. The

Tribespeople dancing in the temporary camp at Nippur. From Hilprecht's Exploration in Biblical Lands *(1903).*

Americans battled to save their effects while the locals gleefully plundered. Half the horses perished, and the Americans also lost valuable guns, saddlebags, and $1,000 in gold. But the antiquities were saved. The expedition retreated in confusion on horseback and boat through the swamps to Al Hillah. Most of the Americans promptly resigned and Peters was recalled to the United States. Twenty thousand dollars had provided but the sketchiest impression of Nippur. The whole season had been an embarrassing debacle.

Somewhat to everyone's surprise, the backers of the first season readily agreed to a second one the next year. Hamdi Bey interceded personally with the grand vizier and the Nippur permit was renewed over the objections of local authorities. Peters again was placed in charge of the expedition, but this time he took no Assyriologists or specialists with him. This extraordinary decision by Peters immediately reduced the excavations from a scientific investigation of a complex site to a form of treasure hunting à la Rassam. Peters was anxious to obtain as many antiquities as possible for the minimum cost and without the interference of scientists. Objects, he felt, would please the public and bring in more money for excavations. He resumed the excavations on January 14, 1890, with a team of 200 workers.

This time the atmosphere at Nippur was quite different. Drought conditions and a major cholera epidemic had so decimated the local people that they were delighted to see the Americans and eager to work for them. Nothing much was said about the incident of the previous year. This time an improved camp was pitched just south of the mounds and built under the protection of a local sheikh. Unfortunately, however, Peters refused to pay a blood indemnity of $44 for the death of the robber, feeling that to do so would be a sign of weakness. This gaffe caused serious problems and constant security worries for the Americans. As rumors of the fabled wealth of the visitors spread far and wide, local tribesmen flocked to the mounds to stare. They were particularly interested in the gold fillings in Peters's teeth, which excited their acquisitive lust.

The Americans were constantly on their guard for raids or conspiracies. Fortunately, they were believed to possess great magical powers, which locals thought had brought on the cholera in revenge for the raid of the year before. Peters cured some minor ailments to reinforce this belief and lost no opportunity to demonstrate his prowess. He might have overdone it when he held a spectacular firework display one evening. During the day he had wandered over a mound near the camp, looking mysterious with a compass and muttering strange incantations. After dark he stole out of camp and ignited several rockets from the bottom of a trench. The workers and their families were at dinner and screamed in fear. Terrified that the stars were falling from heaven, the more timid fled to hide in the huts. "At last we came to *our piece de resistance,* the tomato-can firework. At first this fizzled and bade fair to ruin our whole performance. Then, just as we despaired of success, it exploded with a great noise, knocking us over backward in the trench, behind a wall in which we were hidden, and filling the air with fiery serpents hissing and sputtering in every direction. The effect was indescribably diabolical."[11] Yet, even this impressive pyrotechnical display did not prevent quarrels, thefts, droughts, and floods. But by increasingly shrewd human relations and years of experience, the

Americans at last had mastered what Hilprecht rather charmingly calls the "peculiar dangers of the Babylonian climate."[12]

The first season's excavations had shown that Nippur had been occupied for several thousand years, from prehistoric times right up to the ninth century A.D. Now Peters had to fill in the details of the story. The dig concentrated on the ziggurat. The surroundings of the temple had been protected by two huge walls with watch towers. Storerooms and kitchens, as well as houses, formed an integral part of the walls. Peters broke into the outer shell of the ziggurat and discovered a smaller stepped tower inside it. His tunnels and holes dug like wells revealed a complex architectural history that he was totally incapable of interpreting, despite wild claims to the contrary. The excavations were so haphazard that nothing but a general impression of the temple came to light.[13] Peters's knowledge and archaeological experience were totally inadequate for the complex task that faced him. Wallis Budge, always a tart observer of his colleagues, remarked that "more travelers than one who have seen the site of the American excavations at Nippur have failed to see there any exhibition of scientific digging."[14]

The frenetic pace of Peters's excavations recalled that of Layard and Rassam. He tunneled into Hilprecht's mound and unearthed 2,000 tablets without any notion of the strata they had come from. When a mound on the southeastern side of the site unexpectedly yielded tablets, he moved gangs of diggers to the new locality. Soon they shoveled out a chamber nearly eight meters long and five meters wide and crammed with unbaked tablets that had once been stored on wooden shelves round the walls before the building was burned down. Most were tax lists and business documents of great value for establishing the chronology of the Babylonian kings. Unfortunately, Peters kept few notes. The only plans of the site were those compiled by a visiting Hungarian engineer, who made plans of some of the major structures. Wisely, Peters shipped a large consignment of antiquities downstream before the dig finished. The angry tribesmen, who were still after blood revenge, had planned a raid for the final night. Another dramatic firework display enabled the Americans to slip away unharmed.

∞∞

A third campaign at Nippur lasted three years, from 1893 to 1896. It bore the firm imprint of Peters's excavation strategy but was under the field direction of J. H. Haynes, the photographer and business manager of the first two excavations. A firman was readily granted, partly because Hamdi Bey had great sympathy for the persistence of the Americans, and also because Hilprecht, now recovered from a lengthy illness, had spent many months in Constantinople reorganizing the Imperial Ottoman Museum's Babylonian collections for free. Haynes journeyed to Nippur in August 1892 and put himself under the protection of the local sheikhs. Then he built a permanent base near Peters's camp, a mud-brick structure that was a combined castle, storehouse, and dwelling. In fifteen weeks, his small team of fifty men recovered over 8,000 tablets from a tablet-rich mound near an old canal.

Haynes was about to turn his attention to the complex problems of the ziggurat when a fortunate coincidence put him in touch with a young American architectural graduate student from the Massachusetts Institute of Technology, who readily agreed to spend a year without salary at Nippur. Joseph Mayer was a skilled draftsman who had had some experience in recording ancient monuments in Egypt and Turkey. Haynes, who had been feeling lonely, found him a congenial companion. His notes, hitherto little more than a chronicle of dangers and frustrations, became a record of the unfolding architecture of the Nippur ziggurat. The laborers toiled at the temple mound all through the summer of 1894 while Haynes and Mayer recorded every detail with copious sketches, which, for the time, were adequate enough. Unfortunately, Mayer contracted dysentery and malaria in September and insisted on working until his condition was so serious that he was delirious. He died on December 20, leaving Haynes once again alone, many kilometers from the nearest Westerner and without any skilled assistance.

Wisely, Haynes stopped work on the ziggurat but resumed haphazard digging elsewhere in search of tablets and yet more tablets, the finds that Peters had coveted above all others. His progress reports began to dwell on the dangers around him as the solitude of Nippur began to prey on his mind. Cholera was reported at Al Hillah; and the local people fought the Turkish authorities in a lively engagement that killed seventy-one men. The firing could be heard at Nippur, but the excavations continued. Haynes sometimes had difficulty finding workers to replace his basketmen, who would suddenly drop their tools, seize their weapons with a loud war cry, and prance off to battle. The constant pilfering of cylinder seals, occasional cave-ins and injuries, and all the minor irritations produced by a site far from the regular Euphrates and Tigris caravan routes were just too much for Haynes. Nevertheless, he accelerated the pace of excavation in an attempt to remove as many tablets from the site as possible and to give the impression that Nippur was exhausted. Constant rumors of clandestine donkey loads of tablets traveling between the illegal excavations at Telloh and Babylon haunted Haynes. It was not until July 1895 that he felt he could stop digging for tablets. By that time he had recovered nearly 19,000 of them in three years of digging.

The lonely Haynes spent the last six months of the campaign working on the northwest side of the ziggurat, often in temperatures of 49°C and in the middle of dense sandstorms. When Haynes stopped digging for tablets, the trenches that exposed the temple complex had reached such great depths that the trench walls towered dangerously over the diggers. Peters's huge soil dumps from the earlier seasons made the walls even higher and would have to be moved to thoroughly explore the lower strata of the ziggurat. In August he decided that enough was enough and started to close down the excavations.

Haynes had moved 5,600 cubic meters of earth before the end of the last season. He had collected a huge mass of valuable antiquities. By this time he was in urgent need of a rest. Throughout his long seasons at Nippur he had declined the help of experts, despite urgings from Philadelphia. The excavation committee finally found two young English architects to work with him and sent them out to Nippur without consulting him. They arrived just as he was closing down the dig. Reluctant to leave two inexperienced foreigners alone with the covetous and defiant locals, Haynes took the frustrated Englishmen back to Baghdad with him. The architectural information from his last season was never recorded.

Haynes's excavations were, scientifically speaking, a disaster. They caused increasing concern in Philadelphia, especially among Assyriologists like Hilprecht, who described Haynes's discoveries as isolated and incoherent. His weekly progress reports gave little clue to the true character of the temple of Bel. Everyone assumed he would bring back detailed daybooks describing every feature of the excavation. It turned out that his letters were all the experts had to go on. Only the work completed with Mayer was of scientific value. Haynes had dug through dozens of mud-brick walls, failed to keep accurate measurements, and shoveled away valuable rooms without any concern for their contents. His excavation methods, like those of Peters, showed little improvement over Layard's, for he dug deep shafts and tunnels that penetrated to the deepest layers without adequately exploring the horizons that lay nearer the surface.

The tablets and inscriptions from Nippur gave Hilprecht many hours of arduous detective work. He gained valuable historical information from fragments discovered in the early strata of the ziggurat, especially a celebrated text of Lugalzaggesi, the king of Uruk, 132 lines of which he pieced together from eighty-eight fragments of sixty-four different vases.[15] This important historical text shows how a number of minor early Sumerian city-states were constantly quarreling with one another over land and political matters. The more important rulers gave votive offerings at the shine of Bel at Nippur. Names of the kings of Uruk, Kish, and Ur, hitherto unknown, reentered the stage of world history.

⌒⌒

The University of Pennsylvania conducted a fourth campaign at Nippur from 1898 to 1900. By this time the University Museum had come into being and had taken over the work of the Babylonian Exploration Fund. Hermann Hilprecht was appointed scientific director of the excavations, while Haynes was retained as field director to deal with the practical management of the excavations. Two architects, one English and one American, accompanied the party. By this time there was such bad feeling between Hilprecht and Peters that the trustees of the university set up a special committee to investigate the quarrel, which resulted in Peters' severing further connections with the project. So confident did Haynes feel about field conditions that he was allowed to take his wife along. Because the sultan of Turkey was favorably disposed to the Americans, Hilprecht had to wait but two weeks in Constantinople for the firman.

This time things were very different. The two-year season was budgeted at $30,000, and clear objectives were spelled out. These objectives were to determine the precise character of the temple of Bel and its history, to establish the extent of pre-Babylonian Nippur, to search for city walls and gates, to study burials, and, lastly, to find the temple library. Haynes was given precise instructions about records, notebooks, and photography and was told how to order his priorities. Hilprecht was to arrive at Nippur later.

In January 1899, sixty-two camels, several mules, and six sailing boats carried the expedition from Babylon to Nippur. A Turkish commissioner, 6 soldiers, and 150 workers accompanied the party. The expedition set itself up in considerable style in the fortress-like house, which had been sealed when Haynes had left. The comfort of the mud-brick fortress—it was nothing else—astonished visitors like Hilprecht, who remembered the primitive camps of earlier seasons. Haynes had taken the precaution of digging wells that were piped into the courtyard of the expedition house, just in case the expedition was besieged. Fortunately, political conditions were quieter than in earlier years, partly because of improved Ottoman administration and some agricultural development work, and also because the regular presence of foreign archaeological expeditions had introduced new ideas to the area. Hilprecht found the local people talking with considerable anticipation about the German railroad that was to be built through Mesopotamia.

Haynes started work with 205 men. To the committee's disgust, he quarreled with his architects and continued looking for tablets. It was not until March 1900 that Hilprecht was able to reach Nippur and take over the excavations. Hilprecht stopped all tablet digging, placed the architects under close supervision, and concentrated all efforts on the interpretation of the site. Hilprecht later wrote: "Every trench cut henceforth—and there were a great many—was cut for the sole purpose of examining and gathering necessary data for the history and topography of ancient Nippur. If these trenches yielded tangible museum results at the same time, so much the better; if they did not, I was not troubled by their absence and felt just as well satisfied as if I had packed several thousand tablets, or perhaps even more so."[16]

Hilprecht traced city walls and surveyed all the structures already discovered. He completed the excavation of a Parthian palace, examined over 1,100 post-Christian burials. He dug the ziggurat right down to water level, to centuries earlier than those of Sargon I of Akkad (2700 B.C.). Hilprecht found a huge Sumerian cemetery around the temple. But the most impressive discovery came from his "tablet hill" of the first season, an exploration of the temple library, which was located near some school buildings. Hilprecht was able to recover the lesson tablets used by pupils learning to write cuneiform, as well as scientific works, king lists, hymns, and astronomical records. The library even owned a complete set of multiplication tables from 1 to at least 1,350. The Sumerian literary tablets were the most interesting of all. Sumerian literature was restricted to myths and epic tales, hymns, lamentations, and occasional essays. The earliest works were probably written down about 2500 B.C., and the literature undoubtedly proliferated in later centuries.[17]

By 1900, Hilprecht had 30,000 tablets to examine, which, for the most part, recorded commercial and legal transactions. He was wise enough to realize that the study of the Nippur tablets was a long-term cooperative venture, to last far beyond his lifetime. Indeed, these studies are still in progress. The Nippur tablets were so fragmentary that they took years to study. Each fragment had to be copied by hand, then translated and interpreted. But thanks to the devoted work of Hilprecht, Samuel Kramer, Thorkild Jacobsen, and many others, Sumerian social and economic structure and king lists are now much better known. We know of at least nine Sumerian epic tales, the most famous of which are the epics surrounding the mythical hero Gilgamesh. Work on the compilation of a Sumerian dictionary continues to this day.

Despite these contributions, the Nippur and Telloh excavations were hardly paragons of archaeological virtue. At their worst, they were organized treasure hunts, at their best the first attempts at large-scale scientific investigation of Sumerian civilization. By excavating over many years, the archaeologists were able to train some skilled workers, develop a rapport with the local people, and, above all, gain some insights into the complexities of excavating mud-brick structures and dissecting occupation levels. Without these skills and the long-term commitments to sites that go with them, no archaeologist could hope to study the Sumerians effectively.

NEBUCHADNEZZAR'S BABYLON

In the early days of Near Eastern excavating, mud brick walls were simply not understood and in some cases their very existence was hardly suspected. The normal practice was to go on digging until one reached the stone foundations.

—SETON LLOYD

GERMAN INTEREST IN ASSYRIOLOGY DATED BACK TO THE DAYS OF GEORG Grotefend, who continued to publish cuneiform translations of dubious reliability until his death in 1853 (see Chapter 7). A year after Grotefend died, Kaiser Wilhelm IV had lost a consignment of Assyrian sculptures in the Qurna disaster. Eventually the Berlin Museum bought some bas-reliefs from the Crystal Palace Company in London. This transaction was consummated just as excavations in Mesopotamia entered a twenty-year interregnum. The main interest of the few Assyriologists in Germany, however, was in cuneiform and Asian languages. During the remainder of the nineteenth century the distinguished theologian and linguist Eberhard Schrader followed Henry Rawlinson's work

243

closely and studied the Behistun inscriptions. Schrader was the father of Assyriology in Germany. He accepted Rawlinson's decipherments and used them as a basis for studying the Assyrian text called "Descent of Ishtar into the Underworld."[1] In 1873, he started some private courses in Assyriology in which he dealt with the basic philological principles of the language and discussed the relationship between the Assyrians and the Scriptures. Soon a new and vigorous school of Assyriology was flourishing in Leipzig. Schrader earned international recognition for his book on ancient scripts and the Old Testament, which he published in 1876. His students worshipped him. Wallis Budge described him as "a fine example of the old type of German scholar; his modesty was as great as his learning."[2]

Another German Assyriologist, Friedrich Delitzsch, taught himself cuneiform scripts at an early age and began a precise study of Assyrian grammar and lexicography. He went on to form a class for young Assyriologists and prepared one of the first reading books for students ever published. Delitzsch became the dean of Assyrian scholars in Germany. Never an expert copier, he achieved fame for the quality of his teaching and for the fine students he graduated. It was Delitzsch who was invited to give a series of lectures before Kaiser Wilhelm on the importance of Babylon and Assyria in the context of Biblical studies. In these lectures and in his book *Babel and Bible*, published in the United States in 1903, Delitzsch emphasized the parallels between Mesopotamian myths and the Scriptures.[3] Eloquently, he urged German participation in Mesopotamian archaeology to clarify these parallels. His views were much criticized by Biblical experts but the kaiser encouraged his ideas. The German excavations were to change Mesopotamian archaeology profoundly.

By 1880, the Germans were already digging in other parts of Europe with a precise fervor that reflected both a new concern with scientific reportage and Kaiser Wilhelm's preoccupation with nationalistic prestige. Their revolution in archaeological methods stressed recording of data in the field. When Alexander Conze excavated on Samothrace, in the northern Aegean, in 1873 and 1875, he worked with two architects, a photographer, and the assistance of an Austrian warship. The sumptuous report on the excavations was a model of its kind and illustrated with photographs that recorded architecture and excavation. The German Archaeological Institute came under the control of the Prussian government in 1871. Ernst Curtius and Friedrich Adler worked at Olympia from 1875 to 1880 with an ample budget and specialist architects in the field. The closing season was financed by Kaiser Wilhelm himself. Even more remarkable, the Germans renounced all claims to the finds and even built a small museum at the site. This precise concern for minute architectural details, small artifacts, and, above all, prompt and orderly reporting of field results contrasted sharply with most current archaeological practice. The kaiser wanted to enrich the Berlin Museum, but he argued correctly that sumptuous and prestigious academic publications in the tradition of Napoleon's *Description de L'Egypte* also could reflect favorably on their sponsors.

German interest in Mesopotamia surfaced in the late 1870s, when the Asian studies scholar Ernst Sachan and other German scientists visited Assyria and Babylonia in search of likely sites to excavate. Small parties of excavators followed, looking for long-term projects and gaining experience with local conditions. At one point there was a possibility that the Germans would dig at Nippur, but the University of Pennsylvania preempted them. The Royal Prussian Museum of Berlin was also in the field in early 1887, engaged in a preliminary search for promising excavation sites. Two archaeologists, Bernard Moritz and Robert Koldewey, were able to excavate briefly in two huge tells named Surghul and Al Hiba near Telloh.[4] The mounds were so enormous that they decided to concentrate their efforts on sinking long trenches in order to establish the character of the buildings. They followed mud-brick walls and cleared the contents of chambers, even sectioned deep wells made of terracotta rings. The Germans kept their usual careful records and exposed large numbers of mud-brick houses intersected by long narrow streets only about a meter wide. Many of these structures had crumbled so badly that the archaeologists were forced to trace foundations through dark stains in the soil, a technique of almost unheard-of sophistication in the 1880s. The mound deposits were full of burials and occupation debris, but Moritz and Koldewey's limited time made extended investigation impossible.

Ten years later, Ernst Sachan went to Mesopotamia again, this time to make specific recommendations for likely sites for long-term excavation. Robert Koldewey accompanied the party. They visited all the excavations in progress, then recommended digs at Babylon and Assur. Koldewey had spent two days at Babylon in June 1887. He returned for three more days in December 1897. On each occasion he picked up fragments of enameled bricks that seemed to have formed parts of huge murals. He took the fragments home to Berlin and boldly predicted that they came from Nebuchadnezzar's city. The director general of the Royal Prussian Museum applied for a firman to dig systematically at Babylon. The permit came through in 1899.

∽∽

Robert Koldewey had a lifelong passion for archaeology. He was born at Blankenburg in 1855 and studied architecture, archaeology, and art history in Berlin, Munich, and Vienna. His early archaeological training came in the field at Assos and Lesbos in Greece. After his preliminary digs at Surghul and Al Hiba in 1887, he excavated in Syria, Italy, and Sicily while holding a job as an architectural teacher at Görlitz in extreme eastern Prussia. Koldewey was a lighthearted man with a lively sense of humor. Some of his more single-minded colleagues distrusted him because of his ability to look on the humorous side of his work. When he dug at the Greek city of Selinus in Sicily, he took great delight in describing the gory Carthaginian sieges "in which the ladies of the town took vigorous part." He went on to say: "From this episode, Selinus has not recovered to this day. Because of it, rabbits hop freely through the streets. And because of it, too, I suppose, we have rabbits to eat of an evening now and then."[5]

Despite his sense of humor, Koldewey was a precise and thorough scientific archaeologist. Babylon in all its desolation challenged his inquiring mind. Unlike his predecessors on the site, Koldewey was a trained archaeological observer. Babylon, he was certain, could be studied thoroughly by careful digging, precise recording, and, above all, long-term excavation. Koldewey opened his first trenches at Babylon on March 26, 1899, and continued to dig there every year until 1912. "It involves no depreciation of the labors of our predecessors when we say that they are superseded in almost every detail by the results of our many years of excavations, so far as knowledge of the city ruins are concerned," he was to write in 1914.[6]

Koldewey faced a formidable task: "To those accustomed to Greece and its remains, it is a constant surprise to have Babylon's mounds pointed out as ruins. There are no stone blocks, no columns; even in excavation there is only brickwork."[7] As we have seen, the Babil mound and the Kasr, the most conspicuous landmarks, had been quarried by brick diggers for centuries. Koldewey stopped the quarrying as much as he could by hiring the brick diggers as laborers, but terrible damage had already been done. Because of the unique challenges, he and his colleagues had to develop new archaeological techniques as they went along. Koldewey set out to train special teams of skilled workers who did nothing but trace mud-brick walls. The Germans started with the easy fired-brick structures, then gradually turned their attention to sun-dried brickwork, which was harder to trace as it had dissolved faster in antiquity. They were lucky at Babylon, for the stratification of the various buildings was relatively easy to identify, because the builders had inscribed their bricks with their names.

Koldewey and his colleague Walter Andrae, who started at Babylon and then branched out on his own at Assur, realized that Mesopotamian architecture had changed but little over the centuries. The builders of Babylon and Assur had made their mud bricks by dumping tempered clay into a four-sided wooden mold with an open top and bottom.[8] The clay was smoothed carefully into place with the side of the hand, the mold was removed, and the brick left to dry in the sun. The endless hot and cloudless days of the dry season baked the bricks to such durable hardness that kiln-fired bricks were unnecessary. Koldewey's predecessors had failed to understand the implications of mud-brick architecture and had dug meters of building and walls away in search of stone foundations or the upright stone slabs that formed the lower parts of palace walls in the north. With the weathering of time, the mud bricks had become mud again after the buildings of the city were abandoned. Koldewey realized that the only hope of finding out anything about Babylon was to concentrate on tracing the virtually invisible ancient mud-brick walls.

Season after season, Koldewey's workmen uncovered several kilometers of mud-brick walls. They recovered the layout of the neo-Babylonian city with its vast monumental gateways, elaborate fortifications, major streets, and large palaces. Step by step, the archaeologists recorded the architectural finds with meticulous care, for they realized that only the largest and most massive of mud-brick buildings would survive any length of time after the dig.

Eventually, the Germans found that the best excavation technique was to scrape the ground with hoes while looking for wall faces or changes in soil texture that indicated the junction between a mud-brick wall and the filling behind it. Sometimes a clear line of mud plaster survived on the face of a wall or the pattern of the brickwork could be discerned. Then the expert wall tracer dug carefully into the filling until he had made a hole large enough to squat in. At that point he faced the wall and delicately picked away at the filling until the gentle strokes caused the soil to fall away from the plaster on the wall face. Once the wall face was exposed, the digger simply worked his way round the four walls of the chamber, leaving a layer of filling over the floor and in the center of the room to be removed very carefully later. Thus, the contents of the room could be recorded in place, and evidence for multiple reoccupations recovered.

Over many seasons at Assur and Babylon, Koldewey, Andrae, and their assistants developed a comprehensive method of excavation that influenced the work of all subsequent archaeologists in Mesopotamia. They started by making a topographical survey of the site, then they sunk test pits to obtain a datum baseline for the excavations, a base level, as it were, which provided a yardstick for the untangling of the complicated sequence of cities and buildings. When Koldewey came to investigate the Ishtar Gate at Babylon and the Procession Street that led through it, he found that King Nebuchadnezzar also had had a reason to dig deeply into the ground. In order to reach firm soil undisturbed by earlier occupation, his architects had cut the foundations of their great buildings down to clean sand. The foundation walls built into these deep trenches remained undisturbed for Koldewey to uncover: walls decorated with huge reliefs of dragons and bulls that stand ten meters high. A layer of clay plaster protected the reliefs—they had never been intended to be viewed by the public because they formed part of the building's deep foundations.

The German excavations were part of a sustained, systematic campaign conducted with deliberation and focused primarily on architectural considerations. The excavators were imbued with an almost fanatical passion for detail, so much so that Koldewey was moved to comment that "the gradual progress of the excavations, important and stimulating as it is for the explorers, appears of less interest to those who take little share in it."[9] It is true that their reports make for very dull reading, even for the specialist.

Koldewey had started his dig with a general knowledge of the history of the city, which he had gleaned from cuneiform tablets. His task was to fill in the details. He identified the earliest occupation of Babylon as dating to before the fifth millennium B.C. A few scattered flint implements lay below the water table, the baseline for all his work. The first identifiable city belonged to the time of Hammurabi (1790 B.C.). Subsequent settlements followed the street plans laid out in Hammurabi's time. The Assyrian kings maintained and expanded the temples of their predecessors. But it was Nebuchadnezzar (who reigned from 604 to 562 B.C.) who rebuilt the entire city that was cleared by Koldewey and his colleagues. Nebuchadnezzar had restored the temple on the citadel and several other shrines, built the first stone bridge over the Euphrates, and completed the southern citadel, which included his own great palace. The Procession Street was enlarged and paved with stone, and the Ishtar Gate was completed and decorated with an enameled frieze of animals.[10] He surrounded the entire city with a huge outer wall. The city reached its greatest magnificence under his rule. Babylon began to decline in Nabonidus's time (556–539 B.C.) and never recovered, even when Alexander the Great tried to restore its prosperity. But Alexander died in Babylon before he could complete the restoration. By the time of the Sassanids (A.D. 226–636), Babylon was a ruin and the site occupied by only a few scattered villages.

Koldewey had begun by employing a work force of 250 men on the clearance of the Procession Street, which extended north to south through the inner city. In April 1899 he wrote that he had been digging for two weeks with great success. The secret was his system for wall clearance. Each pickman was armed with two picks: one a small, pointed implement used for tracing walls; the other a larger pick employed for heavier digging. A pickman was supported by sixteen basketmen, who carried away the soil shoveled into their baskets by three shovelmen. The pickmen advanced in a carefully drawn line, peeling off the soil in sloping layers until the walls emerged from the earth. The basketmen carried their loads to a light railroad car used to dump the soil in a place where future digging would be unlikely. The 1899 excavations soon turned up the ends of two parallel walls that formed the boundaries of the Procession Street. This street led to the Ishtar Gate, which Nebuchadnezzar had built as the processional gate for the temple of Marduk. He had paved the street with huge red-and-white marble flagstones that lay on an asphalt and brick substratum. The flagstones bore Nebuchadnezzar's imprint. He had ordered the Procession Street raised almost thirteen meters above the level of the plain. The walls on either side of the street had been faced with glazed bricks that formed a triple frieze of bulls, lions, dragons, and other animals. The lions were white or yellow with yellow or red manes against a blue background. These walls were defensive in intent and led the traveler toward the Ishtar Gate in seclusion from the fine view of Babylon that now stretches on either side of the great walkway. The excavation of the enameled friezes was a long task, for the brickwork behind them had been plundered over the centuries. But Koldewey was able to piece the lions together and estimated that at least 120 animals, each about two meters long, had once adorned the walls of the street.

Koldewey pored over the friezes in an attempt to find out how they had been assembled. He concluded that the sculptors first made a working model, which served as the prototype for clay molds. They assembled the model on a temporary wall, paying careful attention to the jointing of the bricks. Then they made burned-clay molds for each separate brick. The molds were shaped and formed so that the friezes became an integral part of the wall. The contours of the molded and fired bricks were then outlined with a black, vitreous composition, the different courses filled with colored enamels, and the bricks fired to fuse the enamels in brilliant colors. The bricks, duly numbered by the excavators to indicate the correct sequence, were now ready for assembly in the frieze. Conditions were so cramped at the excavation that the brick fragments were shipped back to Berlin for chemical treatment to restore their surfaces. Koldewey insisted that every fragment be numbered so that the friezes could be reassembled later.

This magnificent walkway was but a prelude to Koldewey's most remarkable discovery, Nebuchadnezzar's Ishtar Gate, which he excavated in 1902. The gate lay at the point where the Procession Street passed through the fortifications of the inner city. Koldewey found that the walls of the gate still stood twelve meters high and were covered with horizontal rows of bulls and dragons. Two huge towers flanked the double portals of the gate. Glazed bricks and figures of at least 575

Reconstruction of the Ishtar Gate at Babylon in the Berlin Museum. Bildarchiv Preussischer Kulturebesitz/Art Resource, NY.

bulls and dragons adorned the gate itself, as dragons (described by Koldewey as a "walking serpent") were the sacred animal of Marduk. One hundred and fifty-two of these figures were still in position on the gate. Koldewey decided to remove and incorporate them in a full-size reconstruction of the gate at the Berlin Museum. The task of removal went on until 1912, but the 649 cases of bricks did not leave Iraq until 1926. World War I intervened, the British took over the government of Iraq, and new antiquities laws prevented their release. But eventually the Ishtar Gate went to Berlin in exchange for representative examples of restored panels and two of Koldewey's models of Babylon for the Iraq and Babylon museums.

After several seasons of arduous and unspectacular work, Koldewey was able to disentangle the long history of the Kasr, or citadel, of Babylon. He found that Sargon I had built the first buildings on the site. Then came Nabopolassar's mud-brick palace surrounded by an enclosure wall. His son Nebuchadnezzar completely reconstructed the Kasr, erecting the Ishtar Gate, extending the palaces and temples, and enclosing the entire complex with a massive fortification wall. In the northeast corner of the south citadel, Koldewey found a stone-arched structure associated with a well. These vaulted arches were some of the few stone structures in the entire site. Koldewey combed through the ancient historical sources and concluded that he had found the supports and water supply for the legendary Hanging Gardens of Babylon, one of the classical Seven Wonders of the World. The Hanging Gardens were much more modest than legend would have had the world believe. Nebuchadnezzar's roof garden was an imposing architectural artifice to be sure, but hardly a spectacular wonder to the nineteenth-century archaeologist.

The Procession Street passed along the east wall of the temple of E-Temen-Anki, the great ziggurat of Babylon, which, with Birs Nimrod, had been associated time and again with the Biblical Tower of Babel. An enclosure wall and associated buildings surrounded the ziggurat, but most of the structures had suffered from raids by brick robbers. The complex of buildings in the walls was thought to be priests' houses and pilgrims' accommodations.

Towering over the entire complex, the ziggurat was a colossal structure reached by a huge stairway that extended to the summit. A vast mass of brickwork confronted the excavators. The original temple built by Hammurabi had long since been razed. King Nabopolassar later built a new ziggurat to commemorate the earlier structure: "At that time Marduk commanded me . . . ; to build the Tower of Babylon, which in the time before me had become weak, and had been brought to ruin, to lay its foundation firm on the bosom of the underworld, while its top should stretch heavenwards."[11] His son Nebuchadnezzar boasted that he went even further, raising his temple so that "it might rival heaven." In investigating this stupendous structure, Koldewey had only the base to go on. He studied the foundations and ancient historical records from such authorities as Herodotus and estimated that the base of the ziggurat was ninety meters square and at least fifty, perhaps even seventy-five, meters high. He was almost overwhelmed by the scale of even the ruined structure. He wrote: "The colossal mass of the tower, which the Jews of the Old Testament regarded as the essence of human presumption, amidst the proud pal-

aces of the priests, the spacious treasuries, the innumerable lodgings
for strangers—white walls, bronze doors, mighty fortification walls
set round with lofty portals and a forest of 1,000 towers—the whole
must have conveyed an overwhelming sense of greatness, power, and
wealth, such as could rarely have been found elsewhere in the great
Babylonian kingdom."[12] After the excavations ended, all that was left
of the ziggurat was quarried away for bricks. Thus, nothing remains of
the Tower of Babel today; a swamp now fills the space once occupied
by this legendary structure.

The excavations of the German Oriental Institute at Babylon ran parallel with Walter Andrae's remarkable investigations at Assur in the
north, one of the ancient capitals of the Assyrians. Andrae and his colleagues dug into these extensive mounds with great success from 1902
to 1914. Previously, Austen Henry Layard, Victor Place, and Hormuzd
Rassam had dug there but had found little. Their hectic scrambles for
palaces and bas-reliefs had proved fruitless. Andrae arrived with a season's experience at Babylon behind him, where he had been involved
in the experiments with wall tracing. He soon formed his own specially
trained teams of wall diggers, most of them from local villages; and,
after surveying the site with great care, he set out to probe the depths
of the early Assyrian city. So successful was this experiment that the
villagers became specialists in this type of excavation and passed their
skills on to the archaeologists of the 1930s and 1940s.

Assur had once perched on a heavily fortified rocky spur washed
by the Tigris. At least three ziggurats adorned the summit of the hill, including E-Hassaq-Kurkuma, which was known as the Great Mountain
and House of All Lands. Using his own refinements of Koldewey's
techniques, Andrae traced the city walls, many houses, and temple
precincts.

The Germans' largest and most important operations were directed at one major structure, the temple of Ishtar, the mythical wife of the
city's own god, Assur. Andrae laid out a vertical trench that stripped
off successively rebuilt temples, revealing a long succession of at least
six earlier buildings, until he reached an archaic Sumerian shrine,
which contained stone statues identical to those in Sumerian temples

in the south. Although the Americans had dimly conceived of strati-
graphic layers at Nippur and Koldewey had been able to identify different Babylonian settlements by using inscribed bricks, Andrae was
the first to try to dissect an entire tell to obtain detailed information on
the evolution not only of a temple but of a civilization as well. Assur
was the first site where the Sumerian civilization was found *under* the
Assyrian one. Gone were the destructive excavations of hasty treasure
hunters. Andrae and his colleagues photographed and recorded every
building before they removed it, for they realized that the contents of
the temples and the rituals associated with them were just as important
as statuary or architecture. By their insistence on slow, careful work,
Koldewey, Andrae, and their successors revolutionized Mesopotamian
archaeology at a time when the first professional scholars of archaeology were replacing the amateur archaeologists of earlier times. But
as good as the German excavations were, Koldewey still overlooked
the possible use of pottery for dating, a technique already mastered
by the Egyptologist Flinders Petrie and others along the Nile. Future
generations of German archaeologists were trained in the study of mi-
nutiae and the ordering and classification of artifacts. Soon they began
to use pottery and other finds as a way of developing a chronology
for the early centuries of Sumerian civilization. They employed techniques that had been pioneered by Petrie in the Nile Valley, where
he had developed a technique of sequence dating using Egyptian jars
that extended back to pre-Dynastic times, before 3000 B.C.[13] A similar open-ended chronology developed slowly for Mesopotamia in the
years immediately before and after World War I, and this chronological inquiry took archaeologists on the first steps toward the discovery
of Sumerian origins. This search still continues.

LEONARD WOOLLEY AT CARCHEMISH

The spirit of the place, this ruin set in the wide wind-swept, treeless land is hard to give in words. . . . You are in a strange world wherein anything might happen. To your right the Euphrates runs past in a bold curve, its brown waters eddying and leaping in their haste: the acropolis mound, scarred and seamed with trenches, rises huge and high above the river; landward the sweeping line of the walls shuts out all beyond.

—LEONARD WOOLLEY

THE FIRST SCIENTIFIC EXCAVATIONS IN MESOPOTAMIA TOOK PLACE AGAINST A backdrop of gradual economic, political, and social change. By the end of the nineteenth century, Iraq had begun to feel the influence of European capital and big power politics. The steamer service between Baghdad and Basra was much improved. By the 1870s telegraph lines extended to Baghdad. The Germans eventually built a railroad from southern Turkey to Baghdad that reduced dependence on river transport. But Iraq itself remained a remote and little-understood province of the Ottoman empire. Political conditions outside the towns were still near anarchy, especially in the lower delta. Although many northern sheikhs were now involved in town life and local politics and communications for the traveler were much improved, the tribes of the delta were still in a state of flux, fighting with the Turkish authorities and each other.

The solitary traveler still journeyed at his own peril. Robert Koldewey and his Babylon colleagues felt that they were in an oasis amid the disturbances. The rare Turkish raids against the rebels invariably ended in futile bloodshed and shooting that often stopped steamer traffic on the river. Swampy terrain, unjust landholding laws imposed by the Turks, and profound social turmoil made this a deeply troubled area.

Chaotic as Iraq was, the European powers had their eyes on its future. The Germans and the British were the most aggressive. Diplomatic relations with Germany were established in 1905, when a consul was appointed in Baghdad. The British watched closely. Numerous British and German visitors now came to Iraq to sightsee, trade, spy out potential military strategies, or study archaeological sites.

Many nations sent archaeological expeditions to the country between 1900 and 1915. Most were short-term efforts, like the University of Chicago's expedition to Bismaya, which was headed by the American consul to Baghdad, Edgar J. Banks.[1] The French worked at Kish, also in the south, while Leonard W. King reopened Kuyunjik for the British Museum in 1903. King was a man of great energy and a scholar who loved working out-of-doors. He dug down to a depth of twenty-one meters in the mound, identified three Assyrian levels, and penetrated into a horizon where he found dark earth that contained stone knife-blades and possible pre-Assyrian occupation. Unfortunately, he died in 1919 before he could return to Iraq to continue his work. These and other Mesopotamian excavations were on a small scale compared with the German efforts at Babylon and Assur.

Most of the archaeologists who worked or traveled in Mesopotamia at the turn of the century tended to write popular accounts of their digs, which fall into the tiresome "I was there" category of anecdotal travelogue. Their books did little to advance scholarship or to improve public understanding of archaeology. Few excavators are able to venture successfully beyond the standard travel account or the dull, scientific monograph. But we are doubly fortunate that one of the most gifted archaeologists of the twentieth century, who worked in Mesopotamia for over half a century, could write fluently about it as well.

Charles Leonard Woolley not only dug brilliantly but wrote up his excavations promptly. He was a skilled raconteur who understood the complicated human problems that went with digging an important site. His fascinating accounts of excavation nearly a century ago give us a portrait of the day-by-day hurly-burly of excavation as it was practiced in the days before Arab nationalism completely changed the climate of archaeological research.

Woolley was fond of telling the tale of the casual way he became an archaeologist. The year 1904 was Woolley's last at New College, Oxford, and he was thinking about the future. He had had vague intentions of taking Holy Orders but had changed his mind. A career as a schoolmaster seemed attractive, and it was a job that Woolley had already enjoyed on a temporary basis. One spring day, he received a summons from the warden of New College. He answered the call with considerable trepidation, at a loss to know why Warden Spooner would want to see him. The conversation took a most unexpected turn.

"Ah, Mr. Woolley," began the warden. "Quite so. I think that when you came up to Oxford you had every intention of taking Holy Orders?"

Woolley said yes, it was so, but that he had given up the idea. He waited for what was to come.

"And what do you propose to do?" inquired the warden.

Woolley murmured something about becoming a schoolmaster.

"Oh, yes, a schoolmaster, really?" came the reply. "Well, Mr. Woolley, *I* have decided that you shall be an archaeologist."

"I was not quite sure what an archaeologist was," recalls Woolley. But it was useless to argue with Warden Spooner. Thus, Leonard Woolley became an archaeologist and never regretted it.[2]

He began his career as an assistant keeper at the Ashmolean Museum in Oxford. The Ashmolean was under the direction of Sir Arthur Evans, then at the height of his triumphant career as the discoverer of the Minoan civilization of Crete. Evans had rescued the Ashmolean from a long and neglected oblivion as a repository of curious oddments. He had enriched it with his own collections and from constant field trips to the Balkans and Mediterranean lands. Evans had been a thorn in the flesh of Oxford committees as he fought for his precious museum. When the going became difficult, he would take off for the field, leaving his assistant keeper to respond to all queries with the bland reply, "The keeper, sir, is somewhere in Bohemia."[3]

Woolley was soon in the field, too. He cut his teeth on some crude excavations on Hadrian's Wall in northern England, then spent five years, from 1907 to 1911, working with various archaeologists on the Eckley B. Coxe Expedition to the Sudan. The Sudan was still a wild and remote territory in those days. Woolley fell in love with the desert, excavated cemeteries, and worked on sites of the then little-known Meroitic civilization.[4] His heart, however, was not in the Sudan—he thought it a remote cultural backwater far from the main pulse of Western civilization—but the unspectacular discoveries were more than compensated by the interesting people he met on the digs. Some were trained archaeological workers from Egypt who knew all about archaeology and had worked on many excavations. Others were Sudanis, who were less skilled. The Sudanis taught him much about dealing with laborers in remote areas. At the time, the Nile Valley was one of the finest training grounds for a young archaeologist.

When the Sudanese excavations ended, Woolley was at a loose end just as the British Museum was searching for a director for its recently resumed excavations of the ancient city of Carchemish on the Syrian border. Colleagues recommended the young Egyptologist so strongly that Woolley found himself in charge of a major eastern Mediterranean excavation at the age of thirty-one.

Carchemish was something of a mystery. The ancient city had guarded the main ford of the Euphrates River for centuries. Byzantines and Romans had maintained forts and trading towns on the site. Carchemish was famous from the Scriptures, too. An Assyrian king had conquered and annexed the city in 717 B.C. The earlier history of the site was less certain. Egyptologists knew that the pharaoh Tuthmosis III had fought a pitched battle at Carchemish in about 1455 B.C., a conflict that gave him control of the strategic Euphrates crossing. The city was also known to be a key settlement of the Hittites. But who were the Hittites? Had they ruled over a large area of the eastern Mediterranean world and dealt with Assyrians and Egyptians on terms of equality?

Over fifteen meters of deposits at Carchemish could, conceivably, provide some of the clues. Deep and unexplored prehistoric occupation lay below the Hittite levels, mantling the rocky promontory that gave Carchemish such mastery over the Euphrates.

The British Museum had started operations at Carchemish in 1878. Its deep mounds and extensive fortifications seemed to be a promising treasure house for fine sculpture and possibly clay tablets. At the instigation of the cuneiform expert George Smith, the museum asked the British consul at Aleppo to send a dragoman to Carchemish to dig up sculptures. Although only a few inscribed fragments reached London, they generated considerable interest, for they were among the first known examples of Hittite writing.

The British consul was farsighted. He thought it wise to use his firman to secure title to the site before any other digging started. He journeyed up from Aleppo in state to purchase the old city in the name of the British government. Carchemish was deserted; the local people now lived in the tiny, ramshackle village of Jerablus nearby. The consul found Jerablus flocks grazing on the meadow inside Carchemish's overgrown ramparts. None of the villagers were anxious to claim title to this useless but taxable land except one, a wealthy man who had quietly acquired the title against a rainy day. Ali Agha received the consul courteously but firmly refused to sell Carchemish to the British Museum. Foreigners could dig in the ruins as much as they liked, but he wanted the land for himself. The consul returned to Aleppo empty-handed.

A few months later, Ali Agha was imprisoned in Aleppo, the victim of a sudden arrest on indeterminate charges. His plight was a common but sorry one in Turkish domains, indeed potentially disastrous, for the authorities barely fed their prisoners. Ali Agha was hungry, without funds for bribery, and desperate. Then he suddenly thought of the British consul. A hasty note brought the consul to his cell. Ali tearfully protested his innocence and begged him to intercede on his behalf. The consul tactfully reminded the prisoner that they had some unfinished business at Carchemish. Ali agreed with alacrity. Within a few hours, he was magically freed from prison, all charges dropped. A quarter share in Carchemish duly changed hands in exchange for an embroidered coat, a pair of blue leather boots, and a revolver.

Carchemish lay undisturbed until 1911, when the British Museum again decided to dig the site. Ali Agha's son honored the long-standing agreement and waived all claims to finds within the city walls. The dig began in March 1911 under the directorship of David Hogarth, an experienced archaeologist who had worked with Arthur Evans on the palace of Knossos. Hogarth was a strong personality, known to his Carchemish workmen as Azrael, the Angel of Death, on account of his crotchety temper before breakfast.[5] His junior assistants were Reginald Campbell-Thompson, a cuneiform expert, and a young man named T. E. Lawrence, later to achieve fame for his desert exploits in World War I as Lawrence of Arabia.

Lawrence was to spend four years at Carchemish, Hogarth only two. The preliminary work primarily consisted of shifting the foundations of Roman and other more recent buildings, looking for portable antiquities, and probing the lower levels of the earthworks. The results were sufficiently promising for the British Museum to embark on a long excavation campaign.

Woolley took over an ongoing excavation with an active foreman, a team of unruly Arab and Kurdish laborers, and T. E. Lawrence, who, although fresh from Oxford, was already a veteran of the diggings. Lawrence was well-known for kilometers around, both for his sympathy with and understanding of the local people and also for his impish sense of humor. When Woolley arrived, the workers were still chortling over the trick Lawrence had played on an officious Turkish soldier. The soldier had jeered at Lawrence and challenged his power and authority. Lawrence quietly smiled and said, "I'll show you how powerful I am." He produced two glasses filled with water and two packets of Seidlitz powder, one white, the other an imposing blue. The packets looked impressively magical. In fact, Seidlitz, a village in Bavaria, was famous for its carbonated water, the formula for which was often sold in powdered form.

"Take these two glasses, one in each hand," he told the Turk. "Is the water in them hot or cold?" he then asked.

"Cold, "replied the soldier.

"Right. You ask what powers I have. Can I make the cold water boil without fire?"

"Of course not," was the reply.

Lawrence passed his hands over the two glasses, quietly poured the powders in them, and muttered strange incantations. "Abracadabra!" he finally pronounced. "Pour the water from one glass to the other."

The Seidlitz powder boiled and bubbled furiously. With a terrified howl, the soldier dropped the glasses and fled.[6]

Woolley never revealed his true feelings about Lawrence, even after Lawrence's exploits in Arabia had made him famous. They came to Carchemish together in a humble cart in March 1912, apparently already on good terms. Lawrence took over what he considered congenial tasks — photography, sculpture, and pottery. But Woolley, although liking him, found his work erratic and his attention span short. Fortunately, both men shared a penchant for luxurious living after work. Woolley watched Lawrence throw himself into the role of a Great Personage, teaching lessons to young Arabs, treating diseases, and dressing up in elaborate and incongruous costumes. His evening cloak of gold and silver thread weighed twenty-seven kilograms and had come — cheap — from a thief in the Aleppo market. Carchemish was an formative period in Lawrence's life.

Within minutes of arriving at Carchemish on a Sunday, Woolley had found his camp besieged by people anxious to work as diggers. When Hogarth left, he had arranged for an official guard to be placed on the site to protect it from looters. The guard commander had done his job well. No one had touched anything. But he now refused to let Woolley start work without the permission of the governor of Birecik, a local official who lived forty kilometers away. Woolley wrote this gentleman a polite letter asking for his approval to start work at once, enrolled 120 men to begin on Wednesday, and made final preparations for the dig. The next day, the governor flatly refused permission for any digging at all.

"This was a nasty shock," wrote Woolley later. It was also a tricky situation. If the work did not begin on schedule, he would not only waste valuable time but, even more important, he would lose the respect of his men. Respect was the cornerstone of all Woolley's dealings with the local people. Feeling that a few minutes' conversation would correct any misunderstanding, Woolley and Lawrence rode to Birecik the next morning to interview the recalcitrant official. After cooling his heels in the governor's anteroom for a while, Woolley simply walked in on him. He found an "elderly man with grey hair and pointed beard, sly eyes, and flabby figure." The interview got off to a slow start. Woolley produced his firman from the sultan. The governor refused to take any notice of the British Museum until they communicated with him in Turkish. Woolley argued at length, but to no avail. The governor ostentatiously turned over some papers on his desk to indicate that the interview was at an end. Woolley became insistent. He pointed out that he had engaged 120 men to work on the morrow. "You have only ten men at Jerablus," he told the governor, "and I have a hundred and twenty who want to work." When the governor said he would send more, Woolley lost his temper. "Send all you've got," he said. "I shall still outnumber you and my men are armed." He hoped, he added, that the governor himself would come at the head of his troops. Then he, Woolley, would have great pleasure in shooting him first.

The governor told him he was talking nonsense and refused to budge. Boldly, Woolley called his bluff. He drew his revolver and held it against the governor's left ear. "I will shoot you here and now unless you give me permission to start now," he said with quiet menace.[7] Woolley got his permit that very afternoon and returned to a triumphant welcome from his workers. Lawrence was deeply impressed. These were the days of British arrogance. The Englishmen knew well that a warship would appear promptly in Beirut if they ran into serious trouble.

Woolley's first task on site was to examine the wreckage of the Roman city that stood on the surface. Slowly and deliberately, Woolley removed the Roman city stone by stone. The lower levels were far more important, so the Romans had to go. Woolley carefully recorded every feature he destroyed. "After all," he remarked, "there are perhaps a hundred sites where Roman towns stand better preserved than at Carchemish."[8]

The removal of the Roman city proved to be the costliest of all the excavations at Carchemish. To his great relief, Woolley was able to give the thousands of tonnes of Roman stone to the German engineers who were building the track for the Baghdad railway. The Germans began removing the stone at once. But the owner of Carchemish, Ali Agha's son Hassan Agha, protested that Woolley had given away the stone when the laborers could have made a profit from it. When Woolley told him the engineers would never pay, the story reached the ears of the governor of Birecik. A few days later, a summons from the governor's court arrived for Lawrence. He was to stand trial for stealing stone from Hassan Agha.

The summons was highly illegal. No British subject could be tried in a Turkish court without adequate representation. Furthermore, the court concerned administered Islamic law, which applied only to Muslims. Nevertheless, Lawrence attended the preliminary hearing. The governor promptly confiscated all the papers relating to the site, then adjourned the case.

A few days later, some soldiers arrived to stop the stone removal. They held up the contractors' carts until Woolley devised the brilliant strategy of employing the workers on the Germans' behalf. Then he walked proudly up to the guards at the head of his men. When the guard commander tried to stop him, Woolley asked him what he would do if force was used. "Go ahead," replied the Turk amicably, "for that will clear me with the governor." So Woolley drew his revolver and marched the guard commander to the German dump. The two men quietly smoked cigarettes as several loads of stone arrived safely. The governor was stymied. He retaliated by fining Woolley thirty pounds. Woolley tore to shreds the paper demanding the fine.[9]

Woolley accompanied Lawrence to the next hearing, only to find that the case had again been postponed. Woolley told the governor to convene the court at once, which he did. When the court was assembled, Woolley immediately challenged its legal validity. The prosecution applied for another remand and the archaeologists were asked to sign a lengthy document in Turkish. Woolley firmly informed the judge that the case was over and demanded his papers back. The magistrate refused. When Woolley demanded the presence of the governor, that worthy official refused to attend.

"I'm not going to leave until I get the papers," stated Woolley.

"In that case," replied the magistrate, "you won't leave till next week."

Everyone laughed except Woolley, who got up and leveled a revolver at the magistrate. "You will not leave the room alive unless I get those papers," he shouted. Woolley's foreman also drew his two revolvers. The court was silent. Lawrence was sent to waylay the governor and obtain the missing papers. A few minutes later, the permits were back in Woolley's pocket. He pocketed his revolver as well and left in triumph surrounded by salaaming officials.[10]

A few weeks later, the British consul in Aleppo received a visit from a high local official. "Those English of yours at Jerablus are doing irresponsible things," he complained. "They tried to shoot the governor."

"Did they really shoot him?" inquired the consul.

"Well, they *threatened* to, but they did not actually kill him."

"What a pity," the consul remarked quietly.[11]

And that was almost the end of the matter. When Woolley next called on the British ambassador in Constantinople, he received a somewhat frosty reception. Turkey, he was informed, was a civilized country.

Woolley's acts were, to put it mildly, high-handed. He preferred to brazen it out rather than use finesse. Local conditions were such that he felt he had to be firm. The moment the excavations were bogged down in bureaucracy they were dead. In Woolley's time, Claudius James Rich's terse and famous advice about acting decisively was still applicable. Fortunately for Woolley, an Englishman's word was still law, even to the Turks.

Woolley's predecessor, David Hogarth, had suffered under a series of incompetent and corrupt Turkish archaeological commissioners, none of whom had done anything to settle the constant disputes between the archaeologists and local officialdom. Woolley found himself saddled with Fuad Bey, an Arab from Baghdad who had trained as a civil servant in Constantinople.

Fuad was a puny man, city-bred, who was convinced that the local tribesmen would cut his throat at the slightest provocation. He distrusted Woolley, too, certain that all archaeologists were out to steal everything. At first he insisted that an armed guard sleep outside his tent and tried to set traps for Woolley by leaving antiquities lying around for him to steal. But Fuad soon changed his tune. Woolley was ruthless and, we may surmise, set out to reform the commissioner. Quite what methods he used, we do not know. He seems to have given Fuad a short but intensive course on field archaeology in general and on Carchemish in particular, with a lesson on British customs thrown into the bargain. Within a few months Fuad Bey was working enthusiastically in the laboratories, talking freely to the villagers, and being thoroughly cooperative. "I had reproved him more than once," wrote Woolley. It is unknown what sort of rebukes Woolley used, but Fuad was unswerving in his loyalty to the expedition. Woolley must also have used his full powers of persuasion along with coercion, as he did so often with petty officialdom. One exasperated bureaucrat who had given the expedition trouble over permits admitted defeat when Fuad interceded on Woolley's behalf. "I don't know what you have done to Fuad," he remarked to Woolley, "but he is greatly changed; he seems to be becoming quite English!"[12]

Woolley settled in for a long stay. He organized the labor force into teams of four men. A shoveler and two basketmen supported every pickman. The basketmen carried the discarded soil out of the dig and dumped it in the nearby Euphrates. Everyone wanted to be a pickman, the person who loosened the soil and had the greatest chance of finding new discoveries, which were rewarded with a small payment.

Discoveries brought not only money but considerable personal prestige as well, especially if a basketman found an object overlooked by his superiors. Lawrence and the foreman worked out a system whereby really magnificent discoveries were greeted with a ceremonial volley from the foreman's revolver. The workmen would summon the foreman, who would assess the number of cartridges the find was worth. The resulting salvo announced to the world that another important discovery had come to light. "The whole thing may sound childish," Woolley remarked, "but in fact it is such things that make the work go well, and when digging at Jerablus ceases to be a great game and becomes, as in Egypt, a mere business, it will be a bad thing."[13] Judging from the chronicle of difficulties that confronted the archaeologists, maintaining the game-like atmosphere must have been a considerable strain at times.

The truly great Mesopotamian archaeologists almost invariably got on well with their workers. Leonard Woolley was no exception. He commanded quite extraordinary loyalty from the local people and he and Lawrence lived like kings among them. They built a fine excavation house for seventy-five pounds that suited Woolley's style. It boasted, as Lawrence wrote, "mosaic floors and beaten copper fittings. . . . Woolley fancies himself in the bathroom: a gleaming mosaic floor reflecting his shining body against the contrast of the red-stuccoed walls."[14] A copper bathtub, a large fireplace, many carvings, and thick sheepskin rugs completed the imposing decor. The excavation house was always full of visitors, both Arab and European, gossiping, arguing, and engaged in the constant political intrigue that was an integral part of the Carchemish dig. Visitors were often served coffee in Hittite clay vessels. Lawrence rationalized that the British Museum would be glad of the fragments of any dropped cups.

In 1911 Hogarth had brought to Carchemish a Cypriot foreman named Gregori, who was a veteran of the Minoan palace at Knossos and other digs. Gregori needed a local man to work with him. He chose a redheaded pickman as his new assistant, one Mohammed ibn Sheikh Ibrahim, known to generations of archaeologists as Hamoudi. A tall and gaunt man with a powerful figure and a fiery temper, Hamoudi worked with Leonard Woolley from 1912 to 1946. No Woolley dig was complete without him. He taught himself to read and write, served as Woolley's political assistant in World War I, and became a close family friend. Hamoudi ruled the workers with a firm hand but always with a sense of fun and fairness that made any Woolley excavation a formidable opponent for officialdom because the workers' first loyalty was to Woolley. Many evenings Hamoudi would brew coffee for Woolley and himself. They would smoke and chat until dinner was announced. Woolley could have written a book about these conversations.

"Yes," said Hamoudi one evening many years later, "there have been two passions in my life, archaeology and violence."

Woolley's wife, Katherine, laughed at him. "You wicked old murderer," she exclaimed.

Hamoudi was horrified. "Murderer?" he cried. "I have never in all my life killed a man for money, only for fun!"[15]

This remarkable man had started life as a bandit and an outlaw but abandoned that life to excavate the ruins of Mesopotamia. His four sons followed in his archaeological footsteps and became part of a highly effective team that ran Woolley's later excavations at Ur like clockwork. Hamoudi and Woolley understood each other perfectly and they enjoyed each other's company. Each was a compulsive worker and had a lively sense of humor. As Hamoudi once remarked, they had broken much bread together.

Woolley's house foreman, Haj Wahid, was just as formidable a character. The Haj and Hamoudi hated each other. A large, handsome

Leonard Woolley and his foreman Sheikh Hamoudi, at Ur. Copyright the Trustees of the British Museum.

man, the Haj had spent many years as a courier in the British consulate in Aleppo. Unfortunately, he was devoted to strong drink and firearms. After a heavy bout with the bottle, he would lie down on his flat rooftop with a rifle and fire ineffectually on passersby through the Aleppo city gate that lay below him. Consular couriers had diplomatic

immunity, so the Haj could shoot at the feet of camel drivers with relative impunity. Traffic inevitably ground to a standstill until he tired of
his game.

The Haj's dangerous exploits could go too far. His flirtations with
the daughter of a prominent family so enraged her male relatives that
they seized swords and revolvers and set on him one dark night. The Haj
flailed around him with his official courier's scimitar and discharged
his revolver wildly. A few moments later, four of his assailants lay
dead at his feet, and another was badly wounded. The Haj was found
unconscious the next day and arrested. As the British consul said, a
murder or two could be overlooked but not four in a single night. The
Haj served two years of a life sentence but managed, by some nefari-
ous means, to have his term commuted. There was no way the British
consul could rehire such a turbulent man, so he recommended him to
the Carchemish expedition as a servant. Although some of the Haj's
ways were described by Woolley as "peculiar," especially his habit of
cooking meals with a rifle over his shoulder, he became a loyal protec-
tor of Woolley's — and the British Museum's — interests.

Woolley was to spend most of his time at Carchemish digging the
Hittite city under the Roman settlement. The Hittites were a shadowy
people in 1912. In 1878, an English scholar named Archibald Sayce had
published a paper in which he declared that the Biblical Hittites had
ruled over a large empire in northern Syria and Turkey. The Hittites
were, Sayce argued, a third major political force in the Near East over
3,000 years ago and were treated with respect by both Assyrians and
Egyptians. The Assyrians referred to the Hittites as the "people of
Hatti." Carchemish was one of the small city-states into which the
Hittites were organized.

Sayce's arguments aroused considerable controversy until Wallis
Budge bought the Amarna tablets for the British Museum in 1887.
These cuneiform archives contained frequent references to Hittite raids
on the Egyptians' Syrian domains, proposed marital alliances between
Egyptian and Hittite royalty, and a long history of diplomatic inter-
course between the two empires, which regarded each other as equals.
When the German Assyriologist Hugo Winckler dug into the fortress

mound of Boghazkoy in central Turkey in 1906–1907, he worked out a list of Hittite rulers.[16] One of the kings he identified was the king Suppiluliumas, who, we now know, created the Hittite empire from many smaller city-states by bold military campaigns after 1370 B.C. Suppiluliumas captured the fortress of Carchemish in 1354 B.C. and gained control of the Euphrates crossing. Carchemish remained a Hittite city for 600 years, until its capture by Sargon II of Assyria in 717 B.C.

As the diggers began to uncover the Hittite levels of the city, they found abundant evidence that Carchemish had once been a powerful Hittite settlement. They came across a great wall facing the Euphrates. Its black basalt facing gave way to a massive water gate with intricate carving that led to the Hittite citadel. A broad roadway extended west from the gate to an open space in front of the citadel, which protected the palaces and temple. As the excavators cleared the road, they came across some collapsed sculptured figures, which Woolley replaced in their original positions. They formed a long procession of foot soldiers marching in pairs, following chariots and horses, and shooting down their fleeing foes, as the army marched toward the goddess Ishtar and her temple. From the square at the end of the roadway a wide flight of steps led up to the entrance of the citadel. Imposing basalt lions flanked the door.

Another palace lay on the south side of the square. Lively sculptures of strange and mythical figures, demons, and legendary events adorned its walls. The Hittite sculptors depicted a conquering army marching in triumph to receive the thanks of the seated king and his family. The victorious hosts bear their shields in ceremonial order, helmets in place, bow or javelin at the ready. The captains lead their men and carry olive branches of peace and victory. Musicians and priests parade on the entry walls, watched by an awesome god seated in a lion-drawn chariot. Inside the palace walls, lions and stags prance in relief, pursued by eternal hunters living in a world of easy pleasure.

Unfortunately, Woolley and his colleagues could not relax for a moment and enjoy the luxury of archaeology without distractions. Many of the workers were Kurdish nomads, fiercely proud and independent, from different tribes that were in a constant state of barely suppressed warfare. Everyone, including the archaeologists, carried a firearm. Woolley had to behave like a king, a political equal to the nomad sheikhs who lived across the Euphrates. The Kurds hated the Turks, tolerated the Arabs, and adored Woolley's direct dealings. As a result, he was constantly receiving Kurdish visitors and mediating disputes.

Although Woolley was trusted on all sides, the excavation was far from secure. Kurdish raids were a constant threat, but fortunately one that was never carried out. Because Carchemish commanded a critical ford, Woolley had to be on the alert for raiding parties crossing to attack Aleppo. The fact that such a raid was a definite possibility was confirmed by a local sheikh, who told Woolley he would provide a guard of 2,000 men for the excavations if the attack took place.

Woolley's diplomatic visits with the Kurds took valuable hours away from the excavations. Such niceties, however, could never be ignored, for even a small lapse of etiquette could trigger a major dispute. His particular friend Sheikh Busrawi was fond of strong liquor, something forbidden all Muslims. "We Kurds like drink," Busrawi stated when rebuked. "We are Kurds first and Mohammedans afterward." Woolley, who provided drink, was soon known as "the elder brother of Busrawi." They retained close ties for years.[17]

Second to the Kurds' hatred of the Turks was their loathing for the Baghdad railway that was about to cross their territory. It didn't help matters that the original German engineer in charge of the construction work hated Woolley. On more than one occasion, the archaeologists had to keep the peace between Germans and Kurds. Several times Busrawi eagerly threatened to cut the throats of every engineer. Matters came to a head in 1912, when the Germans asked if they could dig away part of Carchemish's city walls for a railway embankment. Woolley firmly refused and the chief engineer left in a fury. When the excavations closed down for the summer, the Germans quietly moved in and started recruiting men to dig away the walls. Word of the German duplicity came to Haj Wahid, who went at once to see the chief engineer and, on Woolley's behalf, forbade him to start work. His efforts were fruitless. The next morning the Haj took a rifle and two revolvers and lay down on the threatened wall. When the Germans and 300 workers approached, Haj Wahid told them to keep their distance or he would open fire. The standoff continued for three days while Lawrence, warned by telegraph, summoned the authorities, who stopped the work at once.

To make matters worse, at least for the Germans, the laborers they employed would always ally themselves with Woolley and his men rather than with their German employers. The trouble was that the Germans did not know how to handle the locals, for they made no effort to understand them. Some months after the Haj's one-man standoff, Woolley mediated a serious wage dispute between the Kurdish workers and the Germans. By the time he came on the scene, shots were being exchanged between a handful of Germans and 300 furious laborers. The Germans even shot at Lawrence and Woolley. One bullet struck between Woolley's feet. It took two hectic hours and some desperate force before Woolley, Lawrence, Hamoudi, and Haj Wahid could restore order. Even so, one man was killed, which started talk of a blood feud. The whole incident ended with the comic-opera arrival of the Aleppo Volunteer Fire Brigade, brass helmets and all, closely followed by 200 troops. It was a tribute to Woolley's diplomatic skill that he was asked to act as official mediator, a task that took days of patient negotiation before peace was finally restored.

The Carchemish dig ended with the outbreak of World War I. Woolley became an intelligence officer and spent two years after the siege of Kut-al-Amara on the Tigris River in southern Mesopotamia as a Turkish prisoner of war.[18] Lawrence left his full and intense life at Carchemish with deep insights into the Arab character that led to his immortality as Lawrence of Arabia. He never returned to the dig, but Woolley resumed work in 1919 under even trickier conditions than before. A garrison of French soldiers was quartered on the site while Woolley tried to work out the complicated ancient defenses of the town. Woolley again found himself mediating peace and war, this time between the French and the Kurds. After Woolley worked out a peace agreement between the two factions, the Kurds decided to pressure the French to accept the terms of the agreement with some help from the local sheikh. The wily Busrawi, who was forever stirring up trouble between the various factions that passed through Jerablus, asked Woolley when the French ate dinner and quietly scheduled the mock attack on the excavation house for that very hour. For three days the Kurds kept the soldiers busy while their soup got cold. Woolley, however, quietly enjoyed his dinner as the bullets flew overhead and the dig continued without interruption.

The busy world of the dig must have seemed a haven of peace in the midst of all these complications. Woolley felt deeply moved by Carchemish. Its very position by the main ford of the Euphrates ensured the city a lasting place in history. Prehistoric farmers, Hittite kings, Assyrians, Egyptians, and Romans had passed this way. Byzantine officials crossed the Euphrates by the city walls. Modern travelers paused at the Carchemish dig all the time. Woolley dug the city just as the Baghdad railway bridge was built across the Euphrates nearby. The new bridge was, he realized, the final chapter in pages and pages of this historic site. He could stand among the sculptures, eyeing the stately figures of marching soldiers and magnificent kings and imagine the scene as it was 2,000 years and more in the past: the bases of the cedar pillars of the palace worked in elegant bronze, the dry spring dust blowing over a bustling city, and the echo of innumerable footsteps on the worn cobblestones. Twenty-five hundred years ago, he knew, the sculptures had glistened with bright colors and cedar panels covered the dark brick.

Then the image would fade, to be replaced by deserted ruins and the gossip of workers on their lunch break. The place had a subtle charm of its own, one that could come to life as itinerant musicians piped for the dancing workers. "No background more fitting could be found," Woolley wrote years afterward. "The tumbled stones, the steps rising like a theatre set for their outdoor play, the row of sculptured chariots showing off their life against its frozen age."[19]

Carchemish was far more than an excavation. The comfortable images of the past, the regal excavation house, the workers, the constant tumult of political intrigue and petty conflict, all were part of the Carchemish dig as they were a part of other excavations of this time. This tumultuous and perhaps naive world seems as remote today as the Hittites themselves.

SCIENCE AND NATIONALISM

He saw in his mind's eye every building, not as a derelict stump, but complete to the roof up, and in his imagination it was once again refurnished. He led us down the narrow and tortuous streets into brick houses that had been built four thousand years ago. Through the front door and the porter's lodge we went as if we were paying a social call, and indeed we often knew the names of the occupants and much about their business from the cuneiform tablets he had discovered in their offices.

—MAX MALLOWAN

GERTRUDE BELL AND
THE NEW IRAQ

I have not pronounced the word which is the keynote of the 'Iraq. It is romance. Wherever you may look for it you shall find it. The great twin rivers, gloriously named; the huge Babylonian plains, now desert, which were once a garden of the world, their story stretching back into the dark recesses of time—they shout romance.

—GERTRUDE BELL

THE ARCHAEOLOGISTS WHO WORKED IN MESOPOTAMIA JUST BEFORE WORLD War I were dimly aware that major political changes were in the offing. Before the 1870s, Britain had sought to bolster the sultan and his empire against aggressors to protect British trade and strategic communications. The last decades of the nineteenth century saw a change in big-power policy toward the Turks. European nations became less tolerant of Ottoman inertia and gave high priority to economic expansion in western Asia. Concession seeker after concession seeker had persuaded the Turks to mortgage their finances in the hope that railways, new factories, banks, mines, and other industrial developments would lead to prosperity. The Ottoman empire sank deeper and deeper into debt while its outlying possessions evaporated. The 1890s saw civil war in Turkish Crete. The Balkans loosened Ottoman ties early in the new century. The Ottoman empire became known as the "sick man of Europe." Every great power was keenly interested in the political outcome of the final collapse of the sultan's rule.

The progressive weakening of Ottoman authority that climaxed in the Turkish Revolution of 1908 had little effect on the day-to-day governance of Iraq. The newly formed Committee of Union and Progress, which ruled Turkey from 1909 to the outbreak of World War I, governed the obscure province of Iraq substantially as before. Some improvements in the standard of government were made in the last six years of Turkish rule. The Germans were encouraged to extend their railway to Baghdad. The British irrigation expert Sir William Willcocks, who made his reputation along the Nile, headed up efforts to carry out some large-scale flood-control projects in the delta. Archaeologist Gertrude Bell described him as "a twentieth-century Don Quixote, erratic, elusive, maddening, and entirely lovable."[1]

The Iraqis were beginning to demand a greater say in their own affairs. Some Iraqis had attained high office in the Ottoman bureaucracy of Baghdad and were in touch with Arab emigrés in Paris who dreamed of nationhood and a new Iraq. The years between 1908 and 1914 saw a gradual emergence of new ideals among thinking Iraqis, ideas of Arab nationalism, separatism, and local autonomy. Local Iraqi politicians became far more aware of the outside world, of international trends and the strategic importance of their country. Baghdad's newspapers advocated pro-Islamic movements and Arab unity. Some brave souls even displayed anti-Turkish placards in the streets at night. These muted protests were already increasing in number and volume when World War I broke out in 1914, by which time Arabs and Turks found little to agree upon. Most foreigners in Mesopotamia, though sympathetic to the Arabs' plight, felt that their aspirations were premature. They held no sympathy for Turkish rule, but they distrusted the Arabs' ability to govern themselves. Just as it is today, Iraq was a morass of complex political problems, anti-Turkish movements, and tribal and religious conflicts. The tribal communities of the countryside hated the townspeople, different Islamic sects quarreled constantly, and the Kurdish border areas were in a state of perennial ferment.

All of these stirrings had little effect on foreign archaeologists, who continued to work much as they always had, exporting most of their finds and dealing with their laborers and officialdom in an arbitrary, high-handed manner. Only a few archaeologists were aware of the new pulse of excitement in the tents and bazaars. One was the English archaeologist and traveler Gertrude Bell, who had journeyed widely through southwestern Asia in the years before World War I. Bell was fluent in Arabic and gained profound insights into the attitudes and customs of the local people wherever she went. She captured these feelings in one memorable passage: "For the first time in all the turbulent centuries to which those desolate regions bear witness, a potent word had gone forth, and those who caught it listened in amazement, asking one another for an explanation of its meaning. Liberty — what is liberty? I think the question which rang so perpetually through the black tents would have received no better solution in the royal pavilions which once spread their glories over the plain. Idly though it fell from the lips of the Bedouin it foretold change."[2]

The nascent political aspirations of the Iraqis came to an abrupt halt on November 5, 1914, when Turkey entered World War I on the side of the Central Powers. The British government had long made contingency plans to protect their new, vital oil interests at the Iranian city of Abadan, whose installations they could ill afford to lose. On November 6, a brigade of British troops landed and secured both the oil facilities of Abadan and nearby Basra in the face of feeble Turkish opposition. Basra became a British-occupied enclave. The British wondered timidly whether they should advance on Baghdad as well. An abortive campaign up the Tigris in 1915 ended in the disastrous 140-day siege of Kut-al-Amara and the surrender of British forces in April of the following year. Bloody but unbowed, the British spent the rest of 1916 consolidating their Basra bridgehead and setting up a network of roads and service facilities for mechanized transport. They also built airstrips and employed thousands of tribesmen in building light military railways and canals. Communications in southern Iraq were revolutionized in a few short months. Major General Stanley Maude led a successful campaign to recover lost ground up the Tigris in February 1917. On March 11, 1917, British troops entered Baghdad. By the 1918 armistice, they occupied almost all of Iraq as far north as Mosul.

The Iraqis found the British a startling contrast to the Turks. Only a short time after Maude occupied Baghdad, he made a famous speech in which he announced the British government's support of their political ambitions. Meanwhile, the British were faced with the task of setting up a viable and efficient civilian administration from the ruins of Turkish rule. This burden fell on the head of Sir Percy Cox, an Indian political officer of vast experience, who soon became known to the Iraqis as "Cokkus." He found Baghdad in chaos, sanitary conditions shocking, and with no experienced bureaucrats to run Iraq. So he created a British-run administrative service from scratch, designed to be as cheap and efficient as possible. The question of the political status of Iraq had to hang fire until Britain and Turkey made peace.

Nationalist sentiment ran high as international discussions on Iraq's future began. The Conference of San Remo, held in Italy on April 24, 1920, settled her fate. France was granted Syria, and Iraq was mandated to Britain. In July 1920 a serious anti-British insurrection involving tribal rivalries broke out in southern Iraq. It took massive reinforcements from India to put down the revolt, which dragged on for eight months. Cox was recalled from a post in Tehran and appointed British high commissioner in Baghdad. He was immediately confronted with an intricate maze of political maneuvering and mediation.

Once the rebellion was quashed, Cox set up a provisional government in Iraq under the leadership of the *naqib* (mayor) of Baghdad. This caretaker administration gave the British time to search for a national leader. A conference in Cairo in 1921 chose Prince Feisal, the son of King Hussein of the Hijaz (the sharif of Mecca), as the ruler of Iraq. On August 23, 1921, King Feisal was duly proclaimed the elected sovereign. The British tried to cope with the growing tide of Arab nationalism by concluding a compromise treaty with Feisal's new government in 1922. The treaty softened the mandate relationship by giving Iraq limited control of its own affairs. This covenant covered constitutional procedure and guaranteed freedom of religion, education, and missionary enterprise. Although Iraq was to become self-defending within four years, the rights of foreigners were safeguarded. Adequate antiquities legislation was to be implemented under the treaty. Feisal ruled for twelve years, during which time the treaty was renegotiated three times. Britain agreed to terminate the mandate in 1929. On October 3, 1932, Iraq was admitted to the League of Nations and became the first fully independent Arab state.

Iraq was also one of the first places where the British had to face the reality that they could not rule as an imperial power. The transition to independence was achieved with remarkably little disruption or bitterness, considering that the changeover from stagnant Ottoman rule to British imperial governance and then to direct Iraqi control took barely fifteen years. Much of the credit for this remarkable transition must lie with Sir Percy Cox and the small team of administrators and military officers who organized the effective administration of a chaotic Turkish province from the ground up in a few short years. One of Cox's key advisers was Gertrude Bell, by now an extraordinary expert on the Arab world and an accomplished archaeologist. She was the only female official in Cox's administration. In the course of her career, she set the archaeology of Iraq on a radically new course.

Gertrude Bell was born in County Durham, England, on July 14, 1868, the daughter of a well-to-do north country family in the iron business. After private schooling, she went to Oxford in 1886, at a time when few women undergraduates attended the university. Gertrude achieved a brilliant modern history degree in two years. She also swam, rowed, played tennis and hockey, acted, danced, and participated in debates. She emerged from the university with an "Oxfordy" manner, an insatiable appetite for travel, and an honesty and independence of judgment that tended to disconcert her elders. Her travels began in 1892 with a trip to Tehran. The following year she went to Switzerland, Italy, and Algiers. She then traveled around the world and took up mountaineering. After a few seasons, she was recognized as one of the foremost female climbers of her generation. She was, remembered one well-known male climber, an effort to follow.

In November 1899, Bell set out for a seven-month stay in Jerusalem. By this time she had published a travel book on Persia and a volume of her translations of Persian poems. She went to Jerusalem to improve her Arabic and travel in the desert to Petra and Palmyra. This journey was her first experience of the discomforts of desert travel, including tents with black beetles and muddy water to drink. But she chattered away in Arabic to sheikhs and storekeepers and fell in love with the East. During this stay she developed an interest in archaeology. She

Gertrude Bell. Hutton-Deutsch Collection/Corbis.

took over 600 photographs of ancient monuments near Jerusalem, then she spent the next few years alternately traveling in Europe, Morocco, and Egypt and studying archaeology in Rome and Paris.

Bell worked on excavations in western Turkey in 1902 and studied Byzantine monuments in northern Syria and Cilicia in 1905. This latter trip resulted in her second travel book, *The Desert and the Sown* (1907). In 1909, she published a major work on Byzantine Anatolia, a study of the "thousand and one churches" at the Byzantine city of Birbinkilise. Her report is a unique record of a series of sites that effectively no longer exist.

Byzantine ruins were not her first love, for she had lost her heart to the desert. In 1907, she toyed with the idea of a trip through the central Arabian Desert to the town of Ha'il. Sir Percy Cox, who was at the time serving as the British resident in the Persian Gulf, managed to dissuade her from trying this trip in 1909, for the desert tribes were in a state of great political unrest. So she set off from Aleppo for a journey across the desert to the Euphrates and the territory of the Deleim Arabs, who were notoriously dangerous. Her objective was the walled Abbasid palace of Ukhaidir, a huge castle with a fortified enclosure. She spent four days planning and photographing the site, which no one had ever described in detail before. Her soldier escorts refused to set their rifles aside for a moment, so they tumbled all over them as they held her measuring tapes. "I can't persuade them to lay down the damnable things for an instant," she complained.[3] Ukhaidir cast a profound spell on Gertrude Bell. She first described it in the most famous of her books, *Amurath to Amurath,* which was published in 1911. It was in this book that she first hinted at the rising tide of Arab nationalism that she came across in her travels.[4]

In February 1911 Bell took a caravan across the desert in bitter cold. It was so cold she slept in her clothes but still loved the chilly early morning departures, with the Arab tents being struck, the kneeling camels, and warmly wrapped drivers shaking ice off the water skins. Human existence seemed not to have changed since time immemorial.

Bell found time to make a short side trip to her beloved Ukhaidir and found that some of the German archaeologists at Babylon had visited the palace in her absence. They were preparing a volume on the site. Her own study, based on her surveys and the Germans' work, appeared in 1914. She dedicated it to Walter Andrae of Assur fame. "A subject so enchanting and so suggestive as the Palace of Ukhaidir is not likely to present itself more than once in a lifetime," she wrote. "I call to mind the amazement with which I first gazed upon its formidable walls; the romance of my first sojourn within its precincts; the pleasure undiminished by familiarity of my return; and the regret with which I sent back across the sun-drenched plain a last greeting to its distant presence."[5]

From Ukhaidir she journeyed to Babylon and then Baghdad, which she reached safely in late March 1911. She was greeted at both places with the deference due an experienced traveler who enjoyed the confidence of the locals. Everywhere she went she received a steady stream of local sheikhs and dignitaries for ceremonial coffee drinking. In Baghdad, she stayed at the British residency, returning there each evening "to dream of brightly-robed women and far-travelled pilgrims, of the clash and contest of creeds, and of truth, which lies somewhere concealed behind them all."[6]

On her way north, Bell spent three days at Assur with Walter Andrae and his colleague, Conrad Preusser. Andrae was enchanted with his expert visitor and took her over every detail of the excavations. The Germans taught her how to take flashlight photographs, a useful technique for recording dark church interiors. She admired Andrae's "brilliant and comprehensive" views and left, with a heavy heart, for Hatra, where the entire Turkish detachment paraded in her honor.

On her way home, she stopped at Carchemish in the hope of catching David Hogarth, but he had already gone home, leaving Reginald Campbell-Thompson and T. E. Lawrence digging away by themselves. She spent a day at the excavations and later remarked that Lawrence "is going to make a traveler." The visit started badly when she told them that their methods were "prehistoric" compared with those of the Germans. So Campbell-Thompson and Lawrence counterattacked, we are told by the latter, with "a display of erudition." "She was taken (in 5 minutes) over Byzantine, Crusader, Roman, Hittite and French architecture (my part)." Then Campbell-Thompson talked about Greek folklore and Mesopotamian archaeology until Lawrence barged in with "prehistoric pottery and telephoto lenses, Bronze Age metal technique, Meredith, Anatole France, and the Octobrists."[7] Campbell-Thompson ended this animated conversation, which continued through dinner, with a dissertation on "German methods of excavation with the Baghdad railway." Gertrude rode out by 5:30 the next morning, somewhat puzzled to be jeered by the villagers. Years later, she discovered that Lawrence had told them she was too plain to marry.

Neither the British nor the Ottoman authorities approved of her next exploit, a desert journey in 1913 through Jordan and central Arabia to Ha'il, the stronghold of the Rashid Arabs and the place she had attempted to visit before. She was locked up on her arrival and firmly told to leave for Baghdad at once. She did so but only after some forthright protestations. Two months before World War I she returned to England and gave the British intelligence services much new information on Arabia that was to prove of great value. In 1915, she was called out to Cairo to serve in the Arab Intelligence Bureau, where her unrivaled knowledge of central Arabia proved exceedingly valuable.

In the spring of 1916, she was posted to intelligence headquarters in Basra to study tribal politics from the Mesopotamian perspective. The military authorities found a woman rather an embarrassment, so they offered her to Sir Percy Cox as a chief political officer, a line of work she was to pursue for the rest of her life. Bell's position was quite important, as she had to see that agreements made with sheikhs and tribal leaders were actually implemented. When Cox took over as civil commissioner in Baghdad, he arranged for her to be posted there as a member of his new secretariat. She proved useful as a filter between the harassed Cox and the dozens of Iraqi visitors, often of great prestige, who called on him. She flattered, interviewed, gave presents, and briefed her boss on the points he should mention. Within a few months local leaders regarded her as the pro-Iraqi member of the administration, a reputation she resolutely denied, although she wrote that she was sometimes overcome with the sense of being as much an Asiatic as a European. Certainly she enjoyed her frequent meetings with the desert sheikhs, from whom she got most of her news. But she was cautious about the future. "Men living in tents, or in reed huts almost as nomadic as the tent itself, men who have never known any control but the empty fiction of Turkish authority . . . men who have the tradition of personal independence . . . ignorant of a world which lay outside their swamps and pasturages, and . . . indifferent to its interests and to the opportunities it offers, will not in a day fall into step with European ambitions, nor welcome European methods. Nor can they be hastened."[8]

Gertrude Bell lived a hectic but extremely lonely life, which she recorded in a series of letters home to her family. She was a woman full of enthusiasm for all sorts of interests—archaeology, dogs, photography, mountains, languages, and, above all, people. Her intense fascination with the Arabs stemmed at least in part from her sympathy with the fierce loyalties and friendships of the desert. She became a champion of Arab independence, and she was at her best when the government of Iraq was a makeshift affair and personal contacts rather than impersonal memoranda ran the affairs of state.

One issue the new government had to face was that of antiquities legislation. Foreign expeditions were eager to take advantage of the more stable political conditions and conduct large-scale digs at sites like Eridu and Ur. Excavations organized by foreigners meant that national artifacts would likely end up in foreign collections. Indeed, the Germans were pressing for approval to export the crates containing the remains of the Ishtar Gate from Babylon. Clearly something had to be done to improve the antiquated legislation of the Ottoman empire, especially to control the flow of important national antiquities overseas. Within a few months, all archaeological matters were referred to Gertrude Bell. With her characteristic enthusiasm, she sat down to organize a department of antiquities, new excavation legislation, and an Iraqi museum in which to house the nation's artifacts.

In response to Bell's work and lobbying for new legislation and a museum, King Feisal had appointed Bell honorary director of antiquities. When the new antiquities law was proposed, the debates over it were surprisingly acrimonious, for many Iraqis were anxious to protect their country's interests as much as possible and felt that a 50 percent division of finds was too generous to foreigners.

The new law was Bell's cherished project and was made more urgent by pressure from the British Museum to begin fieldwork in Iraq once again. In June and October 1919, the director of the museum at the University of Pennsylvania, George Byron Gordon, had called on Sir Frederick Kenyon, his opposite number at the British Museum, to press for a joint expedition. The University of Pennsylvania was also anxious to return to Iraq to follow up its campaigns at Nippur with a major effort at the same or another location. The two directors agreed to cooperate, for the costs of large-scale excavation were now such that neither could afford to excavate a big tell alone. A long correspondence ensued in which Kenyon stressed the need to wait until a peace treaty was signed and a British mandate for Mesopotamia established. Wrote Kenyon, "It is desirable to impress on the India Office the fact that the civilized world expects facilities for archaeological exploration, and that such facilities should be provided without delay." Meanwhile, the British Museum was influential in obtaining a rider to the peace treaty that obligated Britain to create an antiquities law for Iraq.[9]

Excavations had actually begun in Iraq on a small scale before the end of the war. Campbell-Thompson, who had worked at Carchemish before spending three years on war service in Mesopotamia, started digging at Eridu in 1918, using Indian soldiers. Eridu had long had a reputation for being an extremely ancient city, largely because the Babylonian creation legends stated that it was the primordial settlement. Eridu was the home of the Sumerian god Enki and lay 22.5 kilometers south of Ur in a desolate landscape. Constant winds swept the dust-filled landscape and made excavation a misery. Campbell-Thompson covered the site with small trial pits, about 1.8 meters square, which he excavated with the greatest care. He was frustrated when the trial pits yielded only quantities of loose sand and accumulations of incomprehensible mud brick. He lacked the facilities to reach the mud-brick structures beneath the overburden. His trial-pit method helped but little in locating the early city of Eridu, which had been abandoned in about 2400 B.C. Campbell-Thompson also made small soundings at nearby Ur, and these excavations were so promising that they encouraged the British Museum to work at this hitherto almost untouched site.

The first British Museum excavations at Ur were on a very limited scale. Henry R. Hall, who was later to become keeper of the Department of Egyptian and Assyrian Antiquities in the museum, took charge of the work. He opened trenches at Ur, Eridu, and a small mound near the former named al-'Ubaid. While excavating the Sumerian temple he found there, Hall noticed an unfamiliar type of light-green, black-painted pottery on another part of the mound. He could not afford to open up a larger area of the site, so he simply described this interesting new pottery in his report.[10]

Meanwhile, the correspondence between London and Philadelphia continued with Kenyon telling Gordon that no excavations would be permitted in Iraq until a peace treaty in Turkey was signed and the Iraqi government could afford the expense of administering excavations. Political conditions were also quite unsettled as a result of an insurrection against the British in 1920. In March 1921, Kenyon informed Gordon that the Colonial Office had taken over Iraq and Colonel T. E. Lawrence would be responsible for administration of archaeology. Gordon and Lawrence met in London in fall 1921, but there were further delays until a director of antiquities could be appointed locally. Finally, in January 1922, Lawrence wrote to Gordon, telling him that they were now in a position to consider permit applications. "We are going to be a little particular about the quality of these excavations," he wrote, "because Mesopotamia has suffered so much in the past from unscientific work."[11] A committee in London would vet all permit applications and much would depend on the track record of the excavation's proposed director. By this time Gordon knew that Leonard Woolley might be available for a joint expedition because the country around Carchemish was too unsettled for further excavations there.

The Americans were eager for a survey expedition, but Kenyon stressed that it would be difficult for the museum to join, for its primary objective was to acquire finds on a scale that would not come from a survey.[12] Negotiations went ahead so well, however, that on June 12, 1922, Kenyon was able to write to Philadelphia and agree to a joint expedition to Ur under the direction of Leonard Woolley. The Americans would provide much of the funding, the director's salary would be split between the two institutions, and the British Museum's prestige would be what Gordon called "insurance."

When Woolley arrived in Baghdad on October 29, 1922, he met Gertrude Bell and was told that the new antiquities law was about to be passed. She wrote that King Feisal's assistance had been invaluable. "He's perfectly sound about archaeology, having been trained by T. E. Lawrence." In the meantime, Woolley was to work under a temporary permit. "In Miss Bell we shall of course have a most sympathetic director," Woolley wrote to Gordon. Bell's own correspondence revealed that she was not as thrilled to be working with Woolley. "He's a tiresome little man," she told her father, "but a first class digger and an archaeologist after my own heart, i.e., he entirely backs me up in the way I'm conducting the Department."[13]

After the passage of the antiquities law, Bell began to work on a proposal for an Iraqi museum. In preparation, she began keeping artifacts on a shelf in her home. A year later, the artifacts she had collected and her new finds were housed in a few humble rooms near the palace.

Soon both Woolley and an Oxford University expedition were working in southern Mesopotamia, at Ur and Kish, respectively.[14] Bell supervised the permits and visited the excavations at the end of the season to divide the finds between the newly established Iraq Museum and the excavators. "It took us the whole day to do the division [at Ur] but it was extremely interesting and Mr. Woolley was an angel," she wrote home in March 1923. "We had to claim the best things for ourselves but we did our best to make it up to him and I don't think he was much displeased."[15] Her visits were always traumatic for Woolley, who had to fight hard for his beloved finds. She always took an impartial referee with her to arbitrate over tricky points. On one occasion, in 1926, Woolley lost a hard-fought argument over a statuette of the goddess Bau. The referee supported him, but Bell insisted on keeping the find. The poor referee was quietly addressed by Woolley as "the traitor" for several days afterward as she carried off the find in triumph. But Bell was very fair. "Actually in the division we did very well and have no cause for complaint—though I would not say that to Miss Bell," wrote Woolley after the second season in 1924.[16]

When Bell arrived at Kish, she found the Oxford University expedition, directed by Stephen Langdon and Ernest McKay, sunk in gloom, expecting her to shut them down within an hour by terminating their permit. They were relieved to discover that she was only interested in their finds. She announced that she had the casting vote on what they might take but that she was anxious to oblige them. Her museum was growing daily and she spent more and more time cataloguing and labeling the new finds.

In March 1926 the government gave the Iraq Museum a more permanent home in Baghdad. As she started listing all the Kish and Ur finds, as well as settling the matter of the Babylon finds with the Germans, Woolley helped her design the display cases.

Toward the end of her career in Baghdad, Bell was politically discredited. She had swept aside the British high commissioner's warnings that there would be trouble in the countryside. The troubles duly arrived and she found herself increasingly isolated from the corridors of power. Depressed and mortified, she buried herself deeper and deeper in archaeological matters. Her emotional involvement with Iraq was such that she felt an obligation to shoulder the increasing workload of the museum and the Department of Antiquities. The more overseas universities applied for permits, the harder she worked. King Feisal opened the first room of the museum in June 1926. Although her health was deteriorating rapidly in the debilitating summer heat, she preferred not to resign. Run down and worried about her health and her future, Gertrude Bell took an overdose of sleeping pills and died on July 12, 1926, at the age of fifty-eight. All of Baghdad attended her funeral, including the desert sheikhs, who were perhaps the people with whom she was most comfortable. Three years later the British School of Archaeology in Iraq was founded in her memory. A bust of Gertrude Bell occupied a proud position in the newly opened Iraq Museum. It is now in storage.

Bell was a vivid personality. Max Mallowan, who was to work with Woolley at Ur, remembered her striking appearance and her smart clothes. Her intelligence was legendary, her learning prodigious. Gertrude never suffered fools gladly and fought long and hard for both her adopted country and archaeology. She made many enemies, often people who could not keep up with her. Her reputation in Iraq is somewhat tarnished today, for many Iraqis believe that she gave away too much to foreign excavators. Yet, she was often in an agonizingly difficult position, having to balance the needs of Iraq and the very limited conservation facilities at her disposal with the necessity of satisfying foreign expeditions' backers and making sure she obtained the best possible preservation conditions for unique artifacts. As a scholar, Bell tended to put the interests of science above national goals, which is difficult for Iraqi nationalists to understand. No one can deny her legacy to Iraq and to the wider world of archaeology, for the museum she struggled to organize was to become one of the finest repositories of antiquities in the world.

WOOLLEY AT UR

Nothing relieves the monotony of the vast plain over which the shimmering heat waves dance and the mirage spreads its mockery of placid waters. It seems incredible that such a wilderness should ever have been habitable . . . and yet the weathered hillocks at one's feet cover the temples and houses of a very great city.

—LEONARD WOOLLEY

"EXPEDITION STARTING OUT," CABLED LEONARD WOOLLEY TO GEORGE BYRON Gordon in Philadelphia on October 26, 1922.[1] With this terse message, Woolley embarked on one of the most ambitious and spectacular Mesopotamian excavations ever conducted. He was to work at Ur for twelve seasons, from 1922 until 1934.

Woolley was the unanimous choice of both museum boards for the directorship and ideal for the job. He was short of stature and unprepossessing in appearance, but he had an undisputable presence that impressed even casual acquaintances. This dynamic and formidable leader was by now an archaeologist of international reputation, singleminded of purpose and totally wrapped up in his work. He was an exacting taskmaster who ran huge excavations with the smallest of European staffs, relying heavily on the loyalty and sound training of his foreman Sheikh Hamoudi and Hamoudi's three sons.

Few people had the energy to keep up with Woolley's breakneck work pace. The excavations began each day at dawn and, for the European staff, rarely ended before midnight. Woolley often worked until two or three o'clock in the morning. Anyone working with him was forewarned to expect hard work and somewhat authoritarian direction. His best-known archaeological assistant was Max Mallowan, who, like Woolley, was educated at New College, Oxford. Mallowan had come to Iraq with a general interest in Greek sculpture and a Classical degree but no formal archaeological training. David Hogarth, then keeper of the Ashmolean Museum, recommended him to Woolley, who accepted him after a brief interview, partly because, as always, he was in a hurry and partly because twenty-one years earlier, in 1903, Warden Spooner of New College had likewise gotten him into archaeology.[2] It was a fortunate choice. Mallowan thrived on the hard work and Woolley's style of training, which involved dropping the apprentice pell-mell into the dig and letting him direct the work. Mallowan was warned what to expect. Sir Frederick Kenyon advised him, "You will have your own thoughts: keep them to yourself."[3] Mallowan did so and went on to become a famous Assyriologist himself.

Woolley was the ideal archaeologist for Ur. He could unravel complicated architectural sequences from masses of mud brick with uncanny skill and with far more imagination than the Germans at Babylon and Assur had had. He was a digger of infinite skill, who could dissect the most complicated of temple sequences and with equal facility recover the remains of a fragile wooden harp from the hole left in the ground by its perished case. He had a genius, Mallowan tells us, for finding what he set out to look for and the patience to know when to wait. One of his 1922 trial trenches revealed gold objects, possibly from a cemetery. Knowing the task would stretch his technical abilities to the limit, Woolley waited four years before digging it, until he felt that he had enough experience to tackle it. Iraqi archaeology was in its scientific infancy and few of the objects in the cemetery could be dated accurately. His aim, he wrote, "was to get history, not to fill museum cases with miscellaneous curios, and history could not be got unless both we and our men were duly trained."[4]

Woolley was also a gifted writer with a fluent literary style and the kind of lively imagination that could capture the attention of his readers. To him, Ur was not a dead city but a thronging settlement with busy streets. He would lead his visitors down winding alleys and into abandoned 4,000-year-old brick houses. He actually knew the names of many of the individual owners from cuneiform tablets found inside. He would point out the details of the roof design, drainage contrivances, and even the height of the steps. He had an enthusiasm for the past that brought Ur alive in ways few archaeologists could have done. His preliminary reports were invariably published only a few months after the season's work was completed. He had a natural flair for publicity, too, so a far wider audience than usual followed the Ur excavations. While the public read of royal treasures almost as splendid as those of Tutankhamun and of the discovery of the Biblical flood, his professional colleagues appreciated Woolley's ultimate technical purpose — to discover the origins of Sumerian civilization.

Woolley and Hamoudi deftly controlled the excavations, using similar management styles. Hamoudi organized the unruly mob of workers into the traditional gangs of pickmen, spademen, and four or more basketmen, depending on the distance they had to carry soil to the light railway. He ruled the work gangs with a hand of iron. A master of invective, he was at once sensitive to trouble, happiness, and genuine fatigue. In a moment of genius, he impersonated a tall, singing boatman who used his spade to paddle an imaginary canoe through imaginary reeds to a lilting song as the men shifted piles of heavy soil. Both Hamoudi and Woolley could be relied on to solve a problem, however difficult the situation. The workers enjoyed Woolley's humor, respected his strength, and dreaded his anger. On one occasion, a worker named Zuwair was dismissed for some misdemeanor. He promptly started to cut his throat in public. Woolley recognized what he had to do and pardoned him.

The Ur archaeological team was always a small one, but its small size did not preclude tensions. Some were caused by Woolley's high expectations. Mallowan recalls that Woolley would train his apprentices by putting them in charge of a part of the work, then he would make them read their field notes to him after several days. Invariably they were subjected to devastating criticism, but with a patience and understanding that not only gave a sound training but made the dawn-to-dusk hours bearable. Many of the tensions revolved round Katherine Keeling, who first visited Ur as an unpaid volunteer in 1925. She drew artifacts for the site catalogue and took charge of showing visitors around for two seasons. In 1927 she became Woolley's wife. Katherine Woolley was a dominating and tempestuous personality and also an artist of considerable talent with a gift for interesting the public in the excavations. Her skill at public relations brought much-needed funds to the expedition's coffers. But the combination of her influential position and sudden mood changes caused the staff to live in fear of her. Even the formidable Gertrude Bell trod carefully in her presence. She could be alternately charming and rude to the point of insolence. The laborers, who called her the Khatun, showed her great respect. On one occasion her sudden appearance at the scene of a bloody tribal squabble was enough to separate the antagonists immediately.[5]

Even today, more than eighty years after the dig, few people can speak of Katherine Woolley dispassionately, although they all agree she was a fascinating companion on a remote excavation. She relished the role of being the only woman on the dig, and the Woolleys were careful to allow no other females at Ur. The excavations were immensely enriched by this talented woman, who died at an early age of the ill health that had dogged her entire life.

The Ur experience was by no means all hard work or personal conflicts. Father Leon Legrain, the American epigrapher to the excavation from 1924 to 1926, remembered more congenial moments, such as "our Xmas dinner in good English style with one turkey, one goose, four ducks, two plum puddings, six bottles of champagne, one of gold sherry, two of Vermouth, and no end of whiskey. Don't print that in the Museum Journal please. I like to leave them under the impression of our hardships."[6] The crime novelist Agatha Christie, who visited the Ur excavations and later married Max Mallowan, is thought to have used the personalities at the dig as a basis for her classic mystery *Murder in Mesopotamia.*

The excavations began inauspiciously. Woolley was awakened abruptly by the sound of rifle fire only a few nights after his arrival. Crouching to avoid the bullets that were flying through the tent walls, he peered out to see six riflemen firing at the camp from only twenty-five meters away. By the time the robbers had escaped with some cash and a nice haul of personal belongings, a camp guard was dead and the tented compound like a battlefield. Woolley sent his men in pursuit of the marauders and mobilized the local authorities. Four of the gunmen were captured and much of the loot recovered. The excavations were delayed while Woolley hastened to build a fourteen-room excavation house made of bricks from the ruins at a cost of 200 pounds. The expenditure was worth it for the savings of guards' wages alone. There was no more trouble. It was typical of Woolley that he insisted on employing the convicted robbers as diggers once they had served two years in jail.

Woolley realized that it would take years to dig the site, for Ur was enormous. Even working at high pressure and at times employing up to 400 men, he could not hope to clear even a small portion of the city. The earlier levels were buried deep under many meters of later occupation debris, which was essential to investigate since these levels would throw light on the earliest stages of Sumerian civilization. Woolley had very little information to go on. Colonel James Taylor's and Henry Hall's preliminary investigations at Ur and al-'Ubaid had shown some promising results. Sumerian tablets suggested that the archaeologists would find evidence of kings as early as Ur-Nammu, the founder of the Third Dynasty in 2125 B.C. Sumerian cities certainly went back much earlier than Ur-Nammu and the names of the earlier kings were known from inscriptions, but no one knew when they had reigned, despite Sumerian king lists that extended back over 241,200 years, a period that supposedly covered the reigns of only eight rulers! Scholars wondered if earlier Sumerian history had any basis in fact. Perhaps Ur would provide some explanations.

Woolley began by digging trial trenches over the site to gain some idea of the city's layout. Nebuchadnezzar, that indefatigable builder, had erected a great wall enclosing Ur. Its limits would provide some guidance for the excavations. The trial trench sunk to locate this wall was sited by sheer guesswork, for there were no surface indications to guide the excavation. Woolley, an expert at mud-brick walls, found that most of his trench in fact lay inside the walls. The late Babylonian finds were scanty, so he deepened his cutting and immediately unearthed plentiful finds—including pottery, small bronze objects, and large quantities of glass and stone beads. Whenever the foreman or one of the staff dug in the trench, he found gold beads as well. Curiously, the workers never found any. Woolley rightly surmised that the gold beads were being sold to dealers on weekends. One Saturday, he boldly announced that the work gangs in the area would be paid a large bonus every time Hamoudi or a European found a gold bead. The bonus was three times the dealers' price. The chagrined workers promptly bought back the beads they had sold to the dealers and produced a veritable harvest of gold on Monday. Realizing that he had stumbled across an area of vital importance, Woolley, as mentioned previously, set to work elsewhere, until he and his workers gained sufficient expertise to tackle what might be royal burials. Guards monitored the grave site, but Woolley's laborers knew they would make more through the legal excavation.

As part of his chronological studies, Woolley turned his attention to the small al-'Ubaid mound six kilometers north of Ur. Hall had dug the tell in 1919 and uncovered the remains of a First Dynasty Sumerian temple, a find so important that excavation on a much larger scale was called for. When Woolley returned to al-'Ubaid, he dug into another low mound some fifty-five meters from the temple ruins. The mound was only 1.8 meters high and littered with greenish-colored, black-painted potsherds of a type already found at Eridu and previously noted at al-'Ubaid by Hall. Previously, everyone had labeled this pottery "prehistoric" and left it at that. Woolley was pleased to find that the mound was easy to excavate. A layer of light dust covered a one-meter layer of hard mud mixed with painted potsherds, flint and obsidian (volcanic glass) tools, and the remains of matting houses. He found that this small village had been built on a low hill of clean river silt that had once risen above the marshy plain. A few traces of Sumerian buildings lay in the upper levels, structures contemporary with the First Dynasty temple nearby. Woolley was certain that this small village had been abandoned before the Sumerians had built Ur.

The 'Ubaid people had no metals. Their finest products were their painted pots, which Woolley compared to pottery recovered at faraway Susa. He wondered whether the 'Ubaid people had been the first farmers to settle in southern Iraq, bringing their fine pottery and simple stone hoes with them. Was this simple culture the ultimate ancestor of all later human settlement in the delta? How did al-'Ubaid relate to Eridu and Ur? What was the connection between these simple farmer folk and the earliest stages of Sumerian civilization?

Woolley looked for these connections in the Sumerian temple nearby. The First Dynasty temple at al-'Ubaid had been destroyed in antiquity. The brick walls had been undermined and then pushed over from the inside, so that huge lumps of mud brick with friezes attached to them had to be uncovered and pieced together to obtain a plan of the shrine. The structure turned out to be a solid mass of brick on a platform approached by a flight of steps. Only the substructure remained. The temple itself was gone. One day, a worker handed Woolley a tablet that George Gadd, Woolley's epigrapher during his first two seasons at Ur, joyfully translated: "A-anni-pad-da, king of Ur, son of Mes-anni-pad-a, king of Ur, has built this for his lady Ninkharsag."[7] This foundation stone identified the temple as the work of the son of the first king of Ur's First Dynasty. It took weeks to dissect the remains of the temple, especially a great copper relief of an eagle and stags. The building challenged Woolley's architectural skills. He described it as "very gay and fanciful, the gold and color of its decorations vivid against the white walls."[8] He admired the way the Sumerian architects had graded the decorations and reliefs from ground level up to form an imposing shrine. At the time of its discovery, the al-'Ubaid temple was the oldest building yet found in Iraq. Woolley concluded, rightly, that the equivalent structure at Ur was completely buried inside Ur-Nammu's ziggurat, which still stood.

After four seasons of excavation, Woolley finally felt competent enough to tackle the mysterious cemetery by Nebuchadnezzar's wall, where he found the gold beads. Here, he argued, he might find the links between the al-'Ubaid settlement and the early Sumerians. He soon found that he was dealing not with one cemetery, but two, the later dating to the time of Sargon I of Akkad (ca. 2370 B.C.). The earlier cemetery had been dug into deep mounds of rubbish and provided a mine of information about early Ur society.

The scale of Woolley's cemetery clearance boggles the mind. He cleared 2,000 graves of common people and 16 royal burials in four years. He pegged out the limits of the cemetery very carefully, setting

Leonard and Katherine Woolley excavating the royal burials. Copyright the Trustees of the British Museum.

up base marks for plotting the position of each grave. The staff closely watched the workers, who were trained to stop at once whenever they came upon the fine deposit that marked a grave. Then paintbrushes and knives took over and another burial was recorded and cleared. It was dull work, for the graves were monotonously similar. At least two thirds of them had been plundered or destroyed in antiquity by people reusing the same cemetery or by grave robbers.[9]

The graves of the common people were little more than rectangular shafts from 1.2 to 3.6 meters deep. Each corpse was wrapped in matting or placed in a coffin of basketwork, wood, or clay. The body lay on its side with the legs flexed at hip and knee, the hands in front of the breast. A few personal effects accompanied the dead — a handful of beads and perhaps a dagger or a pin. Some food and drink offerings in pots and some weapons or tools were deposited in the matting-lined grave. The filled-in sepulcher was almost unnoticeable to the excavators, who had little more to go on than a paper-thin wavy line of white powder, the remains of the decayed matting that had lined the grave. The wood and matting survived as impressions, or casts, in the earth that, when photographed, looked like the real thing.

The first royal tomb came to light on the very last day of the 1926–1927 season. The workers found a mass of bronze weapons apparently unassociated with any burial, then a magnificent gold-bladed dagger with a hilt of blue lapis lazuli adorned with gold studs. The gold sheath was worked with a network design in imitation of plaited grass. So unusual was this find that one expert considered the dagger and a gold toilet outfit found nearby to be Arab work of the thirteenth century A.D. The local sheikh guarded the rich grave closely until the following autumn. Then Woolley uncovered a brilliant masterpiece, Prince Mes-kalam-shar's gold helmet, which was in the form of a wig, with the individual locks of hair hammered in relief.

That same season they came across five bodies lying alongside one another in a sloping trench, none of them richly adorned. They lay above a layer of matting, which led the archaeologists to a group of ten women, all wearing elaborate headdresses and necklaces and carefully arranged in two rows. Close to these skeletons Woolley spotted a hole in the ground, then a second one. Suspecting some unusual feature, he poured plaster of Paris into the holes. Carefully he dug around the edges of the cast and was able to recover a decayed wooden harp, complete with its copper bull's head and the shell plaque that had once decorated it.

These finds lay at the entrance to a royal burial chamber containing the remains of a male ruler of uncertain identity. A second stone chamber adjoined it, containing the body of woman named Pu-abi, possibly his wife, who had been buried later. The Sumerian workers who had worked on her sepulcher had quietly quarried into the king's tomb, removed some of the treasures, and then hid their tunnel behind a great clothes chest. After many months of backbreaking and meticulous excavation, Woolley was able to reconstruct not only the tombs and their contents but the burial rites as well. The royal tomb chambers lay at the bottom of an eight-by-fourteen-meter shaft some nine meters deep. A steeply sloping passage led from ground level to the chamber on one side of the shaft. The walls of each burial chamber were of stone and the vaulted roof of brick. Once the mausoleum was ready, the priests carried the royal corpse into the chamber and laid it out in all its finery, along with food offerings in gold and silver vessels. Two or three personal attendants then crouched by the coffin or bier, where they were killed or drugged before the chamber was walled up forever. This step completed the first phase of the funeral.

A long procession of soldiers, courtiers, and male and female servants now filed into the mat-lined burial pit, all of them brilliantly decked out in their uniforms and finest ornaments. The musicians bore their harps; the royal wagons were driven into the pit, with animals led by grooms and drivers in their places. A detachment of soldiers guarded the entrance. Everyone carried a small cup. As music played, each member of the court drank poison from his or her cup, then lay down in his assigned place. Finally, someone came down and killed the oxen and asses that drew the carts — the animals' bodies lay on top of the bodies of their grooms. The same functionary checked that everything was in order before earth fill covered the royal court forever.

The mourners filled the burial pits in stages, the first covering the burial chamber and the courtiers. Woolley reconstructed the later ceremonies from another royal tomb nearby, where he was able to remove the upper levels of the burial shaft layer by layer. He found that a funerary feast had been held at the site of the burial chamber. Then an offering to the god or gods of the underworld had been laid out and covered with a clay bowl before a mud-brick structure was erected over the site. This structure, in turn, was filled with layers of clay, each covered with offerings and the body of a sacrificial victim. The building also contained the coffin of an important personage who was a special sacrifice and completely buried in the earth fill of the shaft. Presumably some form of funerary chapel marked the site of the grave, but no trace of it remained. The elaborate rituals must have extended over a considerable period of time and, to judge from the more or less identical finds in several Ur tombs, were conducted at many royal funerals.

The excavation of these death pits, crowded as they were with delicate objects, challenged the limits of Woolley's archaeological skills. Hamoudi and his sons supervised the removal of the soil in the pits bit by bit until the skeletons were almost exposed, covered only by fragments of brick that had been used as the filling of the shaft. Then the skilled staff moved in, marking out the pit in squares and excavating each skeleton in turn, recording the ornaments and objects in place before removing them. It was slow work, especially when they decided to remove an entire skull with all its ornaments in position.[10] First they cleared away the soil, then they poured liquid paraffin wax over the bones and gold. Next they pressed waxed cloth over the specimen before the entire hardened mass was removed from the soil for later examination. "Queen" Pu-abi's body, for example, lay on a wooden bier with a golden cup near her head. A mass of gold, silver, and semi-precious-stone ornaments covered the upper part of her body. Her elaborate, wig-like gold headdress was crushed by the earth and hid the skull. Fortunately, its parts were so well preserved that Woolley was able to reconstruct the entire piece. It was exhibited in London on a plaster cast of a contemporary skull, which the talented Katherine Woolley had carefully modeled in wax with the features of a Sumerian woman. The headdress was reassembled on the skull using glued wire and paper and probably gave a remarkably accurate impression of the royal queen's appearance.

The preservation of the more delicate objects in the royal cemetery was almost as formidable a task as their excavation. At the time, the Iraq Museum had no conservation facilities so everything was exported to London, where the experts restored some of the most spectacular finds. One was a wooden model of a he-goat with his front legs on branches of a thicket. When Woolley found the statue, it was in a sorry state. The wooden head had decayed to nothing and the animal was a mere silhouette, the shell and lapis-lazuli inlay lay in the earth around the decayed wood. All he could do was pour paraffin wax onto the remains, lift the statue intact, and then restore it in the laboratory. The wax was melted, the earth inside the body removed, and the legs straightened and strengthened. Then the gold leaf of the head was unfolded and reshaped, a jigsaw puzzle in three dimensions. Eventually he restored the statue as close to its original state as was possible.[11]

He applied the same principle to the celebrated Standard of Ur, a panel of wood carved on both sides and inlaid with a lapis-lazuli and shell mosaic. This fragile object, perhaps the remains of a lyre box, had decayed almost completely. By the time Woolley found it, the wood had long since rotted away and only the thousands of tiny shell and lapis-lazuli fragments were left. Fortunately, they lay in place in the ground. Woolley cleared them of dirt, centimeter by centimeter, and poured wax on each section. Now came the tricky part: to separate the mosaics on one side of the standard from those on the other. The two mosaics were lifted as one unit. Woolley then affixed waxed cloth to the exposed parts of the inlays on each side of the lump of soil and mosaic fragments. Each side was, in turn, placed faced downward on glass, and the protective cloth removed by warming the wax. By peering up underneath the glass, Woolley was able to check the design as he removed surplus bitumen and earth. Once the design on both sides was restored, each side, containing thousands of fragments received a new and permanent backing. With the design restored, the standard's design was revealed to consist of two rectangular panels depicting

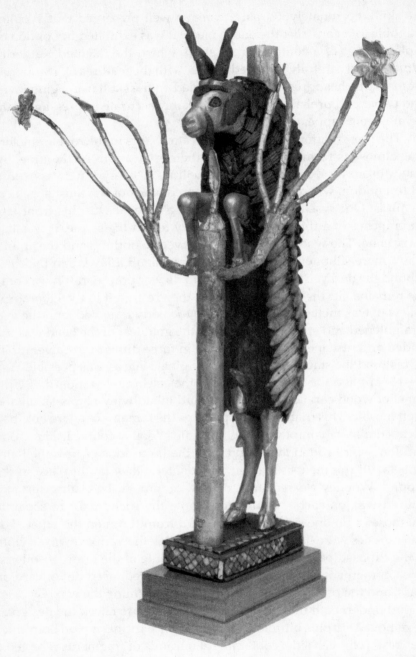

The ram from Ur, an offering stand of gold, silver, and lapis lazuli, reconstructed from fragments by Leonard Woolley. Copyright the Trustees of the British Museum.

peace and war: peace was represented by the king's feasting and judging captives, and war by a depiction of his regiments at war. The standard was designed to be carried in procession and was not only a remarkable art object but a useful historical document. It chronicled the formidable military armory that enabled later Sumerian kings to expand their city-states into an empire of international importance.

All these and other finds from the royal cemetery at Ur are now among the most prized possessions of the British Museum and the University Museum at the University of Pennsylvania. The export of some of them under Gertrude Bell's successors caused considerable local resentment and undoubtedly contributed to the difficulties foreign excavators had after Iraq achieved independence in 1932.

The excavation of the royal cemetery created a sensation almost rivaling that caused by the discovery of the tomb of the Egyptian pharaoh Tutankhamun in 1922. Woolley established the date of the royal graves by using seal impressions and tablets found in the rubbish that overlay and underlay the tombs. The levels above the royal graves date to the First Dynasty of Ur. Those underneath are now dated to between 2500 and 2000 B.C., the earliest period of Iraqi history yielding written records. Although the cemetery throws some light on Sumerian society and the people actually buried in the royal graves, the information is, unfortunately, highly incomplete and experts have been unable to puzzle out the names of several of the rulers. They have also been unable to explain the elaborate rituals in which entire royal households accompanied the ruler in death. It is unknown if such mass self-immolation took place at every royal funeral or if these rituals were reserved only for certain kings who enjoyed divine status. It is also unknown if the women were actual queens. They instead might have been priestesses who held some special position in the Ur temple hierarchy at some point in their lives. The answers can only come from the study of the thousands of Sumerian tablets that still await decipherment and interpretation, a task that will take decades to complete.

The royal cemetery excavations revealed Woolley's genius as an organizer. Every item in the excavation had to be plotted in position, recorded in the catalogue, given emergency restoration, and packed for shipment. The storerooms at the dig were overflowing. "There was gold scattered under our beds," remembered Max Mallowan. One of the exposed royal tombs looked like "a golden carpet ornamented with the beech leaf headdresses of the ladies of the court, and overlaid by the gold and silver harps and lyres."[12]

Woolley's work did not end with the excavations. Archaeology enthusiasts in dozens of countries followed the royal cemetery excavations with bated breath. Here we see Woolley at his worst. By nature a loner, he relied but little on discussion with his staff in interpreting the details of the excavations. Eager to show that the Sumerian civilization was older than the Egyptian, he tended to date the Ur cemetery earlier than his colleagues would have and also overstated his findings in popular books to dramatize his story. Sometimes his own staff was surprised to find him announcing conclusions about their own trenches, which he had never discussed with them. They never received the confidence of Woolley's wider hypotheses about the season's work. Often they first learned of his interpretation of their discoveries in the newspapers.

Woolley's dating and interpretation of the royal cemetery have, naturally, been subjected to some reinterpretation in the past three quarters of a century. Unfortunately, his excavation records are too incomplete to allow a check of his ambitious reconstruction of the funeral rites.

Woolley puzzled over the connections between Ur and al-'Ubaid until the royal cemetery was completely excavated. By this time he was convinced that the spectacular royal burials came from a time earlier than the First Dynasty temple and that they belonged to a highly civilized society, one whose ancestry lay in the lowest levels of the Ur tell. In 1929 he decided to conduct a test excavation into the lowest levels of the mound. His first trench was only 1.5 meters square, a cutting size determined by limited funds and lack of time. The single pickman cut through a meter of occupation debris. Then the finds abruptly ceased and he was digging in sterile river mud. When the worker reported the sterile level, Woolley agreed that he should work elsewhere, but wisely he checked the mud horizon against his site levels and found that the mud was too high. Woolley had never assumed that Ur was built on a hill above the plain but believed that it was built on a low ridge. On a hunch, he told the worker to keep digging, despite the worker's eloquent protests. Two and a half meters lower down, his spade revealed flint implements and 'Ubaid painted pottery.

Woolley leaped into the pit and, after examining the thick zone of mud, wrote hastily in his notebook: "I . . . was . . . quite convinced of what it all meant." But he asked his staff what they thought. They were nonplussed until Katherine Woolley came by, glanced at the trench and remarked casually, "Well, of course, it's the Flood!" That was the very conclusion Woolley had reached, but "one could scarcely argue for the Deluge on the strength of a pit a yard square."[13]

The next year they laid out a huge trench twenty-three by eighteen meters square that ended up going down nearly twenty meters to bedrock. Almost as soon as the workers starting digging, they came across eight levels of houses, the earliest built of mud brick. Five and a half meters of broken pottery lay underneath the houses, the remains of a pottery factory with the broken kilns among the sherds. The fragments came from "seconds," vessels that were cracked or distorted. So the potters smashed them and simply built their kilns on top. The character of the potsherds changed through time, from wares like those found in the ancient houses to distinctive greenish pottery painted with red and black designs.

As he examined the red and black sherds, Woolley recalled Stephen Langdon's recent excavations at Kish, thirteen kilometers east of Babylon. During the excavation Langdon had been shown a low mound named Jemdet Nasr, twenty-nine kilometers northeast of Kish, which he excavated in 1926 and 1928. The mound turned out to be an early town that yielded not only some extremely primitive clay tablets but thousands of black-, yellow-, and red-painted vessels adorned with lattice and check designs. The Kish excavations continued under the direction of French archaeologist Louis Charles Watelin, who dug a pit right through the tell and found Jemdet Nasr pottery under early Sumerian levels. The Jemdet Nasr and Kish finds gave Woolley a useful chronological check for his deep pit and some idea of an earlier society in the region.[14]

Below the Jemdet Nasr vessels were accumulations of plain red pots of a type also found in the lower levels at Uruk. German scholars

Arnold Noldeke and Julius Jordan dug at the site from 1928 to 1939.[15] When they cut a deep shaft through the tell, they found plain red vessels in the lower levels of the site immediately overlying 'Ubaid occupation on virgin soil.

At Ur, Woolley found that some 'Ubaid burials had been dug into the clean and sterile river silt that underlay the centuries-old potters' workshop. The silt was more than three meters deep, a uniform, water-laid deposit of Euphrates mud. And, again, human occupation lay beneath the silt: three superimposed floor levels of mud-brick and reed houses associated with 'Ubaid pottery identical to that from the original al-'Ubaid site. The basal huts lay on a stiff, green clay, where all traces of human activity ceased, once a swampy marsh, and the "bottom of Mesopotamia." Apparently, the first occupants of Ur had tipped their rubbish into the marsh and had gradually built up a low mound that formed the core of the later city.

The Ur dig took Sumerian civilization and its predecessors down to a baseline of sterile soil. Once the German trenches at Uruk were completed, Woolley could define a series of cultural stages that documented southern Mesopotamian society: what had begun as simple peasant villages eventually became a complex urban civilization.

The excavation of the so-called Flood Pit at Ur gave Woolley a unique chance to exercise his fluent pen. Here, he claimed, was not only evidence of a great flood in the area popularly associated with the Garden of Eden but also archaeological confirmation of the great deluge described in Assyrian and Sumerian epics. To Woolley, the 'Ubaid people of pre-flood times had not been obliterated by the deluge but had survived the waters to plant the seeds of Sumerian civilization. "And among the things they handed down to their successors was the story of the Flood; that must have been so, for none but they could have been responsible for it."[16] Woolley pointed out that Noah's flood was not a Hebrew story but a Sumerian one, taken over by the Hebrews with only minor modification. Even much of the phrasing was identical, he claimed. The evidence at Ur suggested a huge flood, an inundation unparalleled in Iraqi history. Even the Sumerian king lists spoke of rulers who reigned before and after the flood.

Woolley traced the extent of the silt deposit by putting down test pits all round the Ur site. He found that the silt was deepest against the north slope of the mound, where the city's deposits had broken the force of the water. Elsewhere the Euphrates scoured away the flood

The great Flood Pit at Ur. The base of the pit dates to ca. 2900 to 2800 B.C. The rectangular hole at the base of the steps leads into the flood deposit. Copyright the Trustees of the British Museum.

silt, which must have covered an area at least 480 kilometers long and 160 across and destroyed hundreds of villages and most settlements except for the oldest cities that were safe on their ancient tells. "It was not a universal deluge," wrote Woolley. "[I]t was a vast flood in the

valley of the Tigris and Euphrates which drowned the whole of the
habitable land between the mountains and the desert; for the people
who lived there that was all the world." Only a few people survived
the disaster, he continued. "No wonder that they saw in this disaster
the gods' punishment of a sinful generation and described it as such in
a religious poem."[17]

Woolley's lucid description of the flood had more impact on the
general public than on his colleagues, most of whom were more interested in the 'Ubaid settlement that lay under the thick layer of
mud. This site, they realized, was a possible baseline for Sumerian
civilization, one that was to be identified as a widespread and prosperous culture in later excavations. Woolley's flood, sensational as
it may have been, had to compete for public attention with evidence
of another flood (more accurately, floods) discovered earlier at Kish.
Woolley had visited Kish before his discovery of flood deposits at Ur,
then returned to his excavation, and promptly found his own alluvial
deposit. The Kish excavators felt that Woolley had cheated them of
credit for the discovery of the flood without mentioning their find in
his announcement.

Later, Max Mallowan argued that neither the Ur flood, dating as
it did to a remote prehistoric period, nor the upper Kish flood could
be the source of the Mesopotamian narratives. Instead, he suggested
that a flood layer discovered at Shuruppak during the University of
Pennsylvania's 1931 excavations might lie behind the Mesopotamian
legends. Mallowan cited literary traditions linking Shuruppak and the
flood, as well as the likely identification of King Ziusudra of Shuruppak
with Ziusudra, hero of the Sumerian flood story. The Shuruppak flood
dates to ca. 2750 B.C. Today, archaeologists and language specialists
alike doubt that the Ur, Kish, or even the Shuruppak floods could
be the source of Mesopotamian flood narratives. They think they are
merely evidence for endemic flooding in the flat terrain of southern
Mesopotamia.

∞∞

Season after season, extraordinary archaeological discoveries continued to come from the ancient city. Woolley's workmen cleared
the great ziggurat of Ur-Nammu, which had been little more than a

sandy hill up which British cavalrymen had ridden their horses in 1915. He worked on Nebuchadnezzar's city and also uncovered dozens of crowded Sumerian dwellings. Innumerable artifacts of diverse types came from these digs, including thousands of cuneiform tablets from all periods of Iraqi history. Eight hundred of these tablets are inscribed with Sumerian literary texts, which have enabled George Gadd, Samuel Kramer, and other cuneiform experts to decipher many Sumerian myths, epic tales, and other literary masterpieces.

The Ur campaigns continued until 1934, when changing political conditions and a feeling that a period of study and publication was needed caused the two museums to shut down excavations. Woolley wrote most of the nine massive volumes that report on the excavation. The epigraphers have published eight volumes of Ur texts so far. Leonard Woolley never worked at Ur again, but enjoyed a long and distinguished career excavating elsewhere in southwestern Asia until his death in 1960. His achievement at Ur can only be described as prodigious. Few archaeologists have ever matched his pace of work and flair for brilliant, scientific discovery.

NATIONALISM AND ARCHAEOLOGY

In spite of occasional mishaps which were due to extremes of cold, heat, rain and wind in turn, we lived in reasonable comfort and fed off the land on fresh food prepared by a succession of cooks, Persian and Indian; some were the worse for drink, others the worse for sobriety; our domestic needs were catered for by an ample supply of Arab servants who arrived thin and left rotund; our Major Domo was a Nestorian named Michael, who might have stepped out of an El Greco painting. Our healthy open air lives made for voracious appetites and apart from the occasional stomach casualties, we suffered from no serious ailments. Life on a dig is conducive to *mens sana in corpore sano*.

—MAX MALLOWAN

THE CLOSE OF LEONARD WOOLLEY'S EXCAVATIONS AT UR MARKED THE END OF A heroic era in archaeology that saw unlicensed treasure hunting replaced by scientific digging focused on solving specific historical problems. The Ur excavations were virtually the last of their kind, a massive operation conducted almost single-handedly by a lone archaeologist who relied on a few assistants to help him supervise the trenches. Woolley employed huge numbers of laborers and moved prodigious quantities of earth with dramatic results. But his excavations, like those of many of his similarly inclined contemporaries, skimped on record keeping and detail, to the point that no one can verify his account of Ur's royal funerals. By 1930, excavation on the grand scale was on the way out.

Woolley and his contemporaries had trained a generation of specialist archaeologists who further refined their digging methods and made the excavation of Sumerian and Assyrian cities a highly specialized craft. The study of cuneiform had also advanced to the point where the linguistic skill needed to make a serious contribution to decipherment and interpretation took years to acquire.

The 1930s and 1940s saw the dawning of the age of the specialist, a period when smaller-scale excavations became the rule of the day and conclusions were based on meticulously researched data. Where gifted amateurs had once worked on excavations and clay tablets, fully qualified professional scholars with interests in cuneiform or some other narrow expertise now took over. As more data came from the new excavations, so academic specializations become ever more narrowly focused and esoteric. This natural fragmentation of specialties was the logical response to large bodies of new information.

As specialization developed, so did team excavations — pioneered on a limited scale by the Germans and by Woolley — in which an archaeologist worked in the field with architects, epigraphers, and other experts in residence on the site. The new teams worked more slowly than their predecessors had. The limited budgets of the Depression often meant smaller budgets and less extensive excavations.

The discoveries of the specialists were not necessarily as spectacular as those of the pioneers. Many of them were little known outside archaeological textbooks or academic journals. Apart from the usual city excavations, the range of archaeological inquiry was extraordinary, encompassing the beginnings of farming in Mesopotamia to over 11,000 years ago, digs into the lowest levels of the great Kuyunjik mound, extensive landscape surveys, and investigations of early Islamic cities. Teams of experts surveyed thousands of kilometers of ancient field and irrigation systems, reconstructed Sumerian temples from almost invisible mud-brick foundations, and discovered an astonishing diversity of Sumerian literature. The research of the 1930s to 1970s produced the first flowing narrative of Mesopotamian history that was rich in detail but still full of unanswered questions. The story of the specialists is no anticlimax but rather the logical and exciting culmination of over a century of intensive archaeological research.

The relatively settled political conditions in Iraq during the late 1920s and early 1930s gave great impetus to the development of specialist excavation. Perhaps the most famous was the German expedition to Uruk, which had been thoroughly probed by Walter Andrae back in 1912. Andrae was also behind the new expedition but the actual field-work was in the hands of two younger archaeologists, Julius Jordan and Arnold Noldeke. The Germans followed the meticulous principles laid down by their predecessors in an excavation campaign that lasted from 1928 to 1939. William Kennett Loftus had worked at Uruk in 1854 and recovered Parthian slipper coffins as well as some Sumerian cone mosaic fragments (see Chapter 11). The Germans arrived at the site with much more background information at their disposal. Andrae had noticed in 1912 that the early levels outcropped near the surface on some eroded portions of the site. The new expedition concentrated on these areas and spent years excavating two temple complexes. As Andrae had done at Assur, the excavators dissected the two shrine areas brick by brick. One complex, known as Eanna, contained a succession of large structures that had been demolished to make room for their successors. The other, Kullaba, consisted of a high terrace upon which stood the so-called White Temple, a building with a long central chamber and rooms arranged symmetrically on either side. The terrace contained the remains of earlier shrines, which, unlike those in Eanna, had not been demolished to make way for later buildings. The unraveling of the complicated sequences of architectural events in these two building complexes turned out to be one of the most demanding feats of excavation ever carried out in Iraq.

When Leonard Woolley excavated the al-'Ubaid site, a settlement of humble reed houses whose inhabitants made black-painted pottery from a greenish clay, he assumed that these "Ubaid people" were the earliest farmers to settle in southern Mesopotamia. Years of subsequent research have suggested that he was probably right. But who were their descendants? How had the primordial farming settlements of the south developed into much more complex societies? Who were the ancestors of the Sumerians?

Walter Andrae was well aware of the potential of the inconspicuous clay potsherd to reveal changes in Mesopotamian society through time. He took careful note of changing pottery styles as he dug a deep cutting into the base of Assur's great mounds before World War I. The lower levels of the mounds contained little but pot fragments, so analysis of these artifacts seemed the most logical way to examine the antecedents of the Sumerians. Because Uruk was known to be one of the earliest of all Sumerian cities, it was a natural place to probe for ancestors. The Germans cut a deep trench into the city in 1930–1931, in an attempt to find the very earliest settlement on the site. They knew there had originally been two religious precincts at Uruk but, as they cut through thick layers below the Sumerian city, they discovered that the two ceremonial zones of earlier times had merged into one, the predecessor of the large Sumerian temples of later centuries.[1]

From these layers the workers recovered thousands of painted potsherds identical to those from the small Jemdet Nasr site near Kish excavated by the English archaeologist Stephen Langdon from 1926 to 1928. Jemdet Nasr pottery also came from the lower levels of Ur, well above the 'Ubaid layers. At Uruk, the Jemdet Nasr vessels gave way to a wheel-made pottery that was, at the time, unique to Uruk; so the Germans named it Uruk ware. The Uruk trench appeared to go back further than an equivalent cutting at Kish, where only Jemdet Nasr pottery came to light. At the base of Uruk, the Germans found traces of a small settlement with characteristic 'Ubaid pot fragments, similar to those at the bottom of Ur.

Here, then, was a credible genealogy for the Sumerians. In 1929, a conference of archaeologists in Baghdad agreed that the 'Ubaid period was the earliest human settlement in southern Iraq, that it was followed by the Uruk and Jemdet Nasr periods, and then by the Early Dynastic period of Sumerian civilization. Two years later the Eighteenth International Conference of Orientalists, held in Leiden, dated the 'Ubaid period from 4000 to 3500 B.C., Uruk from 3500 to 3000 B.C., and Jemdet Nasr from 3200 to 2800 B.C. At this conference, the eminent anthropologist and archaeologist Henri Frankfort argued that the 'Ubaid people had been the original ancestors of the Sumerians.[2] But Julius Jordan, fresh from the Uruk excavations, disagreed. He claimed that the Uruk people were the Sumerians and that they had displaced the 'Ubaid people. At the time, little was known of the 'Ubaid people and their achievements, but, as it turned out, Frankfort was right. Later excavations at Eridu, reputedly the earliest Sumerian city, demonstrated the great degree of cultural continuity between Uruk and 'Ubaid.

But the identity of the earliest Mesopotamian farmers still remained a mystery. Woolley and others believed that they had settled on the southern delta before 4000 B.C. but had probably flourished in the north before then. The search for 'Ubaid ancestors shifted northward to higher ground. Walter Andrae had found pre-Sumerian occupation at Assur, forty-eight kilometers downstream of Nineveh. But how far north had Sumerian civilization and its predecessors extended? Were the origins of the 'Ubaid people to be found in Assyria? Perhaps the answer would come from Nineveh. In 1930 Reginald Campbell-Thompson and Max Mallowan came to Kuyunjik to make a sounding to the base of the great mound once ransacked by Austen Henry Layard and Hormuzd Rassam before being tunneled and undermined by dozens of treasure hunters later in the nineteenth century.[3] Campbell-Thompson had dug briefly at the site with only ten men from 1927 to 1928, completing the excavation of the temple of Tabu, work that had been started in 1905, and digging further in Ashurbanipal's palace.

The easy-going Campbell-Thompson had learned archaeology at Carchemish. He was an epigrapher by training, with little interest in excavation except as a way of recovering clay tablets. He found the region much changed. Mosul had expanded and now boasted plenty of automobiles and a second Bridge of Boats. Many traditional customs, such as the veil, were less prevalent. Nebi Yunus had a new mosque. Campbell-Thompson paid his workmen ten pence a day (Rassam had paid four pence), tolerated some stealing of small antiquities, and controlled his quarrelsome men by letting it be known that instant dismissal awaited brawlers. He even had a truck to transport his finds. The mound had been fortified by the Turks in World War I. He had a moment of excitement when he submitted a sample of a waxlike substance, seemingly a mineral, from a sulphur spring near Kuyunjik to an expert in England for analysis. This substance is not Assyrian at all, came the reply. The sample was highly explosive nitroglycerine!

Campbell-Thompson and Mallowan returned for another season in 1931 with a larger labor force. Campbell-Thompson was chronically indecisive and could not make up his mind where to excavate.

Mallowan argued with him ferociously and took charge of the vertical pit that the expedition sank into the lower, pre-Assyrian levels of the mound in front of the Ishtar temple. Meanwhile, Campbell-Thompson focused on tablet recovery and examining the terrain around the ancient city. A countryman by birth, he had a fine eye for landscape and identified a dam built by King Shalmaneser III some distance from Kuyunjik. Six years later, Thorkild Jacobsen and Seton Lloyd traced the course of a long canal built by the engineer king, complete with an aqueduct that spanned a deep ravine and was constructed with three arches and 2 million stone blocks transported from sixteen kilometers away. The aqueduct doubled as a bridge in the dry season. The winding route of the canal brought water 116 kilometers to Nineveh and was part of a network of eighteen such waterways, eloquent testimony to the importance of irrigation in Assyrian life.[4]

Mallowan laid out a trench twenty-three by fifteen meters on the top of the mound, on the assumption that he would have to dig a very deep cutting indeed. The workmen reached the base of the Assyrian levels at four meters, then dug down for another twenty-two meters of earlier occupation. As the trench grew deeper, the parsimonious Campbell-Thompson tried to stop the dig on the grounds of economy, but Mallowan persisted, pointing out that they would be wasting a great deal of money if they stopped at this point. The vertical trench was difficult to dig, for earth removal was laborious and tricky, even frightening. At first the diggers used a spiral stairway cut into the trench wall. But the upper levels were so soft that the walls had to be sloped to avoid slippage. Eventually a chain of workers standing on wall steps passed baskets of earth from hand to hand. Mallowan reached bedrock at twenty-seven meters below the surface, using a tiny, four-meter-square cutting.

The trench passed through thick Akkadian levels, where Mallowan uncovered a magnificent bronze head of an Akkadian king, possibly Sargon I of Akkad (ca. 2370 B.C.). This head is one of the great art treasures of Iraq, depicting the king as an aquiline-nosed ruler of great authority. Below the Akkadian levels came traces of a prosperous settlement contemporary with the Early Dynastic period of the south. Deep Uruk levels underlay this occupation, themselves preceded by 'Ubaid ware, and beneath that a horizon containing highly characteristic painted pottery, known from the site of Tell Halaf on the Khabur River west-northwest of Nineveh.

Life-sized head in bronze of an Akkadian king, perhaps Sargon I. Found by Campbell-Thompson and Mallowan at Nineveh. Scala/Art Resource, NY.

The Tell Halaf–like potsherds recovered from immediately under the 'Ubaid levels at Kuyunjik caused particular interest. From 1911 to 1914 and in 1929, Baron Max von Oppenheim had excavated the Tell Halaf mound and, in digging an Iron Age palace there, came across earlier levels containing brilliant, polychrome pottery.[5] The potsherds had been brought to the surface by the Iron Age people who had dug the foundations of the palace. No one could date this "Halafian" ware until Mallowan found it at Kuyunjik and estimated it to date from as early as 5000 B.C.

Below the Halaf levels lay a scatter of potsherds of a type found from 1912 to 1914 at Samarra on the Tigris upstream of Baghdad. At the very base of the mound, Mallowan recovered eleven incised potsherds of a hitherto-unknown type. Kuyunjik had been not only a flourishing Sumerian city but a town for centuries before that, probably as long as some of the oldest settlements in southern Iraq. For twelve years the earliest inhabitants of Nineveh were known only from these eleven mysterious potsherds.

The deep trench at Kuyunjik was an extraordinary piece of excavation. "We were all thankful to come out of it alive, except the workmen who thoroughly enjoyed the job," wrote Mallowan many years later, "The like of it had never been done before, and is not likely to be done again."[6] Campbell-Thompson was so economical a digger that the entire operation cost only 1,700 pounds. He solemnly returned the unexpended balance of the grant—eleven pence in postage stamps—to the private sponsor.

Campbell-Thompson had noticed Halafian pottery on the surface of a small mound named Arpachiyah, six kilometers east of Nineveh. In 1932 Max Mallowan spent a season on the site under the aegis of the British School of Archaeology in Iraq.[7] He uncovered four levels of 'Ubaid houses and a contemporary cemetery underlain by eleven earlier settlements of circular, domed clay houses built on stone foundations. Some of the buildings may have been shrines associated with burials. He also uncovered caches of painted pottery and numerous figurines of bulls and women. Some traces of Halafian and early Nineveh occupations came from the lowest levels. Again, these lowermost discoveries were too scanty for anyone to establish their precise relationship to later occupations. But Mallowan had reason to be well satisfied with his excavations. It was now clear that the highly distinctive Halafian culture in the north that had flourished before the 'Ubaid had been preceded by even earlier farming cultures known from a only few potsherds at Kuyunjik and Arpachiyah.

While Mallowan was working at Kuyunjik and Arpachiyah, the Americans excavated in several other areas of Iraq. From the 1930s onward, the University of Pennsylvania dug at the mound of Tepe Gawra, sixteen kilometers northeast of Nineveh near the Zagros foothills. E. A. Speiser embarked on an ambitious excavation to dig the entire twenty-two meters of the mound but soon revised his plans when funds ran low. Still, the expedition found twenty levels of occupation. The earliest, the Halafian, was followed by 'Ubaid and Uruk phases, each of which contained a series of elaborate temple structures. At this site, Speiser traced the development of a small country town that flourished for over 4,000 years, from the sixth to second millennia B.C. The excavations showed that the northern plains had been the home of a prosperous culture in the fourth millennium B.C., a culture that was just as vigorous as those to the south.[8]

In 1919, John D. Rockefeller Jr. financed the Oriental Institute of the University of Chicago, under the directorship of the Egyptologist James H. Breasted, to study ancient civilizations. After some seasons of work in Egypt, the institute extended its operations to Asia Minor and Mesopotamia. In 1927 and 1928, an initial expedition to Khorsabad found the site looted and neglected. A stone head of King Sargon II was being used as a chopping block in a local village. The Oriental Institute's archaeologists had worked in Egypt on less demanding sites and, thus, had to learn the techniques of mud-brick wall tracing from scratch. Serious work at Khorsabad began in 1930, lasted three years, and resulted in the clearance of a temple complex at the foot of the palace mound exploited by Paul Botta and Victor Place.[9]

Later Oriental Institute expeditions were exceptionally well financed and split into several groups. One of these teams worked in the Diyala Valley, where they dug mounds at Tell Asmar and Khafaje, using elderly but skilled workmen from the German dig at Assur to train younger men in wall tracing. The researchers set up a permanent base in the valley and then studied the modern building techniques used by the local people to achieve a better understanding of Sumerian architecture. Pierre Delougaz, the director of the Khafaje excavations, succeeded in uncovering an oval Sumerian temple by using compressed air to clear mud-brick walls and pavements, some bearing the footprints of sacrificial sheep preserved in the dried mud. He even found an imprint from the mesh of a priest's fishing net in the residential quarters of the temple. By the end of the excavations, Delougaz had recovered not only the oval temple but the remains of ten successive rebuildings of the same structure over a depth of nine meters of successive foundations. All this work had been achieved while excavating around the depredations of illicit diggers. Fortunately, the very

irregular placement of their tunnelings made the task of reconstruction rather easier than it would have been had the excavation been
completed by a scientific expedition interested in "total" excavation as
the looters' trenches lay over a large area.[10]

While the Oriental Institute was reopening Victor Place's excavations at Khorsabad and examining mounds in the Diyala Valley, the
French had returned to Ernest de Sarzec's Telloh, the Sumerian city-
state of Lagash. Telloh had been the center of an archaeological scandal in 1924, when an illegally exported collection of statues of Gudea
appeared on the European and American markets and was snapped
up rapidly by collectors (see Chapter 16). The French government
decided to apply for permission to reopen the site and provided a
subsidy and a warship to support the expedition. For four seasons,
from 1929 to 1933, Abbé de Genouillac, André Parrot, and others excavated where Sarzec had left off. They searched unsuccessfully for
royal tombs, recovered a large number of artifacts, and found traces
of Uruk and 'Ubaid occupation in the lower horizons. The French
excavations were not as rigorous as those of the Germans and the
Americans, but they were a team effort, with an architect and epigrapher on-site.[11]

After digging at Telloh, the French turned their attention to Larsa,
southeast of Uruk, a site tested by Loftus from 1853 to 1854 and by
Andrae in 1903.[12] In subsequent years, tomb robbers had tunneled
into Larsa in search of sculptures and portable artifacts. So brazen did
the illegal excavators become that the Iraqi Department of Antiquities
arranged for British Royal Air Force airplanes to buzz and disperse
them, without much success. Officially, the site was put under guard,
but the looting continued until the beginning of the French excavations in 1933. By then, the site looked like a battlefield. Preliminary
diggings were promising and soon yielded a rich harvest of architectural information and over 200 cuneiform tablets. But the project came
to an abrupt end when the antiquities law was reformed in 1934.

The Arpachiyah excavations came at a time when the government began enforcing the antiquities law more strictly than before. The division
of finds from the site proved to be troublesome. Jordan and Mallowan

negotiated for three days in 41°C heat, with the lion's share of the finds going to Iraq. Then it took five months and a vote of the cabinet for Mallowan to be given permission to export his finds. His was the last expedition to be treated so generously in a time of rising nationalistic fervor and increasing resentment of foreign archaeologists and their acquisitive exports.[13]

On October 3, 1932, Iraq became the first fully independent Arab state. King Feisal died in September of the following year and was succeeded by Prince Ghazi, a young and inexperienced ruler. A group known as Iha al'-Watana (the National Brotherhood Party) took control of the government and embarked on a more nationalistic course.

The new climate came with the appointment of a new antiquities director, Yemen-born Sati al-Husri, a celebrated figure in the Islamic world and a once-influential teacher in the Imperial Ottoman Service. He was also a fervent nationalist for Iraq. King Feisal had asked him to reorganize education in Iraq, but al-Husri, realizing his views on the subject were radical compared with those of his future colleagues, accepted the post of director of antiquities instead. Sati recognized that there was strong interest among the younger, restless generation in the new nation's heritage, so he focused his attention on sites dating to the Abbasid caliphate and embarked on restorations of Islamic sites of all kinds, especially monuments in Baghdad.[14]

The Department of Antiquities carried out some notable restorations, but the nationalistic Sati had little taste for foreign excavators. He revised Gertrude Bell's ten-year-old antiquities law in 1934, severely limiting the ability of overseas excavators to remove their finds from Iraq. A propaganda campaign preceded the new legislation, which alleged that Iraq had been robbed of its antiquities by foreign expeditions operating under the previous, more liberal law. The response was predictable. Nearly all foreign researchers withdrew from Iraq. The French were about to shift their attention from Telloh to Larsa but withdrew to Syria and started work at the city of Mari.[15] Max Mallowan left Arpachiyah and started work over the border on Syria's Khabur River. Leonard Woolley, who had already finished his work at Ur, attacked the new restrictions in no uncertain terms and pointed out that eleven expeditions had worked in Iraq in 1933, whereas only three returned in 1935, all of them long-term projects. He defended the export of the Standard of Ur and the two goat figures from the royal cemetery on the grounds that they could not have been restored successfully with local facilities at the time. If, he wrote, there are no concessions, there will be no foreign excavations in Iraq.

The ambitious Sati also planned a new museum to replace the ramshackle buildings of the original institution founded by Gertrude Bell. German architects produced a magnificent design, to be built on the west bank of the Tigris in the heart of Baghdad. There was a danger that some other government department would appropriate the site, so Sati erected an imposing entrance in the Assyrian style, flanked by two winged bulls unearthed some years earlier at Khorsabad. The museum that rose behind this entrance was not built until 1966.

In 1936, two American-trained Iraqis returned from the Oriental Institute, one a cuneiform expert, the other an archaeologist named Fuad Safar. Their arrival gave Sati al-Husri the chance to sponsor Iraqi-led excavations. He set Safar and an architect to work on Islamic sites, notably at Samarra, the short-lived ninth-century capital of the Caliphs, and at Wasit, a once-prosperous city near Kut.

During the 1920s and 1930s, the Iraq Department of Antiquities had made important progress and had developed its own photographic and conservation laboratories. The Iraq Museum was now housed in a large, if old, building and had developed important collections of its own. Increasingly, the Iraqis were taking on responsibility for archaeological research in their country. By the late 1930s the level of foreign activity had dropped sharply. Only some long-term excavations by the Oriental Institute of the University of Chicago and the University of Pennsylvania museum and by the Germans at Uruk were still in progress. Even these shut down as the clouds of World War II gathered on the horizon.

When Jordan was recalled to Germany after serving as adviser to the Department of Antiquities, the Iraqis sought British technical assistance instead. Seton Lloyd was appointed archaeological adviser in 1939.[16] He was present at the department's first large-scale excavations on a non-Islamic site in 1940, at Tell 'Uqair, eighty kilometers south of Baghdad. Tell 'Uqair is a small mound consisting of a temple platform and its associated settlement. The Iraqis scraped the surface of the platform clean and on its summit uncovered the walls of the temple, which were still standing intact to a height of two meters. They also found that the inner walls were decorated with frescoes and ornaments of mosaic cone bricks. The feet and legs of men and animals could be discerned, but the wall tracers discovered that the temple had been filled with mud brick to form the platform for a later structure. The precious frescoes were sticking to the brick fill. Safar and Lloyd had to devise special techniques on the spot. They reduced the fill to a narrow layer, then picked it away in tiny fragments to expose the frescoes underneath. Experiences like this one gave the Iraqis the confidence and training to conduct excavations without foreign support.

A pro-German insurrection in Iraq temporarily disrupted the excavations and also led to the departure of Sati al-Husri from the department. In 1942, an urbane, politically well-connected diplomat, Naji al-Asil, became director, giving the department renewed energy and greater visibility. He encouraged more research on earlier non-Islamic sites.

The Department of Antiquities now embarked on an even more ambitious scheme. The government was carrying out a systematic survey of land ownership throughout the country, so the department arranged for one of its inspectors to accompany each of the survey parties. The inspectors claimed each newly discovered site as state property under the law, collected a bag of surface pottery, and plotted the position of the settlement on official maps. In ten years, over 5,000 tells were located, given numbers, and dated from surface finds, providing a massive database of new information.

In 1942 the department received a bag of potsherds from a mound called Hassuna, thirty-two kilometers from Mosul. The archaeologists who examined the fragments were interested to find that they bore incised decoration similar to that of the eleven sherds Mallowan had found at the base of Kuyunjik. Fuad Safar and Seton Lloyd collaborated on an excavation to investigate the site further. Hassuna proved to be a tiny mound, barely four-and-a-half meters high and ninety-one meters across. Large-scale excavations were relatively easy on such a shallow mound, with a good chance that the true identity of the earliest inhabitants of Kuyunjik might be discovered. The site lay in unadministered tribal territory on the edge of the desert. The locals, remembered Lloyd, had "most liberal ideas about private ownership, and there was usually a good deal of shooting during the night." Car tires were worth at least 100 pounds each in wartime, so everything had to be kept chained down. The excavations continued under these difficult conditions, concentrating on the eastern side of the settlement.[17]

The lowest levels contained the remains of a tiny, temporary encampment. All that remained were transitory hearths, storage jars, and sickles with flint teeth set in bitumen. A larger, more permanent settlement of simple, puddled clay houses followed, forming the nucleus of a tiny farming community. The levels of this village sealed the deposits of the temporary camp at the base of the mound. Thousands of incised sherds and fine vessels littered the camp. A Halafian settlement overlay parts of the Hassuna occupation, confirming the sequence of human cultures found at Kuyunjik and elsewhere. Safar and Lloyd were able to date Hassuna only in general terms, to about 5100 B.C.

By this time, Naji al-Asil had the department working at full throttle. He started an academic journal, *Sumer*, which soon acquired a reputation as an authoritative source on Mesopotamian archaeology. He also arranged for Safar and Lloyd to apply their collective expertise to the ancient city of Eridu in the south, which had resisted the efforts of generations of archaeologists. As their predecessors had complained, working conditions were abominable — the weather alternated between torrential rain and blinding sandstorms.[18] From 1947 to 1949 they dug into the corner of the ziggurat and uncovered a sequence of prehistoric temples and nineteen distinct occupation levels that extended back to about 5000 B.C., to early 'Ubaid times. The sequence of occupation was far longer than that at Ur or Uruk. Gradual changes in pottery styles and temple architecture were documented from each layer, with the result that the ancestry of the Sumerians among the 'Ubaid and Uruk people was established beyond a reasonable doubt. The Eridu people had worshipped at this location, in a precinct that is known to have been sacred to Enki, the Sumerian god of water. Truly, Eridu was one of the oldest cities in the world, as the Sumerians themselves had believed.

Outside the sacred enclosure, Safar and Lloyd found graves of 'Ubaid folk, often buried in pairs and accompanied by their painted pottery and other possessions. Some of the men even lay with their dogs across their chests, with a meatbone close to hand. Wrote Seton Lloyd in a letter to his wife: "You never get over that feeling of being suddenly *among* them when you find the graves."[19]

In the meantime, the Iraqis continued to excavate other sites during and after the war, selecting settlements from all periods of local history so that their personnel could obtain training in a wide range of archaeological problems.

∽∽

As the origins of Iraqi society extended further and further back into prehistory, archaeologists began to search not only for early evidence of Sumerian civilization but for the beginnings of agriculture and animal domestication. Until the 1940s most people assumed that agriculture had first appeared in the Nile Valley rather than in Mesopotamia. Scholars thought vaguely of a solitary genius who had conceived the brilliant idea of growing food rather than gathering it. Then, in the 1930s, a British archaeologist, Vere Gordon Childe, theorized that there were two great revolutions in ancient times, a "Neolithic" (Agricultural) Revolution, when farming began, and the "Urban" Revolution, when cities and civilization had developed about 5,000 years ago.[20] Childe thought of these revolutions as two great watersheds in the human experience, both sparked by technological and economic innovations that took hold in southwestern Asia. The revolutions hypothesis was largely informed guesswork but enjoyed widespread popularity into the late 1940s, when serious research into the origins of agriculture began.

Childe had theorized that farming began along the Nile and estimated that the change came before 4,000 B.C., more than a thousand years before Eridu, Uruk, and other cities appeared in Mesopotamia. His 6,000-year date was merely a carefully reasoned estimate, nothing more. Finding the first farmers became a high priority for foreign expeditions after World War II. Robert J. Braidwood of the University of Chicago brought a research team to northern Iraq and the Zagros Mountains in 1948, the first institute expedition to visit the area since 1937 and the first to search for and excavate small farming villages.[21] Braidwood's group of specialists studied not only pottery and architecture but also animal bones, seeds, and other food remains. Botanists and geologists examined the ancient environment; zoologists searched for evidence of early animal domestication preserved in fragmentary animal bones from the excavations. Braidwood concentrated his efforts on the hilly flanks of the Zagros Mountains that overlooked the lowlands of Mesopotamia, where wild species of goats, sheep, and the ancestors of domesticated cereal crops were to be found.

The researchers examined small village settlements, many of them little more than transitory camps occupied for short periods of time. They excavated Qal'at-jarmo (Jarmo), a small highland farming village occupied for over 4,000 years. The settlement was never more than a cluster of twenty or so houses separated by small alleys and court-yards. The inhabitants farmed barley and wheat, and herded goats and sheep. Nearby lay an even earlier settlement the archaeologists named Karim Shahir, a temporary camp where the inhabitants were probably still hunters and gatherers.[22]

Even just a few years earlier, the dates of Karim Shahir and Jarmo would have been a matter of guesswork, but Braidwood had a new dating method at his disposal developed at his own university. In 1949, physicists Willard Libby and James R. Arnold of the University of Chicago had developed the radiocarbon method, using wartime research in atomic physics. They measured the amount of decay in the radioactive isotope carbon 14 in organic remains, like charcoal and burned bone, found in archaeological sites.[23] At first they dated ob-jects of known age, like ancient Egyptian mummies, then extended their research to artifacts of unknown age from much earlier times. Libby's laboratory received samples from archaeologists in all corners of the world, but Braidwood had an inside track. His Jarmo and Karim Shahir samples received priority. To everyone's surprise, Jarmo dated to 6700 B.C., and the hunting camp at Karim Shahir to about 1,000 years later. The date of farming leapt back 2,000 years in one fell swoop.

Today we can appreciate what a profound scientific revolution radiocarbon dating produced in archaeology. Within a short time, the English archaeologist Kathleen Kenyon had dug into the lowest levels of ancient Jericho in the Jordan Valley and dated a walled farming settlement there, a virtual town.[24] By the time she completed her ex-cavations, a tiny occupation at the very base of the mound had been dated to 7,800 B.C. Later generations of research in the upper Euphrates and southeastern Turkey, combined with more refined radiocarbon dating methods capable of obtaining dates from samples as small as individual seeds, have pushed back the beginnings of agriculture in parts of southwestern Asia to as early as 10,000 B.C. These primordi-al farming settlements show how the changeover from hunting and plant gathering to agriculture took place during a 1,000-year drought, perhaps occuring within a few generations. People had become farmers over 3,000 years before 'Ubaid communities flourished in southern Mesopotamia. Unfortunately, we will probably never know how early their ancestors farmed there. The deep river silt piled up in the southern delta by the Euphrates and Tigris has covered their settlements with meters of fine mud and sand.

Nearly 175 years after Paul Botta and Austen Henry Layard dug into Kuyunjik and Nineveh, we can trace the roots of Mesopotamian civilization back to the frontiers of the last Ice Age.

During World War II, the Department of Antiquities had surveyed large areas of Iraq for archaeological sites, with promising results. It was clear that human settlement patterns, irrigation agriculture, and the boundaries of city-states and larger political entities had changed profoundly over many thousands of years. Rising salinity and shifting river courses had left thousands of hectares uninhabited and caused cities to wither away. During the 1950s and 1960s, the Oriental Institute carried out a series of important landscape surveys in southern Mesopotamia, working not only on the history of irrigation agriculture but also on the changing ancient landscape when Uruk was a flourishing city. These surveys continued the work in the Diyala Valley in Syria that Thorkild Jacobsen had begun in 1935 and were completed in 1957. Robert Adams and other American scholars subsequently returned to the field when they realized that an understanding of changing regional settlement patterns through time was essential to fill out the incomplete portraits of Sumerian civilization obtained from large-scale excavations. Adams and his colleagues showed how the modest schemes of early Sumerian times became the elaborate flood-control and irrigation projects directed by the Babylonian state and the states that followed it.[25] The surveys were conducted with agricultural techniques in mind and were so successful that the archaeologists were able to document an accumulation of silt some ten meters thick, laid down since the arrival of the first farmers at the northern edge of the southern plains. Increased salinity, silt accumulation, and social change all contributed to the progressive deterioration of irrigation and of the cultivation of wheat and barley. But by the time the

Iraqis could no longer grow barley on a large scale because of rising salinity, their strain of barley had become a staple crop all over the Old World.

The Oriental Institute expeditions were by no means the only systematically planned research from the 1950s to 1970s. Max Mallowan was able to work at Nimrud from 1949 to 1960, expanding Layard's excavations and those of his immediate successors.[26] He also recovered a superb series of Assyrian ivories from the North West Palace of Ashurnasirpal, a stela recording the city buildings in the king's time and a great feast at which the monarch claimed to have entertained 69,574 guests to celebrate the rebuilding of Nimrud, and even some cuneiform inscriptions on wax. His workers cleared three wells left untouched by earlier excavators, which yielded magnificent ivory carvings, including a head of a young girl and a plaque depicting a black man being mauled by a lioness in a thicket of papyrus. This fine piece once formed part of Sargon II's throne before he moved to Khorsabad. Agatha (Christie) Mallowan played an important role in the preservation of the damp ivories as they emerged from the deep wells.

Mallowan handed over the excavations to his young colleague David Oates in 1957. Oates investigated a mound at the southeastern corner of the lower city and uncovered the huge royal arsenal of the Assyrian kings, which soon became known as Fort Shalmaneser.[27] The fortress centered around a palace and several courtyards and also contained large storage facilities for storing military equipment and the booty from foreign campaigns. Twelve experts carefully dissected piles of ivories and other fine artifacts lying in confusion in the earthen fills of large storage rooms, a task so enormous that Oates had to leave several of them unexcavated when the field seasons ended in 1963. The huge palace and military precinct of Shalmaneser III yielded yet more superb ivories, its excavation the culminating achievement of the combined efforts of twelve experts. The Department of Antiquities then restored part of the North West Palace for posterity.

These examples are but a few of the fascinating excavations and surveys before the 1970s that filled in many gaps in the complex tapestry of Iraq's past. Increasingly, the Iraqis assumed responsibility for conservation, excavation, and conservation. The character of foreign archaeological research in Iraq changed, too. The British, the French, and the Germans were joined by archaeologists from many other countries, some of whom, like the Canadians, had never worked in

Ivory woman's head from Nimrud. Scala/Art Resource, NY.

Iraq before. As time went on, excavation permits became harder to come by as successive governments fostered a heightened sense of national identity in Iraq. Some involvement in rescue archaeology—survey and excavation designed to save sites in advance of large-scale irrigation or dam schemes—was now considered compulsory for all foreign excavators, whatever their primary academic objectives. The goals of archaeological research meshed with national objectives; the work was increasingly on Iraq's terms and in accordance with the government's wishes and needs. The archaeological wheel had come full circle, from exploitation to scientific excavation, and from wholesale plundering and export to partial and then almost total local control of archaeological finds.

Unfortunately, the tragedy of dictatorship and two wars stopped all research in its tracks and unleashed, once again, the forces of uncontrolled looting and destruction.

CATASTROPHE

Today, the smuggling of ancient art is the single most devastating development for the antiquities of Iraq. If it continues unchecked, it will destroy much archaeological evidence that has not been studied or published. For certain types of collectors the provenance of their objects is immaterial. For archaeologists, however, it is of vital importance.

—SELMA AL-RADI

BY THE 1970S, IRAQ—IN ITS ANTIQUITIES AUTHORITY, AS THE DEPARTMENT OF Antiquities was now called—had one of the best cultural heritage organizations in the world. The museum, now called the Iraq National Museum, in Baghdad flourished in a modern building—finally built behind the Assyrian-style gate built decades ago—and boasted of fine exhibits, including a children's wing. Iraq also had thirteen regional museums, displays at many important sites, 1,600 site guards, and a growing number of Iraqi expert field archaeologists, conservation specialists, and curators. More than 10,000 archaeological sites were known, of which about 1,500 had been investigated. Many more awaited discovery. In 1974, the government tightened existing antiquities law even further, allowing the export of nothing except scientific samples and study materials. Looting under what was essentially a draconian dictatorship with absolute powers was virtually nonexistent. Looters were sometimes shot on the spot. Ten people were executed for cutting up a Nineveh winged bull for sale abroad.

The Iraqi Antiquities Authority also undertook restorations at major sites, a daunting task given the friable nature of mud brick. Even the most expert conservators are still baffled by the problem of mud-brick conservation, despite years of experimentation. The Iraqis dealt with the problem by erecting modern walls around such major structures as the Ur ziggurat and doing extensive reconstruction work on-site at Nimrud and elsewhere. A major interdisciplinary project by Iraqi and Italian experts in the 1960s and early 1970s carried out controlled experiments at Seleucia, Hatra, and Nineveh. They tried spraying chemicals on walls; capping walls with a mixture of mud, sand, and portland cement; and covering ancient structures with bricks of mud, sand, and 8 percent portland cement. Testing the success of conservation measures requires their monitoring over long periods of time. Thirty years after the mud-brick experiments, we know that covering the structures with newly made bricks is the most successful. The bricks were made in the traditional way, tempered with straw, and allowed to dry slowly to prevent cracking. The conservators then walled in existing structures, covered large horizontal surfaces (such as courtyards), and filled gaps in ruined walls. The greatest damage to the reconstructed structures came not from natural processes but from shepherds grazing their flocks on-site. Despite large-scale conservation efforts, many of Iraq's greatest sites were deteriorating before the Gulf Wars effectively prevented any further conservation work.[1]

Spectacular discoveries continued under Saddam Hussein's regime. In 1951, Max Mallowan excavated a room in the royal living quarters of Nimrud's North West Palace.[2] There, he unearthed a bath-shaped coffin containing a richly adorned woman. Nearly thirty years later, Iraqi archaeologists Muayard Damerji, Donny George, and Muzahim Mahmud Hussein carried out further excavations in the same area. While doing so, Hussein noticed an uneven floor in one of the rooms.

He examined the surface closely and found a shaft that led to a flight of stairs and a vaulted, earth-filled chamber whose ridge had caused the unevenness in the floor overhead.[3] A sarcophagus at the far end of the chamber contained the skeleton of a woman aged fifty to fifty-five. She wore fine gold earrings, gold beads that had once formed several necklaces, and an array of gold bracelets, five on her left forearm alone. These pieces were some of the few known examples of Assyrian jewelry, for the Medes and Babylonians had sacked Nimrud thoroughly in 612 B.C.

The following year, Hussein observed another inconspicuous ridge to the side of a courtyard. Another meticulous search eventually located the entrance to a more elaborate tomb that led down some steps into a small antechamber. Two huge doors opened into the main burial chamber, with a stone sarcophagus at the end. This time the tomb was waterproof and free of the earth that had seeped into the previous year's sepulcher. Everything was exactly as it had been when the chambers were sealed.

A niche in the antechamber wall held a clay tablet, which identified the owner of the tomb as Queen Yaba, the wife of King Tiglath-Pileser III (744–727 B.C.). Queen Yaba had laid a curse on anyone who violated her burial: "By command of the great gods of the underworld, mortal destiny caught up with Queen Yaba in death, and she travelled the path of her ancestors. . . . Whoever in time . . . removes me from my tomb, or places anyone else with me, or lays hand on my jewellery with evil intent, or breaks open the seal of this tomb, let his spirit wander in thirst in the open countryside."[4] The queen went on to invoke the gods of the underworld to condemn the violator to permanent restlessness and a dearth of offerings.

Nevertheless, someone had violated the tomb soon after the royal funeral. The sarcophagus contained not one but two women. Queen Yaba was probably the lower body, which had been buried first. The later one had been cooked to a temperature of 100°C to 200°C before burial. Conceivably, she had died elsewhere and then been heated, perhaps to preserve the body while it was transported back to the palace for burial. But who was the second person? Fortunately, the two skeletons lay with three gold bowls, each inscribed with the name of a different queen. One belonged to Yaba; a second bore the name of Atalya, the wife of King Sargon II (721–705 B.C.); and the third (and also a mirror cover) bore the name Banitu, the queen of King Shalmaneser, who reigned between Tiglath-Pileser III and Sargon II. The two deceased appear to be Yaba and Atalya, the latter having inherited some of the possessions of her predecessor. Some experts believe that Yaba and Atalya were mother and daughter, each married to an Assyrian kings.

Unfortunately, concerns about the security of leaving the undisturbed tomb overnight meant that the sepulcher was excavated in a single afternoon. The excavators worked feverishly to recover the bodies and grave goods as carefully as possible. They established that both women had been buried fully clothed. Fragments of their garments survived, which, when analyzed, revealed an absence of animal products. This discovery meant that the queens probably wore linen clothing, which was adorned with over 2,000 gold add-ons and other trinkets in various shapes. The gold objects from the tomb included a crown and diadem, seventy-nine earrings, six necklaces (combined with strings of semi-precious stones), thirty finger rings, fourteen armlets, four anklets, and fifteen vessels—over fifteen kilograms of gold alone. A superb mirror with a finely carved handle inlaid with agate and gold lay on top of the bodies.

Four months later, another even more spectacular tomb came from an adjacent room. Again, a ridge in the floor provided the clue, but this time robbers had emptied the sepulcher in antiquity. The excavators entered through the hole dug by the thieves and descended into the burial chamber with its empty sarcophagus. An inscription on the lid revealed that it had belonged to Queen Mullisu, wife of King Ashurnasirpal (883–859 B.C.). This tomb was the earliest of the three. The doors to the antechamber could not be opened from the inside, so the investigators searched for the proper entrance and eventually found it. To their astonishment, the antechamber held three large bronze coffins, two lying side-by-side, the third stacked on top of them. There were thirteen skeletons in the caskets and also a large quantity of treasure, most of it in one coffin.

The treasures were astounding. One was a gold crown made of two parts, with a trellis vine on top and a circlet adorned with gold daisies and pomegranates that fitted around the forehead. Winged figures joined the two halves. Blue lapis-lazuli grape bunches hung from the lower edge. Over 530 earrings, some tasseled diadems, many necklaces, and numerous small trinkets that once decorated clothing accompanied a golden ewer and a bowl inscribed with the name of

Shamshi-ilu, who served as commander-in-chief to three Assyrian kings between 782 and 745 B.C.

Seven adults and six children lay in the three coffins. One strongly built man of sixty to sixty-five may have been Shamshi-ilu himself. All of the deceased were buried some time after the royal burial had been looted. Who owned the treasure found with the bodies is unknown, but the objects were buried long after the queen died, one of them dating to a century after her death.

A fourth tomb was discovered in 1990 but had been thoroughly looted except for the terracotta sarcophagus and two bronze saucer lamps still in their niches, where they had provided light for the interment.

These dramatic discoveries came just as Saddam Hussein invaded Kuwait and the First Gulf War began. The finds were hastily cleaned and examined and then stored in a vault in the Central Bank in Baghdad, where they remained until after the Second Gulf War in 2003.

The invasion of Kuwait and the First Gulf War stopped all archaeology in Iraq in its tracks.

The Iraq National Museum was the crown jewel of the Antiquities Authority.[5] The collection that originally had been stored in Gertrude Bell's informal rooms had become a world-class museum. Under Bell's leadership, the museum had moved from a temporary location within a government building to a new structure near the al-Shuhada Bridge in 1926 (see Chapter 19). It wasn't until 1966 that the collection finally moved to the site on the west bank of the river where Sati al-Husri had established its Assyrian-style entrance many years before (see Chapter 21). The new two-storey brick structure had a basement and courtyard and was a suitably impressive home for the Iraq National Museum, as it was now called. The museum was extended twenty years later with another courtyard and now had a total of twenty galleries covering 11,000 square meters. The Assyrian gallery with its fifteen meters of bas-reliefs and winged, human-headed bulls was the highlight for most visitors. More then 10,000 objects, some tiny cylinder seals, others huge statues, chronicled 10,000 years of Iraqi history. The museum storerooms held more than 100,000 cuneiform tablets, including proto-cuneiform writing from Uruk and the neo-Babylonian archives from Sippar, which date to 625–529 B.C. The Iraq National Museum had become one of the great cultural repositories of the world.

The First Gulf War, in 1991, and the United Nations sanctions that followed effectively dismantled the Iraq Antiquities Authority. Severe budget cuts forced layoffs of site guards and regional museum staff. Mobs looted nine of the thirteen local museums, including the one at Mosul, where the robbers were apparently well prepared with photographs of prize artifacts taken before the war. By 2001, the Palace of Sennacherib at Nineveh, which in the twentieth century had been restored as a museum to protect the significant amount of decoration still remaining in situ, was robbed of its roof, which had been stolen for raw materials. The exposed bas-reliefs became porous in the heavy winter rains and cracked when ice formed in the interstices. Thieves broke off the smaller fragments and sold them to dealers. With no funds for conservation or guards, looting resumed throughout the country, fueled by an insatiable demand from hard currency dealers and collectors in the United States, Switzerland, Great Britain, and Japan and the high prices fetched by cuneiform tablets. Senior members of Saddam Hussein's government and some of his immediate family participated in the black market activity. The Antiquities Service tried valiantly to stem the robbery and to carry out salvage excavations at vandalized sites, but to little avail. Foreign collectors, and even some major museums, cared nothing for the historical context of the artifacts they craved.

To make matters worse, the Ministry of Communications, a prime bombing target early in the First Gulf War, lay across the road from the museum. Several glass cases shattered and the museum was closed. The staff believed the war would be over soon, so they removed only smaller objects and stored them in trunks in the basement. But the bombing continued, electricity supplies faltered, and the pumps that emptied groundwater from the basement stopped working. The floors flooded and the trunks corroded. Bacteria and humidity attacked the packing materials. The collections disintegrated before the staff's eyes, for they were unable to obtain chemicals to treat them because of United Nations sanctions. Fortunately, damage to major sites from military activities was relatively minor, except for some destruction at the Ur ziggurat and to the brick vault over the Sassanian audience hall at Ctesiphon, which had been admired by Claudius James Rich and many of his successors.[6]

After the war, a UNESCO mission headed by archaeologist Selma Al-Radi made valiant attempts to catalogue the extent of the loss and sent a list of looted objects to interested authorities, including Interpol. Unfortunately, almost none of the stolen artifacts looted after the First Gulf War have come to light. On a brighter note, the artifacts taken by Saddam Hussein's occupying forces from the Kuwait Museum were repatriated successfully under UNESCO auspices. By 1995, the Iraqi government was making progress toward restoring its archaeological infrastructure and might have been able to stem looting activity and resume conservation had official priorities allowed it. But the Second Gulf War, Operation Iraqi Freedom, descended on Baghdad in 2003.

In advance of the second war, a delegation of Mesopotamian specialists provided the Pentagon and the State Department with background information and a map of 5,000 major archaeological sites in the war zone. They also stressed the importance of Iraq's museums and the need to safeguard cultural resources. Unfortunately, some government officials paid virtually no attention to these specialists, preferring to meet with the American Council for Cultural Policy, whose membership mostly comprises museum curators and private collectors. At the time, the council's treasurer was a lawyer who represented the National Association of Dealers in Ancient, Oriental, and Primitive Art. Not surprisingly, the group pressed for, and continues to advocate, more relaxed cultural heritage administration in post–Saddam Hussein Iraq so that the antiquities laws can be amended to allow the export of selected Iraqi antiquities.

In late March 2003, the Pentagon sent a memorandum to the Coalition Forces Land Component Command that listed buildings to be secured as soon as Baghdad was captured.[7] Together with the Central Bank, the museum was at the top of the no-strike list. But circumstances played havoc with good intentions. As American forces entered Baghdad, Republican Guards occupied the 4.5 hectare museum compound with automatic weapons and rocket-propelled grenades, in violation of international laws of armed conflict. Lying only 900 meters from a strategic bridge across the Tigris, the museum became a fortress in a battle zone. On April 9, a tank company from the only U.S. forces in that area of Baghdad took fire from about 100 to 150 fighters in the compound, many of them in the Children's Museum building. When American tanks approached, they continued to take fire from the troops holed up in the museum before firing a single 120mm round into the museum's facade, taking out the rocket grenade position inside. Still, the firing continued. Instead of attacking and destroying the museum, the tank commander pulled back his tanks, thereby saving the compound from certain destruction.

The first looters appeared on April 10, by which time the fighters inside had withdrawn. As many as 300 or 400 of them approached through the back of the compound. Intense fighting still surrounded the buildings, which prevented American forces from securing the building; however, the museum staff and some journalists managed to enter the building and the curators and technicians chased the looters out, but not before significant damage was done. For unknown reasons, it took the U.S. Army four days to secure the compound, which was done on April 16. In the meantime, the staff had guarded the museum and the looters had not returned.

Marine Colonel Matthew Bogdanos, a reserve officer in anti-terrorism and intelligence, is a New York assistant district attorney in civilian life. He is also a boxer, a ballet dancer, and a voracious reader, as comfortable with the works of Shakespeare and Voltaire as with military training manuals — and he has a background in classics. A forthright man with little patience for procrastinators, he received reluctant permission in 2003 to form a small, handpicked multi-agency team of investigators, which he led to Baghdad to investigate the looting while trying to recover as many antiquities as possible. This task was challenging in a city still reeling from the sudden invasion, where crime and violence were on the rise. Fortunately, Bogdanos was blessed with great patience, terrier-like persistence, and a gift for getting on well with people on the street. He was the ideal man for a job that would have defeated most archaeologists who lacked his legal background and military planning experience.

No one knows exactly how many people, some pushing carts and wheelbarrows, broke into the museum on April 10, 2003. Much of the looting appears to have been caused by anger at Saddam Hussein, who had closed the museum except by special invitation and seemed to treat it as his personal gift shop. The intruders stole statues and pottery, cuneiform tablets, and anything portable, leaving empty, shattered offices behind them. The Iraq National Museum was devastated. Initial news reports spoke of broken museum cases and over 170,000 artifacts spirited away. Archaeologists throughout the world shuddered.

Colonel Bogdanos and his colleagues lived in the museum library for six months while they attempted to inventory the extent of the loss. It soon became apparent that the reported loss of 170,000 objects did not mesh with what he found still intact in the galleries. He turned to the museum inventory records, which turned out to be incomplete and byzantine in their complexity. The museum's staff had been too small and undertrained to maintain good records. Colonel Bogdanos could not even establish when many artifacts first had gone missing. After months of painstaking detective work, an amnesty that brought back a significant number of looted artifacts, and many days spent drinking tea in cafés and haunting bazaars, Bogdanos identified three types of thieves—professionals, people off the street, and insiders.

Professionals had removed forty of the museum's most treasured objects from twenty-eight galleries and the conservation room. These were expert thieves, who may even have slipped into Iraq before the war with a "shopping list" and the connections to smuggle their loot out of the country in short order. Their expertise was evident as they removed the most exquisite cuneiform bricks from an exhibit that displayed many such items from Sumerian to neo-Babylonian times, leaving the more prosaic ones behind. A copy of the stela bearing Hammurabi's law code was left standing, because the thieves surely knew that the original is in the Louvre. One thief removed the Sacred Vase of Warka (Uruk), the earliest such vessel in the world. Fortunately, it was returned under the amnesty, broken once again into the fourteen fragments in which it had been found. No one knows who was waiting to buy these well-known and widely illustrated artifacts, for they could never display them in public. The identity of these collectors remains a complete mystery, as does that of the dealers who commissioned the thefts. It may be years before purchasers are found for much of the more famous loot.

The casual looters were more promiscuous in their activities, hauling heavy items across the floors, knocking over statues, and trying to drag them away. Their activities damaged twenty-five major artifacts or exhibits, including what remained of the Golden Harp from Ur. Fortunately, the original golden head had been removed to the vaults of the Central Bank before the First Gulf War. In total, about 3,100 pieces, including some copies and gift shop items, vanished in the looters' hands.

The thievery Bogdanos attributed to the museum staff was mostly of small pieces of jewelry, coins, and cylinder seals, which appeared to have been taken by people with inside knowledge of the museum. In all, about 10,000 items were taken by these insiders; some of these items were returned to the restoration room during the amnesty, but a significant number are still missing.

It also appears that over 3,000 items from excavations were stolen from the museum's aboveground storage rooms, although the number may increase when inventories are complete. The looters even swept entire shelves of artifacts into sacks with their arms. Fortunately, they did not succeed in opening lockers containing many valuables, but they still removed 5,144 cylinder seals and also 5,542 pins, amulets, and jewelry items. They also did not breach a bricked-up vault crammed with lockers containing 8,366 valuable items such as jewelry and ivories from the galleries.

There is no question that the losses were tragic and irreplaceable but at least they were not as bad as once feared. An estimated 14,000 objects were lost, about 5,500 of which have been recovered. Fifteen of the forty artifacts removed by professional thieves have been tracked down, including a well-known clay mask from Uruk. So far, little has surfaced on the international market, but that is just a matter of time.

But where were the treasures from Nimrud and Ur? The museum staff was sure they were stored in the vaults of the Central Bank, which were flooded with sewage. Bogdanos agreed with them. It was one thing to suspect they were there, quite another to recover them. Fortunately, television producer Jason Williams was on hand and had a film budget, which paid for the pumps that emptied nearly 13 million liters of water from the basement. The investigators found that a rocket-propelled grenade had scarred the steel door of the vault before the flood waters cascaded into the bank. The body of the drowned shooter lay in the approach passage. On June 1, 2003, the bank's former manager opened the vault. The sealed boxes were waterlogged and allowed to dry before being opened four days later. It was an emotional moment for the museum staff. Four boxes contained the treasures of Ur, another the Nimrud gold. In celebration, the museum put the trea-

Phoenician gold and ivory inlay of a lioness nuzzling a man from Nimrud. One of the masterpieces missing from the Iraq National Museum. Scala/Art Resource, NY.

sure of Nimrud on exhibit under heavy security for a single day on July 2, 2003. Since then, the museum has been sealed off for security reasons. No one knows when it will reopen.

Bogdanos received a National Humanities Medal from the president for his efforts but is haunted by the items that are still missing.

∞∞∞

Colonel Bogdanos has not been the only one to offer help to Iraq. The British Museum, the National Geographic Society, the University of Chicago's Oriental Institute, and the Italian government were among the organizations that gave assistance to the museum and sought to stop the uncontrolled, blatant site looting that broke out as the war wound down. Interpol and UNESCO, as well as law enforcement authorities around the world, received information on known stolen items. Colonel Bogdanos lectured to archaeological societies and academic groups on both sides of the Atlantic. English Heritage, the Getty Conservation Institute, and the World Monuments Fund are among the international organizations that are providing conservation and conservation training, developing computerized site inventories, and lending their expertise in electronic survey methods.

The illegal pillaging of antiquities is a multibillion-dollar international business, behind only drug dealing and arms sales in its scope. At least 150 sites in southern Iraq have been looted, among them Larsa and Telloh. Looting in Iraq is now on an industrial scale and not simply the work of impoverished farmers with families to feed. At Umma in the south, 200-person teams with earthmoving equipment working nightly have turned the site into a lunar landscape.[8] Farming antiquities has become a business in a country with untold archaeological riches and little or no official supervision, despite the formation of a new 1,300-guard security unit.

Military activity has also destroyed some of Iraq's monuments. Although most sites escaped bombing or artillery fire in both of the wars, a large air base and helicopter pad destroyed two temples at Babylon; the base subsequently was closed. Shellfire damaged the reconstructed ziggurat at Ur in the First Gulf War, but far more serious damage has resulted from uncontrolled looting.

Although the security situation continues to be volatile, attention is beginning to shift from looters to smugglers and dealers. It will be difficult to stop the illegal export of artifacts because of the amount of money involved. An artifact that a farmer sells for $50 in Baghdad can fetch $200,000 to $300,000 in New York; thus, cuneiform tablets continue to leave the country by the truckload. When customs officers try to confiscate them, they sometimes pay with their lives, as happened in October 2004, when eight inspectors were murdered on the road from Syria to Baghdad. This replay of tablet and antiquities theft is on a scale that dwarfs that of Wallis Budge's and Hormuzd Rassam's day.

With so much being lost to history, it seems that the Iraqi government would be eager to protect as many sites as possible. Like everywhere else, however, the government has to strike a balance between spurring economic development and preserving cultural heritage. For example, the construction of the Makhul Dam on the Tigris, 130 kilometers downstream of Mosul, will create a lake that will run upstream more than 30 kilometers and flood the city neighborhoods of Assur. The citadel will survive, but the water table from the lake will cause severe damage. There is no money to pay for a coffer dam to protect the ancient Assyrian capital, where German archaeologists have worked since the early twentieth century. When given a choice between economic and cultural interests, almost invariably economics wins.

How important are the concerns about the loss of Iraq's cultural heritage in a world driven by environmental crises, global warming, local conflicts, and widespread hunger and poverty? For the Iraqis, these concerns are critical and the damage is devastating. The loss of their past hits at the very core of their culture and history, at their national identity. Iraq has long been a country divided by factionalism and tribal rivalries. The rich tapestry of more than 10,000 years of their past is one of the few ways in which the country can forge a shared national identity. Since 1923, the Iraq National Museum has been a symbol of that emerging identity for all Iraqis, regardless of religious or tribal affiliation.

The loss to all of humanity is incalculable, too. Mesopotamia was a center of very early farming and, along with the Nile, the cradle of urban civilization. The roots of Western civilization lie ultimately in the land between the rivers, a place where many of our cherished cultural and religious beliefs began. Our values and our identity—and that of all humankind—reside in its history. A long line of artistic, aesthetic, philosophical, and scientific influences connect the modern world to Egypt and Mesopotamia through the later cultures of Rome and Greece.

Southern Iraq was the birthplace of history as we study it today, a place that inspired some of the great works of early literature, among them the *Epic of Gilgamesh*, inscribed on clay tablets. Now this heritage has become a crop to be harvested and sold to the wealthy and acquisitive, usually to people with no concern for the historical importance of their purchase. McGuire Gibson, a professor of Mesopotamian archaeology at the University of Chicago's Oriental Institute, recalls visiting a Bond Street dealer in London some years ago. He was shown a bag of more than 100 cylinder seals from Iraq. The dealer apologized for their quality. He had already sold the best ones to Japanese and Taiwanese collectors a few days before.[9]

Those who condone the looting of ancient Mesopotamia have little concern for preserving the cultural identity of a great people, nor do they care whether the world's cultural heritage vanishes in the name of profit. They are selling Iraq's birthright and the cultural heritage of all humankind, which we all should collectively hold in trust for generations as yet unborn.

Does archaeology have a future in a world obsessed with celebrity, profits, and immediate gratification? In Mesopotamia, the scene of so many scientific triumphs, we are witnessing the past vanishing as if it had never been. Essentially, we have returned to the freewheeling days of the nineteenth century. Will this scenario of destruction and virtually uncontrolled looting be allowed to continue? Will there ever be a new generation of archaeological research that builds on the solid accomplishments of earlier scholars? Unfortunately, the study of Iraq's fascinating and important past remains a low priority in the face of an insurgency and breakdown in law-and-order. There is unlikely to be any significant reordering of priorities for a while, and it may soon be too late.

NOTES

CHAPTER 1: A LEGACY OF CIVILIZATIONS

The epigraph to this part is drawn from George Noel Gordon, Lord Byron, *The Destruction of Sennacherib* (1815), stanza 3 (based on II Kings 19–35).

The epigraph to this chapter is drawn from Genesis 2:10–12.

1. Austen Henry Layard, *Nineveh and Its Remains* (London: John Murray, 1849), 5. The term *Mesopotamia* comes from the Greek word for "Land between the Rivers" and refers to the floodplain between the Euphrates and Tigris rivers in what is now Iraq.

2. William Kennett Loftus, *Travels and Researches in Chaldea and Susiana* (London: J. Nisbet, 1857), 163. Loftus (1820–1858) was a geologist and naturalist who traveled extensively in Mesopotamia, visiting Ur and excavating at

Susa. Erech (in Arabic Warka) was one of the oldest of all Mesopotamian cities and contained a revered shrine.

3. Zephaniah 2:13.

4. Napoleon took more than 150 scientists—including antiquarians, cartographers, and farming experts—to Egypt with his army. His soldiers called them "donkeys." The research of these experts produced the first clear portrait of ancient Egyptian civilization, published lavishly in the *Description de l'Egypte*, one of the great publications of Egyptology.

5. Austen Henry Layard, *Nineveh and Babylon* (London: John Murray, 1853), 245.

6. There are numerous translations of the *Epic of Gilgamesh*. One of the most accessible is the Penguin Classic translated by Nancy K. Sandars, *Epic of Gilgamesh: An English Version with an Introduction*, rev. ed. (Baltimore: Penguin Books, 1960).

7. Genesis 11:2–4.

8. Samuel Kramer's *The Sumerians* (Chicago: University of Chicago Press, 1963) contains vivid translations of these and other Sumerian tablets. The quotes are from pages 112 and 115.

9. John Malcolm Russell's *Sennacherib's Palace without Rival* (Chicago: University of Chicago Press, 1991) is the definitive study of this remarkable structure. The quote is from page 227.

10. Byron, *Sennacherib*, stanza 1.

11. Akkad is named after the city of Agade near modern-day Baghdad, founded by King Sargon in about 2200 B.C. The kingdom was north of Sumer in southern Mesopotamia.

12. Nahum 1:1, 4, 5.

CHAPTER 2: EARLY TRAVELERS

The epigraph to this chapter is drawn from Dante Gabriel Rossetti (1828–1882), *The Burden of Nineveh*, privately printed poems, 1869, from the Rosetti Archive: http://www.rossettiarchive.org/docs/1-1870.tb2.fiz.rad.html.

1. Herodotus, *The Histories*, trans. Robin Waterfield (Oxford: Oxford University Press, 1998), is an excellent translation. Quotes are from Book 1:181, 79. A stade is about 128 meters, the length of the Olympic footrace at Olympia, whence the word *stadium*.

2. Xenophon, *The Persian Expedition* (Harmondsworth, England: Penguin, 1979), 162–163.

3. Jonah 4:11.

4. Al-Masudi (ca. 888–957) was born in Baghdad and traveled extensively in India, southwestern Asia, and Africa. His *Meadows of Gold: The Abbasids* has been translated by Paul Lunde and Caroline Stone (London: Kegan Paul, 1989).

5. Ibn Batuta (1307–1377) set out for Mecca in 1325 and just kept traveling, covering more than 120,000 kilometers in 29 years. He traveled as far afield as China, Spain, the Russian steppes, and Timbuktu. The quote is from Saul Lee, *The Travels of ibn Batuta* (London: John Murray, 1829), 49. Yunus is the Arabic form of Jonah. The mound is today called Nebi Yunus.

6. Little is known of Benjamin of Tudela. He was born in about 1127, began his journey from Saragossa in about 1160, and visited over 300 cities during his wanderings. Benjamin returned to Castille in Navarre in 1173. See Marcus Nathan Adler, *The Itinerary of Benjamin of Tudela: Critical Text, Translation, and Commentary* (New York: Phillip Feldheim, 1907), 34 (quotation). See also Sandra Benjamin, *The World of Benjamin of Tudela* (Madison: Farleigh Dickinson University Press, 1995). A *parasang* is an ancient Persian measure of distance equivalent to about 5.6 kilometers, or the distance that can be traversed on foot in an hour.

7. Quotes in this paragraph are from Adler, *Itinerary of Benjamin of Tudela,* 35.

8. Quotes in this paragraph are from ibid., 36.

9. Sir John Mandeville's *The Voyages and Travels of Sir John Mandeville, Knight* (London: R. Scott, 1677) was a best seller in its day. Quote is from chapter 6. The book is not a firsthand traveler's account but a compilation of travelers' tales combined with medieval lore. Mandeville himself is a mystery. Apparently, he was a fourteenth-century Englishman, born at St. Albans, who spent much of his time on the continent. Many scholars think that Mandeville was a pseudonym for Jean d'Outremeuse (1338–1400), a writer of fabulous histories. The authorship controversy remains unresolved. See J. W. Bennett, *The Rediscovery of Sir John Mandeville* (New York: Modern Language Association of America, 1954); and also Tamarah Kohanski, *The Book of Sir John Mandeville* (Tempe: Arizona Center for Medieval and Renaissance Studies, 2001).

10. Bennett, *Rediscovery of Sir John Mandeville,* chapter 6.

11. Johann Schiltberger (1381–?1440) was a nobleman from Bavaria who became an officer in the king of Hungary's army. He was captured by the Turks in 1396 and became a courier during their campaigns in Mesopotamia and Egypt. He then became a slave to the Central Asian conqueror Timur and one of his sons, traveling widely through Armenia and Georgia. He eventually escaped from servitude and wrote an account of his experiences in 1427, including the first European account of Mecca, which appeared at Augsburg in about 1460. See John Buchan Telfer, trans., *The Bondage and Travels of Johann Schiltberger, a Native of Bavaria, in Europe, Asia, and Africa, 1396–1427* (London: Hakluyt Society, 1970). Quotes are from page 46.

12. The Mameluks (or Mamelukes) were a warrior caste recruited from non-Muslim slaves. They were influential in southwestern Asia and along the Nile for more than 700 years, forming dynasties of sultans in Egypt, Syria, and elsewhere from A.D. 1250.

13. Karl H. Dannenfeldt, *Leonard Rauwolf, Sixteenth Century Physician, Botanist, and Traveler* (Cambridge: Harvard University Press, 1968), 133.

14. John Eldred traveled widely and became one of the wealthiest and best known merchants of his day. In later life, he was associated with the Virginia Company and early colonization efforts at Jamestown. His crossings of the Syrian desert brought him to Babylon, where he saw what he called "the ancient tower of Babel." He lived in Babylon for two years and called it a "great place of trade." Quotes in these paragraphs on Eldred are from Richard Hakluyt, *The Principall Navigations: Voiyages and Discoveries of the English Nation* (Cambridge: Cambridge University Press, 1965), 1:234ff.

15. Sir Anthony Sherley (1565–?1635) was an adventurer, driven from England by family debt. He described his travels to Mesopotamia in *Sir Anthony Sherley: His Relation of his Travels into Persia* (London: N. Butter and I. Bagset, 1613; reprinted, Norwood, NJ: W. J. Johnson, 1974). Quote is from page 111.

16. Samuel Purchas, *Hakluytus postumus, or Purchas his Prilgrimes: containing a history of the world in sea voyages and lande travels by English* (London: William Jenkins, 1625; reprinted, Edinburgh: John Maclehose, 1905–1907).

17. Archbishop William Laud (1573–1645) was Archbishop of Canterbury during the reign of King Charles I. He was executed (unjustly) for treason. Richard Pococke (1704–1765) traveled widely in Egypt in 1737–1738 and published a best-selling book on the subject in 1743. Sir Thomas Roe (or Row) (ca. 1581–1644) served with distinction as a diplomat in Mongol India and at Constantinople. He was a famed negotiator and collector of manuscripts.

18. Pietro Della Valle's *The travels of Sig. Pietro delle Valle, a noble Roman, into East-India and Arabia Deserta* (London: John Martin and James Allestry, 1665) is the best source on this remarkable traveler.

CHAPTER 3: CARSTEN NIEBUHR AT PERSEPOLIS

The epigraph to this chapter is drawn from John Milton, *Paradise Regained,* trans. Anthony J. Wyatt (London: W. B. Clive, 1900), 56.

1. Johann David Michaelis (1606–1667) was a Biblical scholar and a teacher who rose to become a distinguished professor at the University of Göttingen. He had strong interests in antiquities and natural history as well as geography. Michaelis was a pioneer in the study of the lives of ancient Hebrews and their influence in the ancient Near East.

2. Thorkild Hansen, *Arabia Felix: The Danish Expedition of 1761–1767,* trans. James McFarlane and Kathleen McFarlane (New York: Harper & Row, 1962), 14.

3. Niebuhr's diary, quoted in ibid., 89–90.

4. Eric Schmidt, *Persepolis I: Structures, Reliefs, Inscriptions* (Chicago: Oriental Institute of the University of Chicago, 1953), 63.

5. Carsten Niebuhr, *Travels in Arabia and Other Oriental Countries* (London: N.p., 1808–1814).

6. The story of his travels appears in Abbé Jean de Beauchamp, *Journal de Sçavarr* (Paris: J. Payot, 1791).

7. André Michaux (1746–1802) visited Mesopotamia during his early years. Subsequently, he was sent to New York to start a nursery that would export trees and plants to France. He traveled widely in North America while botanizing and acquired a reputation as a garden designer. Michaux died of fever while on an expedition to Madagascar.

CHAPTER 4: CLAUDIUS JAMES RICH

The epigraph to this part is drawn from Henry Creswicke Rawlinson's comments on the correct behavior for Europeans on diplomatic or official business overseas, quoted by George Rawlinson, *A Memoir of Major-General Sir Henry Creswicke Rawlinson* (London: Longmans, Green, 1989), 57.

The epigraph to this chapter is drawn from Claudius James Rich's comments on the Nebi Yunus mound, quoted in *Narrative of a Residence in Koordistan and on the Site of Ancient Nineveh* (London: James Duncan, 1836), 39.

1. The Scottish philosopher and writer Sir James Mackintosh (1765–1832) took the post of recorder at Bombay in 1804 with the idea that he would have ample leisure for scholarly pursuits. He was kept so busy adjudicating corruption cases that he had no time for his own work. He returned to Britain on account of ill health in 1811. Quote from G. Rawlinson, *Memoir*, 27.

2. Constance Alexander, *Baghdad in Bygone Days* (London: John Murray, 1928), 33.

3. James Silk Buckingham, *Travels in Assyria, Media, and Persia* (London: Henry Coburn, 1829), 2:214.

4. Alexander, *Baghdad*, 66.

5. Ibid., 68.

6. Ibid., 32.

7. Quotes in this paragraph are from Claudius James Rich, *Narrative of a Journey to the Site of Babylon in 1811* (London: Duncan and Malcolm, 1839), 1.

8. Ibid., 22.

9. Birs Nimrod, the site of ancient Borsippa, was built by King Hammurabi (1792–1750 B.C.). The city prospered under King Nebuchadnezzar of Babylon after 604 B.C. and was destroyed in the fifth century B.C. by the Achaemenid king Xerxes I. The city's Ezia Temple was dedicated to the god Marduk, the national god of the old Babylonian empire. Quotes in this paragraph are from Rich, *Narrative*, 46.

10. Claudius James Rich, "Memoir on the Ruins of Babylon," *Fundgraben des Orients* 3 (1813): 129–162.

11. Claudius James Rich, *Second Memoir on Babylon* (London: Longman, Hurst, and others, 1818).

12. Lord Byron, *Don Juan* (1819–1824), Canto the Fifth. For a discussion of Assyria in early nineteenth-century society, see Fredrick A. Bohrer, "Inventing Assyria: Exoticism and Reception in Nineteenth-Century England and France," *The Art Bulletin* (June 1998):1–14.

CHAPTER 5: DIPLOMACY AND ARCHAEOLOGY IN BAGHDAD

The epigraph to this chapter is drawn from Claudius James Rich's comments on Babylon, quoted in Rich, *Narrative*, 45.

1. Joseph Freiherr von Hammer-Purgstall (1774–1856) was a prolific scholar, who published numerous books on diverse subjects connected with Asia. His work had many defects, but he did much for Asian studies, as Sir William Jones had done for England and Silvestre de Sacy for France. He was what was once called an "Orientalist," a term now considered politically incorrect.

2. Buckingham, *Travels*, 2:221.

3. James Silk Buckingham (1786–1855) settled in India after visiting Baghdad. There he started a newspaper but was expelled when it criticized the East India Company. Subsequently, he founded two periodicals in England, wrote numerous travel books, and became a member of Parliament.

4. A tarboosh is a rimless red hat, usually made of felt and often worn by Turkish officials.

5. Buckingham, *Travels*, 2:221.

6. Ctesiphon, some thirty-two kilometers south of Baghdad on the Tigris, was the capital of the Parthian empire during the first century B.C. It was attacked by the Romans under Trajan and later became the capital of the Sassanian empire. The famous Arch of Ctesiphon is all that remains of the city, a favorite tourist destination for generations. The site was also the scene of a battle between the British and Turks in 1915, which resulted in the invader's retreat. The ruins of Ctesiphon were further damaged in the First Gulf War.

7. Buckingham, *Travels*, 2:427.

8. Ibid., 2:428.

9. The devout and perceptive Sir Robert Ker Porter (1777–1842) was a painter of some note, well-known in particular for his battle scenes, including his painting of the storming of Seringapatam in India in 1799 that was nearly thirty-seven meters long. In 1804 Porter had traveled to Russia, where he became painter to the czar. He also wandered extensively in Central Asia before heading south to Baghdad in 1818 via Persepolis on his way to sketch at Babylon. Ker Porter was the first Western artist to sketch Behistun, eleven square meters of inscriptions in Old Persian, Elamite, and Babylonian cuneiform commemorating King Darius's victory over rebel kings in 522 B.C. "What

a treasure of information doubtless was there to the happy man who could decipher [the scripts]," he wrote in his *Travels in Georgia, Persia, Armenia, and Ancient Babylon* (London: Longmans, 1821), 2:274.

10. Ibid., 2:177.

11. Ibid., 2:274.

12. Quotes in this paragraph and the next are from ibid., 2:306–309.

13. Isaiah 13:21.

14. Carl Bellino, "Account of the Progress Made in Deciphering Cuneiform Inscriptions," *Journal of the Bombay Literary Society* 1 (1818):2–23.

15. Claudius James Rich, *Narrative of a Residence in and on the Site of Ancient Nineveh*, ed. Mary Rich (London: James Duncan, 1836), 39.

16. *Tell* is the Arabic word for "mound" and is often applied by archaeologists to abandoned city mounds.

17. Quotes in this paragraph are from Rich, *Koordistan*, 40–41.

18. Ibid., 44.

19. Ibid., 45.

20. Ibid., 46.

21. Unlike many other southwest Asian cities, Nimrud (Biblical Calah) was not a long-lived settlement. Assyrian king Shalmaneser I founded it in the thirteenth century B.C., but its heyday was during the reign of King Assurnasirpal II (884–859 B.C.), who made it the capital of Assyria. It remained the capital until about 710 B.C., when the capital moved to Khorsabad and then Nineveh. The city's ziggurat was dedicated to Ninurta, the goddess of rain, fertility, and war.

22. Bushire is now known as Bushehr.

23. For details about Rich's visit to Persepolis, see Rich, *Narrative*, 232–236.

CHAPTER 6: THE EUPHRATES EXPEDITION

The epigraph to this chapter is drawn from Francis Chesney's letter from Baghdad to Sir John Hobhouse, president of the India Board, October 1, 1836, quoted in John S. Guest, *The Euphrates Expedition* (London: Kegan Paul, 1992), 124.

1. Ker Porter, *Travels*, 2:210.

2. In the closing days of the plague, Groves's wife and child died. He withdrew to India, where he served as a missionary for many years.

3. The Scottish traveler and writer James Baillie-Fraser (1783–1856) is known for his explorations of the Himalayas and journeys through Asia Minor to Tehran on horseback.

4. Quotes in this paragraph: James Baillie-Fraser, *Mesopotamia and Assyria from the Earliest Ages to the Present Time* (Edinburgh: Oliver and Boyd, 1842), 2:111.

5. Sir Stratford Canning, Viscount de Redcliffe (1786–1880), made his name as a brilliantly successful British ambassador in Constantinople, where he served from 1824 to 1829 and again from 1842 to 1858. Previously, he had worked in both Switzerland and Washington. Canning had an abrupt manner, which occasionally caused diplomatic ripples. He is mainly remembered for his sponsorship of Austen Henry Layard's excavations at Nimrud and Nineveh, described in Chapter 9.

6. Details of the prolonged debates over the expedition will be found in Guest's *Euphrates*, chapters 1 and 2, which includes an interesting discussion of early steamship technology.

7. Captain Francis Chesney (1785–1872) was the son of an Englishman who had emigrated to South Carolina and fought on the wrong side in the Revolutionary War. A diminutive, wiry man, Chesney was a difficult if brave commander with an expertise in surveying. Years after his Suez survey, Ferdinand de Lesseps, who built the canal, met him in Paris and called him the father of the canal. Chesney later served in Hong Kong and Ireland and eventually rose to the rank of general. Quote from Guest, *Euphrates*, 126.

8. Discussed in Guest, *Euphrates*, chapter 5.

9. Congreve rockets were widely used during the early nineteenth century. Developed by Sir William Congreve (1772–1828), the slow-flying rockets had a range of about 2,750 meters and were fired from tubes set on tripods.

10. For the wreck of the *Tigris* and subsequent details of the expedition, see Guest, *Euphrates*, chapters 9–14.

CHAPTER 7: CUNEIFORM DECIPHERED

The epigraph to this chapter is drawn from Henry Rawlinson's letter to his sister Maria, July, 1836, quoted from Lesley Adkins, *Empires of the Plain: Henry Rawlinson and the Lost Languages of Babylon* (New York: St. Martin's Press, 2003), 80.

1. Ker Porter, *Travels*, 2:158.

2. In the interests of brevity, I don't cite the early philological contributions of Münter and others, as they are of interest only to specialists. For a survey, see Adkins, *Empires*, chapter 5.

3. Abraham Hyacinthe Anqueil-Duperron (1731–1805) lived in India for seven years and was France's earliest expert on Asian languages. Antoine Isaac, Baron Silvestre de Sacy (1758–1838), started off as a civil servant, learning Semitic languages in his spare time and working on the Persepolis inscriptions. He became a professor of Arabic in the newly founded school of living Eastern languages in 1795 and enjoyed a successful, high-profile career as one of the pioneers of Asian studies in France.

4. Adkins, *Empires*, 61–63.

5. Ibid., chapters 1–8, describes Rawlinson's early career.

6. Eugène Flandin, *Voyage en Perse de MM Eugène Flandin, peintre, et Pascal Coste, architecte* (Paris: Gide et J. Baudry, 1851), 1:451.

7. Adkins, *Empires,* 151–152, describes Fahed in the residency.

8. H. C. Rawlinson, "The Persian Cuneiform Inscriptions at Behistun, Deciphered and Translated; with a Memoir," *Journal of the Royal Asiatic Society* 10 (1864–1851):pts. 1–3; quote is from part 1.

9. For an accessible description and analysis of Hincks's and Rawlinson's research, see Mogens Trolle Larsen, *The Conquest of Assyria: Excavations in an Antique Land* (London: Routledge, 1996), chapter 20. Larsen is especially good at describing the intricate, and often touchy, relationship between the two men.

10. Quoted from Adkins, *Empires,* 322.

11. Described by Adkins in ibid., 337–341.

CHAPTER 8: EXCAVATIONS AT KHORSABAD

The epigraph to this part is drawn from an inscription from the Assyrian king Sennacherib at Nineveh, quoted from Russell, *Sennacherib's Palace,* 246.

The epigraph to this chapter is drawn from Paul Émile Botta, *Monuments de Ninive* (Paris: Imprimerie Nationale, 1849), 16.

1. Brian Fagan, *The Rape of the Nile,* 2nd ed. (Boulder, CO: Westview, 2004), describes these activities.

2. Julius von Mohl (1800–1876) was born in Germany but went to Paris in 1823 to study under Silvestre de Sacy. He was appointed professor of Persian at the College de France in 1847.

3. Captain E. de Verninac Saint-Maur, *Voyage de Luxor* (Paris: Payot, 1835), quoted in Leslie Greener, *The Discovery of Egypt* (New York: Viking, 1965), 157–158.

4. Paul Émile Botta, *Relation d'un voyage dans l'Yémen* (Paris: Benjamin Duprat, 1841).

5. Edward L. Mitford, *A Land March from England to Ceylon Forty Years Ago,* 2 vols. (London: W. H. Allen, 1884), 1:280.

6. Julius von Mohl, ed., *Lettres de M. Botta sur ses découvertes a Khorsabad, près de Ninive* (Paris: Imprimerie Royale, 1845), 2:10. Botta's letters were translated into English and published in London in 1850.

7. Eugène Napoléon Flandin (1803–1876) was born in Naples to French parents. He was a painter of historical scenes, portraits, and rural and urban landscapes. He was known for his Islamic expertise, having traveled with the French Army to Algiers in 1837. In 1840, he was sent on a mission to Persia, where he inventoried monuments, including the Great Rock at Behistun, as far south as Persepolis, returning through Mosul and Constantinople. He was a logical and triumphant choice to work at Khorsabad.

8. Assyrian palaces were adorned with large blocks of carved limestone or alabaster quarried in northern Assyria. The decorated slabs served as paneling

and were decorated with hunting and military scenes and also deities and animals. The massive bulls with human heads at the palace entrances were calm statements of dominant majesty. They created a profound impression in the minds of Victorian museum visitors.

9. Paul Émile Botta, *Monument de Nineve découvert et décrit par M. P. E. Botta, mesuré et dessiné par M. E. Flandin* (Paris: Imprimerie Nationale, 1849).

CHAPTER 9: LAYARD OF NINEVEH

The epigraph to this chapter is drawn from Henry Rawlinson's letters to Henry Layard, quoted from Larsen, *Conquest,* 102–103.

1. Quoted from Gordon Waterfield, *Layard of Nineveh* (London: John Murray, 1963), 27.

2. Petra, in modern-day Jordan, is famous for its rock-cut temples and tombs. The city came into prominence during the first century B.C. as a spice trading center and major city of the Nabateans. The Nabateans were conquered by the Roman general Pompeii in 64–63 B.C. Petra became the capital of the Roman province Arabia Petraea in A.D. 106 and prospered as a caravan city and Christian bishopric. Petra declined in the sixth century when trade routes changed direction and a massive earthquake leveled much of the city.

3. Layard, *Nineveh,* 4–5.

4. Susa lies in the Khuzistan highlands of southwestern Iran and was occupied from the late fifth millennium B.C. to early medieval times. The city was the capital of an important Elamite state and maintained relationships with both lowland Mesopotamia and the Iranian plateau to the east.

5. Dr. Dover's Powder was a mixture of ipecac and opium developed by the British physician Thomas Dover in 1732. It was a pain-reducing potion that could not be taken in large quantities because of its emetic qualities. The powder was a popular medication for more than two centuries but went out of use as aspirin became popular and addictive opiates were banned from the marketplace. Layard described his Bakhtiari exploits many years later in his *Early Adventures.*

6. Quoted from Waterfield, *Layard,* 85–86.

7. Ibid., 102.

8. British Library document 58161, letter dated July 22, 1843, quoted from Larsen, *Conquest,* 26.

9. Quoted from Arnold Brackman, *The Luck of Nineveh* (London: Methuen, 1980), 121.

10. Quotes from a letter to Sir Stratford Canning dated November 28, 1845, quoted by Waterfield, *Layard,* 123. Finds also described in Layard, *Nineveh,* 35.

11. Layard, *Nineveh,* 32.

12. Quoted from Waterfield, *Layard,* 127.

13. Layard, *Nineveh,* 49.

14. Waterfield, *Layard,* 154.

15. Layard, *Nineveh,* 95.

16. Ibid., 228.

17. Ibid., 263–264.

18. Quotes and details of the discovery are from Waterfield, *Layard,* 168.

19. *Morning Post,* March 3, 1847. J. A. Longworth was a respected and adventurous journalist with a yen for the romantic. He traveled widely in Russia and Circassia for the *London Times.*

20. The Prussian expedition to the Nile from 1842–1845 was led by Karl Lepsius (1810–1884) and was a great success. Lepsius and his team collected more than 15,000 artifacts. The resulting monograph, *Denkmäler aus Ägypten und Äthiopien,* in seventeen volumes (1856 onward), is a fundamental source for Egyptologists.

21. Waterfield, *Layard,* 182.

22. Ibid., 188.

23. *Times,* February 9, 1849.

24. Quotes in this paragraph from Layard, *Nineveh,* 324–325.

CHAPTER 10: NIMRUD AND KHORSABAD

The epigraph to this chapter is drawn from Layard's comments on the Nimrud lions, quoted from his *Nineveh and Babylon,* 202.

1. Henry James Ross (1820–1902) spent much of his life doing business in the eastern Mediterranean world. He corresponded with Layard at intervals during his life, especially about Turkish and Crimean war questions.

2. Layard's and Rawlinson's accounts of the visit differ somewhat in the details, but they agree that the site tours were very brief. Layard quote from Adkins, *Empires,* 270.

3. The interested reader will find an admirable discussion of the chronology issue in Larsen, *Conquest,* 208–214. Canning quote is from page 212.

4. Layard, *Nineveh and Babylon,* 114.

5. Russell, *Sennacherib,* 101.

6. Layard, *Nineveh and Babylon,* 117.

7. Nahum 3:13.

8. Layard, *Nineveh and Babylon,* 121.

9. Russell, *Sennacherib,* 272.

10. 2 Kings 18:13.

11. Layard, *Nineveh and Babylon,* 169.

12. Ibid., 203.

13. Spectacular ivories came from later excavations into Fort Salmaneser at Nimrud by Max Mallowan over a fifteen-year period from 1947, described in Max Mallowan, *Nimrud and Its Remains* (London: Collins, 1966).

14. An Assyrian vassal, Samanuha-shar-ilani, ruled Arban, now in eastern Syria, in 883 B.C.

15. Layard, *Nineveh and Babylon,* chapter 10; quote is from page 263.

16. Ibid., 338.

17. Ibid., 345.

18. Quotes in this paragraph are from ibid., 347.

19. Ibid., 487.

20. Ibid., 499.

21. Nippur (Layard called it Niffer), 257 kilometers southeast of Baghdad, was excavated extensively during the last decade of the nineteenth century (see Chapter 16). This Sumerian city of the third millennium B.C. did not enjoy political autonomy but housed an important shrine of the god Enlil, lord of the universe.

22. Layard, *Nineveh and Babylon,* 562.

23. Ibid., 589.

24. Sculptures from Sennacherib's reign show religious symbols, winged bulls, and the monarch engaged in cult activities. There are also three long inscriptions, one so inaccessible that Layard had himself lowered on ropes to copy it.

25. A technical assessment of Layard's excavation by two archaeologists, one of them Max Mallowan of Nimrud fame, can be found in Waterfield, *Layard,* 484–490.

CHAPTER 11: EXCAVATIONS IN BABYLONIA

The epigraph to this part is drawn from James Felix Jones, *Memoirs by Commander James Felix Jones, I.N.* (Bombay: Records of the Bombay Government, 1857), 431.

The epigraph to this chapter is drawn from Henry Rawlinson's comments on the aftermath of his discovery of dedication cylinders in the Birs Nimrod ziggurat, quoted from H. C. Rawlinson, "On the Birs Nimrod, or the Great Temple of Borsippa," *Journal of the Royal Asiatic Society* 18 (1861):1–34.

1. Quotes from Loftus, *Travels,* 124–125.

2. Ibid., 199.

3. The Parthian period lasted from 320 B.C. to A.D. 620, a time of constant political change in the region. Mesopotamia was one of the "lower kingdoms" of the eighteen Parthian satrapies.

4. Quotes are from Loftus, *Travels,* 181, 183.

5. Ibid., 188.

6. H. C. Rawlinson, "Birs Nimrod," 3.

7. J. E. Taylor, "Notes on the Ruins of Muqeyer," *Journal of the Royal Asiatic Society* 15 (1855):260–276.

8. Daniel 13:5–6.

9. J. E. Taylor, "Notes on Abu Shahrein and Tell el-Lahm," *Journal of the Royal Asiatic Society* 15 (1855):404–412.

10. Jules Oppert, *Expédition scientifique en Mésopotamie*, 2 vols. (Paris: Imprimerie Impériale, 1859–1863).

CHAPTER 12: A ROYAL LION HUNT

The epigraph to this chapter is drawn from Hormuzd Rassam's description of Ashurbanipal's lion hunt, quoted from Rassam, *Asshur and the Land of Nimrod* (New York: Eaton and Mains, 1897), 28.

1. Léon Faucher (1804–1854) worked as a literary translator before becoming a member of Parliament and then the minister for Public Works after the 1848 revolution. He later served as minister of the Interior for a short while and was well-known for his writings on economics.

2. Maurice Pillet, *Un Pionnier de l'assyriologie* (Paris: Cahiers du Société Asiatique, 1962), 11.

3. Royal Asiatic Society, *Annual Report*, May 1853, xix.

4. Felix Jones served as British resident for the Persian Gulf from 1856 to 1862. Quote from *Memoirs*, 459.

5. For additional details, see Place's *Nineve*. A photographer, Gabriel Trenchand, was present at the excavations and took some of the earliest photographs of an archaeological dig anywhere, using the calotype technique that produced negatives on paper. Thomas Septimus Bell had brought such a machine with him to Mosul a few years before but never used it.

6. Excellent analyses of this complex man are found in Larsen, *Conquest*, chapters 33–36, and Seton Lloyd, *Foundations in the Dust*, rev. ed. (London: Thames and Hudson, 1980), chapter 11.

7. Rassam, *Asshur*, 28.

8. Ibid., 28.

9. The disaster is well summarized in Larsen, *Conquest*, chapter 36.

10. Lloyd, *Foundations*, p. 147.

CHAPTER 13: THE DELUGE TABLETS

The epigraph to this chapter is drawn from George Smith's comments on tablet sorting from his *Assyrian Discoveries: An Account of Explorations and Discoveries at the Site of Nineveh during 1873 and 1874* (New York: Scribner, Armstrong, 1875), 13.

1. Rawlinson quoted in *The Athenaeum*, May 31, 1862, 728.

2. Edwin Norris (1795–1872) wrote a number of articles on the lesser known languages of Africa and Asia. His unfinished three-volume *Assyrian Dictionary* was published posthumously.

3. Joachim Menant (1820–1899) was a magistrate and Asian scholar who became a member of the French Court of Appeals. He was, however, best known for his cuneiform studies, which were published in many papers and monographs, among them the two-volume *Les Langues perdues de la Perse et d'Assyrie* (Paris: Ernest Leroux, 1885–1886). Menant collaborated frequently with Jules Oppert.

4. Samuel Birch (1813–1885) was a parson's son with a taste for esoteric research. After a few years in the Government Record Office, he was appointed to the British Museum's antiquities department on account of his knowledge of Chinese and Egyptology. He soon extended his research to Assyriology, but his primary task was the cataloging of the Egyptian collections. Quote from Wallis Budge, *By Nile and Tigris,* 2 vols. (London: John Murray, 1920), 1:21, where a short biographical sketch can also be found.

5. Ibid., 1:35.

6. Ibid., 1:8.

7. British Museum, *Cuneiform Inscriptions of Western Asia* (London: British Museum, 1861–1884).

8. Quotes from Reginald Campbell-Thompson, *A Century of Exploration at Nineveh* (London: Luzac, 1929), 49.

9. *Times,* December 4, 1872.

10. Campbell-Thompson, *Century,* 50.

11. A guinea is equivalent to one pound plus a shilling, a unit of currency now defunct but was often used to buy and sell racehorses, antiques, and objets d'art.

12. Quoted from Campbell-Thompson, *Century,* 52.

13. Quoted from ibid., 55.

14. George Smith's diary, August 18, 1876, British Museum.

15. Rassam has been much vilified for his archaeological work, but there is no question that his deeds in Abyssinia from 1866 to 1868 were remarkable. He was imprisoned there for two years while on a diplomatic mission until rescued by Sir Charles Napier's invading force. He also served diplomatically during the Russo-Turkish War, investigating conditions among the Christian communities of Asia Minor and Armenia. For an obituary that assesses his diplomatic service, see the *Times,* September 17, 1910.

CHAPTER 14: GATES AND PALACES

The epigraph to this chapter is drawn from Rassam, *Asshur,* 205.

1. Osman Hamdi Bey (1842–1910) was the eldest son of a Grand Vizier, which gave him impeccable social and political credentials in Constantinople. He studied law in Paris and developed an interest in archaeology and history while Director of Foreign Affairs for Baghdad. After serving as Assistant Director of Palace Protocol, he was appointed director general of the museum.

Hamdi Bey was founder of the School of Fine Arts, developed antiquities legislation with teeth, and continued painting throughout his life. He was also founder of Constantinople's Archeology Museum, which opened in 1891.

2. Details of Layard's turbulent but successful diplomatic career can be found in Waterfield, *Layard,* parts 4 and 5.

3. The German excavations at the Shrine of the Cabiri on Samothrace and at Olympia were led by Alexander Conze and Ernst Curtius, financed in part by the kaiser, and took place with a warship present some of the time. The Germans renounced their finds, built site museums, and employed architects, artists, and photographers on-site. These historic excavations marked the beginning of scientific archaeology in the eastern Mediterranean. The excavators published their fieldwork promptly in sumptuous monographs.

4. Quotes in this paragraph from Rassam, *Asshur,* 200.

5. Ibid., 208.

6. Ibid., 216.

7. Ibid., 267.

8. Ibid., 276.

9. Ibid., 289.

10. Ibid., 290.

11. Sippar was an important Babylonian city, occupied from the fourth millennium B.C. until 481 B.C. Belgian and Iraqi excavations have added much to Rassam's investigations, including numerous tablets and temple records.

12. Sargon I of Akkad was the founder of the Akkadian Dynasty and conquered the Sumerian king Lugalzaggesi in about 2370 B.C. Sometimes called "the Great," Sargon I ruled over a confederacy of city-states that extended from Sumer to the Mediterranean. His capital has never been found. Sargon II, the Assyrian king who ruled from 721–705 B.C., built the great palace at Khorsabad near Nineveh, discovered by Paul Botta in 1843.

13. Rassam, *Asshur,* 411. Kuthah was an important Babylonian city with a temple dedicated to the god Negral, a solar deity.

CHAPTER 15: A SCRAMBLE FOR TABLETS

The epigraph to this chapter is drawn from Hormuzd Rassam's comments while at Abu Habbah, 1880, quoted in his *Asshur,* 399.

1. William St. Chad Boscawan (1854–1913) wrote extensively on the Biblical associations of Assyrian history.

2. Ernest Alfred Thompson Wallis Budge (1857–1934), or rather Sir Wallis Budge as he became in 1920, entered British Museum service in 1883 and traveled widely in Egypt, Mesopotamia, and the Sudan collecting for the museum. He was unpopular in his day with many of his colleagues, who distrusted his methods and his gossipy manner. He was also a prolific author of popular books on Assyria, Egypt, and Mesopotamia.

3. Budge, *By Nile and Tigris,* 1:10.

4. Budge's escapades in Egypt are described in more detail in Fagan, *Rape,* chapter 13.

5. The Amarna tablets are described in detail by William L. Moran in *The Amarna Letters* (Baltimore: Johns Hopkins University Press, 1992).

6. Quotes from Budge, *By Nile and Tigris,* 1:224–227.

7. Ibid., 1:229.

8. Ibid., 1:240.

9. Ibid., 2:8.

10. Ibid., 2:128.

11. Ibid., 2:129.

12. The Sumerian city of Der, modern Tell Aqar, was severely damaged by the Iraqi Army, which converted it into earthworks during the Iran-Iraq War. Their trenches cut through a 4,500-year-old temple.

13. Budge, *By Nile and Tigris,* 2:258–259.

14. Ibid., 2:266–267.

15. Waterfield, *Layard,* 479. A biased account appears in Budge, *By Nile and Tigris,* 2:appendix 2.

16. *Times,* July 4, 1893.

17. *Daily News,* July 4, 1893.

CHAPTER 16: SUMER DISCOVERED

The epigraph to this chapter is drawn from a Sumerian epic quoted by Samuel Kramer, *History Begins at Sumer,* 2nd ed. (Philadelphia: University of Pennsylvania Press, 1981), 170–171.

1. Lloyd, *Foundations.*

2. Telloh was a city in the city-state of Lagash. The actual Lagash is the Al Hiba site.

3. Gudea ruled the city-state of Lagash from ca. 2144 to 2124 B.C. An influential ruler, he also built temples at Nippur, Ur, Uruk, and other cities. He styled himself "god of Lagash" but chose the title of *ensi* ("governor"). Inscriptions tell us that he fostered irrigation agriculture and imported all manner of commodities from many parts of western Asia. At least twenty-six statues purporting to show Gudea are known.

4. Leon Heuzey (1831–1922) headed the French School of Archaeology in Athens and carried out important work in Macedonia before assuming his appointment at the Louvre.

5. H. G. Wells, *Phoenix* (London: Secker and Warburg, 1942), 31.

6. Hermann Hilprecht, *The Excavations in Assyria and Babylonia* (Philadelphia: Holman, 1904), 290.

7. Ibid., 294.

8. The beginnings of the project are described in ibid., 299ff.

9. Ibid., 304.

10. Quotes in this paragraph from ibid., 304–306.

11. Ibid., 314.

12. Described in ibid., 306ff.

13. Ibid., 326.

14. Wallis Budge, *Rise and Progress of Assyriology* (London: Martin Hopkinson, 1925), 202.

15. Lugalzaggesi (there are several spellings) ruled Uruk from ca. 2360 to 2335 B.C. and unified much of Sumer by force and diplomacy. His successor was Sargon of Akkad to the north.

16. Hilprecht, *Excavations*, 446.

17. Samuel Kramer summarized Sumerian writings for a general audience very ably in his *History Begins*, which includes both commentary and translations.

CHAPTER 17: NEBUCHADNEZZAR'S BABYLON

The epigraph to this chapter is drawn from Seton Lloyd, *Mounds of the Near East* (Edinburgh: Edinburgh University Press, 1963), 23.

1. Eberhard Schrader (1836–1921) was professor of theology at the University of Zurich, later taking up an appointment as professor of Oriental languages at the Friedrich Wilhelm University in Berlin. His work on Ishtar, *Die Höllenfahrt der Ishtar* (Berlin: J. Ricker'sche Buchhandling), was published in 1874.

2. Budge, *Rise and Progress*, 213.

3. Friedrich Delitzsch (1850–1922) was one of the finest teachers of his generation. His *Babel and Bible* (Chicago: Open Court Publishing Company, 1903) was widely read for many years.

4. Surghul (ancient Nina) was a center of the goddess Nanshe, sister of Inanna (Ishtar). She was the deity of fish and fishing, and also a soothsayer. Many rulers of Lagash claimed that she chose them.

5. Selinus was founded by Dorian Greeks in about 628 B.C., quarreled with its nearby rival Segesta, and was sacked by the Carthaginians in 409 B.C. Carthage finally destroyed the settlement in 250 B.C. The city is famous for its fine Doric architecture. Robert Koldewey and Oscar Pushstein, *Die Grieschen Tempel in Unteritalien and Sicilien* (Berlin: Rugen, 1899), 5.

6. Robert Koldewey, *The Excavations at Babylon* (London: Macmillan, 1914), ix.

7. Ibid., 14.

8. Tempered clay is clay that has had some form of bonding agent, such as sand or crushed shell, added to it.

9. Koldewey, *Babylon*, v.

10. The Ishtar Gate was the eighth gate for the inner city of Babylon. King Nebuchadnezzar ordered its construction in 575 B.C. The gate was finished

with blue glazed tiles. A processional way ran through the gate, lined with walls adorned with lions on glazed bricks. A reconstruction can be seen in Berlin's Pergamon Museum.

11. Quoted in Koldewey, *Babylon,* 193.

12. Ibid., 196.

13. The definitive biography of Flinders Petrie, which describes these experiments, is Margaret D. Drower's *Flinders Petrie: A Life in Archaeology* (London: Victor Gollancz, 1985).

CHAPTER 18: LEONARD WOOLLEY AT CARCHEMISH

The epigraph to this chapter is drawn from Leonard Woolley's comments on Carchemish, from *Dead Towns and Living Men* (London: H. Mitford, 1920), 79.

1. Bismaya has never been properly published. Banks excavated a temple dating to at least 2550 B.C. and an administrative center, a residential quarter, and what he described as a palace, all dating to the Akkadian period, ca. 2335–2155 B.C. The Banks excavations are currently being prepared for belated publication.

2. Woolley, *Dead Towns,* 9.

3. For a comprehensive biography of Arthur Evans, see Joan Evans, *Time and Chance* (London: Longmans, 1943).

4. Eckley B. Coxe came from a wealthy coal and mining family and supported numerous archaeological expeditions to the Nile Valley. The Meroitic civilization flourished at the confluence of the Blue Nile and White Nile and further downstream in what is now the Sudan from 593 B.C. to ca. A.D. 350. Its African rulers were consummate traders and aped the pharaohs.

5. David G. Hogarth (1862–1927) was keeper of the Ashmolean Museum from 1909 until his death. He traveled and excavated widely in Cyprus, Crete, Egypt, and Syria and also investigated the Temple of Artemis at Ephesus.

6. Woolley, *Dead Towns,* 72–72.

7. Quotes in these paragraphs are from ibid., 114–117.

8. Ibid., 74.

9. Story and quotes in these paragraphs from ibid., 122–124.

10. Ibid., 125–128.

11. Ibid., 128.

12. Ibid., 99.

13. Ibid., 101.

14. Quoted in John E. Mack, *A Prince of Our Disorder* (Boston: Little, Brown, 1976), 81–82.

15. Woolley, *Dead Towns,* 143.

16. Hugo Winckler (1863–1913) wrote extensively on Assyrian and cuneiform and became professor of Oriental languages at the University of Berlin in 1904. He excavated Boghazkoy from 1906 to 1912 with support from the

German Oriental Society. The excavations yielded thousands of tablets written in the hitherto unknown Hittite language and allowed Winkler to reconstruct Hittite history in the fourteenth and thirteenth centuries B.C. He also showed that Boghazkoy was the center of the Hittites' great empire.

17. Woolley, *Dead Towns,* 169.

18. Woolley edited an account of British POW experiences in Turkish captivity: C. L. Woolley, ed., *From Kastamuni to Kedos, Being a Record of Experiences of Prisoners of War in Turkey, 1916–1918* (Oxford: Blackwell, 1921).

19. Woolley, *Dead Towns,* 80.

CHAPTER 19: GERTRUDE BELL AND THE NEW IRAQ

The epigraph to this part is drawn from Max Mallowan's comments on Woolley's guided tour of Ur, from his "Memories of Ur," *Iraq* 22 (1960):9.

The epigraph to this chapter is drawn from Gertrude Bell's unpublished essay titled "Romance of Iraq," quoted by H.V.F. Winstone, *Gertrude Bell* (London: Jonathan Cape, London, 1978), 257.

1. Quoted by Winstone, *Gertrude Bell,* 115. Bell's statement is a little unfair, for Willcocks was a brilliant irrigation engineer who carried out important work in India, Mesopotamia, and the Nile Valley.

2. Quoted by Winstone, *Gertrude Bell,* 117.

3. The Abbasid palace of Ukhaidir lies about 190 kilometers southwest of Baghdad and was built by Isa ibn Musa in A.D. 774 and 775. The fortress/palace is remarkable for its elliptical barrel vaulted architecture. Quote is from Janet Wallach, *Desert Queen* (New York: Nan Talese/Doubleday, 1996), 87.

4. See Gertrude Bell, *Amurath to Amurath* (London: Heinemann, 1911), preface.

5. Gertrude Bell, *Palace and Mosque at Ukhaidir* (Oxford: Clarendon Press, 1914), ix.

6. Bell, *Amurath,* 197.

7. Letter from Lawrence to his mother, quoted by Wallach, *Desert Queen,* 93–94.

8. This astute analysis by Bell is quoted from Wallach, *Desert Queen,* 177.

9. George Byron Gordon (1870–1927) was director of the University Museum at the University of Pennsylvania from 1910 to 1927, a period of major expansion for the institution. Sir Frederick Kenyon (1863–1952), director and principal librarian of the British Museum, was a distinguished papyrologist and an authority on the poets Robert Browning and Elizabeth Browning. The correspondence between the two directors is excerpted in Robert H. Dyson, "Archival Glimpses of the Ur Expedition in the Years 1920 to 1925," *Expedition* 20:1 (1977):5–23. Quote in this paragraph is from page 7.

10. Henry R. Hall, *A Season's Work at Ur, al'Ubaid, Abu Shahrain, and Elsewhere* (London: Methuen, 1930).

11. Dyson, "Archival," 9.

12. This correspondence is analyzed in Winstone, *Woolley*, 115–117.

13. Woolley's quote in this paragraph is from Dyson, "Archival," 10, 12. Bell on Woolley: letter from Bell to her father, Sir Hugh Bell, November 1, 1922, quoted by Winstone, *Woolley*, 117.

14. Kish lies on an ancient branch of the Euphrates forty kilometers south of Baghdad. It was founded before 3000 B.C. and was an important city-state in the early third millennium B.C. Occupation of the city's forty mounds continued until A.D. 650.

15. Quotes in this paragraph are from Winstone, *Woolley*, 135.

16. Traitor comment is from Mallowan, "Memories," 11. Woolley's quote is from Dyson, "Archival," 13.

CHAPTER 20: LEONARD WOOLLEY AT UR

The epigraph to this chapter is drawn from C. L. Woolley, *Excavations at Ur* (New York: Barnes and Noble, 1954), 11.

1. Dyson, "Archival," 12.

2. M.E.L. Mallowan, *Mallowan's Memoirs* (New York: Dodd, Mead, 1977), 28–29.

3. Mallowan, "Memories," 7.

4. Woolley, *Excavations at Ur*, 13.

5. Winstone, *Woolley*, in particular pages 159–161, offers insight into Katherine Woolley's tortuous personality.

6. Dyson, "Archival," 15.

7. Woolley, *Excavations at Ur*, 93.

8. Ibid., 97.

9. The classic popular description of the royal graves is in Woolley, *Excavations at Ur*, chapter 3. The final report appears in C. L. Woolley, *Ur Excavations*, vol. 3, *The Royal Cemetery* (Oxford: Oxford University Press, 1934). There have been frequent specialized reassessments of the contents of the tombs, and these reassessments are described in the technical literature. The description here follows Woolley for obvious historical reasons.

10. Described in general terms by Woolley in *Excavations at Ur*, 71–75.

11. Ibid., 27–28.

12. Mallowan, *Mallowan's Memoirs*, 32.

13. Woolley, *Excavations at Ur*, 34.

14. The Field Museum in Chicago is now working on a Web-based catalog of the finds from the Kish excavations, which have never been published.

15. Julius Jordan, who worked for the German Oriental Institute (formerly called the German Oriental Society), was director of the Iraq Museum from 1931 to 1934. He was an accomplished musician and an ardent Nazi supporter.

16. Woolley, *Excavations at Ur*, 36.

17. C. L. Woolley, ed., *Ur Excavations*, 9 vols. (Oxford: Oxford University Press, 1927–1946), 110–111.

CHAPTER 21: NATIONALISM AND ARCHAEOLOGY

The epigraph to this chapter is drawn from Max Mallowan's comments on life at Nimrud; from his *Memoirs*, 290. Contrast Mallowan's experiences with those of Layard.

1. The German excavations at Uruk are described in Julius Jordan, *Uruk-Warka nach dem Ausgrabungen durch die Deutsche Orient Gesellschaft* (Leipzig: J. C. Hinrichs, 1928), and subsequent volumes.

2. Henri Frankfort (1897–1954) was born in Amsterdam but emigrated to the United States. He was an expert on the cultural history of Mesopotamia and southwestern Asia and was associated with the Oriental Institute of the University of Chicago and the Warburg Institute of the University of London. He worked at Tell Asmar and Khorsabad.

3. Mallowan, *Memoirs*, 69–85, gives an informal account of the Kuyunjik research.

4. Thorkild Jacobsen and Seton Lloyd, *Sennacherib's Aqueduct at Jerwan* (Chicago: Oriental Institute Publications, vol. 24, 1935).

5. Baron Max von Oppenheim (1860–1946) trained in the law but became an inveterate traveler in southwest Asian lands, also serving as a diplomat in Cairo. He traveled widely in Syria, where he complained of signs of "progress" at Palymra, including metal bedsteads for tourists and numerous graffiti left by tourists from many nations. A meticulous observer, he became interested in archaeology with his discovery of Tell Halaf. Unfortunately, his foundation and site museum were destroyed by bombing and looting at the end of World War II. Oppenheim lost all his possessions in the notorious Dresden raid of February 1945 and died two years later.

6. Mallowan, *Memoirs*, 84.

7. Ibid., chapter 5, describes the excavations. See also M.E.L. Mallowan, *Twenty-Five Years of Mesopotamian Discovery* (London: British Museum, 1956).

8. Charles Bache and A. J. Tobler, *Tepe Gawra* (Philadelphia: University of Pennsylvania Press, 1950).

9. George Loud. *Khorsabad*, vol. 1 (Chicago: Oriental Institute, 1936).

10. Pierre Delougaz and Seton Lloyd, *Pre-Sargonid Temples in the Diyala Region* (Chicago: Oriental Institute, 1942). A general summary appears in Lloyd, *Mounds*, 34–42.

11. André Parrot (?–1980) later achieved fame by excavating the city of Mari in Syria over a forty-one-year period, from 1933 to 1974. Excavations today focus on Mari's landscape and economic base.

12. Larsa was a city-state that was powerful in the first two centuries of the second millennium B.C. Larsa's ruler Rim-Suren was overthrown by Hammurabi of Babylon in about 1800 B.C.

13. Mallowan, *Memoirs,* 100.

14. This discussion is based on Lloyd, *Foundations,* 193–203.

15. Mari ruled over a kingdom on the west bank of the Euphrates during the third millennium B.C. The city was an important trade hub with a magnificent palace, where records of costumes and important archives were recovered.

16. Seton Lloyd (1902–1996) originally trained as an architect, did his first archaeology at el-Amarna in Egypt, and became a site supervisor for the Oriental Institute at Khafaje. He later became director of the British Institute of Archaeology in Ankara and professor of western Asiatic archaeology at the University of London. The Tell 'Uqair excavation is summarized in Lloyd, *Mounds,* 55–57.

17. Hassuna excavations are summarized in Lloyd, *Mounds,* 70–74; quote is from page 71.

18. For more on the Eridu excavations, see Lloyd, *Mounds,* 57–64.

19. Lloyd, *Foundations,* 202.

20. Australian-born Vere Gordon Childe (1892–1957) was one of the great archaeologists of the twentieth century, best known for his comprehensive works of synthesis that linked southwestern Asia with Europe. His Marxist ideas and notion of using ancient cultures like historical personages, exercised an enormous influence on several generations of archaeologists. His work has generated an expanding specialist literature. His ideas on revolutions can be found in his *New Light on the Most Ancient East* (New York: Appleton, 1934).

21. Robert Braidwood (1907–2003) trained in architecture, was hired by James Breasted at the Oriental Institute, and then excavated in Syria's Amuq Valley during the 1930s, where he developed some of the survey and excavation techniques he used in his later work. His wife, Linda, was a close partner in his work.

22. The sites are summarized in Robert J. Braidwood and Bruce Howe, *Prehistoric Investigations in Iraqi Kurdistan* (Chicago: Oriental Institute, 1960). See also Robert J. Braidwood and Linda S. Braidwood, eds., *Prehistoric Archaeology Along the Zagros Flanks* (Chicago: Oriental Institute, 1983).

23. Willard Libby, *Radiocarbon Dating* (Chicago: University of Chicago Press, 1955).

24. Kathleen Kenyon, *Excavations at Jericho,* vol. 3 (Jerusalem: British School of Archaeology, 1981).

25. The surveys are described in Robert M. Adams, *Heartland of Cities* (Chicago: University of Chicago Press, 1981), and Robert M. Adams and Hans J. Nissen, *The Uruk Landscape* (Chicago: University of Chicago Press, 1972).

26. Described in Mallowan, *Memoirs,* part 4, and, of course, in the same author's *Nimrud and Its Remains.*

27. See Joan Oates and David Oates, *Nimrud: An Assyrian Imperial City Revealed* (London: British School of Archaeology in Iraq, 2001).

CHAPTER 22: CATASTROPHE

The epigraph to this chapter is drawn from Selma al-Radi, "The Ravages of War and the Challenge of Reconstruction," in *The Looting of the Iraq Museum, Baghdad: The Lost Legacy of Ancient Mesopotamia*, ed. Milbry Polk and Angela M.H. Schuster (New York: Harry Abrams, 2005), 211.

1. For a detailed analysis, see Friedrich T. Schipper, "The Protection and Preservation of Iraq's Archaeological Heritage, Spring 1991–2003," *American Journal of Archaeology* 109 (2005): 521–572.

2. Joan Oates and David Oates's *Nimrud* is an excellent source for excavations since the 1840s.

3. Andrew Selkirk and Nadia Durrani, "The Nimrud Treasure," *Current World Archaeology* 11 (2005):12–20, is an excellent popular account. Unfortunately, I was unable to obtain illustrations of the finds.

4. Selkirk and Durrani, "Nimrud Treasure," 16.

5. Polk and Schuster, *Looting*, 1–33, has an account of the Iraq National Museum's history.

6. Schipper, "Protection," 253ff.

7. The paragraphs that follow rely on Colonel Matthew Bogdanos's remarkable account of the investigation into the thievery at the museum. An assistant district attorney in New York, Bogdanos brought both a military and a cool, dispassionate investigator's eye to the situation. He was able to show that many initial media reports—and claims by archaeologists—were inaccurate. Anyone seriously interested in the challenges of rebuilding the museum and its collections should read Matthew Bogdanos (with William Patrick), *Thieves of Baghdad* (New York, Bloomsbury, 2006).

8. For more information, see Schipper, "Protection." See also the bibliographies in Polk and Schuster, *Looting*, and Bogdanos, *Thieves*. There are also numerous Web pages devoted to the subject, including an account of the UNESCO mission in August 2003 at http://www.archaeological.org/.

9. Quoted from Bogdanos, *Thieves*, 248.

GUIDE TO FURTHER READING

THE RESEARCH FOR THIS BOOK COVERED NOT ONLY A BEWILDERINGLY DIVERSE ARCHAEO-logical literature but the work of scholars in many other disciplines as well. I relied heavily on contemporary travelers' accounts and nineteenth-century archaeologists' writings. Published works were amplified with archival sources whenever possible, desirable, or practicable. In general, I have cited historical sources instead of specialist references or modern works; this is, after all, a work of history rather than contemporary archaeology. This guide is organized by chapter and provides some general references, which may also appear in the more detailed notes. For obvious reasons, some chapters have been combined into one section. At times, I have identified a god, a site, or a person to amplify the text.

CHAPTER 1: A LEGACY OF CIVILIZATIONS

An excellent and concise account of the geography of Mesopotamia can be found in the Great Britain Naval Intelligence Division Handbook titled *Iraq and the Persian Gulf* (London: H. M. Stationery Office, 1944). Published many years ago, it's useful as background to earlier archaeological enterprises. The archaeology of Iraq is admirably summarized in a number of readily available volumes, including Seton Lloyd's *The Archaeology of Mesopotamia* (London: Thames and Hudson, 1978). Seton Lloyd's *Twin Rivers* (London: Oxford University Press, 1943) is an admirable account of Mesopotamia that is very useful for the later, historical periods. See also Harriett Crawford, *Sumer and the Sumerians*, 2nd ed. (Cambridge: Cambridge University Press, 2004); Charles Maisels, *The Early Civilizations of the Old World: The Formative Histories of Egypt, the Levant, Mesopotamia, India, and China* (London: Routledge, 2001); and Nicholas Postgate, *Early Mesopotamia: Economy and Society at the Dawn of History* (London: Kegan Paul, 1993).

The Gulf Wars and terrorism have produced a flood of books on Islam, almost to the point of saturation. Philip K. Hitti's *A Short History of the Arabs*, 10th ed. (New York: Palgrave Macmillan, 2002) has been described rightly as a masterwork. John L. Esposito's *The Oxford History of Islam* (New York: Oxford University Press, 2000) is also authoritative.

Guy Le Strange's *The Land of the Eastern Caliphate* (Cambridge: Cambridge University Press, 1905) is still an excellent source on the Arab scholars. Translations of the Arab geographers' works can be found in most large university and college libraries and also on the World Wide Web.

CHAPTER 2: EARLY TRAVELERS
and
CHAPTER 3: CARSTEN NIEBUHR AT PERSEPOLIS

In this chapter, we introduce the reader to Seton Lloyd's *Foundations in the Dust*, rev. ed. (London: Thames and Hudson, 1980), an entertaining and literate account of early Mesopotamian archaeology. Lloyd covers the exploits of the early travelers well and should be read in conjunction with Mogens Trolle Larsen, *The Conquest of Assyria* (London: Routledge, 1994), who focuses mainly on the nineteenth century. Sarah Searight's *The British in the Near East* (London: Weidenfeld and Nicholson, 1969) is a mine of information on the Ottoman empire and early travelers.

CHAPTER 4: CLAUDIUS JAMES RICH
and
CHAPTER 5: DIPLOMACY AND ARCHAEOLOGY IN BAGHDAD

Claudius Rich's papers have never been published. The only sources currently available on this fascinating man are his *Collected Memoirs*, edited by his wife, Mary (London: John Murray, 1833), and Constance Alexander's enchanting *Baghdad in Bygone Days* (London: John Murray, 1928), which was based on the Rich family papers. Mary Rich also published her husband's *Narrative of a Residence in Koordistan*, 2 vols. (London: John Murray, 1836), which contains an account of their visit to Nineveh. Sir Robert Ker Porter's *Travels in Georgia, Persia, Armenia, and Ancient Babylon* (London: Longmans, 1821) contains some references to Rich and provides fascinating information on Behistun and other sites. James Silk Buckingham's *Travels in Assyria, Medea, and Persia*, 2 vols. (London: Henry Coburn, 1829) is probably the most entertaining Mesopotamian travel book of the period and contains charming vignettes of Baghdad and desert travel.

CHAPTER 6: THE EUPHRATES EXPEDITION

James Baillie-Fraser's *Travels to Koordistan, Mesopotamia, etc.*, 2 vols. (London: Longmans, 1840) is rather tiresome except for its vivid descriptions of the plague in Baghdad. John S. Guest, *The Euphrates Expedition* (London: Kegan Paul, 1992), draws on primary sources for a definitive account of the project. The best firsthand account is by William Ainsworth, the expedition surgeon, whose *A Personal Narrative of the Euphrates Expedition* (London: Kegan Paul and Trench, 1888) is full of evocative description and local color. Colonel Chesney's tomes are heavy going, but his *Narrative of the Euphrates Expedition* (London: Longmans, 1868) is rather easier to read than his two-volume report published in 1890 and the maps produced by the expedition surveyors are exquisite.

CHAPTER 7: CUNEIFORM DECIPHERED

Andrew Robinson's *The Story of Writing: Alphabets, Hieroglyphs and Pictograms*, rev. ed. (London: Thames and Hudson, 2007) is an excellent popular account of ancient scripts in general, including cuneiform. Samuel Kramer's *The Sumerians* (Chicago: University of Chicago Press, 1963) is a good source for understanding the significance of cuneiform texts and contains some information on decipherment. Wallis Budge, *By Nile and Tigris*, 2 vols. (London: John Murray, 1920), gives useful insights into the early cuneiform experts. For more information on Edward Hincks, see Edward F. Davidson, *Edward Hincks: A Selection from his Correspondence with a Memoir* (Oxford: Oxford University

Press, 1933). For additional information about Henry Rawlinson, see George Rawlinson's *Memoir of Major General Sir Henry Rawlinson* (London: Longmans, Green, 1898). Lesley Adkins's *Empires of the Plain: Henry Rawlinson and the Lost Languages of Babylon* (New York: St. Martin's Press, 2003) is the only modern biography. Having read many of Henry Rawlinson's letters in the British Museum, I'm not surprised at the dearth of biographical works. His writing resembles the cuneiform scripts that he deciphered in all their complexity. Wallis Budge's *The Rise and Progress of Assyriology* (London: Hopkinson, 1925) is also valuable on early decipherment efforts.

CHAPTER 8: EXCAVATIONS AT KHORSABAD

Currently, there is no biography of Paul Botta; however, Mogens Trolle Larsen, *The Conquest of Assyria* is especially good on him (chapters 2ff). Seton Lloyd's *Foundations in the Dust* also has a useful description (chapter 7). Some hours spent looking at Paul Émile Botta's *Monuments de Ninive* (Paris: Imprimerie Nationale, 1849) is a joyful experience, especially for Eugène Flandin's pictures. This is a rare book and obtainable only in reprint form or in special collections of large academic libraries. The text of this work was a major source for this chapter.

CHAPTER 9: LAYARD OF NINEVEH
and
CHAPTER 10: NIMRUD AND KHORSABAD

Austen Henry Layard is a well-known figure of nineteenth-century history and left a copious paper trail behind him. Gordon Waterfield's *Layard of Nineveh* (London: John Murray, 1963) is a comprehensive biography. Layard's own writings are also worth reading. His *Early Adventures in Persia, Susiana, and Babylonia* (London: John Murray, 1887) is an autobiographical sketch of his early days. *Nineveh and Its Remains* (London: John Murray, 1849) and *Discoveries in the Ruins of Nineveh and Babylon* (London: John Murray, 1853) are archaeological classics and adventure stories. My account of Layard's exploits is largely based on his correspondence, which is preserved in the British Museum. See also Cyril J. Gadd, *The Stones of Assyria* (London: Chatto and Windus, 1936). Larsen's *The Conquest of Assyria* (chapters 4–31) offers an excellent scholarly analysis.

CHAPTER 11: EXCAVATIONS IN BABYLONIA

The best source on early excavations in the south is Hermann Hilprecht's *The Excavations in Assyria and Babylonia* (Philadelphia: Holman, 1904), which is almost too thorough in its blow-by-blow descriptions of the pioneer digs. William Kennett Loftus's *Travels and Researches in Chaldea and Susiana* (London: J. Nisbet, 1857) is saved from being pedestrian by its lively accounts of early excavations at Uruk. For more information on the French scientific expedition, see Maurice Pillet, *L'Expédition scientifique et artistique de Mésopotamie et de Médie, 1852–1855* (Paris: E. Champion, 1922).

CHAPTER 12: A ROYAL LION HUNT

Hormuzd Rassam's papers appear to be lost, so we are forced to rely on his *Asshur and the Land of Nimrod* (New York: Eaton and Mains, 1897), which at best can be described as a self-serving document. Victor Place remains a rather shadowy figure, except for Maurice Pillet's biographical sketch, *Un Pionnier de l'assyriologie* (Paris: Cahiers du Société Asiatique, 1962), a study that includes some fascinating early photographs of the Khorsabad dig. Place's three-volume *Ninive et l'Assyrie* (Paris: Imprimerie Nationale, 1869) is a grandiose description of Sargon's palace.

CHAPTER 13: THE DELUGE TABLETS

George Smith's *The Chaldean Account of Genesis* (New York: Scribners, 1876) is a good starting point. The best popular account of the significance of his discoveries is Edmond Sollberger's *The Babylonian Legend of the Flood* (London: British Museum 1971). Samuel Kramer's *The Sumerians* (Chicago: University of Chicago Press, 1963) gives a broad account of the antecedents and significance of the deluge epics. See also Adkins, *Empires of the Plain*, chapter 19.

CHAPTER 14: GATES AND PALACES
and
CHAPTER 15: A SCRAMBLE FOR TABLETS

For information on Hormuzd Rassam, I used the sources listed for Chapter 12, amplifying them with archival materials in the British Museum, especially correspondence with Layard and the trustees preserved in the Layard archives. An atmosphere of low comedy always seems to surround Wallis Budge in my mind, although I realize this association is unfair. One source on his activities is his *By Nile and Tigris,* a book best described as a gossipy compendium of information on his trips to Mesopotamia and on academic doings in Assyriology in the closing decades of the nineteenth century. Budge's *Rise and Progress of Assyriology* (London: Martin Hopkinson, 1925) is also useful for filling in details.

CHAPTER 16: SUMER DISCOVERED

Hermann Hilprecht's *Explorations in Biblical Lands* (Philadelphia: A. J. Holman, 1903) is a useful source on the events that led to the excavations at Telloh and on the Nippur digs. John P. Peters's *Nippur, or Explorations and Adventures on the Euphrates,* 2 vols. (New York: Putnams, 1899) is rather prosaic compared with Hilprecht's book and adds little to Hilprecht's expert account. André Parrot's *Archéologie mesopotamienne* (Paris: Michel, 1946) is informative on Telloh and the early French excavations. Ernest de Sarzec and Léon Heuzey's *Decouvertes en Chaldée* (Paris: E. Leroux, 1884–1912) is the basic source on the earliest work on the Sumerian city.

CHAPTER 17: NEBUCHADNEZZAR'S BABYLON

The Germans were reticent to write about their work for the general public, but Robert Koldewey's *The Excavations at Babylon* (London: Macmillan, 1914) gives an outline, and a rather dull description, of the many campaigns at the site. Joan Oates gives an admirable description and analysis from a modern perspective in her *Babylon* (London: Thames and Hudson, 1986). For Assur, see Walter Andrae's *Das Wiedererstandene Assur* (Munich: Beck, 1977).

CHAPTER 18: LEONARD WOOLLEY AT CARCHEMISH

Harry V.F. Winstone's *Woolley of Ur: The Life of Sir Leonard Woolley* (London: Heinemann, 1992) is a comprehensive biography of this remarkable archaeologist. Leonard Woolley always wrote up his excavations thoroughly, both for the specialist and for the general public. His most entertaining books were anecdotal, especially his *Dead Cities and Living Men* (New York: Philosophical Library, 1956), in which he describes the lighthearted side of Carchemish. The stories he tells seem historically accurate but are obviously sometimes overstated; T. E. Lawrence was upset by their first publication. Two excellent biographies of Lawrence served me for this chapter: John E. Mack's *A Prince of Our Disorder* (Boston: Little, Brown, 1976) and Desmond Stewart's *T. E. Lawrence: A New Biography* (New York: Harper and Row 1977). For the Hittites, see James G. MacQueen, *The Hittites and their Contemporaries in Asia Minor,* rev. ed. (London: Thames and Hudson, 1996).

CHAPTER 19: GERTRUDE BELL AND THE NEW IRAQ

Accounts of political developments between 1905 to 1932 are well summarized by Stephen Longrigg's *Iraq, 1900 to 1950* (London: Oxford University Press, 1953). The same author's *Four Centuries of Modern Iraq* (Oxford: Clarendon Press, 1925) is also widely admired by experts. There are many

Bell biographies, but Harry V.F. Winstone's *Gertrude Bell* (London: Jonathan Cape, 1978) is widely quoted and Janet Wallach's *Desert Queen* (New York: Nan Talese/Doubleday, 1996) is definitive. Bell's writings still give pleasure, especially *The Desert and the Sown* (London: Heinemann, 1907) and *Amurath to Amurath* (London: Heinemann, 1911). Her letters were published by her mother in heavily expurgated form; see Lady Bell, *The Letters of Gertrude Bell*, 2 vols. (New York: Boni and Liveright, 1927). The correspondence between the University of Pennsylvania and the British Museum was excerpted by Robert H. Dyson in "Archival Glimpses of the Ur Expedition in the Years 1920 to 1925," *Expedition* 20:1 (1977):5–23. Full publication of the Bell archives in the University of Newcastle and of the University of Pennsylvania files will reveal a mass of new material on this period.

CHAPTER 20: LEONARD WOOLLEY AT UR

Winstone's *Woolley of Ur* is the only biography of this remarkable archaeologist. Leonard Woolley himself is the best contemporary source on the Ur excavations. In writing this chapter, I used the expedition monographs and preliminary reports as well as Woolley's summary *Excavations at Ur* (New York: Barnes and Noble, 1954). Sir Max Mallowan's autobiography *Mallowan's Memoirs* (New York: Dodd, Mead, 1977) is not particularly entertaining but contains useful memories of the Ur excavations. Further historical material on Ur can be found in a 1960 volume of the academic journal *Iraq*, which was offered in tribute to Woolley and published soon after his death. Agatha Christie's *An Autobiography* (London: Collins, 1977) is a delightful vignette of her archaeological and literary life, while her *Come Tell Me How You Live* (London: Collins, 1943) tells of later diggings in southwestern Asia after Ur.

CHAPTER 21: NATIONALISM AND ARCHAEOLOGY

Seton Lloyd's *Foundations in the Dust* (chapter 14) is the best general source for this chapter. Other key references are Seton Lloyd's *Mounds of the Near East* and the basic syntheses listed for Chapter 1. Max Mallowan's *Nimrud and Its Remains* (London: Collins, 1966) is a magnificent account of his remarkable ivory discoveries at Nimrud and of work there since Layard's day. Robert Braidwood and Bruce Howe's *Excavations in Iraqi Kurdistan* (Chicago: Oriental Institute, 1960) summarizes the team approach that resulted in the excavation of Jarmo and other sites. Robert Adams's *Land Behind Baghdad* (Chicago: University of Chicago Press, 1965) and *The Uruk Countryside* (Chicago: University of Chicago Press, 1972) summarize the results of the Oriental Institute irrigation surveys. Thorkild Jacobsen's *The Treasures of Darkness* (New Haven: Yale University Press, 1976) is a superb account of

Mesopotamian religion that places the Biblical legends and Sumerian (and later) beliefs in a broad perspective.

CHAPTER 22: CATASTROPHE

Much of Chapter 22 is based on two major sources: editors Milbry Polk and Angela M.H. Schuster's *The Looting of the Iraq Museum, Baghdad: The Lost Legacy of Ancient Mesopotamia* (New York: Harry Abrams, 2005) is a beautifully illustrated account of the museum and also a survey of Iraqi history; Matthew Bogdanos (with William Patrick) in his *Thieves of Baghdad* (New York, Bloomsbury, 2006) offers an engrossing popular account of the raping of the museum and the subsequent investigations.

INDEX